CRITICAL ISSUES IN THE
STUDY OF CRIME
A Book of Readings

CRITICAL ISSUES IN THE STUDY OF CRIME

A BOOK OF READINGS

Simon Dinitz and
Walter C. Reckless
THE OHIO STATE UNIVERSITY

Little, Brown and Company · Boston

FOREWORD

Critical Issues in the Study of Crime is designed to present a field-oriented view of the crime problem in America. In addition to the inclusion of traditional materials and topics, this volume is unique in its focus on the criminal and legal processes and on critical and controversial policy matters. For this reason, we have relied very heavily on the reports of the President's Commission on Law Enforcement and Administration of Justice, as well as on other government and professional association publications. This unique emphasis—on processes and on policy—is specifically geared to supplement current texts used in criminology, penology, and correctional administration courses in American universities and colleges. Some of the materials should also prove to be invaluable in criminal law and procedure courses. The authors also have in mind its special usefulness as a basic orientation to the problem of crime and its control for in-service training courses which are offered to law enforcement officers as well as to personnel in the field of corrections which handles the custody, treatment, and supervision of juvenile and adult offenders.

A deliberate attempt has been made to assemble articles and reports which present critical, central, unresolved, and emerging issues by outstanding professional persons who have close contact with the field on varying levels—legal, administrative, enforcement, and correctional. The more formal and theoretical assessment of the problem of crime is left to the textbooks in sociology and in law, while the varying presentations of accepted practices in law enforcement and in the several fields of corrections are left to the specifics of inservice-training programs.

It is becoming more and more obvious that certain basic topics deserve special attention in a field-oriented study of the crime problem. The authors have undertaken to capture first-hand observations and insights into the following aspects of crime:

1. Crime, delinquency, and social change;
2. The relation of crime and law;
3. The reporting of crime;
4. The range of criminal behavior;
5. Involvement of juveniles in delinquency;
6. The major behavioral deviations related to crime;
7. The role of the victim;

8. New developments in law enforcement and criminal justice;
9. Punishment and correctional substitutes.

Simon Dinitz
Walter C. Reckless

COLUMBUS, OHIO
JANUARY, 1968

TABLE OF CONTENTS

OVERVIEW | THE CHALLENGE OF CRIME
IN A FREE SOCIETY*

There is much crime in America, more than ever is reported, far more than ever is solved, far too much for the health of the Nation. Every American knows that. Every American is, in a sense, a victim of crime. Violence and theft have not only injured, often irreparably, hundreds of thousands of citizens, but have directly affected everyone. Some people have been impelled to uproot themselves and find new homes. Some have been made afraid to use public streets and parks. Some have come to doubt the worth of a society in which so many people behave so badly. Some have become distrustful of the Government's ability, or even desire, to protect them. Some have lapsed into the attitude that criminal behavior is normal human behavior and consequently have become indifferent to it, or have adopted it as a good way to get ahead in life. Some have become sus-

* Reprinted from *The Challenge of Crime in a Free Society: A Report by the President's Commission on Law Enforcement and Administration of Justice* (Washington, D.C.: Government Printing Office, 1967), pp. 1–15.

picious of those they conceive to be responsible for crime: adolescents or Negroes or drug addicts or college students or demonstrators; policemen who fail to solve crimes; judges who pass lenient sentences or write decisions restricting the activities of the police; parole boards that release prisoners who resume their criminal activities.

The most understandable mood into which many Americans have been plunged by crime is one of frustration and bewilderment. For "crime" is not a single simple phenomenon that can be examined, analyzed and described in one piece. It occurs in every part of the country and in every stratum of society. Its practitioners and its victims are people of all ages, incomes and backgrounds. Its trends are difficult to ascertain. Its causes are legion. Its cures are speculative and controversial. An examination of any single kind of crime, let alone of "crime in America," raises a myriad of issues of the utmost complexity.

The underlying problems are ones that the criminal justice system can do little about. The unruliness of young people, widespread drug addiction, the existence of much poverty in a wealthy society, the pursuit of the dollar by any available means are phenomena the police, the courts, and the correctional apparatus, which must deal with crimes and criminals one by one, cannot confront directly. They are strands that can be disentangled from the fabric of American life only by the concerted action of all of society.

Of the everyday problems of the criminal justice system itself, certainly the most delicate and probably the most difficult concern the proper ways of dealing individually with individuals. Arrest and prosecution are likely to have quite different effects on delinquent boys and on hardened professional criminals. Sentencing occasional robbers and habitual robbers by the same standards is clearly inappropriate. Rehabilitating a drug addict is a procedure that has little in common with rehabilitating a holdup man. In short, there are no general prescriptions for dealing with "robbers." There are no general prescriptions for dealing with "robbery" either. Keeping streets and parks safe is not the same problem as keeping banks secure. Investigating a mugging and tracking down a band of prudent and well-organized bank robbers are two entirely distinct police procedures. The kind of police patrol that will deter boys from street robberies is not likely to deter men with guns from holding up storekeepers.

Crime and society's response to it resemble a gigantic disassembled jigsaw puzzle whose pieces the Commission was asked to assemble into as complete and accurate a picture as it could. It was charged with discovering whether the popular picture of crime in America is how it really looks and, if not, what the differences are; with determining how poverty, discrimination and other social ills relate to crime; with ascertaining whether America's system of criminal justice really works the way the public thinks it does and the books say it should and, if it does not, where, when, how, and why it does not.

TOWARD UNDERSTANDING AND PREVENTING CRIME

A skid-row drunk lying in a gutter is crime. So is the killing of an un-faithful wife. A Cosa Nostra conspiracy to bribe public officials is crime. So is a strong-arm robbery by a 15-year-old boy. The embezzlement of a corporation's funds by an executive is crime. So is the possession of marihuana cigarettes by a student. These crimes can no more be lumped together for purposes of analysis than can measles and schizophrenia, or lung cancer and a broken ankle. As with disease, so with crime: if causes are to be under-stood, if risks are to be evaluated, and if preventive or remedial actions are to be taken, each kind must be looked at separately. Thinking of "crime" as a whole is futile.

In any case it is impossible to answer with precision questions about the volume or trends of crime as a whole, or even of any particular kind of crime. Techniques for measuring crime are, and probably always will be im-perfect. Successful crime, after all, is secret crime. The best, in fact almost the only, source of statistical information about crime volumes is the Uni-form Crime Reports of the FBI. The UCR is the product of a nationwide system of crime reporting that the FBI has painstakingly developed over the years. Under this system local police agencies report the offenses they know of to the FBI; the UCR is a compilation of these reports. This compilation can be no better than the underlying information that local agencies supply to the FBI. And because the FBI has induced local agencies to improve their reporting methods year by year, it is important to distinguish better report-ing from more crime.

Obviously the most serious crimes are the ones that consist of or employ physical aggression: willful homicide, rape, robbery, and serious assault. The injuries such crimes inflict are grievous and irreparable.

Controlling violent crime presents a number of distinct problems. To the extent that these crimes occur on private premises, as most murders and rapes and many assaults do, they are little susceptible to deterrence by police patrol. To the extent that they are the passionate culmination of quarrels between acquaintances or relatives — as again many murders and assaults are — there is little that can be done to increase the deterrent effect of the threat of punishment.

Only 13 percent of the total number of Index Crimes in the UCR for 1965 were crimes of violence. The remaining 87 percent were theft: thefts of $50 or over in money or goods, automobile thefts, and burglaries (thefts that involve breaking into or otherwise unlawfully entering private prem-ises). Of these three kinds of stealing, burglary was the most frequent; 1,173,201 burglaries were reported to the FBI in 1965, approximately one-half of them involving homes and one-half commercial establishments. Bur-glary is expensive; the FBI calculates that the worth of the property stolen by burglars in 1965 was some $284 million. Burglary is frightening; having one's home broken into and ransacked is an experience that unnerves almost anyone. Finally, burglars are seldom caught; only 25 percent of the burglaries known to the police in 1965 were solved, and many burglaries were not reported to the police.

Larceny — stealing that does not involve either force or illegal entry — is by far the most frequent kind of stealing in America. It is less frightening than burglary because to a large, perhaps even to a preponderant extent, it is a crime of opportunity, a matter of making off with whatever happens to be lying around loose. Only 20 percent of reported major larcenies are solved, and the solution rate for minor ones is considerably lower.

A unique feature of the crime of automobile theft is that, although only a quarter of all automobile thefts — and there were 486,568 reported to the FBI in 1965 — are solved, some 87 percent of all stolen automobiles are recovered and returned to their owners. The overwhelming majority of automobile thefts are for the purpose of securing temporary transportation, often for "joyriding."

These three major crimes against property do not tell the whole story about stealing. In fact, the whole story cannot be told. There is no knowing how much embezzlement, fraud, loan sharking, and other forms of thievery from individuals or commercial institutions there is, or how much price-rigging, tax evasion, bribery, graft, and other forms of thievery from the public at large there is. The Commission's studies indicate that the economic losses those crimes cause are far greater than those caused by the three index crimes against property.

Businessmen who defraud consumers promote cynicism towards society and disrespect for law. The Mafia or Cosa Nostra or the Syndicate, as it has variously been called, is deeply involved in business crime, and protects its position there by bribery and graft and, all too often, assault and murder. White-collar crime and organized crime are subjects about which the criminal justice system, and the community as a whole, have little knowledge. Acquiring such knowledge in a systematic way is an extremely high-priority obligation of those entrusted with protecting society from crime.

"Crimes without victims," crimes whose essence is providing people with goods or services that, though illegal, are in demand, are peculiarly vexatious to the criminal justice system. Gambling, narcotics, and prostitution offenses, and their like, are not only numerous, but they present policemen, prosecutors, judges, and correctional officials with problems they are ill-equipped to solve. Since such crimes have no direct victims, or at any rate no victims with complaints, investigating them obliges policemen to employ practices like relying on informants who may turn out to be accomplices, or walking the streets hoping to be solicited by prostitutes.

Finally, there are "petty offenses" and "breaches of the peace" like public drunkenness and public quarreling, which are the most numerous of all crimes. Most Americans have never actually seen a serious crime committed, but every American has seen a petty offense. Such offenses are undoubted public nuisances against which the public has every right to protect itself. Yet a curious thing about them is that usually the only person who suffers real damage from one of these crimes is the offender himself. Breaches of the peace are the most exasperating everyday problem of the criminal justice system. Petty offenders, many of whom, like chronic alcoholics, are repeated and incurable lawbreakers, occupy much of the time of policemen, clog the lower courts and crowd city and county jails.

Two striking facts that the UCR and every other examination of American crime disclose are that most crimes, wherever they are committed, are committed by boys and young men, and that most crimes, by whomever they are committed, are committed in cities. Three-quarters of the 1965 arrests for Index crimes, plus petty larceny and negligent manslaughter, were of people less than 25 years old. More 15-year-olds were arrested for those crimes than people of any other age, and 16-year-olds were a close second. Of 2,780,015 "offenses known to the police" in 1965 — these were Index crimes — some 2 million occurred in cities, more than half a million occurred in the suburbs, and about 170,000 occurred in rural areas. The number of city crimes per hundred thousand residents was over 1,800, the suburban rate was almost 1,200, and the rural rate was 616.9. In short, crime is evidently associated with two powerful social trends: the increasing urbanization of America and the increasing numerousness, restlessness, and restiveness of American youth.

What appears to be happening throughout the country, in the cities and in the suburbs, among the poor and among the well-to-do, is that parental, and especially paternal, authority over young people is becoming weaker. The community is accustomed to rely upon this force as one guarantee that children will learn to fit themselves into society in an orderly and peaceable manner, that the natural and valuable rebelliousness of young people will not express itself in the form of warring violently on society or any of its members. The programs and activities of almost every kind of social institution with which children come in contact — schools, churches, social-service agencies, youth organizations — are predicated on the assumption that children acquire their fundamental attitudes toward life, their moral standards, in their homes.

That there are all too many ambiguities and lacks in the community scarcely needs prolonged demonstration. Poverty and racial discrimination, bad housing and commercial exploitation, the enormous gap between American ideals and American achievements, and the many distressing consequences and implications of these conditions are national failings that are widely recognized. Their effects on young people have been greatly aggravated by the technological revolution of the last two decades, which has greatly reduced the market for unskilled labor.

And so there are two continually growing groups of discontented young people: those whose capacity or desires for becoming educated has not been developed by their homes or schools (or both), and who therefore are unemployed or even unemployable; and those whose entry into the adult working world has been delayed by the necessity of continuing their studies long past the point at which they have become physically and psychologically adult. Young people today are sorely discontented in the suburbs and on the campuses as well as in the slums.

It is with the young people and the slum dwellers who have been embittered by these painful social and economic pressures that the criminal justice system preponderantly deals. Society insists that individuals are responsible for their actions, and the criminal process operates on that assumption. However, society has not devised ways for ensuring that all its members have the ability to assume responsibility. It has let too many of them grow up untaught, unmotivated, unwanted. The criminal justice system has a great potential for dealing with individual instances of crime, but it was not designed to eliminate the conditions in which most crime breeds. It needs help. Writing on poverty, inadequate housing, and unemployment, is warring on crime. A civil rights law is a law against crime. Money for schools is money against crime. Medical, psychiatric, and family-counseling services are services against crime. More broadly and most importantly every effort to improve life in America's "inner cities" is an effort against crime. A community's most enduring protection against crime is to right the wrongs and cure the illnesses that tempt men to harm their neighbors.

AMERICA'S SYSTEM OF CRIMINAL JUSTICE

The system of criminal justice America uses to deal with those crimes it cannot prevent and those criminals it cannot deter is not a monolithic, or even a consistent, system. It was not designed or built in one piece at one time. Its philosophic core is that a person may be punished by the Government if, and only if, it has been proved by an impartial and deliberate process that he has violated a specific law. Around that core layer upon layer of institutions and procedures, some carefully constructed and some improvised, some inspired by principle and some by expediency, have accumulated. Parts of the system — magistrates' courts, trial by jury, bail — are of great antiquity. Other parts — juvenile courts, probation and parole, professional policemen — are relatively new. The entire system represents an adaptation of the English common law to America's peculiar structure of government, which allows each local community to construct institutions that fill its special needs. Every village, town, county, city, and State has its own criminal justice system, and there is a Federal one as well. All of them operate somewhat alike. No two of them operate precisely alike.

Any criminal justice system is an apparatus society uses to enforce the standards of conduct necessary to protect individuals and the community. It operates by apprehending, prosecuting, convicting, and sentencing those members of the community who violate the basic rules of group existence. The action taken against lawbreakers is designed to serve three purposes beyond the immediately punitive one. It removes dangerous people from the community; it deters others from criminal behavior; and it gives society an opportunity to attempt to transform lawbreakers into law-abiding citizens. What most significantly distinguishes the system of one country from that of another is the extent and the form of the protections it offers individuals in the process of determining guilt and imposing punishment. Our system of justice deliberately sacrifices much in efficiency and even in effectiveness in order to preserve local autonomy and to protect the individual. Sometimes it may seem to sacrifice too much. For example, the American system was not designed with Cosa Nostra-type criminal organizations in mind, and it has been notably unsuccessful to date in preventing such organizations from preying on society.

The criminal justice system has three separately organized parts — the police, the courts, and corrections — and each has distinct tasks. However, these parts are by no means independent of each other. What each one does and how it does it has a direct effect on the work of the others. The courts must deal, and can only deal, with those whom the police arrest; the business of corrections is with those delivered to it by the courts. How successfully [the] corrections [system] reforms convicts determines whether they will once again become police business and influences the sentences the judges pass; police activities are subject to court scrutiny and are often determined by court decisions. And so reforming or reorganizing any part or procedure of the system changes other parts or procedures. Furthermore, the criminal process, the method by which the system deals with individual cases, is not a hodgepodge of random actions. It is rather a continuum — an orderly progression of events — some of which, like arrest and trial, are highly visible and some of which, though of great importance, occur out of public view.

What has evidently happened is that the transformation of America from a relatively relaxed rural society into a tumultuous urban one has presented the criminal justice system in the cities with a volume of cases too large to handle by traditional methods. One result of heavy caseloads is highly visible in city courts, which process many cases with excessive haste and many others with excessive slowness. In the interest both of effectiveness and of fairness to individuals, justice should be swift and certain; too often in city courts today it is, instead, hasty or faltering.

At the very beginning of the process — or, more properly, before the process begins at all — something happens that is scarcely discussed in lawbooks and is seldom recognized by the public: law enforcement policy is made by the policeman. For policemen cannot and do not arrest all the offenders they encounter. It is doubtful that they arrest most of them. A criminal code, in practice, is not a set of specific instructions to policemen but a more or less rough map of the territory in which policemen work. How an individual policeman moves around that territory depends largely on his personal discretion.

That a policeman's duties compel him to exercise personal discretion many times every day is evident. Crime does not look the same on the street as it does in a legislative chamber. How much noise or profanity makes conduct "disorderly" within the meaning of the law? When must a quarrel be treated as a criminal assault: at the first threat or at the first shove or at the first blow, or after blood is drawn, or when a serious injury is inflicted? How suspicious must conduct be before there is "probable cause," the constitutional basis for an arrest? Every policeman, however complete or sketchy his education, is an interpreter of the law.

Every policeman, too, is an arbiter of social values, for he meets situation after situation in which invoking criminal sanctions is a questionable line of action. It is obvious that a boy throwing rocks at a school's windows is committing the statutory offense of vandalism, but it is often not at all obvious whether a policeman will better serve the interests of the community and of the boy by taking the boy home to his parents or by arresting him. Who are the boy's parents? Can they control him? Is he a frequent offender who has responded badly to leniency? Is vandalism so epidemic in the neighborhood that he should be made a cautionary example? With juveniles especially, the police exercise great discretion.

Finally, the manner in which a policeman works is influenced by practical matters: the legal strength of the available evidence, the willingness of victims to press charges and of witnesses to testify, the temper of the community, the time and information at the policeman's disposal. Much is at stake in how the policeman exercises this discretion. If he judges conduct not suspicious enough to justify intervention, the chance to prevent a robbery, rape, or murder may be lost. If he overestimates the seriousness of a situation or his actions are controlled by panic or prejudice, he may hurt or kill someone unnecessarily. His actions may even touch off a riot.

In direct contrast to the policeman, the magistrate before whom a suspect is first brought usually exercises less discretion than the law allows him. He is entitled to inquire into the facts of the case, into whether there are grounds for holding the accused. He seldom can. The more promptly an arrested suspect is brought into magistrate's court, the less likelihood there is that much information about the arrest other than the arresting officer's statement will be available to the magistrate. Moreover many magistrates, especially in big cities, have such congested calendars that it is almost impossible for them to subject any case but an extraordinary one to prolonged scrutiny.

In practice the most important things, by far, that a magistrate does are to set the amount of a defendant's bail and in some jurisdictions to appoint counsel. Too seldom does either action get the careful attention it deserves.

In many cases the magistrate accepts a waiver of counsel without insuring that the suspect knows the significance of legal representation.

The key administrative officer in the processing of cases is the prosecutor. Theoretically the examination of the evidence against a defendant by a judge at a preliminary hearing, and its reexamination by a grand jury, are important parts of the process. Practically they seldom are because a prosecutor seldom has any difficulty in making a prima facie case against a defendant. In fact most defendants waive their rights to preliminary hearings and much more often than not grand juries indict precisely as prosecutors ask them to. The prosecutor wields almost undisputed sway over the pretrial progress of most cases. He decides whether to press a case or drop it. He determines the specific charge against a defendant. When the charge is reduced as it is in as many as two-thirds of all cases in some cities, the prosecutor is usually the official who reduces it.

In the informal, noncriminal, nonadversary juvenile justice system there are no "magistrates" or "prosecutors" or "charges," or, in most instances, defense counsel. An arrested youth is brought before an intake officer who is likely to be a social worker or, in smaller communities, before a judge. On the basis of an informal inquiry into the facts and circumstances that led to the arrest, and of an interview with the youth himself, the intake officer or the judge decides whether or not a case should be the subject of formal court proceedings. If he decides it should be, he draws up a petition, describing the case.

When a prosecutor reduces a charge it is ordinarily because there has been "plea bargaining" between him and a defense attorney. The issue at stake is how much the prosecutor will reduce his original charge or how lenient a sentence he will recommend, in return for a plea of guilty. There is no way of judging how many bargains reflect the prosecutor's belief that a lesser charge or sentence is justified and how many result from the fact that there may be in the system at any one time ten times as many cases as there are prosecutors or judges or courtrooms to handle them, should every one come to trial.

Plea bargaining is not only an invisible procedure but, in some jurisdictions, a theoretically unsanctioned one. In order to satisfy the court record, a defendant, his attorney, and the prosecutor will at the time of sentencing often ritually state to a judge that no bargain has been made. Plea bargaining may be a useful procedure, especially in congested urban jurisdictions, but neither the dignity of the law, nor the quality of justice, nor the protection of society from dangerous criminals is enhanced by its being conducted covertly.

In the juvenile system there is, of course, no plea bargaining in the sense described above. However, the entire juvenile process can involve extra-judicial negotiations about disposition. Furthermore, the entire juvenile process is by design invisible. Though intended to be helpful, the authority exercised often is coercive; juveniles, no less than adults, may need representation by counsel.

An enormously consequential kind of decision is the sentencing decision of a judge. The law recognizes the importance of fitting sentences to individual defendants by giving judges, in most instances, considerable latitude. Even when a judge has presided over a trial during which the facts of a case have been carefully set forth and has been given a probation report that carefully discusses a defendant's character, background, and problems, he cannot find it easy to choose a sentence. In perhaps nine-tenths of all cases there is no trial; the defendants are self-confessedly guilty.

In the lower or misdemeanor courts, the courts that process most criminal cases, probation reports are a rarity. Under such circumstances judges have little to go on and many sentences are bound to be based on conjecture or intuition. When a sentence is part of a plea bargain, which an overworked judge ratifies perfunctorily, it may not even be his conjecture or intuition on which the sentence is based, but a prosecutor's or a defense counsel's. But perhaps the greatest lack judges suffer from when they pass sentence is not time or information, but correctional alternatives.

The correctional apparatus to which guilty defendants are delivered is in every respect the most isolated part of the criminal justice system. Much of it is physically isolated; its institutions usually have thick walls and locked doors, and often they are situated in rural areas, remote from the courts where the institutions' inmates were tried and from the communities where they lived.

The most striking fact about the correctional apparatus today is that, although the rehabilitation of criminals is presumably its major purpose, the custody of criminals is actually its major task. On any given day there are well over a million people being "corrected" in America, two-thirds of them on probation or parole and one-third of them in prisons or jails. However, prisons and jails are where four-fifths of correctional money is spent and where nine-tenths of correctional employees work. Furthermore, fewer than one-fifth of the people who work in State prisons and local jails have jobs that are not essentially either custodial or administrative in character. Many jails have nothing but custodial and administrative personnel. Of course many jails are crowded with defendants who have not been able to furnish bail and who are not considered by the law to be appropriate objects of rehabilitation because it has not yet been determined that they are criminals who need it.

Most authorities agree that while probationers and parolees need varying degrees and kinds of supervision, an average of no more than 35 cases per officer is necessary for effective attention; 97 percent of all officers handling adults have larger caseloads than that. In the juvenile correctional system the situation is somewhat better. Juvenile institutions, which typically are training schools, have a higher proportion of treatment personnel and juvenile probation and parole officers generally have lighter caseloads. However, these comparatively rich resources are very far from being sufficiently rich.

Except for sentencing, no decision in the criminal process has more impact on the convicted offender than the parole decision, which determines how much of his maximum sentence a prisoner must serve. This again is an invisible administrative decision that is seldom open to attack or subject to review. It is made by parole board members who are often political appointees. Many are skilled and conscientious, but they generally are able to spend no more than a few minutes on a case. Parole decisions that are made in haste and on the basis of insufficient information, in the absence of parole machinery that can provide good supervision, are necessarily imperfect decisions. And since there is virtually no appeal from them, they can be made arbitrarily or discriminatorily.

In sum, America's system of criminal justice is overcrowded and overworked, undermanned, underfinanced, and very often misunderstood. It needs more information and more knowledge. It needs more technical resources. It needs more coordination among its many parts. It needs more public support. It needs the help of community programs and institutions in dealing with offenders and potential offenders. It needs, above all, the willingness to reexamine old ways of doing things, to reform itself, to experiment, to run risks, to dare. It needs vision.

THE FOUNDATIONS OF A CRIME CONTROL PROGRAM

The many specific needs of the criminal justice system — for manpower, for equipment, for facilities, for programs, for research, for money — are interlocking. Each one must be filled with the others in mind. Equipment cannot be operated, facilities manned, programs initiated or research conducted without personnel of many different kinds. It would be useless to seek to recruit more and better personnel if there were not more and better jobs for them to do. Programs cannot be conducted without equipment and facilities, and cannot be conducted effectively without research. Money is needed for everything. This discussion of the system's needs assumes that every need is dependent on the others.

The problem of personnel is at the root of most of the criminal justice system's problems. The system cannot operate fairly unless its personnel are fair. The system cannot operate swiftly and certainly unless its personnel are efficient and well-informed. The system cannot make wise decisions unless its personnel are thoughtful. In many places — many police departments, congested urban lower courts, the understaffed county jails, the entire prison, probation and parole apparatus — more manpower is needed. Probably the greatest manpower need of all, in view of the increasing — and overdue — involvement of defense counsel in all kinds of cases, is for lawyers who can handle criminal cases. Everywhere more skilled, better trained, more imaginative manpower is needed. Some positions are hard to fill. Often the pay is bad and the working conditions are difficult. In addition, an odd and injurious notion is widespread that there is something disreputable about being a policeman or a criminal lawyer or a prison guard. The fact is that there are few fields in which people have more opportunities to do important and responsible work than the criminal justice system. Recruiting such people in large numbers, training them fully and giving them the pay, the opportunities for advancement and the responsibility they deserve is a matter of great urgency.

Probably the single greatest technical limitation on the system's ability to make its decisions wisely and fairly is that the people in the system often are required to decide issues without enough information. A policeman who has just set out in pursuit of a speeding and suspicious looking car should be able to get immediate information as to whether or not the car is wanted; a judge about to sentence a criminal should know everything about him that the police know; and the correctional authorities to whom that criminal is delivered should know everything about him that the judge knows. When they make dispositional decisions, judges and corrections officials should be able to draw on the experience of the system in dealing with different offenders in different ways. Existing procedures must be made more efficient; and new procedures must be devised, so that information can flow more fully and swiftly among the system's many parts.

Each time a citizen fails to report an offense, declines to take the commonsense precautions against crime his police department tells him to, is disrespectful to an officer of the law, shirks his duty as a juror or performs it with a biased mind or a hate-filled heart, or refuses to hire a qualified man because he is an ex-convict, he contributes his mite to crime. That much is obvious. A further duty of every citizen is to familiarize himself with the problems of crime and the criminal justice system so that when legislatures are considering criminal laws or appropriations for the system he can express informed views, and when politicians make crime an election issue he will not be panicked or deceived. The money that is needed to control crime will come, ultimately, from the public. That, too, is obvious.

Beyond this, controlling crime depends to a great degree on interaction between the community and the criminal justice system. The need for the system and the universities to work together on research into crime and the ways to prevent or control it has been mentioned. Similarly, effective policing of slums and ghettos requires programs designed to improve relations between the police and the residents of such neighborhoods and enable them to work together. Community-based correctional programs require that organizations of many kinds, and individuals as well, involve themselves actively in the job of reintegrating offenders into the life of the community. Programs designed to reduce juvenile delinquency require the same kind of public involvement.

Above all, the Commission inquiries have convinced it that it is undesirable that offenders travel any further along the full course from arrest to charge to sentence to detention than is absolutely necessary for society's protection and the offenders' own welfare. Much of the congestion throughout the system, from police stations to prisons, is the result of the presence in the system of offenders who are there only because there is no other way of dealing with them. One of the system's greatest needs is for the community to establish institutions and agencies to which policemen, prosecutors, and judges can refer various kinds of offenders, without being compelled to bring the full force of criminal sanctions to bear on them. Doubtless, devising and instituting alternative ways of treating offenders is a long and complicated process. It must begin with an understanding by the community of the limited capacity of the criminal justice system for handling the whole problem of "crime." Until the public becomes fully aware of what the system can do and what it cannot do, it cannot give the system the help it needs.

The inertia of the criminal justice system is great. More than 30 years ago the Wickersham Commission described the scandalous way in which justice was being administered in many of the country's "lower" courts, and urged that they be abolished; few of them have been abolished and many of the remaining ones are still a scandal. For centuries the imposition of money bail has discriminated against poor defendants, but only in the last few years has the movement to eliminate money bail for most defendants gained any momentum, and even so money bail is still used for almost everyone in the overwhelming majority of courts. State prisons that were built before 1850 and became obsolete before 1900 are still in operation. Police departments continue to insist that all policemen start their careers at the bottom and rise through the ranks slowly, despite the clearly damaging effect this has on the recruitment and effective use of able personnel. A third of the arrests and convictions in America every year are for drunkenness, though for many years almost everyone in the criminal justice system and out of it has recognized that the criminal process is an irrational means of dealing with drunks. The list of examples could extend for pages.

Many of the criminal justice system's difficulties stem from its reluctance to change old ways or, to put the same proposition in reverse, its reluctance to try new ones. The increasing volume of crime in America establishes conclusively that many of the old ways are not good enough. Innovation and experimentation in all parts of the criminal justice system are clearly imperative. They are imperative with respect both to entire agencies and to specific procedures. Court systems need reorganization and case-docketing methods need improvement; police-community relations programs are needed and so are ways of relieving detectives from the duty of typing their own reports; community-based correctional programs must be organized and the pay of prison guards must be raised. Recruitment and training, organization and management, research and development all require reexamination and reform.

The Commission believes that the first step toward improvement is for officials in all parts of the system to face their problems. The lower courts never will be reformed if their officials do not grapple with the hard fact that the quality of justice that is dispensed in them is disgracefully low. Any program to rehabilitate prisoners must begin with the acknowledgement of the fact that most prisons today do not even try to do this job. Until the police recognize that they exercise great discretion about whom they arrest and how they investigate, no effort to ensure that that discretion is exercised wisely can be made. It is futile to consider ways of making plea negotiation an open, regular procedure as long as prosecutors and defense attorneys state ritually to judges that pleas are not negotiated.

The Commission finds, first, that America must translate its well-founded alarm about crime into social action that will prevent crime. It has no doubt whatever that the most significant action that can be taken against crime is action designed to eliminate slums and ghettos, to improve education, to provide jobs, to make sure that every American is given the opportunities and the freedoms that will enable him to assume his responsibilities. We will not have dealt effectively with crime until we have alleviated the conditions that stimulate it. To speak of controlling crime only in terms of the work of the police, the courts and the correctional apparatus, is to refuse to face the fact that widespread crime implies a widespread failure by society as a whole.

The Commission finds, second, that America must translate its alarm about crime into action that will give the criminal justice system the wherewithal to do the job it is charged with doing. Every part of the system is undernourished. There is too little manpower and what there is is not enough trained or well enough paid. Facilities and equipment are inadequate. Research programs that could lead to greater knowledge about crime and justice, and therefore to more effective operations, are almost nonexistent. To lament the increase in crime and at the same time to starve the agencies of law enforcement and justice is to whistle in the wind.

The Commission finds, third, that the officials of the criminal justice system itself must stop operating, as all too many do, by tradition or by rote. They must reexamine what they do. They must be honest about the system's shortcomings with the public and with themselves. They must be willing to take risks in order to make advances. They must be bold.

1 | PERSPECTIVES ON CRIME, DELINQUENCY, AND SOCIAL CHANGE

INTRODUCTION

This chapter contains five articles covering a wide range of concerns about criminal behavior in the United States and abroad. The breadth of these essays illustrates the enormous complexity of the crime problem, its universality, its relationship to social change, its economic costs, and its concentration in lower class and minority group life.

In "Criminality and Social Change," James Bennett argues that crime is neither inherent in social change nor in the migrations of populations in the wake of technological change, especially not in the economically underdeveloped countries. He strongly suggests the need for better planning so that newcomers can be integrated in the urban areas. Urban community planning is regarded as the chief method of crime prevention in the face of rapid social and economic change.

Daniel Glaser is also deeply concerned with the social consequences of technology. In "Crime in a Great Society," Glaser is convinced that the distinctive feature of industrial societies which bears particularly on delinquency and crime is the emergence of a youth subculture with its own values, standards, language, dress, and orientation. Drawing heavily on, and especially attractive to, out-of-school and out-of-work youth, the effects of this isolation from adults is seen in increased narcotics usage, in the increasing extent to which crime is a phenomenon of youth. For many youths, crime may thus be thought of as compensation for failure in legitimate pursuits.

In "The Cost of Crime," Raymond Galvin attempts to estimate, even if only very crudely, the economics of crime in the United States. The losses sustained in the traditional crimes such as burglary, robbery, grand larceny, and auto theft — the least costly of criminal activities — are estimated to amount to some $600 million annually. The cost of white collar crime — undoubtedly the most expensive of all criminality — cannot even be estimated. Employee theft alone, however, runs to at least $1 billion a year. In the organized criminal sector, racketeering probably drains $7.5 billion annually while illegal gambling — the most lucrative of all syndicate activities — is pegged at $17 billion a year. These estimates fail, of course, to indicate how huge an industry crime really is. If the indirect costs — law enforcement, court, and corrections — were included, the crime problem would easily rival some of our largest industries.

As a change of pace, two articles dealing with crime and delinquency elsewhere are included. In the first, Walter Lunden presents a fascinating picture of the crime problem in London, since the Second World War. "Crimes in London, England, 1945-64" indicates the startling increase in the number of reported crimes in this period, the very small percentage of personal crimes in the total, and the fact that American cities of comparable size have five to ten times as high a murder rate. Lunden also emphasizes the British view that the foot patrolmen can and should play a major role in police work.

Franco Ferracuti shows that crime and delinquency problems besetting cities in continental United States are paralleled by those in Puerto Rico. His major point is that the improved economic situation in Puerto Rico is being offset by the increasing problems of social pathology. A fivefold increase in delinquency, a tremendous number of new addicts, mostly adolescent, but fortunately no juvenile gangs as yet, have come to characterize the situation in Puerto Rico in the last decade.

CRIMINALITY AND SOCIAL CHANGE *

JAMES V. BENNETT

1. Criminality is not necessarily a consequence of social changes accompanying economic development in less developed countries. Social changes and economic development are both welcome, and under proper circumstances, may even contribute to a decrease in criminality. The term "less developed countries" refers only to a state of economic development.

2. The question of the types of criminality connected with social changes and accompanying economic development in less developed countries is one to which inadequate attention has been given and on which insufficient reliable data is available. Therefore conclusions and recommendations on this topic are tentative and subject to verification based on sound research.

3. Criminality which may be related to social changes accompanying economic development in less developed countries may not be new in the sense of forms of behaviour not previously otherwise observable. Attention should therefore be focused on the increases in criminality in general in relation to social change and not limited to concern with special types of criminality.

4. Cultural instability, the weakening of primary social controls and the exposure to conflicting social standards, which have a relationship to criminality, are intensified when social change is disorderly, when the degree of social change is high and when the gap between the breakdown of old social institutions and the creation of new institutions is great.

5. Social change is subject to a certain degree of control and should be a matter for national planning.

6. Migration, and especially internal migration,

* Reprinted from Agenda No. 4, entitled "Prevention of Types of Criminality resulting from Social Changes and accompanying Economic Development in Less Developed Countries," duplicated in Appendix IV of the Report of the United States Delegation to the Second United Nations Congress on the Prevention of Crime and the Treatment of Offenders, London, England, August 8-20, 1960, prepared by James V. Bennett, Chairman of the Delegation, January 4, 1961, mimeographed.

which is to be found associated with social changes accompanying economic development in less developed countries has sometimes been erroneously assumed to be a cause of criminality. It is not migration, *per se*, that is conducive to criminality, but perhaps the cultural instability, the weakening of primary social controls and the exposure to conflicting standards of behaviour associated with migration that are to be identified with crime causation. This same conclusion is to be applied to urbanization and to industrialization.

7. The unfavorable results which may accompany rapid migration to urban centers may be ameliorated by providing to the rural areas the social and economic advantage in search of which the rural inhabitant leaves the land for the city.

8. In connection with rural-urban migration, one essential element in maintaining the social integrity of the individual is the preparedness of the migrant for this experience and the preparedness of the urban community to receive him. In both instances, community development, now occupying a major role in national economic and social policy in many countries, has an important role to play. Indeed, urban community development may prove a principal instrument for the prevention of criminality resulting from social changes and accompanying economic development in less developed countries. Urban preparedness also involves providing reception and orientation services (including temporary shelter), town planning including housing, educational and vocational opportunities for the new population and family and child welfare services.

9. Programmes for the prevention of criminality should be closely coordinated, if possible by an agency organized for this purpose, and constituted by persons highly qualified in this field. It is recommended that this agency operate as an integral part of a coordinated scheme for national social and economic planning since, as stressed in United Nations social surveys, there is an urgent need to eliminate compartmentalization of thought and to integrate social and economic objectives in countries undergoing rapid development.

10. In considering the question of criminality and social change, emphasis is generally laid upon the urban center. This may be warranted, but it would be advisable to assess the impact of social change on rural areas as well, since this may uncover the roots of crime which later manifests itself in the urban setting.

11. The penal code must be in harmony with and reflect social change. Individualization of justice must be envisaged so as to allow rational adjudication and treatment which take into consideration both the social order and the special circumstances of the individual.

12. Research is urgently required to assess the many factors of social change which have the potentiality to contribute to criminality, and research is equally urgently required to evaluate measures of prevention. To this end, there must be a marked increase in the adequacy of

statistical techniques and procedures, to which national attention should be called and international assistance sought. As an adjunct to statistical methods of research, reliance should be placed on case studies, field observations by teams of qualified experts and pilot projects. The United Nations should be asked to assume primary responsibility for carrying out this research in the regional institutes for the prevention of crime and the treatment of offenders organized with its cooperation, and/or by undertaking pilot studies with the cooperation of Governments, the specialized agencies of the United Nations, appropriate non-governmental organizations, and other competent resources. The scope of the research should vary in order to provide proper attention to factors which may be worldwide, regional or local in character.

CRIME IN A GREAT SOCIETY *

DANIEL GLASER

It is an old truth in social science that technological change occurs at an exponential rate. Not only are we changing rapidly, but our speed in changing is increasing all the time. This can be illustrated in innumerable ways. For example, some people in this audience may, like me, recall the 1920's or 1930's, when they travelled across the country by automobile or train at a speed which rarely exceeded 50 or 60 miles per hour. It was not until the late 1940's and the 1950's that airplane travel became a very popular method of long distance travel, and it made our speed more than double, for propeller driven planes flew at from 150 to 250 miles per hour. But only six years ago the mode of cross-continental travel changed once more, again more than doubling our speed. Today in commercial jet liners we think nothing of travelling 550 to 650 miles per hour.

We should, of course, realize that it is not just technology that changes, but also social life, since it is highly dependent on technology. We have all seen social consequences of the mechanization of agriculture, the tremendous increase in automobiles (now exceeding one per household) and the appearance of television in almost all households in less than 20 years. With the remarkably rapid disappearance of the horse and mule, the South's sharecrop and tenant farming system largely dissipated, and most of its rural populations moved into the cities of the North and South. Our civil rights con-

* Reprinted with permission from "Correctional Institutions in a Great Society," *Criminologica*, III, Nos. 2-3 (August–November 1965), 3-5.

troversy and the Negro revolt stems in large part from the development of mechanical cotton pickers which shifted most cotton growing from East to West of the Mississippi in the 1950's, and changed the pattern of rural life in the South.

With advanced industrialization today we are approaching a distribution of income which will change from the pyramid to something like a diamond shape. There will be relatively few very poor people and relatively few extremely rich people in comparison with the larger numbers in a middle income range. We have already moved far in this direction, and this movement seems likely to be much accelerated in the next ten or fifteen years.

Automation today is progressively reducing the number of unskilled and semi-skilled low productivity jobs. At the moment about one-fifth of our population is described as in a state of poverty, with family incomes of less than $3,000, but our so-called war on poverty eventually will make considerable inroad on this chronic problem group, so many of whose members are perpetually on relief. We are investing heavily in paying people to learn to work at jobs where their services can command a reasonable income. New school programs should reduce the frequency in the next generation of the educational deficiencies which today handicap so many persons who are chronically poor.

Although disparity in income is the main problem related to crime on which we are concentrating our national attention, there is another consequence of rapid technological change and urbanization that should concern this National Institute on Crime and Delinquency. I refer to the changed pattern of transition from childhood to adulthood which distinguishes advanced industrial society. A distinctive feature of modern life is the increased extent to which children interact primarily with persons of their own age level. Formerly, there was more work in the home which required interaction between children and parents, and gave children responsibility to the rest of the family. Now the reduction of drudgery in housework, with new appliances and prepared foods, has reduced household demands on both parents and children. With a larger proportion of the married women employed, and with the increased size of our schools, children have a larger percentage of their time in personal relationships exclusively with their own age mates. This is in contrast also with former days when a large proportion left school early and stepped immediately into an apprenticeship relationship to an adult skilled workman.

Isolation of children in their own world is especially characteristic of the most crowded sections of our city, the slum areas where crime and delinquency come most dramatically to our attention. However, it is also more now than previously a characteristic of better residential areas in metropolitan regions, and even of rural life. It is especially the out-of-school and out-of-work group which lives in a social world that is homogeneous in age. Increasingly, youth who are isolated socially from other age groups have the distinctive characteristic of any isolated social group, the development of their own standards and styles of life. They have their own goals of consumption, standards of dress and language, and value systems. While this condition has always existed to some extent, it has been progressively made more extensive as a result of the technological changes which make age homogeneity a larger part of life between childhood and adulthood.

These social changes bring shifts in the nature of crime. Most notable is the reduction of the former linkage between young delinquents and adult professional criminals. The latter are no longer so concentrated in the slum areas, as their income and organization permits them to live in better residential locations, and they need not operate on the streets as predominantly as they once did. The slum itself, with dislocated populations from housing projects and urban renewals, no longer includes such close-knit communities as integrated the criminal world in the 1920's and 1930's, when the classic accounts of slum life, delinquency, and crime were written.

One dramatic change in the nature of crime which is distinctly associated with this increase in the age homogeneity of youth social life is the change in the nature of narcotics usage. In the 1930's and early 1940's most of the commitments to the federal narcotics hospital were from rural areas, with Texas being the state with the largest contribution. Today a majority of the commitments are from New York City, even though there are local narcotics hospitals there. Formerly, the narcotics addict was disproportionately white and middle-aged, while now he is disproportionately from minority groups and most are under 28. Previously crime seemed to follow a narcotics habit, if it was linked with it at all, whereas increasingly now narcotics follows an introduction to delinquency and crime, in an out-of-school and out-of-work youth population. The narcotics addict today expresses a sub-culture in our society with new goals, in which the youth work hard to procure what they conceive as distinctive elite experiences. They conceive of themselves, from the perspectives of their peers, not as escapists, but as persons with a sophistication which those of the "square" world do not share. This compensates them psychologically for their failure in legitimate pursuits.

Another indication of the impact on crime of the increasing age homogeneity in youth social life in the adolescent and youthful years is simply the increase in the extent to which crime is a phenomenon of youth. Auto theft is committed by persons most of whom are less than seventeen years of age. Half of the persons arrested for burglary in this country, and half of those arrested for larceny, now are less than eighteen years of age. Half of those arrested for robbery are less than twenty-two. More of what crime we have seems to be expressive conduct of youth in a world of their own.

Another interesting phenomenon which has not yet affected the crime situation radically is the greatly increasing extent to which persons in old age live in isolation from younger people. Not only are we losing the three-generation household in which grandparents, parents and children are in contact with each other, but the extension of life by medicine, the development of social security, and especially the growth of private pensions systems, separates the social world of the aged. In conjunction with the great geographical mobility of our population now, there is more disorganization in old age. The evidence of the relationship of old age to crime is found mostly in the misdemeanor courts, particularly with the arrestees from Skid Row, but it is a phenomenon likely to grow.

What I have been saying thus far is that more rapid change than ever is likely, and it is well for us to be able to anticipate it. I have been saying that we are likely to see some changes in the characteristics of crime, and in its age distribution. I am not pessimistically forecasting that we shall necessarily see an increase in actual crime. There are several reasons for believing that the actual rate of crime may already be on the decline. If so, one factor may well be the increased investment of government agencies in effective means of combatting crime. The war on poverty is placing more and more youth into work experience and increasing their qualifications to continue work on their own in adult roles. Although this process is wasteful and frequently unsuccessful in the short run, it should offset what would be otherwise an increasingly prolonged transition from childhood to adulthood for the out-of-school, out-of-work population. Police service also is becoming more efficient, despite its problems in the courts. Most important, it is becoming increasingly preventive in the juvenile areas.

But the primary anti-crime factor in the immediate future, in my opinion, is the general educational up-grading of our population. It has always been true that violent reaction to rebuffs, and willingness to risk arrest and prosecution by stealing, are more accepted — even expected — among the less educated than among the more educated. The more educated have most to lose by overt crime, and are more conditioned against it. I am, of course, not referring to so-called "white-collar" crime, but to the offenses most often prosecuted in our felony courts.

It may well be that much of our crime rate on paper is not something that represents more crime now than we had 30 or 60 years ago. It may simply be a greater use of public agencies, notably the police, in dealing with crime, now that societies are scattered and communities are more disorganized worlds of strangers than ever, so that there is less settlement of conflict outside of police offices and courts. One suggestion of a decline in actual crime is the fact that murder rates have been cut almost in half in the past 30 years.

THE COST OF CRIME*

RAYMOND T. GALVIN

Upon hearing the phrase "the cost of crime," many people are likely to conjure up images of burglarized homes, beaten robbery victims, and the like. However, such losses constitute only a minute portion of the total cost of crime. Indeed, there are costs associated with other types of crime and costs of other than a monetary nature which need to be explored, if an accurate picture is to be drawn.

In order to deal with such a complex matter it is useful to devise a system of classification so that the question may be treated in a logical manner. Crime, as most commonly known, seems to best fall into three major categories. First is the traditional form of criminality. It is traditional in the sense that it has long been publicly recognized as deviant behavior. Traditional crime may be subdivided into two groups, crimes against the person such as murder, assault, rape, etc., and crimes against property like arson, burglary, forgery and larceny. The second major category is that of organized crime. This classification has received considerable public attention since the days of Prohibition. It embraces such diverse activities as gambling, prostitution, trading in narcotics, and the protection racket. The third category is that of white collar crime. This area has only recently been subjected to extensive general scrutiny. It includes a variety of illegal and unethical acts by executives in both the private and public sectors and all forms of theft by employees.

Besides defining the types of crimes, some comment must be made concerning the nature of the costs resultant from their commission. These criminal acts bring about monetary losses in both cash and goods, social costs such as those related to the administering of criminal justice and the loss to society of individual productive capacity, and consumer costs, those losses which are suffered by business and passed on to the consumer in the form of higher prices. Any attempt to evaluate the true losses brought about by such behavior must consider their costs under each of these forms.

It is, of course, impossible to give precise figures on the various costs of the different types of crime on a nation-wide basis, or even on a state-by-

* Raymond T. Galvin, "The Cost of Crime," *The Michigan Economic Record*, VII, No. 9 (November 1965), 1, 2 & 8. Reprinted by permission of the publisher, the Bureau of Business and Economic Research, Division of Research, Graduate School of Business Administration, Michigan State University.

state basis. Crime by its very nature is not something which lends itself to simple study and easy measurement. There are, however, some general statements which can be made about the costs of the different forms of crime in relation to one another.

Examining first the traditional crimes, it is rather quickly apparent that they account for only a small portion of the total monetary cost. Losses of this type are, generally speaking, confined to the victim of the crime. They are limited to property losses in the cases of crimes against property, and to medical expenses, losses of income due to lost work time, etc., in the cases of crimes against the person. However, here are often discovered the greatest social losses. These involve the vast amounts of the public money expended to apprehend, try, incarcerate and attempt to rehabilitate the perpetrators of these acts. Add to this waste of potentially productive human resources, the immeasurable cost in terms of suffering, shame, and humiliation on the part of victims and the families of perpetrators, and it is easy to see the extent of the cost, intangible though it may be.

Several of the traditional crimes also result in extensive monetary losses in the form of consumer costs. While it is often indicated that ten to fifteen dollars is lost by employee theft for every dollar that is lost to shoplifters, the customer costs in this area are seldom mentioned. The amount of capital that a company spends in deterring and apprehending shoplifters in undoubtedly sizeable. The expenditures made by a retail store for security personnel and the installation of security devices such as burglar alarm systems and wide-angle mirror layouts are recovered by increasing the sales prices on their merchandise. Thus, the consumer pays the costs.

A recent article in *The Wall Street Journal* indicated another major area of economic loss due to traditional crime. The offenses of burglary, robbery, serious larceny and auto theft cost an estimated $600 million in property annually. While this sum alone is staggering, the holder of an insurance policy of this type is also victimized through the related constant increases in his premiums. And even though rates show a continuous upward trend, the nation's casualty insurance companies paid out in claims $104.60 for each $100.00 of revenue they took in on burglary and theft policies in 1963. Unfortunately, the end is not in sight, as the commission of these crimes is still on the upswing both in Michigan and across the nation (see Table 1 [page 27]).

The second category is that group of activities commonly referred to as organized crime, or commercialized vice. Organized crime is big business. Its operations and income are extensive. Its annual revenues from non-gambling enterprises have been calculated at over $7.5 billion. It even emulates big business in its organization and practice. This type of crime has, over the past thirty years, shown a steady shift from crimes involving force and outright thievery to crimes which are more in the nature of a supply-demand relationship and require considerably more sophistication.

They run the gamut from prostitution, boot-legging, narcotics, and gambling, to the infiltration for illegal purposes of labor unions, providing "protection," and finally, the infiltration of various legitimate business enterprises.

The infiltration has occurred in two ways. First there has been a direct takeover in certain areas, such as linen supply, and the supply of mechanical amusement equipment such as jukeboxes and pinball machines. The second form of infiltration is more covert and comes about through the investment of illegal income in what are otherwise legitimate areas of business. The Kefauver Report noted that over fifty fields have received such money, including advertising, appliances, baking, banking, cigarette distribution, construction, drug stores, florists, football, hotels, insurance, etc.

The movement of organized crime into the area of legitimate business is causing law enforcement officials great concern. Under the mantle of legitimate commerce, criminal elements are gaining huge profits at the expense of the public. Large-scale tax frauds are constantly perpetrated. The profits from quasi-legal enterprises often go to strengthen clearly illegal ventures. Legal competitors of such firms are forced to fight questionable trade practices. Finally, the consumer in some areas is faced with monopolistic tactics and required to purchase inferior products.

Many of the activities of organized criminals are nothing more than traditional vice activities which have been placed on a commercial basis to increase profits. These are costly in several ways. There are large social costs involved, particularly with narcotics addiction and prostitution. The former usually drives its victims to the commission of traditional crimes in order to support their habit, and the latter brings about the spread of venereal disease.

Gambling, an activity participated in by millions of otherwise law-abiding citizens, takes in billions of dollars each year in illegal profits. One recent estimate placed the total illegal gambling figure at $48 billion annually; Michigan's share of this enormous sum was $5 billion.

A more conservative and probably more trustworthy estimate of the yearly illegal gambling in this country indicates the following totals: illegal book-making, $8 billion; numbers (policy, lottery, etc.), $6 billion; slot machines, $3 billion, for a total of $17 billion (see Table 2 [page 27]).

Regardless of how one makes an estimate, there can be no doubt that organized crime relieves the American public of sums running into the billions each year.

Besides the deprivation of individual citizens, there are extensive losses to the various levels of government in unpaid taxes. Without arguing either the morality or the propriety of the state of Nevada's position on this matter, the fact is that Nevada's governmental jurisdictions realize over $15 million annually in tax revenues from the approximately $5 billion in legal gambling that occurs in the state. Indeed, the desire to emulate Nevada's success in this area and to collect errant tax dollars has led a number of states to look upon legalized gambling as a promising source of revenue. New Hampshire has approved and held a lottery, and New York seriously considered controlled off-track betting during a recent legislative session. A congressman from New York also recently issued a statement urging the approval of a national lottery, stating: "Our states and nation need government controlled and operated gambling to make gambling profits work for and not against the people." This flurry of activity emphasizes the fact that gambling is an important economic enterprise.

White collar crime is the third major classification which is extremely close to the nation. White collar crime as defined here includes a somewhat broader range of activities than is usually the case. The term as normally used means the dishonest acts of men in the upper socio-economic levels of American society which are committed as part of their normal business or professional practices. Here, however, it will also be taken to include thefts from a firm or an individual by an employee.

In his now classic first study, Sutherland examined the history of seventy large American corporations. He found that the seventy had accumulated a total of 980 legal decisions against them. Of these, 16 percent were criminal decisions for offenses ranging from unfair labor practices and violation of trust to misrepresentation in advertising and rebating. The recent conviction of several top officials of General Electric indicates that this type of criminality is still very much with us. It is, understandably, almost impossible to estimate the monetary cost of such acts. Unfortunately, there are more than monetary costs at stake. Such acts may have grave moral consequences in other areas of American life. How can we expect honesty from the average citizen when he sees our largest and supposedly most honored business firms engaging in dishonest practices?

The other form of white collar crime, as described here, is theft by employees. This covers a wide range of behavior, all the way from embezzlement to taking home a box of company stationery for personal use. Here again are found hidden costs to the consumer. In many businesses the losses suffered due to employee theft are made up by simply raising prices enough to cover them. As stated earlier, it is estimated that for every dollar lost to shoplifters, there are ten to fifteen dollars lost to dishonest employees. There have been instances of such theft taking the form of well organized rings which divert shipments of goods. Needless to say, extensive security measures must be taken against such losses, which most estimates place at upwards of $1 billion yearly. At the risk of over-emphasizing a point, consider that *one* security agency reported that of $60 million in business thefts in 1963, 60 percent were attributable to employee theft. The Pinkerton Detective Agency estimates that 75–80 percent of all employee thefts are of non-cash items. The effect that such practices have on this nation's character are obviously inestimable.

It has long been known that embezzlement is an extremely costly form of criminality. One embezzler can do more damage than can one hundred

TABLE 1

Growth of Selected Conventional Crimes in United States and Michigan 1959–1964

	Robbery	Burglary	Auto Theft	Larceny Over $50
1959				
U.S.	71,535	685,862	288,337	403,428
Michigan	4,714	39,652	13,666	17,561
1964				
U.S.	111,753	1,110,458	402,971	704,536
Michigan	7,113	51,990	21,011	33,163
Numerical increase				
U.S.	40,218	424,596	174,634	301,108
Michigan	2,399	12,338	7,345	15,602
Percentage of increase				
U.S.	56.2	61.9	51.5	74.6
Michigan	50.8	31.1	53.7	88.2

TABLE 2

Estimated Annual Cost of Selected Crimes in the United States

Type of Crime	Estimated Cost
Conventional Crime (Robbery, Burglary, etc.)	$ 600,000,000
White Collar Crime (Employee Theft only)	$ 1,000,000,000
Organized Crime (Racketeering)	$ 7,500,000,000
Illegal Gambling	$17,000,000,000

burglars. The American Bankers Association estimates that $9 million was lost to embezzlers in American banks in 1963. A related form of offense for which no reports are available is the bilking of trust funds and estates, many of which are probably never uncovered.

The cost of crime to the American public is staggering. Billions of dollars which could be better employed to defeat poverty, disease and ignorance are lost annually. Even greater is the loss experienced by society in human misery and in the waste of human resources. These deprivations are not as remote to the individual citizen as he would like to think. Each one finds his life conditioned directly and indirectly by the greed and violence of the criminal element, whether white collar, traditional, or organized.

CRIMES IN LONDON, ENGLAND, 1945-64*

WALTER A. LUNDEN

Within the past eight years, the great metropolis of London, England, with 8,177,600 inhabitants, has been confronted with a serious increase in crimes, as much as many cities in the United States. In 1963, the London police reported 229,107 indictable offenses or 7 per cent more than the previous year. In his annual report for the year, Commissioner J. Simpson stated that there were "more crimes reported to the police than ever before."

Between 1945, the last year of World War II, and 1963, the population of London increased 18 per cent; but for the same years serious crimes rose more than 75 per cent or about four times faster than the number of inhabitants. In the same period of time, arrests for all offenses rose 103 per cent. Confronted with this sharp increase in crimes and arrests, Commissioner Simpson remarked:

The basic causes for crime have been the same for centuries but perhaps the most distressing feature of the rise in crime today lies in the fact that neither the absence of real poverty nor the more progressive methods employed in dealing with delinquents appears to have done anything to reduce the volume of crime.

The British Home Office has not been unmindful of the same situation. The 1959 Home Office Report opens with the following statement.

It is a disquieting feature of our society that in the years since the war, rising standards in material prosperity, education and social welfare have brought no decrease in the high rate of crime, . . . on the contrary, crime has increased and is still increasing.

In spite of similarities in the increase of crimes in London and cities in the United States, there are marked differences in the amount of offenses.

* Reprinted with permission from "Crimes in London, England, 1945-64," *Police* (May-June 1966), pp. 1-3, Charles C Thomas, publisher.

TABLE 1

Crimes Known to Police in London,
England, 1945–63
(Indictable Offenses and Arrests Only)

Year	Crimes Known	Arrests for All offenses
1945	128,954	58,759
1946	127,796	59,695
1947	127,458	67,529
1948	126,597	77,092
1949	106,077	70,373
1950	100,304	73,993
1951	111,091	81,198
1952	109,392	81,480
1953	99,454	77,545
1954	93,937	78,333
1955	95,262	76,416
1956	108,582	82,393
1957	125,754	99,005
1958	151,796	106,354
1959	167,343	104,254
1960	188,396	96,625
1961	196,854	103,684
1962	214,120	112,864
1963	229,107	119,249

SOURCE: *Report of the Commissioner of Police of the Metropolis for Year, 1963.* July, 1964. (Cmd. 2408) London, p. 48 and 100. Arrests are for all persons dealt with at Magistrates' Courts and Assizes or Quarter Sessions.

Table 2 shows the number of murders in London, in three large American cities, and for all of England and Wales, together with the population and the strength of the police forces for three years.

London, in 1964, had a force of 16,131 men in the "Uniform Branch," 1,820 in the Criminal Investigation Division and thirty-eight police women. In the same year, thirty-six homicides occurred in the city. In 1964, the greater New York metropolitan area with a population of 11.3 millions accounted for 690 murders. The total police force consisted of 26,000 officers and civilian employees. In the same year, the City of Chicago, with the surrounding districts, reported 462 murders. There were 11,835 police serving the 6.3 millions of inhabitants. In 1964, the City of Los Angeles with 6.6 million inhabitants reported 321 homicides. The total police force in the city amounted to 6,150 officers and employees.

TABLE 2

Murders in London, New York, Chicago,
Los Angeles and England and Wales, 1962–64

City	Population in Millions	Murders 1962	1963	1964	Police Force
London (1)	8.1	38	26	36	18,000
New York (2)	11.3	550	583	690	26,000 (a)
Chicago (2)	6.3	440	419	462	11,835 (a)
Los Angeles (2)	6.6	325	306	321	6,150 (a)
Total England and Wales (3)	41.1	159	153	(b)	(b)

(a) Includes Civilian Employees.
(b) No data available.

SOURCES:
(1) Report of the Commissioner of Police of the Metropolis for the year 1964, London, 1965.
(2) Uniform Crime Reports, 1964, Crimes in the United States, 1965. New York includes Bronx, Manhattan, Queens, Richmond, Nassau, Rockland, Suffolk, and Westchester Counties.
Chicago includes Cook, DuPage, Lake, McHenry, and Will Counties.
Los Angeles includes Los Angeles County.
(3) Criminal Statistics England and Wales, 1963, Cmnd. 2525, 1964.

Although Chicago and Los Angeles had fewer people than London, these cities had ten times more murders. In all of England and Wales, with a population of 41.1 millions, there were only 153 murders in 1963 or fewer than all three of the American cities.

As in other cities, there were more crimes against property in London than against persons. The 5,620 offenses against persons in 1963, which comprised only 2.5 per cent of the total, consisted of twenty-six murders, forty manslaughters, forty-nine cases of rape, 3,268 "woundings" and others. Property crimes made up 96 per cent of all offenses, larceny 78.5 per cent, and breaking 17.5 per cent.

It may be assumed that as the volume of crimes increased in London, the number of crimes cleared by arrest decreased. In 1956, of the 108,582 offenses known to the police, 31.1 per cent were cleared by an arrest. Six years later, the percentage for the 214,120 crimes fell to 24.6 and finally in 1964 to 21.9 per cent. Table 4 reveals the changes in percentages for six crimes for a ten-year period.

TABLE 3

Indictable Offenses Known to the Police,
London, 1963

Crime Against	Number	Per Cent	Per cent Increase Over 1962
Persons	5,620	2.5	5.5
Property			
Breaking	40,136	17.5	8.5
Larceny	180,327	78.5	6.6
Others	3,024	1.3	13.3
Total	229,107	100.0	7.0

From 1955 to 1964, the percentage cleared by arrest for burglary decreased from 42.4 to 30.5 per cent. Clearance for housebreaking declined from 20.2 to 13.2 per cent and robbery from 59.1 to 27 per cent. Larceny from persons declined from 20.5 to 13.8 per cent and larceny from motor cars fell from 25.5 to 17.4 per cent. The percentage of shoplifting cases which amounted to 97.8 per cent in 1955 decreased to only 94.4 per cent for the same years.

In contrast to the police system in the United States, the major portion of the London police carry out their duties "on foot" in assigned areas. This practice follows the traditional plan which enables the officers to maintain

TABLE 4

Percentage of Crimes Cleared by Arrest in
London, England, 1955 and 1964

Crime	1955 (Per Cent)	1964 (Per Cent)
Shoplifting	97.8	94.4
Robbery	59.1	27.0
Burglary	42.6	30.5
Housebreaking	20.2	13.2
Larceny from Person	20.5	13.8
Larceny of Motor Cars	25.5	17.4

NOTE: Irrespective of when the crime occurred, it is cleared at the time the person is arrested, therefore some of those cleared in one year may have taken place earlier.

close contact with the public. "I know that this is out of keeping with modern American conceptions of preventive policing but we in this country feel that the traditions upon which our Force was founded and has well succeeded are those of contact between the policemen and the general members of the public. It may be wasteful in manpower but from the preventive point of view it is essential, and even more essential for maintaining the spirit of co-operation between the members of the general public and the force." *

It is highly probable that the "Police on Foot" system used in London could be used to good advantage in the subways and public places in the United States in order to prevent violence while at the same time providing better protection for the people. One of the major complaints at present is that streets and subways in American cities are not safe. In some cases, subway stations have been closed during certain hours because of assaults and violence. In not a few cities, business firms provide special transportation for employees who may be required to work late hours. The motorized police may cover more territory but what may be gained in miles covered is lost in effective control of crimes and the protection of the public.

Not unlike their counterparts in the United States, the police in London have been hampered by criminals who make false claims under the guise of interference with civil rights and individual liberties. England does not have the Fifth Amendment but offenders have made use of the policies advanced by the National Council of Civil Liberties in trying to avoid arrest and conviction in court. In certain cases, criminals lodge complaints against law enforcement officers as a means of embarrassing the police. These open attacks by criminals and others have diverted the efficiency of the police and lessened the protection to the public. Casting doubt on the police has another dimension which has been and is related to subversive elements within a nation. While these persons harass, make false claims against the police, and make libertarian demands, they shun their civil responsibilities as citizens. As it often happens, they *want everything but refuse to support the society that protects their rights and liberties. They have not learned that rights and duties cannot be separated.*

* Quoted from a letter to the author from Sir Joseph Simpson, Commissioner of Police.

JUVENILE DELINQUENCY AND SOCIAL CHANGE IN PUERTO RICO*

FRANCO FERRACUTI

Few countries of the Western World have been exposed to the rapid rate of change that has taken place in the Commonwealth of Puerto Rico. The island has an estimated population of 2,625,600 units. The rate of growth of the population was 18.3 per cent in the decade from 1940 to 1950, but only 6.3 per cent in the decade 1950 to 1960. Migration to the continental United States is one of the important factors, together with the increase of the educational level, in the change of the rate of increase of the population. The population density is 767.5 persons per square mile, one of the highest in the world.

The peaceful racial climate of the Island has caused the distinction between the original Indian, Negro and Spanish white stocks to disappear into a principal central nucleus of unclear racial status. In 1965, 48.1 per cent of the total population was 19 years of age or less. The population over 65 years of age composed only 5.8 per cent of the total. This situation, common to many developing countries, puts, of course, a strain on the educational, labour and productivity resources of the Island.

Illiteracy, although still high (16.6 per cent of the population over 10 years of age) is rapidly decreasing. The school system, however, suffers from a high rate of drop-outs, particularly in the high school levels.

Puerto Rico has now 55 cities compared with 17 in 1899. The San Juan Metropolitan Area includes a population of approximately 700,000. The urban proportion of the population, from 14.6 per cent in 1899, has now reached a level of 44.2 per cent. The external migration has always been directed to the continental United States; migration to other Latin American countries has never been economically attractive. Predictably, migration has followed the economic fluctuations of the U.S. economy and labor market. It reached a peak in the 1951–1960 decade, with an average of 41,212 migrants per year, and it has now decreased to an average of 1,200 units per year for the period 1961 to 1964. Seasonal migration has always had an important role. In recent years, the increase of labor opportunities, the

* From *International Understanding* (published by the International Council of Psychologists, Inc.), Volume 3, Autumn 1966. Reprinted by permission of the author and the editor of *International Understanding*, Dr. Cecily Grumbine.

phenomenon of the retiring Puerto Rican and the reduction of travel costs has increased the rate of the returning Puerto Rican migrant. A conservative estimate of a total of 150,000 persons can be classified as "return migrants." It is difficult if not impossible to find any community in Puerto Rico where no member has been exposed, even briefly, either through migration, or through military service, or through tourism, to the tempo and patterns of life in the United States.

Although products, life patterns, and institutions are more and more North American oriented, English is spoken with any degree of fluency only by about 40 per cent of the population. The traditional Puerto Rican values face the challenge of erosion by contact with continental values and by change due to urbanization, industrialization and increase in mass media use. The emphasis on material wealth (and on its symbols), the expansion of education, the urbanized competitive life patterns, the changing family roles, and the political uncertainties which are the lot of the Puerto Rican "man-in-the-street" result in occasional passivity and/or in the cultural confusion and maladjustments which many authors have described for many developing countries.

The per capita Gross National Product, from a level of 150 dollars in 1940 has increased to about 1,000 in 1964. The entire economic structure of the Island has been altered by a number of planned and unplanned transformations. Agriculture in 1940 accounted for 31 per cent and manufacturing for 12 per cent of the National Income. Twenty-five years later, these percentages are 20 and 23 per cent respectively. Many statistics could be quoted to substantiate the spectacular economic transformation experienced by the people of Puerto Rico. In psychological terms, the dependency and despair which characterized the Puerto Rican life of the thirties have changed to optimism and to a dynamic pattern of expectations for the future. In sum, the Island constitutes a striking example of the "revolution of rising expectations."

Another important side of the general picture is that provided by the improvement of health conditions. Health statistics show a great reduction of infant mortality (from 113 per thousand births in 1940 to 44 in 1965), the life expectancy at birth raised to 70 years thus reaching about the same level as the United States. It was 38 years in 1910.

The optimistic picture which the economic indexes convey is somewhat offset by an analysis of the indexes of "social pathology." Of these, we shall focus our attention on those related to delinquency.

If we take the number of police interventions on juveniles (one of the most reliable figures in the field), we note that the figure of 2,542 interventions in 1956 shows a 600 per cent rise in 1963 (15,070 interventions) and a 509 per cent rise in 1964 (12,768 interventions). Although delinquency is on the rise in almost all countries, Puerto Rico shows certainly one of the most serious and alarming changes. A parallel increase is shown in the number of juveniles referred to court for adjudication. More recent years show the beginning of a declining trend, which probably indicates an adjustment of the control and judicial institutions to the large increase of the 1956–1963 period.

Related to it is the phenomenon of narcotic addiction. Until recently, virtually unknown in the Island, it has, in the last 6 years, become a major problem with a total estimated number of addicts between 10,000 and 12,000. Most addicts are in the adolescent group. Most, predictably, engage in some form of delinquent behavior to maintain the habit; thefts of various kinds are the rule of behavior in this group.

Delinquency begins in early prepuberal and puberal years, mostly in boys of the lower socio-economic group. It is an urban phenomenon, most frequent in newly urbanized families, where other social problems are present. A large percentage of delinquents come from government-sponsored housing projects. Absence from school, either as a primary or as a secondary concomitant, is almost universal in the delinquent population. Although group or associated (often with adults) delinquency is frequent, there is no evidence of gang activity as a way of life pattern on the vast scale [as] found in continental (U.S.) metropolitan areas. A large percentage [as high as 50 per cent in a recent random group of 30 cases from the San Juan Metropolitan Area] shows evidence of handicaps in intellectual abilities or in personality structures. Organic factors are frequent, and compound or are compounded by, the social deviant forces which operate in the environment. A distinction, or even a differential weighting of the relative importance of biological and social "causes" is impossible in practice, and an interdisciplinary multifactor approach to etiology of delinquent behavior is in order. School maladjustment and dropping out are often the first visible symptoms after which addiction or delinquency or more frequently both occur and mark definitely the subject as a candidate for a career which starts with a probationary sentence and progresses to institutionalization. Several studies and reports have demonstrated the inadequacy of the existing preventive and treatment policies in the Island. The social action against delinquency is dispersed among a variety of agencies, from the Police, to the Judiciary, to Health, with little coordination and little agreement on aims, procedures, and policies.

The prevalence of organic handicaps and factors in the delinquent population is, of course, not surprising to students of epidemiological aspects of developing countries. In the struggle for bettering the health standard of a raising society, preventive measures on maternal and birth care come, as a rule, only after more serious problems of infectious diseases have been solved; this, plus the raise in medical technology and the resulting decrease in child mortality, created a limited backlog of less-than-adequate individuals with evidence of infant organic injury to the central nervous system. Standard measuring instruments must be adapted to the biological and social reality of the culture. This is particularly true of intelligence testing.

The factors which sociologists have regarded as responsible for the genesis of delinquent behavior: culture conflicts, anomie, subcultural drifts and allegiances, are all present in a society which exhibits the rates of change, in terms of industrialization, urbanization, migration and other factors, which are recorded for Puerto Rico. However, a minority may be biologically and/or socially unequipped for these changes. This minority may choose delinquency or addiction as alternate solutions to their adjustment problems.

Patterns of social pathology like the ones outlined above are certainly not peculiar to Puerto Rico. In fact, they are all too common in most developing countries, and in a way, they represent the almost inevitable price a free society has to pay for progress and change.

Another element of interest is the fact that, although economic planning has undoubtedly been a success in Puerto Rico (in contrast to the somewhat pessimistic outlook for other developing nations), no major social planning has evolved to control the negative developments of delinquency. The economic planner has once more got the lion's share of governmental bureaucratic attention, to the possible detriment of the less concrete, less obvious, but no less important social planner.

Awareness of the seriousness of the problem is now increasing and several efforts are under way to coordinate the existing resources. Their effectiveness will be a problem for future evaluation. The cost of delinquency treatment and the risk of failure are always greater than the cost of prevention. But prevention is difficult and, in a free and mobile society, not easy to formulate and implement. After this brief and incomplete sketch of the Puerto Rican scene, some concluding remarks seem in order:

1. Delinquency, addiction and other forms of social pathology are more often than not the concomitant of rapid social change unless preventive measures are undertaken.

2. Prevention is a broad action program, which must be planned centrally and carried out in a variety of ways, from health measures to social measures; it must be envisaged and planned simultaneously with economic planning for social change.

3. The benefits obtained by change can be seriously offset by resulting social pathologies. Delinquency is one of the most visible and most acute of the concomitants of social change. Its cost in dollars and suffering is beyond calculation.

4. Preventive work must be based on a broad interdisciplinary approach. Social theories of deviancy must be integrated with existing biopsychological problems.

5. Economic planning without social preventive planning is, at best, hazardous, and, at worst, imprudent. The Puerto Rican experiment should be of interest to other developing countries in as far as its elements are comparable.

2 | CRIME AND THE LAW

INTRODUCTION

Whatever else crime may be behaviorally, symbolically or socially, it is first and foremost a violation of one or more criminal codes or statutes. Nothing is quite as central, therefore, as some understanding of criminal law — its origins, evolution, types, function, relationships to other kinds of law, and utilization as a formal mechanism of social control. While it is obviously impossible to consider even all of the more important aspects of the criminal law, the five articles in this section will at least introduce some of the major themes and arguments regarding the criminal law and social control.

In "The Concept of Crime," P. J. Fitzgerald first distinguishes the notion of crime from civil wrongs. Crimes are the concern of the state; civil wrongs merely of the individual wronged. Crimes, therefore, make the wrongdoer subject to punishment while civil wrongs obligate him to compensate his victim. One interesting question is why and how some acts come to be defined as criminal while others, seemingly of equal or even more harm,

37

are defined as civil wrongs. Fitzgerald also suggests that there are two major types of criminal acts — those intrinsically wrong and those which are bad because they are defined as illegal. This distinction between *mala in se* and *mala prohibita* crimes is not uniformly accepted by many as valid. The student might well ponder the validity of these types.

The second selection, "Law as a Type of Social Control," deals with social control as a process whereby persons are persuaded to behave in accordance with group norms. The mechanisms of social control may be either formal or informal, or both. Informal controls — gossip, ridicule, and laughter, for example — are most effective in the small community characterized by primary group relationships. Mass society relies, therefore, on formal social controls of which the most obvious is law. In this article, F. James Davis discusses the nature of law as a mechanism of social control. He distinguishes substantive and procedural, public and private, civil and criminal, and enacted and common law. An especially interesting aspect of the article is the notion of law as an index of social solidarity.

C. Ray Jeffery in "Criminal Justice and Social Change" traces the evolution of law from the private law and self-help notions of primitive society through its development as public law in archaic societies and its evolution as state law. Professor Jeffery covers the role of the feud, vengeance, banishment and compensation, and the transition to punishment. Finally, the article describes the emergence of two types of criminal procedure — the accusatorial and the inquisitional systems.

In his essay "Is Criminal Behaviour Deviant Behaviour?" Richard Quinney challenges the widely embraced assumption that violations of the criminal law also represent deviations from other social norms. He argues that the extent of social differentiation is so great in complex societies that many criminal laws are simply not supported by most persons. Many laws ("blue laws," white-collar crime laws) are probably out of step with the social norms of the general population or of specific subgroups. Apart from social differentiation, Quinney also cites the processes in the formulation of criminal law and the disproportionate influence of some groups on this process as a major factor creating the gulf between legal and other norms. The difficulty in enforcing laws on which there is little or no consensus is seen as one major outcome of this disparity.

The effect of criminal law on moral judgments is considered in a timely article by Nigel Walker and Michael Argyle. In the United States, in particular, there has been increasing agitation for the decriminalization (legalization) of traditionally morally reprehensible acts such as addiction, abortion, and homosexuality. How would the decriminalization of these and other such behaviors affect our moral judgments of these acts? In a short but very provocative contribution, the authors seek to evaluate empirically the "declaratory argument." This argument holds that the repeal of a legal prohibition gives the impression that the conduct in question is no longer to be regarded as morally wrong. In "Does the Law Affect Moral Judgments?" Walker and Argyle conclude that there is not much empirical support for the "declaratory argument."

THE CONCEPT OF CRIME *

P. J. FITZGERALD

The criminal law is part of public law. Public law consists of those fields of law which are concerned with the state and its relationship with the individual, as opposed to private law, which deals with relationships between individuals. The criminal law falls under the heading of public law because it is concerned with those wrongs of which the state takes cognizance. The general aim of the criminal law is to discourage and prevent certain types of the conduct in question, together with the assignment of a punishment for disregard of the prohibition.

Attempts to provide an adequate definition of the notion of a crime have been complicated by the fact that there are really two different questions involved here. The first problem is to explain what is entailed by the stigmatization by law of any conduct as criminal. The second is to ascertain the distinguishing feature common to all the different types of conduct which are by law classified as criminal.

First, crimes are the concern of the state, whereas civil wrongs such as breach of contract and tort are the concern merely of the individual wronged. This means that the initiative with regard to crimes rests with the state, whereas in the case of civil wrongs it is up to the victim to decide whether to go to law against the wrongdoer. If, for instance, Jones refuses to pay a debt to Smith, it is purely a matter for Smith whether or not to take legal action against Jones. If, on the other hand, Jones were to break and enter and steal something from Smith's house, this would become a matter for the state, and whether or not Jones was prosecuted would be no concern of Smith.

The second consequence of criminality is that whereas a man who is proved to have committed a civil wrong will be made to compensate the victim, one who is convicted of a criminal offence is liable to be punished. If A by negligent driving were to injure B, B could bring an action against him whereby A would be made to compensate B. If, however, A were violently to assault B, then A would be prosecuted and on conviction would be liable

* Reprinted from P. J. Fitzgerald, *Criminal Law and Punishment* (1962), pp. 1–7, by permission of the Clarendon Press, Oxford.

to punishment. This distinction between the consequences of a criminal act and an act which is only a civil wrong is to some extent blurred by the fact that in certain cases the Criminal Courts may decline to punish an offender; for example, the judge may think it preferable to take a more lenient course such as discharging the accused absolutely. Secondly, in certain cases, the Civil Courts may punish a defendant by ordering him to pay exemplary damages to the plaintiff, as frequently happens in libel actions. Nevertheless, it remains true that the essential object of criminal procedure is to punish the accused and so prevent further offences, whereas the essence of civil proceedings is to compel the defendant to compensate the plaintiff for the injury done to him.

To define crime merely as conduct prohibited by law under pain of certain special consequences has seemed to some writers insufficiently informative. There must be something, it has been felt, common to all the different criminal offences known to the law other than the mere possession of the legal label of criminality. Accordingly, some intrinsic common quality has been sought by which to distinguish criminal from non-criminal conduct.

One candidate for this has been the quality of harmfulness. Crimes, it has been suggested, consist only of those acts which are particularly harmful to the community. It is true that this quality of harmfulness to the community is to be found in many of the more serious crimes, such as treason and other attacks on the institution of the state, murder and other offences of violence which threaten the peace and order of society, and offences against property, which is one of the basic institutions of our community. But this quality will not suffice to indicate with certainty whether an act is a crime or not. There are some criminal offences where little in the way of harm or danger to the public at large could be found. Certain offences of gross indecency, acts of homosexuality between consenting adults, violations of the Blue Laws would, by many people, be thought to fall into the category of conduct constituting no particular threat to society in general. On the other hand, there are certain types of conduct which do not amount to criminal offences, but which may be harmful to the community. Breaches of contract, negligence leading to the destruction of property, and adultery resulting in the break-up of a marriage, while all outside the purview of the criminal law, can cause widespread injury to society. The attempt to elucidate the test of criminality in terms of harmfulness to the public is not, therefore, wholly successful.

Another suggestion is that crimes consist of acts which are wrongful or immoral. This too is not without some basis, in that people do in general think of crimes as wrongful acts, quite apart from the law. Many people would be surprised to learn that acts not intrinsically wrong such as speeding are criminal offences. Certainly the term "criminal" is generally reserved for those who commit crimes of violence and dishonesty. Those with several convictions for careless, dangerous, and even drunken driving would not usually be referred to as criminals. But the law makes no distinction here between crimes consisting of acts considered wrong in themselves, and acts not wrong in themselves, but merely prohibited by the law. Both are alike criminal offences.

Crime and sin are, in fact, intersecting circles. There are many types of conduct, generally looked on as immoral, which are quite outside the view of the criminal law. Equally, there are many criminal offences such as betting in a public house, shooting game on Sunday, which few people would consider wrongful, apart from their illegality. Many of these offences are the creation of statute and other legislation passed to regulate the welfare of society.

The distinction between crimes which are morally wrong and crimes which are merely legally wrong is certainly one which is popularly made. This distinction of crimes into those intrinsically wrong, *mala in se,* and those merely legally wrong, *mala prohibita,* has also been made by judges and certain authors.

On the other hand the distinction has incurred considerable disfavor at the hands of certain academic writers. Their attack has been launched on two different flanks. Men's views of what is right and wrong, it is argued, vary from place to place and from time to time; some communities think it wicked to smoke, drink, and gamble, while others seem to devote all their energy to such activities. Euthanasia, though practised in ancient Sparta and by certain Eskimo peoples in recent years, is not countenanced in this country. From this, the conclusion is drawn that no offence can be said to be intrinsically wrong. This attack is misconceived. Important as it is to realize that no code of morality commands universal acceptance, it is a mistake to think that this realization commits us to abandon what is suggested by the distinction between *mala in se* and *mala prohibita.* The distinction claims that there are certain offences which can only be condemned on legal grounds, types of behaviour which, had they not been legally prohibited, would incur no blame, and that there are other offences such as murder which can be condemned not only on legal but also on moral grounds, types of behaviour which would incur blame quite apart from their illegality. The only reason for our duty to abstain from the former is our general duty to obey the law, while there are extra reasons for abstaining from acts of the second class. Admittedly different societies at different times take different views about what conduct is right and wrong; and whether a crime is thought wrong in itself or only legally wrong will depend on the moral code current in a society. But acknowledgement of the relativity should not blind us to the fact that moral codes are current in societies.

Those who have wanted to define crime in terms of wrongfulness or tendency to injure the community were right in feeling that Parliament and the courts have not acted arbitrarily in creating crimes and that the reason why many acts have become crimes is because of their tendency to injure the community. This principle can be seen at work underlying the judicial creation of such criminal offences as incitements, attempts, and public mischief. It is interesting to note that negligent conduct has for the most part remained outside the criminal law, with the exception of those cases where negligence may be particularly harmful, e.g. on the roads. Moreover, there have been written into the criminal law certain general principles limiting criminal liability, such as those principles relating to lack of choice, lack of intention, mistake, duress, and so forth. A full understanding of the notion of crime must take into account these general principles, which are, of course, common to all criminal offences.

LAW AS A TYPE OF SOCIAL CONTROL*

F. JAMES DAVIS

SOCIAL CONTROL *is the process by which sub-groups and persons are influenced to conduct themselves in conformity to group expectations.* A group is any number of persons among whom social interaction (meaningful mutual influence) occurs. The expected behavior in a smaller group, such as a delinquent gang, may be antisocial from the standpoint of a larger group of which it is a part. In this event, both the pressures exerted by the deviant group to get its members to follow its ways and the influences the larger group uses to bring the subgroup into conformity with the dominant expectations are social controls as defined here.

The character of the process varies with the type and size of the group, and controls may be classified from several points of view. Social control may be exerted unconsciously or deliberately, and the controlled person(s) may or may not be conscious of the process. All actions that influence conduct toward conformity may be treated as the means of social control. Specific means of control may be classified as to whether they are formal or informal; examples of the latter are flattery, gossip, ridicule, and praise. From another standpoint, the particular means of control may be classed as to whether they are suggestive, persuasive, or coercive. Suggestion and persuasion are usually accomplished by verbal symbols; coercion may involve language symbols or physical force. The use of physical force, even when

* Reprinted with permission of The Macmillan Company from *Society and the Law: New Meaning for an Old Profession,* by F. James Davis, Henry H. Foster, C. Ray Jeffery and E. Eugene Davis, pp. 39–57, 60–61. © The Free Press of Glencoe, a Division of The Macmillan Company, 1962.

unaccompanied by words, is social control when the effect is to support group patterns of conduct.

Those means of social control that involve a reward or penalty are often referred to, respectively, as *positive* and *negative sanctions*. Some discussions of sanctions indicate that all social controls involve some kind of reward or penalty. It may be noted that diffuse sanctions (those brought into play by anyone in the group) are informal means of control, and that organized sanctions (those employed only by designated officials) are formal means of control.

To the degree that men act in conformity to group expectations, others can predict what they will do in given situations. When such predictability is not possible, for whatever reasons, orderly group life is impossible. Shared understandings about what people will do under given conditions are indispensable if the group is to retain its unity and ultimately its very existence. Social control thus facilitates social order and group unity.

Since the maintenance of orderly group life involves encouraging the person and placing restraints upon him, social controls influence personality development. The person may develop a relatively permanent set of habits and attitudes that conform to group expectations, but he does not automatically do so. There may be no lasting, measurable influence of particular controls, and under certain conditions the person may develop antipathies towards group expectations. However, whenever orderly group life is maintained, the attitudes and habits of group members generally coincide with the values and expectations of the group. A group expectation is but the agreement of a number of persons as to what conduct is right and what is wrong for persons playing roles in a given situation. Such a consensus may become established in the personality structure of the individual, may become a part of what is called conscience, and may operate as a motive. When this occurs we may say that the pressure of those external stimuli we call social controls has resulted in conformist self-control.

As soon as he begins to understand language symbols the small child encounters social controls, at first chiefly in the form of parental ordering and forbidding. Social controls continue to influence conduct and personality development throughout life. Social control and socialization are thus intimately related but different; the former refers to pressures on the person to conform and the latter to the effects of these pressures on the personality. The one involves learning stimuli, the other the actual learning of expected ways or the unlearning of contrary ones. The pressures are brought to bear on persons as they play particular social roles. When people conform, their conduct indicates that they have learned the attitudes and habits the group expects them to adopt in playing given roles.

Law is defined as *the formal means of social control that involves the use of rules that are interpreted, and are enforceable, by the courts of a political community*. This is intended to be consistent with Pound's definition of law as "the systematic and orderly application of force by the appointed agents" of politically organized society. Pound has noted that law has been used to mean three different things: (1) the legal order, or "the regime of adjusting relations and ordering conduct by politically organized society," (2) the authoritative materials (including rules) that guide administrative and judicial decisions, and (3) the judicial process. It appears that Pound has identified law as the first of these and that when law is so defined it includes the other two. Rules and other authoritative materials (such as annotations and historical interpretations) are tools that constitute an important part of the legal order, and the judicial process refers to the operations of an essential part, the court and law-enforcement machinery.

In this [article] the term "laws" will often be used synonymously with legal rules, and "a law" will mean a particular rule. "Law" will include legal rules but will encompass the various agencies and procedures by which the rules are made, applied, and enforced, including that "law" which is at the end of a policeman's nightstick.

This definition of law is inconsistent with the much broader usages only in the sense that it delineates a smaller segment of social control. The reasons for restricting the definition of law to the political community are that it is the dominant usage among American legal scholars, political scientists, and sociologists, and that the authors wish to center attention on the Anglo-American legal system. The usage of this definition is not intended to support the idea that the expressed will of the state is absolutely sovereign. Neither is it intended to preclude the use of materials about preliterate or other systems of social control that do not have courts or other requisites of law as defined above. The line must be drawn somewhere for analysis and communication, yet the greatest amount of understanding of law will come when it is related to total knowledge in the field of social control.

Formal social control is characterized by (1) explicit rules of conduct, (2) planned use of sanctions to support the rules, and (3) designated officials to interpret and enforce the rules, and often to make them. Informal controls, spontaneously employed by any member of a group, are powerful supporters of expectations in small, homogeneous groups. But as life becomes more complex and anonymous these controls become increasingly inadequate for many purposes, and the group establishes formal controls to maintain conformity to its expectations. Law is often said to be at the extreme formal end of the continuum of social control.

Many methods of social control, both formal and informal, are used in multigroup societies. Law and other formal controls become increasingly important as social organization grows more complex; but ostracism, shaming, gossip, and other informal controls continue to influence conduct toward conformity. The conditions under which the two types of control reinforce each other, and under which they are opposed, are not yet clearly understood. In this connection it should be noted that despite their relative impersonality, formal organizations characteristically contain informal group structures that influence their operation. Even law, then, may be expected to be closely related to certain informal controls, and should be viewed as an approximation to the ideal type of formal social control.

Informal social controls operate largely with reference to implied rules of conduct; formal social controls involve clearly expressed rules. It has been maintained that handwriting is essential to formal control because of the need for keeping records. Accounts of legal rules, rule interpretations, and rule enforcement must somehow be kept. The fact that the members of such groups as the Icelanders and the Ifuago of the Philippines have memorized a great number of precise regulations suggests that writing and printing are not essential to express rules, but they do greatly facilitate explicitness. It is difficult to conceive of modern legal systems apart from the masses of printed materials.

Legal rules specify proper conduct for the citizen, but they are also guides to the conduct of the various officials charged with enforcing the rules. Many rules or parts of rules are directed specifically toward legal officials. This is true of statements of sanctions. A negative sanction, such as the punishment specified by a criminal law, directs the appropriate officials to impose certain penalties when a given rule of conduct is not heeded. Positive legal sanctions, such as laws providing for rewards for informants or pensions for public servants, also are sets of directions for certain officials. Rules of procedure are also guides for rule-makers, rule-interpreters, advocates of the parties to a dispute, enforcement officers, or occupants of other legal roles.

In specifying proper conduct, social rules are guides for the behavior of persons playing different roles in the same situation. The rights of one are the duties of the other. If the role rights and duties are clearly understood by all parties, predictability and social orderliness are possible; but otherwise, there can be only confusion. Particularly in heterogeneous, dynamic societies, social rules are often formulated explicitly to clarify role expectations. Legal rules clarify role rights and duties, and also provide sanctions to support them. A law that grants a right to Person or Group A imposes a legal duty on Person or Group B. The same legal rule that confers a legal privilege on A withholds from B the right to make the corresponding demand.

In all formal agencies of control, provisions are made for designated persons to play specialized roles, and law has many and varied specialists. Unless there are official agencies to decide disputes by interpreting and applying legal rules to given situations — that is, unless there are courts — there is no law as defined here. Unless there is at least one specialist whose function it is to preside over formal sessions and to adjudicate contested cases, there is no court. There must be judges, and their decisions must be justified by reference to rules rather than to caprice, or there is no law. Weber's approach sounds like an insistence upon formal control when he writes that law is a regulatory order that requires an enforcement staff; but he includes even the clan under the concept of staff and does not require the presence of a court. Hoebel insists that there be a court and characterizes it as having responsibility, authority, and method.

Law as defined above is a means of control employed by a political community. A political community involves "forcible maintenance of orderly dominion over a territory and its inhabitants." How much power do political communities have, and what are the implications for the legal system? This question will be discussed primarily with reference to the state. One political community may contain lesser ones, and in each there is law if the unit can use force to get its inhabitants to obey its rules. The state is the supreme political community, privileged to use force to maintain order in the entire territory.

Law defies exact classification and is often called a "seamless web." Yet the vastness and complexity of the subject require that some attempt at subdivision be made. Classifications from three different standpoints will be considered here: (1) the content of law, (2) the origin of law, and (3) the degree of rationality in the legal system. In the first two instances attention is focused on legal rules, but these categories also refer to the agencies and procedures by which the rules are made, interpreted, and enforced.

The content of law may be classed as *substantive* or *procedural*. The former consists of rules concerning rights, powers, duties, and other legal relations, that courts are established to administer. Procedural law, often called *adjective law* and sometimes *remedial law,* has to do with the administration of the substantive law; it provides means for maintaining legal rights or for obtaining redress when they are invaded.

Although it is difficult to maintain a clearcut distinction, a division is sometimes made between *public* law and *private* law. The former has to do with the structure of government, the duties and powers of officials, and the relationship between the individual and the state. It includes such subjects as constitutional law, administrative law, regulation of public utilities, criminal law and procedure, and law relating to the proprietary powers of the state and its political subdivisions. Private law, on the other hand, refers to the rules, both substantive and procedural, governing relationships between individuals, such as the law of torts, contracts, and property.

A distinction more familiar to the practitioner is that between *civil* and *criminal* law. Criminal law has to do with the definition of crimes and the prosecution and penal treatment of offenders. Civil law, as used in this context, means all law other than criminal law, and would thus encompass private law, as defined above, and a large portion of public law.

Law is sometimes classified on the basis of its origin, which is often suggested by the form of the rule under examination. The basic distinction here is between (1) *legislation,* that is, rules of general application, enacted by a law-making body in politically organized society, and (2) *case law,* which is a byproduct of decisions in particular controversies and is expressed with considerable literary freedom by judges in explaining their decisions.

Included in *legislation,* so defined, are constitutions, treaties, statutes, ordinances, administrative regulations, and court rules. Statutes have been further subdivided in many ways. In one scheme, statutes are classed as to whether they are enabling, remedial, or penal. Enabling statutes confer new powers; remedial statutes correct abuses or some other undesirable situation; and penal statutes provide negative sanctions.

The term *common law* is sometimes used as a synonym for "judge-made" law or "case law," as distinguished from legislation, or "enacted law." Much of Anglo-American common law is thought to have been derived from the customs of long ago. Customs, whether local or general, become law when officially adopted by the courts or law-making agencies of a political community. If the body of rules resulting from judicial decisions is of general application within the realm, whether it originated in custom or not, it is *common law.* The distinctive feature of Anglo-American common law has been its emphasis on logical development, with decisions in particular cases resting for the most part on precedents found in earlier cases.

As a part of society's system of social control, law is an aspect of the social organization of the political community. It is a part of the culture — the habits, attitudes, and ideas that are transmitted from one generation to another. Specifically, it is an aspect of the institutionalized part of the culture. Social institutions are organized, and their expectations are stated, as explicit rules that are obligatory and that are supported by specialists.

Social institutions, including legal ones, are interrelated. Nobody has put forth the proposition that law completely determines the culture; but many writers have contended that law is completely determined by other social factors, especially economic forces. Law cannot exist independently, of course; all legal acts concern economic, family, educational, or other areas of life. But this does not mean that law is not itself an element of culture, and that it has no influence on the areas of life it seeks to control. Law is instrumental in making choices and in organizing value systems. Searches for immutable connections between legal institutions and other cultural elements have not been successful, but the evidence at least seems capable of supporting the conclusion that *law and other cultural elements influence each other*

The values supported by other social institutions perhaps determine the limits within which legal controls operate. Certain values are considered essential and others are subordinate or secondary. What matters most at a given time and place ordinarily will be reflected in law. Where there is ambivalence or disagreement as to the priority of values, legal decisions and the law's enforcement will likely be uncertain and equivocal. For example, we expect law in our time and place to support monogamy but not prostitution and concubinage. Yet prostitution and concubinage may thrive if the policy favoring monogamy takes the form of withholding divorce for whatever cause or limiting it to the grounds of adultery, or if marriages are matters of "convenience." Systems of law have grown out of particular cultural systems, those that are already institutionalized to a considerable degree; but at the same time law helps in the process of value integration.

Some sociologists have maintained that law is so intimately connected with other institutions that it can serve as an index of at least the most cherished values. One view is that law indicates those forms of conduct believed to be most dangerous to the welfare of the political community.

The idea that law is a measure of the type of solidarity or unity in a society was stated by Durkheim. He observed that the division of labor was rapidly increasing and that the basis for social cohesion was changing apace. In homogeneous societies, Durkheim reasoned, the basis for group unity is similarity in habits, attitudes and ideas. He called this mechanical solidarity. Early law, he maintained, was repressive, and this penal law was invoked in support of nearly unanimously supported rules of conduct — those reflecting mechanical solidarity. Later, in societies with much division of labor, the basis for group unity came to be the interdependence of widely different persons and groups performing a great variety of functions. Durkheim characterized this as organic solidarity, and contended that a new kind of law—restitutive law—was developing to help cement the new type of society together. Stated concisely, his proposition is that penal law reflects mechanical solidarity, while restitutive law is an index of organic solidarity.

CRIMINAL JUSTICE AND SOCIAL CHANGE*

C. RAY JEFFERY

Law is a social rule, the violation of which calls into action some official of a politically organized society. A state has a monopoly over the legitimate use of force as a means of social control. *Law,* sanctioned by coercive force, can be distinguished from *custom,* which has the sanction of group disapproval, from *religion,* which has a supernatural sanction, and from *morality,* where the sanction is the super-ego or conscience.

* Reprinted with permission of The Macmillan Company from *Society and the Law: New Meaning for an Old Profession,* by F. James Davis, Henry H. Foster, C. Ray Jeffery & E. Eugene Davis, pp. 264–71, 274–75. © The Free Press of Glencoe, a Division of The Macmillan Company, 1962.

It is difficult to differentiate law and custom in primitive societies since they have not developed special social institutions for handling problem cases. For this reason anthropologists have taken two extreme views concerning primitive law. One view is that all primitive law is custom, and primitive man is governed by "the cake of custom." The other view is that there is no law in primitive societies since there are no courts, judges, or territorially organized communities.

Malinowski rejects the notion that custom is automatically obeyed in primitive societies. He also rejects the idea that a politically organized society is necessary before a social code can be labeled "legal." He argues that custom is enforced in primitive societies by a system of reciprocal relationships that create personal obligations that, if not satisfied, lead to a breakdown in economic, family, and friendship patterns. He included in "reciprocal relationships" the sanction of group disapproval. Other writers have been critical of this definition of law and point out that he is not discussing legal control but social control in general.

The view of primitive law taken by Seagle, Radcliffe-Brown, Redfield, and Hoebel is that law involves the use of organized force by the community. Radcliffe-Brown quotes as a definition of law Pound's statement: "social control through the systematic application of the force of politically organized society." Primitive law is private law, and the unit involved in enforcing the sanction is the kinship group. The sanction is expressed by personal revenge in the form of the blood feud. An injury is regarded as a private affair to be settled by the injured party with the aid of his family and friends.

Later the feud was replaced by the payment of compensation. One reason compensation (or composition) is preferred is because feuding is costly in terms of lives and property. It also destroys the peace of the community. Gluckman regards the maintenance of peace as dependent upon a system of conflicting allegiances that men have in the community. He concluded that the feud is not waged in the immediate group, but force is used to settle disputes between outlying groups with weak interpersonal relations. "The feud is waged and vengeance taken when the parties live sufficiently far apart, or are too weakly related by diverse ties." "The more his ties require that his opponents in one set of relationships are his allies in another, the greater is likely to be the peace of the feud."

Hoebel notes that primitive law is private law since for these people kinship is more real than the total community. The growth of public law is limited to groups that are more mature and complex in organization. The more civilized a society becomes, the greater is the need for law.

Integration of primitive communities, then, is achieved without the use of legal sanctions. Custom, tradition, ridicule, tabus, witchcraft, and magic are powerful agents of social control in a primary group dominated by personal, informal relationships. The feud rests upon the solidarity of the kindred. Social organization of such groups is characterized by homogeneous groupings. As societies become complex and heterogeneous, the primary agents of social control decline in importance, and law fills the vacuum. An urban society is much more in need of law than a rural society.

Sir Henry Maine's *Ancient Law* represents an early attempt to trace the developments from private to public law. The unit of ancient society was the family, and one's status in the family determined one's legal rights. As the family was replaced by the state, as tribal sovereignty was replaced by territorial sovereignty, status was replaced by the free agreement of individuals or the law of contract. Maine saw the evolution of law as being from "status to contract" and noted: "the penal law of ancient communities is not the law of Crimes; it is the law of wrongs . . . or torts."

In ancient Greece and Rome, banishment, the feud, and the payment of compensation were found at an early stage of legal development. There emerged the figure of the arbitrator, a prominent member of the community who arranged the settlement of the dispute, and a change from voluntary to compulsory arbitration occurred. Offenses were no longer a private matter to be settled by feuding families. Also, during the early stages of legal development, the successful litigant was left with the task of executing the judgment of the arbitrator; at a later date the legal process included public means of enforcing a judicial judgment.

Von Bar and Esmein describe early continental criminal procedure in terms of feuds, self-help, private vengeance, and compensation. The tribal units of France, Germany, and the Scandinavian countries had a system of private family law. "The community appears to have been concerned in the crime in so far as it arranged the peace between the hostile parties, the offender and the party injured." The defendant was outlawed if he rejected the offer of compensation, or if he refused to appear before the court.

The early law of Anglo-Saxon England was the law of self-help, which also took the form of trial by battle, oath, and ordeal. Pollock and Maitland state that personal injury was a first cause of the feud between the kindreds of the wrongdoer and the person injured.

The system of compensation, or composition, was devised contemporaneously with the advent of money as a medium of exchange. At first these payments were an alternative to the feud, but by the time of Alfred compensation had to be offered and refused before the injured party could resort to the feud.

As the kinship system disintegrated it was replaced by a feudal system. Payments were then made to the lords and kings. The defendant was allowed to "make his fine" with the king, to pay compensation in lieu of punishment.

Simpson and Stone state that "the cardinal characteristic of an emergent political society is that kinship is no longer the main bond of social cohesion. Stated affirmatively, this means that political organization has been superimposed upon kin organization to the extent that it reduces the latter to mere protegé, albeit still an all-important one, of organized society." "A tremendous change takes place when the tribal tie gives way to the territorial tie."

The feud was limited by the concept of *mund* or peace. Lords, bishops, and kings had special *munds,* which meant that no violence or feuding could occur in their presence. Gradually this concept of the king's peace was applied to special occasions, special cities, special highways, and special days. The peace was gradually extended to more places and occasions until finally it came to be regarded as a general law of the land. Finally, all pleas came to be *pleas of the crown.*

As a result of the development of the concept of the king's justice, the common law of England came into being. Itinerant justices traveled throughout England administering the law of the King's Court to people who at an earlier date had depended upon lords and bishops for justice. Writs of various types were issued by the king through his officials. The Curia Regis came to be four different courts, replacing the hundred court and shire court. Under William I ecclesiastical and territorial jurisdiction were separated, and a separate secular court system and professional bar emerged.

One of the major sources of private disputes at this time was the seizure of land and/or cattle by one person from another. The individual involved had to resort to self-help in order to regain possession of his property, and often the offender was a lord whereas the offended party had no recourse available to him. Common law actions, such as the Writ of Right, the *assize of novel disseisin,* and the *assize mort d'ancestor* were developed and used by plaintiffs to regain land illegally seized from them. The common law actions of detinue, replevin, account, and the Writ of Mesne were used to recover chattels illegally taken or unlawfully detained by a defendant. The aggrieved party had in these common law actions legal remedies with which to regain land or chattels without resorting to self-help.

The most important common law action in this respect was the action of trespass, which was used as a substitute for self-help from the thirteenth century on. This action declared that the defendant did with force and arms and against the king's peace violate the rights of the plaintiff. Trespass actions were recommended by Britton and others at this time because of their advantage to the plaintiff. Trespass was preferred to private appeal because the plaintiff could collect damages, the pleadings were much simpler, trial by battle was eliminated, and there was no amercement or payment to the Crown in the case of an unsuccessful action as there was for an unsuccessful private appeal. "On the same facts an appeal, an indictment, and an action of trespass might be open to the aggrieved party." However, there was no restitution of stolen property unless the case was brought on an appeal of felony. The Writ of Restitution of 1529 allowed the plaintiff to recover his stolen property in a case brought by way of an indictment if the plaintiff gave evidence at the trial.

The law of wrongs developed into the law of torts and the law of crimes.

One led to compensation, the other to punishment. The distinction between the two must be sought in the legal remedy, not in the nature of the act. Most crimes are torts, and most torts are also crimes. "For almost every crime admits of being treated as a tort so that the person wronged by it can sue the wrongdoer for pecuniary compensation."

By the twelfth century, payment of compensation had disappeared for certain offenses. The use of physical punishment such as mutilation, death, outlawry, or transportation appears to be intimately related to the inability of the defendant to pay compensation.

From the thirteenth to the seventeenth centuries, criminal procedure worked to the disadvantage of the accused. He was not allowed to prepare a defense or hire counsel, he could not look at the indictment or evidence, and he could not call witnesses on his behalf. There were no rules governing the introduction of evidence, and the accused was not allowed to cross-examine his accusors. As the state grew stronger, it granted more rights to the accused. Judges were made independent of the Crown after 1688, and, in Bushel's case of 1670, juries were freed from despotic judicial control. After 1688, procedural reforms were made that allowed the defendant right to counsel, the right to a jury trial, the right to call witnesses, the right to face his ac- cusors, and the right to know the nature of the charges against him. A strict legal definition of crimes, as defined in statutes, replaced arbitrary decisions of judges.

Two different types of criminal procedure developed: the accusatorial system, which is found in Anglo-American law, and the inquisitorial system, found on the Continent. The accusatorial system is a sham battle between the two contestants. The action is regarded as a private affair and is initiated by a private party by way of an appeal. The judges act as umpires. The trial is public and oral, and witnesses are confronted by the accused.

In the inquisitorial system the prosecution and detection of crime are in the hands of the state. The prosecution is handled by a public prosecutor, evidence is gathered in secret, and witnesses are heard in secret. The judge is a partisan party: he gathers evidence, questions witnesses, and cross-examines the accused. Coerced confessions are common. The decision is given not by a trial jury, but by a board of judges.

The weakness of the accusatorial system is that it leaves the prosecution of cases in the hands of private parties who may not act because of lack of funds, interest, or power. The weakness of the inquisitorial system, on the other hand, is that it places in the hands of the state great power that is subject to grave abuse.

IS CRIMINAL BEHAVIOUR
DEVIANT BEHAVIOUR?*

RICHARD QUINNEY

One of the basic assumptions in the study of criminal behaviour is that behaviour in violation of the criminal law also represents deviation from other norms. The criminologist in his research usually proceeds on the premise that the criminal law embodies important social norms and that these norms are held by most persons in society. While these assumptions are rarely questioned in most studies of criminal behaviour, a few criminologists have nevertheless recognised that the relationship between the criminal law and social norms is problematic.

This paper will explore, on the one hand, the relation between criminal law and social norms and, on the other, the relation between crime and deviation. It is suggested that these relationships may be taken as objects of study in their own right. The strategy becomes one of exploring the relationships rather than taking them for granted. The degree of correspondence between criminal violation and normative deviation poses significant problems for study. Likewise, the relation between criminal law and social norms presents a number of important research problems.

Criminal law may be regarded as an instrument of formal social control whereby an organised effort is made to regulate certain areas of behaviour. As a particular type of formal social control, criminal law is characterised by (1) explicit rules of conduct created by political authority, (2) provisions for punishment, (3) designated officials to make, interpret and enforce the rules, and (4) uniform administration of the codes for all persons within a given territory.

Law has grown increasingly important as a means of social control as societies have grown in complexity. In preliterate and peasant societies where norms are relatively uniform, stable and consistent, intimate personal relationships exist to such an extent to control human interaction. The more modern societies, on the other hand, have become highly differentiated in terms of values and norms. Various social groupings have arisen with their own sets of values and norms. In these heterogeneous societies there are many values and norms which are agreed upon by most members, but there are many values and norms which are unique to the diverse groups.

* Reprinted with permission from *The British Journal of Criminology*, V, No. 2 (April 1965), 132–40.

Criminal law, therefore, has emerged as a formal system of maintaining social order in differentiated societies. Other means of social control have proved inadequate in the uniform regulation of many areas of behaviour. Where correct conduct cannot be agreed upon, the criminal law serves to control the behaviour of all persons within a given political jurisdiction.

It is unlikely, then, that all criminal law incorporates the most cherished values and norms of all persons in a society. There are values and norms supported by some or possibly all persons which are not part of the law, and the law includes values and norms which are not important to some persons. It is going too far to argue that "there is no surer way of ascertaining what kinds of behavior are generally regarded as immoral or anti-social by the people of any community than by reference to their criminal code, for in theory, at least, the criminal code embodies social judgments with respect to behavior, and perhaps, more often than not, fact conforms to theory," or that "most of the people in any community would probably agree that most of the behavior which is proscribed by their criminal law is socially un-desirable." Such thinking on the similarity between criminal law and other social norms ignores (1) social differentiation in modern society, (2) processes in the formulation of criminal law, and (3) the relation of social change to criminal law and social norms.

Some legal norms forbidding certain behaviours are supported by nearly all segments of a society, while others find little support. Many of our recent laws do not have the support of the majority of the people. There is little question that the traditional laws regarding such conventional crimes as murder, larceny, and robbery find support in public opinion. However, it is unlikely that laws which define such behaviours as restraint of trade, false advertising and misuse of trade marks as criminal are supported by most persons. These latter laws are unrelated to the social norms of the vast majority of the population.

Due to the heterogeneity of modern society, with varied and often oppos-ing subcultures, there cannot be complete arrgement on all norms. "To a large number of persons who live in such a culture, certain life situations are governed by such conflicting norms that no matter what the response of the person in such a situation will be, it will violate the norms of some social group concerned." Thus, many people in modern society, depending upon their particular attachments, do not regard the official, legal norms as legitimate. The criminal law may not overlap the social norms of some groups and thus may not be supported by some individuals. The result is that there is selective obedience to the law for most persons. Some laws are obeyed and others are not according to a person's own values and the norms of his groups.

Another reason for the lack of agreement between criminal law and other social norms is due to the particular processes that operate in the formulation of the law. Cultural diversity creates special groups, and certain of these groups become organised to an extent that they are in a position to exert influence at strategic points in the formulation of criminal law. The values and norms for some groups become a part of the criminal law, while other groups are not represented in the law which is binding upon all persons and groups.

The content of the criminal law, then, including the kind of conduct prohibited and the nature of sanctions attached, depends upon the norms of those groups in society which influence legislation, court decisions, and administrative rulings. In addition, these influential groups may not be in the majority in numbers or even represent the interests of the majority in the population.

The ability of groups to influence the formulation of law is related to the power positions of the particular groups. A group that can get in a strategic power position can determine the content of criminal law. Furthermore, the criminal law changes as the values and norms of the dominant groups are modified and as the place of these groups is altered in the power structure itself. Therefore, what is defined as criminal behaviour in a society is related to the success of certain groups in influencing legislation, the values and norms of these groups, the compromises of these groups, and shifts in the power structure of the society. In addition the determination of what is criminal extends into the interpretation and enforcement of the law. The values and norms of groups in positions of power can enter at any point in establishing the criminality of any behaviour.

The degree of correspondence between criminal law and social norms is also affected by the changes in a society. For instance, many criminal laws lag behind the changing societal norms. The well-known "blue laws" are an example of criminal laws which were once related to the norms of several groups or segments of society but have since become dated and obsolete because of normative modifications and changes.

It is also the case that some laws precede the norms that will some day become established for a large portion of the society. In fact, law can serve as a device to induce social change. The recent civil rights legislation in the United States in reference to negro-white relations is forcing a change in social norms in some segments of the population. As has been noted by Segerstedt, social codes — or imperatives — create social customs. Thus, in a number of ways, criminal law is related to social change. Social change and changes in the law are constant and interacting processes.

It can therefore be seen that the relationship between criminal law and social norms is a function of a number of factors, of which the most important appear to be social differentiation, processes in the formulation of criminal law, and social change. It is clear that the relationship between criminal law and social norms is a problematic one. Criminologists cannot take the relationship — in terms of complete correspondence — for granted. The nature of the relation of any criminal law to other social norms is far from certain.

Much of what is called criminal behaviour may thus be viewed as behaviour that is oriented to norms other than those embodied in the criminal law. Such illegal behaviour is, of course, in a sense deviant behaviour in that there is deviation from a norm, the legal norm. Deviant behaviour represents "behavior which violates institutionalized expectations — that is, expectations which are shared and recognized as legitimate within a social system." Similarly, deviant behaviour consists of "only those situations in which behavior is in a disapproved direction, and of sufficient degree to exceed the tolerance limit of the community." While behaviours in violation of many of a society's legal norms deviate from institutionalised expectations and exceed the tolerance limit of the community, it is also true that some crimes are not in violation of expectations (or social norms) and are not disapproved to such a degree as to exceed the tolerance limit of the community. Criminal behaviour and deviant behaviour can thus be treated as two separate orders of behaviour.

The problem of the correspondence between deviant behaviour and criminal behaviour becomes particularly crucial in the study of white collar crime — or occupational crime. The question arises whether or not the behaviours which have been defined as criminal — many of them only recently — are also deviations from the normative structure of the occupation. If it can be established that the behaviours are regarded as deviant, as well as criminal, by the occupational members, the criminal violations can truly be studied as deviations from occupational norms, thus eliminating the cumbersome problem — usually not resolved — that criminal behaviour may not be normative deviation from the standpoint of the group being studied.

The relation between legal norms and other norms has consequences for violation and enforcement of the criminal law. In general, those laws which are in accord with the important extra-legal norms of most of the population are realised in actual behaviour. Enforcement becomes a problem when there is a lack of agreement on the norms embodied in the criminal law.

Finally, in reference to the relation between criminal law and social norms, it may be suggested that much criminal behaviour in modern, heterogeneous society represents a normal response to the accumulation of criminal laws. There is a tendency in modern societies to make laws as a first reaction to situations which are defined by some as difficult and unpleasant. The result is that today our criminal codes consist of many laws which contradict one another and many which are antiquated. Each year there are thousands of new laws added to the statute books, creating many new crimes. It has been estimated that since 1900 in the United States the number of offences for which a person can be arrested has doubled. Many of the laws no longer incorporate the social norms on which they were once based. Changes both in norms and scientific knowledge have made many laws obsolete. Such laws are likely to meet with resistance. Violation may occur where the usefulness of the proscribed action is doubtful. Violation of these laws may be the only possible solution to present-day problems and situations.

Several undesirable consequences result from such an unwieldy accumulation of criminal law. A genuine disrespect and disregard for the particular laws may be created and, what is more, even for law in general. This may be furthered when law enforcement agencies must often ignore the offence when the law is obsolete but still exists on the statute books. Enforcement and administrative procedures in general tend to break down. Furthermore, there may be an outright attempt by the public to outwit the law enforcement agencies in violation of these laws and others.

When criminal laws no longer receive social support, or the laws become obsolete because of scientific knowledge, the laws should be changed with old and inefficient ones repealed and, if necessary, new ones enacted. It may also be desirable to bring within the scope of the criminal law behaviours which deviate from the basic values of the society. Thus, as has been suggested by several writers, the study of criminal law by criminologists could provide the necessary knowledge for rational legislation. Further investigation of the relation between criminal behaviour and deviant behaviour could contribute to this purpose.

DOES THE LAW AFFECT MORAL JUDGMENTS?*

NIGEL WALKER and MICHAEL ARGYLE

In the course of debates about the propriety of using the criminal law to discourage certain types of conduct an argument is often used which may be called "the declaratory argument." It asserts that, whether a legal prohibition operates as a deterrent or not, to repeal it would give the impression that the conduct in question is no longer regarded by society as morally wrong.

The "declaratory theory" seems capable of being tested empirically, at least to the extent of discovering whether people's moral judgments are affected by their knowledge or belief as to the state of the law.

The Suicide Act of 1961, which provided that attempted suicide should no longer be a criminal offense, created a situation in which one sort of test

* Reprinted with permission from *The British Journal of Criminology*, IV, No. 6 (October 1964), 571–79.

could be applied to the declaratory hypothesis, since at any given date some people would, while others would not, know of the change in the law. In the summer of 1962, therefore, about a year after the Act received the Royal Assent, interviewers were recruited from two undergraduate societies and, after briefing, carried out 403 interviews with men and women in different parts of the country.

Among the questions in the survey were the following, in the order shown:

10. "Do you regard attempted suicide as
    morally wrong?
    not morally wrong?
    not morally wrong if . . .
    (here any special circumstances offered by the respondent were noted)
11. "Should it be treated as a crime? . . .
    (if the answer was "yes," the respondent was asked how it should be dealt with)
12. "Is it against the law now?"

Sixteen per cent of those interviewed knew that the law had been changed; nine per cent were unsure; the remainder believed that attempted suicide was still criminal. If the change in the law had affected the moral judgments of those who knew of the change, there should have been a lower percentage of those who definitely regarded attempted suicide as morally wrong.

There are obvious limitations, however, to this sort of evidence. In particular, it relates only to attempts at suicide, which is not an act which most people seriously consider the possibility of committing themselves. Since no other crime (excluding offenses under emergency legislation and analogous measures) has been removed from the statute book in the last hundred years, the prospect of a similar opportunity to test the declaratory hypothesis by a field survey about other types of conduct is remote.

Each group of subjects was invited to take part in a survey of views on questions of law and morality by completing an anonymous questionnaire. The questionnaires described a number of actions of different sorts, which the subjects were asked to rate on a six-point scale, ranging from "as wrong as possible" to "very right." The questionnaire told the subjects whether the action in question was a criminal offense or not. Thus the first question explained the law on abortion, and then asked subjects to record their judgments on a doctor who performed an abortion "because the baby is likely to be deformed," "because the baby would be illegitimate," and so on.

The next questions dealt similarly with unintentional litterdropping, negligent injury, public drunkenness, prostitution, and the use of obscene language in public. But whereas the law on abortion was correctly summarized in all the questionnaires, the law on these types of behavior was differently stated in different questionnaires. In tests (i)–(iii) half the questionnaires described each type of behavior as being a criminal offense, while the other half described it as not being an offense. If the declaratory theory were true, the version of the question which described the conduct as an offense should elicit more censorial moral judgments from the respondents.

Two methods of testing the "declaratory theory" of the function of the criminal law produced the following results:

1. A survey of moral attitudes towards a type of act which had recently ceased to be criminal (attempted suicide) showed no significant difference between those who knew of the change in the law and those who did not.
2. It was found possible to devise a "laboratory" situation in which measurable alterations in the moral judgments of young adults in the direction of the "majority view" were induced by telling them the results of a fictitious survey of their peers.
3. There were minorities who believed that legislation which made heavy smoking an offense would make it morally wrong.
4. Those apart, however, no significant differences of the kind predicted by the declaratory theory appeared to occur between those who were told that a given type of conduct was a criminal offense and those who were told that it was not.
5. On the other hand, in some cases there appeared to be a slight tendency for those who were told that certain forms of conduct were criminal offenses to react by taking a less censorious moral view of it.
6. Nor were significant differences of the predicted kind produced by adding fictitious descriptions of cases in which the "offender" had been fined. Indeed, in the case of public drunkenness this may even have been responsible for a slight shift towards greater moral tolerance in the case of male undergraduates.

These results cast considerable doubt on the "declaratory" argument that alterations of the criminal law are likely to weaken moral attitudes. It is true that they are concerned only with the possibility of short-term effects; and supporters of the declaratory theory could argue that the creation or abolition of offenses has long-term effects on attitudes — in other words that the legislation of one generation is the morality of the next. But in the fact of the apparent absence of short-term effects, the onus of proof seems to lie very definitely on those who believe in long-term effects.

3 | THE REPORTING OF CRIME

INTRODUCTION

Few things preoccupy the public and the press quite as much as the latest statistics on the extent and types of crime in the United States. The release of the annual crime data as reported in the FBI publication, *Uniform Crime Reports,* never fails to arouse controversy about the facts and figures presented and the degree to which they fairly reflect the lawlessness in this country. So much confusion exists about the collection of these data that even criminologists are sometimes baffled by the meaning of it all. We know, of course, that most criminal acts, for a variety of reasons, go unreported and result in no action, official or otherwise. We also know that many of the acts which are reported to the police go unrecorded and are not counted as crimes even though known. There is also considerable "give" in the data on offenses cleared by arrest, the characteristics of persons arrested, persons charged, and a variety of other important aspects of the crime problem. As a result, many criminologists, though neither the general public nor press, have just about decided that the official data are perilously close to being worthless and may do more harm than good if taken too seriously. Criminologists are agreed that far more emphasis than warranted is placed on the crime index data as indicative of the extent and fluctuations in crime. Without actually altering the situation at all, it is possible to introduce increases or decreases of great magnitude in the crime problem simply by making only minor changes in the reporting and recording sphere. Although there are just three articles in this section, each is of such range that together they cover not only the present methods used in the reporting and recording of crime but the principal weaknesses of the system.

The first contribution is taken from the FBI handbook on how to prepare the Uniform Crime Reports tabulation sheets which are distributed to the various police departments in this country. These instructions specify the minimum standards for the record system to be kept by the police. Even more important are the rules to be followed in tallying major, or Part I, offenses. These rules are illustrated by examples of problems and solutions. In reading these rules, special note should be taken that when several different offenses are committed by one or more persons at the same time, only the most serious of them is tallied. This rule, of course, results in gross underreporting but is obviously the only sensible way of dealing with the problem of multiple offenses as part of the same criminal event sequence. Again, attention is directed to the rules governing the recording of offenses against the person, against property, of handling "unfounded" complaints, of the clearance of crimes, Part II offenses, the involvement of juveniles, and all the other Tally Sheet materials. Perusal of Return Forms A, B, and C should also aid in the understanding of this very complex subject of the reporting and recording of crime.

In the second contribution on criminal statistics, Peter P. Lejins raises some very relevant issues concerning the Uniform Crime Reports. In general, he discounts many of specific faults attributed to the Uniform Crime Reports and is specially pleased that the FBI has been able to accomplish the difficult goal of national coverage in police statistics. One very interesting point raised by Lejins is that criminologists are loath to utilize court rather than police statistics even though the court data are not subject to the same difficulties as the police data. Lejins attempts to explain this reluctance to employ court rather than police data. He also explores the reasons criminologists are so enamored of the dictum by Sellin regarding the best point in the criminal and legal process to gather the most reliable and valid reports about the extent of crime.

The third and final contribution to this section on the comprehensive reporting and recording of crime is a review by Roland J. Chilton of some of the "Persistent Problems of Crime Statistics." These persistent problems include: the issue of the general utility of crime data; the possibility that reporting agencies will be evaluated in terms of such data and therefore have a stake and investment in these statistics above and beyond that warranted in purely objective terms; the interpretation of this information; the lack of uniformity in the gathering of these statistics, and in achieving the cooperation of thousands of enforcement agencies; and in the general fragmentation of efforts to arrive at reasonably coherent crime statistics.

UNIFORM CRIME REPORTING*

Not all crimes come readily to the attention of the police — embezzlement for example. Some important crimes happen infrequently, such as kidnapping (often this is for the purpose of robbery or other crime and not for ransom). So, the International Association of Chiefs of Police, for practical purposes, limited the reporting of "offenses known" to the following crime classifications because they are crimes which are most likely to be reported to police and they occur with sufficient frequency to provide an adequate basis for comparison:

(1) Criminal homicide (subdivided as to 1a, murder and non-negligent manslaughter and 1b, manslaughter by negligence); (2) forcible rape; (3) robbery; (4) assault (subdivided as to aggravated and simple); (5) burglary (breaking and unlawful entering); (6) larceny — theft (except auto theft) (subdivided as to $50 and over in value and under $50 in value); and (7) auto theft.

These are the Part I classes of the uniform crime classification. All other crimes and violations are reported under the Part II crime classes. No "offenses known" data is collected for the Part II classes, only arrest information.

Persons arrested for all violations except traffic in the reporting jurisdictions are represented in the annual report on arrests, Age, Sex, and Race of Persons Arrested. This return deals only with *persons arrested* and all arrests are included even though the person is later released without being formally charged. It provides a wide range of information on crime and some characteristics of persons arrested for crimes.

The annual Return C provides police with a form wherein they can report the number of *persons* they formally *charge* for criminal acts (turn over for prosecution) and how these persons are disposed of by the courts, including both adults and juveniles.

* Reprinted from *Uniform Crime Reporting Handbook*, Federal Bureau of Investigation, United States Department of Justice (Washington, D.C.: Government Printing Office, 1965), pp. 2–4, 8, 39–44, 47–48, 56–60, 67–71.

To insure that you have the needed information, your record system should meet the following standards:

1. A permanent written record is made of each crime as soon as the complaint is received. All reports of crimes and attempted crimes are included, regardless of the value of property involved.

2. Staff, or headquarters, control exists over the receipt of complaints. This is to insure that each is promptly recorded, properly classified and subsequently counted.

3. An investigative report is made in each case. It shows fully the details of the offense as alleged and as disclosed by the police investigation. Each case is closely followed to see that reports are made promptly.

4. All reports are checked to see that the crime class conforms to the uniform classification of offenses.

5. The offense reports on crimes cleared by arrest or by exceptional means are so noted.

6. Arrest records are complete, special care being taken to show the final results of the charge.

7. Records are centralized; records and statistical reports are closely supervised by the chief administrative officer; periodic inspections are made to see that the rules and regulations of the local agency on records and reports are strictly followed.

8. Statistical reports meet the Uniform Crime Reporting standards and regulations.

The monthly form used to collect "Offenses Known" data is the Return A. It is important that you count on your report all Part I crimes, "Offenses Known," that occur in your jurisdiction. Reports are collected for urban places (cities or towns) and rural areas. Police count crimes that happen within the city (urban) limits. Sheriffs, county and state police count crimes that happen in the county (rural area) outside urban places of 2,500 or more inhabitants.

For crime reporting, cities are places that have 2,500 or more people according to the latest U.S. census. There are a few places that are designated as urban under a special rule.

Offenses (crimes) come to the attention of a law enforcement agency in a number of ways. Check over your record system to be sure that all possible sources are covered by the records to be used in preparing crime reports:

(1) The telephone brings most of them to your attention.

(2) Also, a citizen may walk into your office and report that a theft or other crime has occurred.

(3) An officer on duty sees or hears of a crime. A record should be made even though there is no arrest.

(4) An officer on duty makes an arrest during, or shortly after, the commission of a crime. He makes the arrest before any complaint or report is received at headquarters. For example, a shop-keeper calls to a policeman on

the street and reports a shoplifting. The policeman sees the thief and makes an arrest. This is referred to variously as an "on view," "pickup," or "original" arrest. Include such incidents in the records used in compiling crime reports.

(5) Sometimes crimes are reported by citizens to the prosecuting attorney or judge. Generally, you can arrange to have these officials notify you of the crime that has occurred in your jurisdiction. Also, urban police can arrange to be notified if a sheriff's office, county police, county detectives, or state police receive the first notice of a crime that has happened in a city (urban place).

(6) If you receive a warrant of arrest and it is your first notice of a Part I offense in your jurisdiction, the offense should be counted.

One of the primary objectives of the Uniform Crime Reporting Program is to provide reliable and meaningful data for administrative and operational use of law enforcement agencies. One of the means utilized to attain this goal is the use of the "crime index." Seven selected offenses are used in an attempt to measure the extent, fluctuation and distribution of crime in the United States. The count is based on the number of these selected offenses being reported to police or coming to their attention (offenses known). The following offenses are used in compiling the crime index:

(1) Murder and non-negligent manslaughter, (2) forcible rape, (3) robbery, (4) aggravated assault, (5) burglary, (6) larceny $50 and over, and (7) auto theft.

(Note: Manslaughter by negligence, simple or minor assaults and larceny under $50 are not included in the crime index.)

As noted above, *police count those crimes that occur within the city limits; a sheriff counts only those crimes that occur in the county outside the cities.* This avoids duplication.

If the crime occurs in another city or another county, do not count it. This is true even though you may arrest the offender. *Examples:* (1) The Maple City Police arrest an auto thief in an auto stolen in Oak City. Oak City counts the crime. (2) The Locust County Sheriff arrests the murderer of a woman killed in Locust City, the county seat and an urban place. The sheriff does not count the murder on his report because it occurred in Locust City and the Locust City Police Department will report it.

The FBI mails supplies each month to contributors. If your agency is on our mailing list of contributors, you will receive these basic supplies:

(1) Tally Sheet for Return A — this is a handy worksheet that you keep in your office;

(2) Return A — for mailing to the FBI after you have filled it out;

(3) Self-addressed return envelope requiring no postage.

The box in the lower left corner of the monthly Return A is for the purpose of providing a count of total arrests made by your agency during the month for which the return is being submitted. (Include arrests for both Part I and II offenses.) Enter here two figures: one for adults arrested and one for juveniles arrested, for all offenses, *except traffic*.

Only count arrests for offenses committed in your jurisdiction. Do not count arrests you make for other police agencies. In counting juveniles use your state definition as to who is a juvenile.

The same rules apply for counting arrests in this box as are used in scoring arrests on the annual return Age, Sex and Race of Persons Arrested. If you have a doubt as to when a juvenile is considered as arrested, refer to p. 72 for an explanation.

The figures placed in this box represent a count of *persons* arrested as opposed to *offenses* scored on the remaining portion of the Return A.

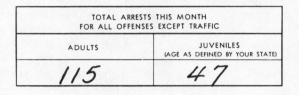

TOTAL ARRESTS THIS MONTH FOR ALL OFFENSES EXCEPT TRAFFIC	
ADULTS	JUVENILES (AGE AS DEFINED BY YOUR STATE)
115	*47*

If several different offenses are committed by a person or a group of persons *at the same time,* glance down your list of Part I offenses and stop at the first crime you recognize from your set of facts.

Examples:

Problem: A holdup man forces a husband and his wife to get out of their automobile. He shoots the husband and leaves in the automobile after taking money from the husband. The husband dies as a result of the shooting.

Solution: From the several crimes in the problem, you recognize class 1a, murder and non-negligent manslaughter, as the first crime in the list. Stop at that classification — it is the only one that will be used for scoring the problem. (For crime reporting you ignore the other crimes in the set of facts — this does not affect the number of charges for which the defendant may be prosecuted in your courts.)

Problem: Three men break into a public garage after closing hours. They steal cash from the garage office lockbox and two automobiles from the shop.

Solution: Here is forcible entry burglary, theft, and auto theft. Following the rule, we find forcible entry burglary first. This is the only classification used.

Problem: An automobile is stolen and a short time later it is used as a getaway car in an armed robbery.

Solution: Note this does not illustrate several crimes occurring at one time. Here we have two separate crimes at different times (different operations). So, this *does not* fall within our rule of classifying by the first crime in our list. Class as a robbery and also as an auto theft.

RETURN A
MONTHLY RETURN OF OFFENSES KNOWN TO THE POLICE

TO BE FORWARDED TO THE FEDERAL BUREAU OF INVESTIGATION, U.S. DEPARTMENT OF JUSTICE, WASHINGTON, D.C., 20535 BY THE SEVENTH DAY AFTER CLOSE OF MONTH.

1 CLASSIFICATION OF OFFENSES (PART I CLASSES)	2 OFFENSES REPORTED OR KNOWN TO POLICE (INCLUDE "UNFOUNDED" AND ATTEMPTS)	3 UNFOUNDED, I.E., FALSE OR BASELESS COMPLAINTS	4 NUMBER OF ACTUAL OFFENSES (COLUMN 2 MINUS COLUMN 3) (INCLUDE ATTEMPTS)	5 NUMBER OF OFFENSES CLEARED BY ARREST THIS MONTH	
				a TOTAL OFFENSES CLEARED**	b BY ARREST OF PERSONS UNDER (INCLUDED IN 5)
1. CRIMINAL HOMICIDE					
a. MURDER AND NONNEGLIGENT MANSLAUGHTER	2	1	1	1	0
b. MANSLAUGHTER BY NEGLIGENCE *	2	1	1	1	1
2. FORCIBLE RAPE TOTAL	2	0	2	1	1
a. RAPE BY FORCE	1		1	1	1
b. ASSAULT TO RAPE - ATTEMPTS	1		1	0	0
3. ROBBERY TOTAL	9	1	8	4	2
a. ARMED - ANY WEAPON	4	0	4	3	1
b. STRONG-ARM - NO WEAPON	5	1	4	1	1
4. ASSAULT TOTAL	9	1	8	8	4
a. GUN	1	1	0	0	0
b. KNIFE OR CUTTING INSTRUMENT	1	0	1	1	0
c. OTHER DANGEROUS WEAPON	0	0	0	0	0
d. HANDS, FISTS, FEET, ETC. - AGGRAVATED	0	0	0	0	0
e. OTHER ASSAULTS - NOT AGGRAVATED *	7	0	7	7	4
5. BURGLARY TOTAL	30	2	28	14	5
a. FORCIBLE ENTRY	17	0	17	10	2
b. UNLAWFUL ENTRY - NO FORCE	11	2	9	4	3
c. ATTEMPTED FORCIBLE ENTRY	2	0	2	0	0
6. LARCENY - THEFT (EXCEPT AUTO THEFT)					
a. $50 AND OVER IN VALUE	12	2	10	2	1
b. UNDER $50 IN VALUE	66	4	62	14	9
7. AUTO THEFT	24	1	23	8	7
GRAND TOTAL	156	13	143	53	30

TOTAL ARRESTS THIS MONTH FOR ALL OFFENSES EXCEPT TRAFFIC	
ADULTS	JUVENILES (AGE AS DEFINED BY YOUR STATE)
115	47

January 2, 1965
DATE

John Doe
PREPARED BY

Clerk
TITLE

Richard Roe
CHIEF, COMMISSIONER, OR SUPERINTENDENT

▼ December, 1964
◄ MONTH AND YEAR

Aberdeen, Nebraska
CITY AND STATE

DO NOT USE THIS SPACE	
	INITIALS
RECORDED	
REVIEWED	
PUNCHED	
VERIFIED	
ADJUSTED	

* Not used in computing the Crime Index.
** Does not include the number of persons arrested—only the offenses cleared.

SCORING

This means the number of offenses to be counted in any criminal event. *Only two general rules* are needed for scoring if we group our Part I crimes as to (1) crimes against the person and (2) crimes against property.

OFFENSES AGAINST THE PERSON (Criminal homicide, forcible rape, and assault.)

Count one offense for each victim. This means that the number of offenses scored equals the number of persons unlawfully killed, raped, maimed, wounded, or assaulted, plus attempts.

Example: An unknown man murders three persons. There are 3 victims, so count 3 offenses.

Assault is sometimes troublesome. If the facts are in dispute and you can't tell the aggressors from the victims, count the number of persons assaulted as the number of offenses.

Example: Answering a "riot" call, police find that seven persons were in a fight. A variety of weapons are strewn about. None of the participants is particularly cooperative. Each one claims innocence but is vague as to who is responsible for the assault. Three of the seven are severely wounded and receive emergency medical treatment. All seven are arrested. While all the facts of the fight are not known, we do know that three persons are severely wounded. Count three offenses of aggravated assault, 4d, cleared. Also count four offenses in 4e, other assaults, cleared.

OFFENSES AGAINST PROPERTY (Robbery, burglary, larceny-theft, and auto theft.)

Count one offense for each distinct operation or attempt.

Robbery examples:

Forty patrons are present in a nightclub when it and the 40 patrons are held up by armed bandits. This is *1 distinct operation*, count 1 offense. (The number of people held up makes no difference if it is one distinct operation in an offense against property.)

Three men "strong-arm" and rob a man on the street. One operation, one offense.

Burglary — Forcible or Unlawful Entry Examples: Special "Hotel" rule — consider hotels and lodging houses as single units without regard to the number of rooms entered at one time.

Example: Six rooms in a hotel are broken into by 2 "sneak thieves" on 1 occasion. Under the "Hotel" rule *count just one offense.*

Apartment houses — count one offense for each apartment entered ("Hotel" rule does not apply to apartments).

Offices — Count one offense for each suite of offices entered in a building.

Example: One night a building is broken into. In all, 21 offices (rooms or partitioned spaces) are ransacked. These offices are occupied by (1) a lawyer, (2) a doctor, (3) Apex Co., and (4) Elite Co., who do not share their space and are not related in a business way (four separate units or "distinct operations," four offenses).

Larceny-theft: One article or several articles stolen from one place on the same occasion is a distinct operation. Count one offense. This is true even if several articles belonging to different persons are stolen at the same time from one place.

Attempts: Count opposite "Under $50" in value. The article may be worth more, but no value is obtained.

Auto theft: Count one for each vehicle stolen. Also count each attempt. You may recover a car very soon. This does not change the rule: A car stolen by a person not having lawful access to it must be counted as an actual offense (a car taken for temporary use and actually returned by the taker to the owner is not counted).

UNFOUNDED COMPLAINTS

"Unfounded" means that the investigation proves that the crime did not happen or was not attempted. All "unfounded" complaints (Part I crimes) are listed on the Return A in columns 2 and 3.

Example: You receive a report of a burglary. Investigation shows that a man climbed through the window of his own home. He locked himself out by mistake. A neighbor thought it was a burglar and called the police.

OFFENSES CLEARED BY ARREST

An offense is "cleared by arrest" when at least one person is (1) arrested, (2) charged with the commission of the offense, and (3) turned over to the court for prosecution (whether following arrest, court summons or police notice).

A clearance by arrest can be taken when the offender is a person under 18 and he is cited to appear in Juvenile Court or before other juvenile authorities. This clearance can be taken even though no actual physical arrest was made.

Keep clearly in mind that *offenses* and not *arrests* are being counted. It makes no difference how many are arrested. There can be no more offenses cleared than offenses that occurred.

If several persons commit 1 crime and only 1 is arrested and charged, list the crime in column 5 of Return A as cleared by arrest. When the other offenders are arrested (say, in the next month) do not list a clearance by arrest a second time for the one offense.

Several crimes may be cleared by the arrest of one person.

Examples:

1. A man commits murder. He is arrested, charged, and turned over to

the court. You score 1 offense of murder and 1 offense of murder cleared.

2. Five thieves break into a warehouse. You arrest and charge one of them. Score 1 offense of burglary — forcible entry, and 1 such offense cleared by arrest. Later the other four thieves are arrested and charged. No entry is made on Return A. The one offense has already been listed as cleared by arrest.

3. You identify a suspect with five forcible entry burglaries. You arrest him and charge him with the five offenses. These 5 offenses are cleared by the arrest of 1 person.

In compiling data for the annual returns which are discussed in the following sections of this Handbook, both Part I and Part II of the Uniform Classification are used for compiling facts about *persons arrested* and *persons charged*. It is just as essential to have maximum uniformity in collecting these figures as it is in getting statistics for the monthly returns.

Although schedules of Part II offenses have not been prepared for each State, the description of the classes appearing in the following section will serve all practical purposes. They are representative of the types of offenses to be found in the penal codes of the 50 States and territorial jurisdictions. Violations of municipal ordinances as well as State laws are to be included.

Definition of Part II Classes. In November, 1932, the FBI adopted a Standard Classification of Offenses for the compilation of criminal statistics. This classification was devised and adopted in order that police, judicial, and penal statistics might be uniformly compiled in terms of a single classification of offenses. The Standard Classification is substantially the same as the Uniform Classification with the exception of certain changes in the Part II classes of offenses. The brief list of offenses under each of the following classes of Part II indicates the general content and scope of the class. Although the offenses listed here may not be identical in name with those in local jurisdictions, they are sufficiently descriptive to serve as a guide in determining what offenses should be included in or excluded from each class. The offense classes which follow are numbered in accordance with the listing shown under the Part II classes of offenses included on the annual returns.

8. *Other Assaults*
9. *Arson*
10. *Forgery and Counterfeiting*
11. *Fraud*
12. *Embezzlement*
13. *Stolen Property; Buying, Receiving, Possessing*
14. *Vandalism*
15. *Weapons; Carrying, Possessing, etc.*
16. *Prostitution and Commercialized Vice*
17. *Sex Offenses*

18. *Narcotic Drug Laws*
19. *Gambling*
20. *Offenses Against the Family and Children*
21. *Driving Under the Influence*
22. *Liquor Laws*
23. *Drunkenness*
24. *Disorderly Conduct*
25. *Vagrancy*
26. *All Other Offenses*
27. *Suspicion*
28. *Curfew and Loitering Laws — (Juveniles)*
29. *Run-away—(Juveniles)*

Annual reports under this program are:
   (1) Return B — Offenses Known.
   (2) Age, Sex and Race of Persons Arrested.
   (3) Return C — Persons Charged.
   (4) Police Employee Data.
The FBI mails these and tally sheets annually at the end of the calendar year to all contributing law enforcement agencies. If you need more, write to the FBI for additional supplies.

Police, sheriffs, state police and other participating agencies are requested to furnish annual reports. Those who have not prepared them in the past are urged to do so at the end of the current year.

RETURN B — ANNUAL RETURN OF OFFENSES KNOWN

The purpose of Return B is to summarize the figures submitted on the 12 monthly Return A's and to provide an opportunity to make any necessary adjustments in the monthly figures submitted previously. Return B is illustrated on page 73.

Return B is the same as Return A except the Return B is, in effect, the Return A *for the year*. Return B is prepared by adding the figures on the 12 monthly Return A reports for the year.

If year-end adjustments are necessary, they can be made in the Return B figures. If there is a difference between the totals in column 4 of Return B and the sum of the 12 monthly Return A's, briefly state on the Return B the reason for the difference and denote which figures are correct.

AGE, SEX, AND RACE OF PERSONS ARRESTED

This is the basic report for the collection of arrest data. The purpose of this return is to provide police with a record of their total arrest activity for criminal acts in all the crime classes and to furnish basic data concerning personal characteristics of persons arrested during the year.

Figures tallied on the form represent *persons arrested, and are a count of arrests, not charges.* You may arrest the same person several times during the year for similar or several different violations. Each separate arrest should be counted. You may arrest a person on several charges at one time; however, only one arrest is scored.

The form provides for a compilation of arrest totals broken down by specific age groups, by sex and by race for all Part I and Part II offense classifications, except traffic violations.

Data for persons 18 years of age and over is tabulated on the white Age, Sex and Race of Persons Arrested form while arrests of persons under 18 are scored on the pink portion of the form. Arrests are tallied by sex within certain age groups. (See illustrations pages 75–77.)

Arrests are tallied also by race. The race designations are: White, Negro, Indian, Chinese, Japanese, and All Other. Persons of Mexican birth or ancestry who are not definitely Indian or of another nonwhite race should be counted as members of the *white race.*

HOW TO PREPARE THE AGE, SEX, AND RACE OF PERSONS ARRESTED RETURN

Show in this report *all persons* taken into custody during the past calendar year for committing an offense of the indicated types *in your local jurisdiction.* This includes:

(1) Those persons you arrest and release without any formal charge being placed against them.

(2) Juveniles taken into custody or arrested but who are warned and released without being charged.

Enter opposite each offense the number of persons taken into custody listing them according to age and sex of the persons arrested and according to race without regard to sex.

Persons whom you arrest for other jurisdictions are not counted on the return. This is to avoid duplication. The agency for whom you make the arrest will report it on their return.

With respect to arrests for Federal offenses in those cases where the arrest is for a Federal crime occurring in your jurisdiction and the offense is also a crime under your state penal code, when you make the arrest independent of a Federal agency or assist in making the arrest, it *should be* counted on your Age, Sex and Race of Persons Arrested form.

JUVENILES

For purposes of Uniform Crime Reporting, a juvenile should be counted as "arrested" when the circumstances are such that if he or she were an adult, an arrest would be tallied. Juveniles taken into custody should be listed opposite the classification of the offense for which they were taken into custody. For example, if a juvenile is arrested for committing an offense of larceny he should be listed opposite the larceny-theft classification on this report, even though the technical charge placed against him is "Juvenile de-

RETURN B
ANNUAL RETURN OF OFFENSES KNOWN TO THE POLICE

State _____ Agency _____ Group _____ Div. _____

Place __Aberdeen__ State of __Nebraska__ for year ending December 31, 19__64__

1 CLASSIFICATION OF OFFENSES (Part I classes)	2 OFFENSES Reported or Known to Police (include "Unfounded" and Attempts)	3 Unfounded, i.e., False or Baseless Complaints	4 Number of Actual OFFENSES (Column 2 Minus Column 3) (include attempts)	5 Number of OFFENSES Cleared by Arrest This Year	
				a Total Offenses Cleared	b By Arrest of Persons Under 18 (included in 5a)
1. CRIMINAL HOMICIDE					
a. Murder and Nonnegligent Manslaughter	7	1	6	5	1
b. Manslaughter by Negligence	5	2	3	3	
2. FORCIBLE RAPE TOTAL	8		8	6	1
a. Rape by Force	5		5	4	1
b. Assault to Rape - Attempts	3		3	2	
3. ROBBERY TOTAL	21	7	14	5	1
a. Armed - Any Weapon	14	5	9	3	1
b. Strong-arm - No Weapon	7	2	5	2	
4. ASSAULT TOTAL	53	9	44	34	11
a. Gun	2		2	2	
b. Knife or Cutting Instrument	10	4	6	5	2
c. Other Dangerous Weapon	4		4	2	
d. Hands, Fists, Feet, etc. Aggravated	6	2	4	3	1
e. Other Assaults - Not Aggravated	31	3	28	22	8
5. BURGLARY TOTAL	343	21	322	124	56
a. Forcible Entry	238	13	225	91	42
b. Unlawful Entry - No Force	81	6	75	29	13
c. Attempted Forcible Entry	24	2	22	4	1
6. LARCENY - THEFT (except auto theft) a. $50 and Over in Value	389	7	382	74	22
b. Under $50 in Value	844	27	817	197	82
7. AUTO THEFT	138	17	121	53	27
GRAND TOTAL	1,808	91	1,717	501	201

If the entries in column 4 above do not agree with the sum of your monthly returns, briefly state reasons for difference. __agree__

Do your entries in column 4 of Return B include all offenses of the designated types known to have been committed in your jurisdiction last year? (Note: All thefts reported to the police should be included even though the value of the property stolen was small. Attempted crimes should be included.) _____ __yes__

The entries in columns 5a and 5b should not represent the number of persons arrested, but the number of offenses cleared by arrest. Include offenses reported in prior years, but not cleared until this year.

DO NOT WRITE IN THESE SPACES	
Recorded _____	
Reviewed _____	
Punched _____	
Verified _____	

__John Doe__   __Clerk__
Prepared By   Title
__Richard Roe__
Chief, ~~Sheriff, Commissioner or Superintendent~~
Date __January 7,__ _____ , 19__65__

linquency." Police "contacts" with juveniles where no offense has been committed should not be scored as arrests. Instances where a juvenile is taken into custody for his own protection, such as "neglect," and no crime committed, should not be listed as an arrest.

Violations growing out of local juvenile acts other than runaway and curfew and loitering law violations should be included in the "all other" classification. This would include "arrests" in the usual sense and also any situation where the young person, in lieu of an actual arrest, is summoned, cited, or notified to appear before the juvenile or youth court or similar official for a violation of the law. Provision is made on the pink section of the form to enter arrests for runaway and curfew and loitering law violations.

SCORING

The unit of scoring is the person arrested or summoned and *not* the number of charges placed against the person. One is counted for each person as follows:

(1) Count one for each person on each separate occasion (day) he is arrested or charged. (Note the difference between this and a case where a person is charged with several crimes after *one* arrest.)

Example: Adam Adamson is arrested and charged with burglary on May 5. One month later he is arrested and charged with drunkenness. He is counted as *one person arrested for each incident.*

(2) If 2 or more persons are arrested for committing 1 offense, each is counted as a separate arrest or charge.

Example: Two thieves are arrested and charged with burglary of a tire shop. Count two persons arrested opposite burglary — breaking or entering.

(3) If a person is arrested for committing a burglary and while in custody you determine he has committed another local burglary, do not score an additional arrest. Score one arrest only for the offense on which he was originally arrested.

(4) If the person who was arrested for burglary is released on bond and then you discover he has committed another local burglary and you arrest him again, this would constitute two persons arrested.

RETURN C — ANNUAL RETURN OF PERSONS CHARGED

The object of the annual Return C is to show the total number of persons who are formally charged by the police and turned over to the courts. The return gives a complete picture of the number of persons dealt with by the courts. This return provides information relating to the final step in the handling of an offender by police. It is a record of what happened to those individuals held and turned over to the courts for prosecutive action.

The figures collected on the Return C will not be the same as those reported on the Age, Sex and Race of Persons Arrested return because many

AGE, SEX AND RACE OF PERSONS ARRESTED
under 18 years of age
(Include those released without having been formally charged)

CLASSIFICATION OF OFFENSES		SEX	AGE						Total Under 18	RACE					
			10 and Under	11-12	13-14	15	16	17		White	Negro	Indian	Chinese	Japanese	All Other
Murder and Nonnegligent Manslaughter	01a	Male													
		Female													
Manslaughter by Negligence	01b	Male													
		Female													
Forcible Rape	02	Male													
		Female													
Robbery	03	Male													
		Female													
Aggravated Assault (Return B-4a-d)	04	Male													
		Female													
Burglary--Breaking or Entering	05	Male													
		Female													
Larceny-Theft (Except Auto Theft)	06	Male													
		Female													
Auto Theft	07	Male													
		Female													
Other Assaults (Return B - 4e)	08	Male													
		Female													
Arson	09	Male													
		Female													
Forgery and Counterfeiting	10	Male													
		Female													
Fraud	11	Male													
		Female													
Embezzlement	12	Male													
		Female													
Stolen Property; Buying, Receiving, Possessing	13	Male													
		Female													
Vandalism	14	Male													
		Female													
Weapons; Carrying, Possessing, etc.	15	Male													
		Female													
Prostitution and Commercialized Vice	16	Male													
		Female													
Sex Offenses (Except Forcible Rape and Prostitution)	17	Male													
		Female													
Narcotic Drug Laws Total	18	Male													
		Female													
Opium or Cocaine and Their Derivatives (Morphine, Heroin, Codeine)	a	Male													
		Female													
Marijuana	b	Male													
		Female													
Synthetic Narcotics - Manufactured Narcotics Which Can Cause True Drug Addiction (Demerol, Methadones)	c	Male													
		Female													
Other - Dangerous Non-Narcotic Drugs (Barbiturates, Benzedrine)	d	Male													
		Female													
Gambling Total	19	Male													
		Female													
Bookmaking (Horse and Sport Book)	a	Male													
		Female													
Numbers and Lottery	b	Male													
		Female													
All Other Gambling	c	Male													
		Female													
Offenses Against Family and Children	20	Male													
		Female													
Driving Under The Influence	21	Male													
		Female													
Liquor Laws	22	Male													
		Female													
Drunkenness	23	Male													
		Female													
Disorderly Conduct	24	Male													
		Female													
Vagrancy	25	Male													
		Female													
All Other Offenses (Except Traffic)	26	Male													
		Female													
Suspicion	27	Male													
		Female													
Curfew and Loitering Law Violations	28	Male													
		Female													
Run-Aways	29	Male													
		Female													
TOTAL															

AGE, SEX AND RACE OF PERSONS ARRESTED
18 years of age and over
(Include those released without having been formally charged)

CLASSIFICATION OF OFFENSES		SEX	AGE									
			18	19	20	21	22	23	24	25-29	30-34	35-39
Murder and Nonnegligent Manslaughter	01a	Male / Female										
Manslaughter by Negligence	01b	Male / Female										
Forcible Rape	02	Male / Female										
Robbery	03	Male / Female										
Aggravated Assault (Return B-4a-d)	04	Male / Female										
Burglary--Breaking or Entering	05	Male / Female										
Larceny--Theft (Except Auto Theft)	06	Male / Female										
Auto Theft	07	Male / Female										
Other Assaults (Return B-4e)	08	Male / Female										
Arson	09	Male / Female										
Forgery and Counterfeiting	10	Male / Female										
Fraud	11	Male / Female										
Embezzlement	12	Male / Female										
Stolen Property; Buying, Receiving, Possessing	13	Male / Female										
Vandalism	14	Male / Female										
Weapons; Carrying, Possessing, etc.	15	Male / Female										
Prostitution and Commercialized Vice	16	Male / Female										
Sex Offenses (Except Forcible Rape and Prostitution)	17	Male / Female										
Narcotic Drug Laws Total	18	Male / Female										
Opium or Cocaine and Their Derivatives (Morphine, Heroin, Codeine)	a	Male / Female										
Marijuana	b	Male / Female										
Synthetic Narcotics - Manufactured Narcotics Which Can Cause True Drug Addiction (Demerol, Methadones)	c	Male / Female										
Other - Dangerous Non-Narcotic Drugs (Barbiturates, Benzedrine)	d	Male / Female										
Gambling Total	19	Male / Female										
Bookmaking (Horse and Sport Book)	a	Male / Female										
Numbers and Lottery	b	Male / Female										
All Other Gambling	c	Male / Female										
Offenses Against Family and Children	20	Male / Female										
Driving Under The Influence	21	Male / Female										
Liquor Laws	22	Male / Female										
Drunkenness	23	Male / Female										
Disorderly Conduct	24	Male / Female										
Vagrancy	25	Male / Female										
All Other Offenses (Except Traffic)	26	Male / Female										
Suspicion	27	Male / Female										
TOTAL												

CLASSIFICATION OF OFFENSES	SEX	AGE						TOTAL	RACE					
		40-44	45-49	50-54	55-59	60-64	65 and over		White	Negro	Indian	Chinese	Japanese	All Other
Murder and Nonnegligent Manslaughter 01a	M													
	F													
Manslaughter by Negligence 01b	M													
	F													
Forcible Rape 02	M													
	F													
Robbery 03	M													
	F													
Aggravated Assault (Return B-4a-d) 04	M													
	F													
Burglary--Breaking or Entering 05	M													
	F													
Larceny--Theft (Except Auto Theft) 06	M													
	F													
Auto Theft 07	M													
	F													
Other Assaults (Return B-4e) 08	M													
	F													
Arson 09	M													
	F													
Forgery and Counterfeiting 10	M													
	F													
Fraud 11	M													
	F													
Embezzlement 12	M													
	F													
Stolen Property; Buying, Receiving, Possessing 13	M													
	F													
Vandalism 14	M													
	F													
Weapons; Carrying, Possessing, etc. 15	M													
	F													
Prostitution and Commercialized Vice 16	M													
	F													
Sex Offenses (Except Forcible Rape and Prostitution) 17	M													
	F													
Narcotic Drug Laws Total 18	M													
	F													
Opium or Cocaine and Their Derivatives (Morphine, Heroin, Codeine) a	M													
	F													
Marijuana b	M													
	F													
Synthetic Narcotics - Manufactured Narcotics Which Can Cause True Drug Addiction (Demerol, Methadones) c	M													
	F													
Other - Dangerous Non-Narcotics Drugs (Barbiturates, Benzedrine) d	M													
	F													
Gambling Total 19	M													
	F													
Bookmaking (Horse and Sport Book) a	M													
	F													
Numbers and Lottery b	M													
	F													
All Other Gambling c	M													
	F													
Offenses Against Family and Children 20	M													
	F													
Driving Under The Influence 21	M													
	F													
Liquor Laws 22	M													
	F													
Drunkenness 23	M													
	F													
Disorderly Conduct 24	M													
	F													
Vagrancy 25	M													
	F													
All Other Offenses (Except Traffic) 26	M													
	F													
Suspicion 27	M													
	F													
TOTAL														

of the persons you arrest or "book" (and tally on the Age, Sex, and Race of Persons Arrested) will be released without prosecution. By the same token, the figures on the Return C will not balance out with those on the Return B since the Return B deals with *offenses known or criminal acts* while the Return C has to do with *persons arrested and charged* — those who commit the criminal acts or violations.

Figures for persons charged are collected for all offenses contained in both the Part I and Part II crime classes.

Count on Return C all persons charged by you for committing offenses (Part I and Part II) within your jurisdiction who are turned over to the courts for prosecution. Do not include persons arrested and released by police. Do include those persons charged and released at any prosecutive level. For purposes of this Program a person is considered charged when he is held for prosecution before any court of jurisdiction for any criminal offense. This includes persons whose cases will be heard by justices of the peace, magistrates, or other judicial officers who have authority to impose punishment for the offense committed. A person also is considered charged when he pays a fine or forfeits bail on any citation or summons.

Count persons actually physically arrested and *persons summoned, cited, or notified to appear.*

Scoring — All persons you arrest are not held for prosecution or charged. On Return C count only those individuals who are (1) arrested and turned over for prosecution, and (2) those who are summoned, notified, or cited. *Do not count* on Return C persons arrested and later released without any formal charge being placed against them. *Do not count* arrests you made for other authorities (Federal, other states, cities, towns, counties, etc.). Score one person charged for each person arrested and held for prosecution. The unit of count is each person. Several persons may be arrested and formally charged for one crime. Each is counted as a person charged. One person may be arrested and formally charged more than once in a year. Each separate occasion is counted.

Column 2. — Persons arrested and held for prosecution are tallied in this column.

Column 3. — Persons responding to court summonses and police notices are counted in this column (persons who waive trial, plead guilty and pay a fine are included).

Column 4. — Enter opposite the proper class the total number of persons charged who are turned over to the courts for prosecution. This is the sum of columns 2 and 3.

Juveniles are included on the Return C only when they are turned over or referred to juvenile court jurisdiction (including probation to department, etc.) or when they are waived to criminal court jurisdiction. Juveniles who are arrested, summoned or notified should be included in columns 2 or 3

RETURN C. -- ANNUAL RETURN OF PERSONS CHARGED

(Please Read Instructions on Reverse Side)

Classification of Offenses (1)	Persons Charged by Police			Disposition					
	Arrested (Held for prosecution) (2)	Summoned, Notified or Cited (3)	Total Persons Charged (Columns 2 and 3) (4)	Adults Guilty		Acquitted or Otherwise Dismissed (7)	Referred to Juvenile Court Jurisdiction (8)	Other (Include pending prosecuted elsewhere in lieu of your jurisdiction, etc.) (9)
				of offense charged (5)	of lesser offense (6)			
Part I Classes								
1. Criminal Homicide:								
(a) Murder and Nonnegligent Manslaughter	5		5	3		1	1	
(b) Manslaughter by Negligence _ _ _ _ _	3		3	2		1		
2. Forcible Rape _ _ _ _ _ _ _ _ _ _ _ _ _ _	7		7	4	1	1	1	
3. Robbery_ _ _ _ _ _ _ _ _ _ _ _ _ _ _ _ _	2	3	5	4	1		1	
4. Aggravated Assault (Return B-4a-d)_ _ _	16		16	9	1	2	3	4
5. Burglary -- Breaking or Entering _ _ _ _ _	142	4	146	64	16	10	41	15
6. Larceny -- Theft (except auto theft) _ _ _	217		217	90	14	29	46	38
7. Auto Theft _ _ _ _ _ _ _ _ _ _ _ _ _ _ _	45		45	14	2	4	22	5
TOTAL, Part I Classes _ _ _ _ _	437	7	444	190	35	48	115	62
Part II Classes								
8. Other Assaults (Return B - 4e) _ _ _ _ _ _	29		29	9	3	5	7	5
9. Arson _ _ _ _ _ _ _ _ _ _ _ _ _ _ _ _ _ _	3		3	3				
10. Forgery and Counterfeiting _ _ _ _ _ _ _ _	19		19	11	1	4		3
11. Fraud _ _ _ _ _ _ _ _ _ _ _ _ _ _ _ _ _ _	11		11	8	2	1		1
12. Embezzlement _ _ _ _ _ _ _ _ _ _ _ _ _	12		12	6	1	1	3	1
13. Stolen Property; Buying, Receiving, Possessing_ _ _ _ _ _ _ _ _ _ _ _ _ _ _	2		2			1	1	
14. Vandalism _ _ _ _ _ _ _ _ _ _ _ _ _ _ _	45		45	9		16	12	9
15. Weapons; Carrying, Possessing, etc. _ _	4		4	3		1	1	
16. Prostitution and Commercialized Vice_ _	2		2	1		1		
17. Sex Offenses (except 2 and 16) _ _ _ _ _	33		33	17	3	6	2	5
18. Narcotic Drug Laws _ _ _ _ _ _ _ _ _ _ _	1		1	1				
19. Gambling _ _ _ _ _ _ _ _ _ _ _ _ _ _ _	44		44	35	2	3		4
20. Offenses Against the Family and Children _ _ _ _ _ _ _ _ _ _ _ _ _ _ _ _	20		20	12	1	5		2
21. Driving Under the Influence _ _ _ _ _ _ _	54		54	39	3	2		10
22. Liquor Laws _ _ _ _ _ _ _ _ _ _ _ _ _ _	20		20	14	1	2	2	1
23. Drunkenness _ _ _ _ _ _ _ _ _ _ _ _ _ _	208		208	163	16	15	3	13
24. Disorderly Conduct _ _ _ _ _ _ _ _ _ _ _	542		542	334	7	130	27	44
25. Vagrancy _ _ _ _ _ _ _ _ _ _ _ _ _ _ _ _	32		32	27	1	3		1
26. All Other Offenses (except traffic) _ _ _	77		77	55	1	12	4	5
TOTAL, Part II Classes _ _ _	1,158		1,158	747	42	208	62	104
GRAND TOTAL _ _ _ _ _ _ _	1,595	7	1,602	937	77	256	177	166

Traffic Arrests

Physical custody and warrants served 930

Citations issued 19,002

Total traffic arrests 19,932

Date January 7 , 19 65   John Doe   Clerk   Richard Roe

                 Prepared By   Title   Chief, ~~Sheriff, Commissioner or Superintendent~~

To be forwarded to the Federal Bureau of Investigation, U.S. Department of Justice, Washington, D. C. 20535, by January 22 and 4. Juveniles who are handled by the police through warning and release are *not* considered as being *formally* charged by police.

DISPOSITION

Columns 5, 6, 7, 8, and 9 are provided to show what happened to the persons who were charged (column 4). If cases of persons charged last year were disposed of this year, those dispositions may be included in the appropriate disposition column but they are not entered as charged again in column 4. Show the disposition only in such cases.

ADULTS GUILTY (COLUMNS 5 AND 6)

You will notice "Adults Guilty" dispositions are separated into two columns: "of offense charged" and "of lesser offense." Adults charged by the police who are found guilty by the courts during the calendar year are entered in one of these two columns.

Guilty of offense charged (column 5) means the person was found guilty in court of:

(1) The same charge as was placed against him by the police (if there was more than one charge or count, he must be found guilty of the most serious); or,

(2) A different charge *with the same penalty as the original or with a greater penalty.*

Guilty of lesser offense (column 6) means the person was found guilty of (1) a lesser offense than the one charged by the police, or (2) an offense less than the most serious if there was more than one charge (or count).

Disposition of cases involving juveniles which are waived to adult court should be handled the same as adults, with the disposition scored in column 5, 6, 7, or 9. Disposition of juvenile cases handled by the juvenile court are *not* entered in columns 5, 6, or 7, but are entered in column 8 *only*.

There is no provision on the Return C to show persons arrested and released.

ACQUITTED OR OTHERWISE DISMISSED (COLUMN 7)

In column 7 count all adults whose cases were disposed of through dismissal of the charges *at any prosecutive step*. This includes subsequent dismissal of a case by the local prosecutor when prosecution has been previously authorized by him and legal process obtained. Include nolle prosequi, dismissed due to death of defendant, etc. Score in this column all defendants who were acquitted by a judge, jury, magistrate or in any other legal proceeding after having been charged, notified or summoned.

When juveniles whose cases are waived to criminal court are acquitted, enter the acquittal in column 7.

REFERRED TO JUVENILE COURT JURISDICTION (COLUMN 8)

This column pertains only to juveniles and shows *police* disposition of juvenile cases. Once the juvenile is turned over by police to the juvenile court, probation department or officer within the jurisdiction of the juvenile court, the case is considered disposed of by the police for purposes of Return C.

Juvenile dispositions should *not* be tallied in columns 5 or 6 when they are considered as guilty. For purposes of this return all juveniles turned over to juvenile court jurisdiction are included in column 8 only. It is not necessary, therefore, to determine the final disposition of the case by juvenile authorities in order to complete the Return C although this information would be valuable for your own administrative and investigative purposes.

Juvenile dispositions shown in column 8 will be only those juveniles previously entered in column 4 as arrested and charged. Dispositions of juveniles whose cases are waived to criminal court are treated the same as adults and entered in columns 5, 6, 7 or 9.

When you arrest a juvenile for a crime committed in your jurisdiction but turn him over to another jurisdiction for handling, enter the disposition in column 9.

Juveniles you arrest and release to parents with a warning are not considered to be charged and would not be entered on the Return C. (Juvenile arrests of this type are counted on the Age, Sex, and Race of Persons Arrested return.)

OTHER (COLUMN 9)

This is a residual column where you will enter dispositions of cases included in column 4 but which cannot be entered in columns 5, 6, 7 or 8. The following types of cases would be some of those most frequently entered in column 9:

(1) Persons arrested and charged by police whose cases remain pending or undecided at the year's end.

(2) Persons charged by police for a local crime but who were tried elsewhere.

POLICE EMPLOYEE DATA

The primary purpose of the form is to gather information relating to the number of full-time police employees, both officers and civilians. When counting the number of officers, the chief should be included in the tally. Do not include in your count persons performing guard and protection duties who are not paid from police funds, school crossing guards, special officers and merchant police.

Civilian employees to be counted include only such persons as clerks, radio dispatchers, meter maids, stenographers, mechanics, etc., *who work full-time, but do not have police powers. Persons not paid from police funds should not be counted.*

In preparing your count, include any employees on leave *with pay.*

POLICE KILLED AND ASSAULTED

The second purpose of this form is to collect data concerning the number of police officers killed or assaulted in line of duty. The count of police officers killed should include accidental deaths which occur in line of duty, such as automobile, motorcycle, and airplane accidents, falls, etc.

Assaults on police are separated into two categories: (1) those where the officer was injured, and (2) those where no injury was sustained. In order to place an assault in the first category, the extent or seriousness of the injury is not a consideration. A slight injury (sprain, bruise, etc.) is sufficient to include the assault in (1).

Each separate assault is counted as one offense. For example, if Officer Jones is attacked once in January and again in July, with injury resulting on both occasions, two assaults resulting in injury would be scored on the Police Employee form.

UNIFORM CRIME REPORTS *

PETER P. LEJINS

The Uniform Crime Reports, which are the only source of cumulative data concerning the national crime situation, deal with the total volume of crime, the figures on major offense categories, and the changes in this picture from year to year.

The Reports are the only compilation of crime statistics on a National scale that provide as high a degree of completeness and uniformity. In the United States there are neither comprehensive judicial criminal statistics nor comprehensive statistics at any other step of the criminal procedure on a national scale: no national probation statistics, no national parole statistics, and no national statistics of cases and their dispositions by grand juries or through the information procedure. It should be noted, however, that the need for these various types of criminal statistics has been recognized for some time.

* Reprinted with permission from *The Michigan Law Review,* LXIV, No. 6 (April 1966), 1011–1030.

It has generally been recognized that the difficulty in producing criminal statistics on a national scale is in large measure due to the basic organizational structure of law enforcement in the United States, that is, the fact that it is organized and operated as a responsibility of local government — the state, county, and the municipality — rather than of the federal government. At the same time, there is no authority capable of requiring cooperation in reporting the data.

The difficulties encountered in compiling criminal statistics under the circumstances could perhaps be considered as falling within three distinct categories. First, the absence of a central authority to require cooperation in any kind of national program results in complete dependence upon voluntary participation for all contributions. Second, since a potential contributor of data to the national program does not have complete control over the entire law enforcement system in his own locality, but only of a segment, he very often cannot secure uniform data because the rest of the local units cannot be modified, either by him or by the national program, so as to provide comparable information. Third, the divergence of views on the value of various kinds of data and their usefulness for law enforcement which exists among the personnel of law enforcement systems is apt to cripple the needed voluntary cooperation.

The following conditions must remain satisfied even at the sacrifice of all other characteristics of the program: (1) the agency which manages the national program must enjoy a very high level of prestige among the law enforcement personnel expected to supply the data; (2) the agency carrying out the program must have a very strong motivation in performing the task, which requires patience, perseverance, resourcefulness, and energy; (3) excellent public relations must exist between the central agency and the local law enforcement authorities; (4) the local authorities must share the belief that the collection of the information is useful for law enforcement in general and is in line with their own purposes and interests; (5) the tasks to be performed for the program by the local authorities must not tax their time, personnel, and budget beyond a level they consider tolerable; and (6) the meaning of the data requested must be understandable to the local personnel in light of their criminological sophistication.

The Federal Bureau of Investigation, which in 1930 was given by Congress the responsibility for developing and operating the Uniform Crime Reporting system as planned by the Committee on Uniform Crime Records of the International Association of Chiefs of Police, and which is still operating it with the advice and cooperation of that Committee and Association, has managed to develop extremely high morale among the police of this country with regard to the need for their assistance in gathering comprehensive statistics on offenses known to the police and arrests. The magnitude of the FBI's accomplishment is also placed into proper perspective by the already

mentioned failure of a similar attempt by the Bureau of the Census to secure the cooperation of the judiciary throughout the United States to develop judicial crime statistics.

In evaluating the Reports as a statistical series, it should be kept in mind
that from the point of view of both the agency producing these statistics and
the budget allotment to that agency, the Reports are intended to be a compilation of police statistics on crime and certain other data of importance to
the police. Indeed, the Reports are intended to be a statistical house organ
of the police in the United States. This fact is so obvious to anyone familiar
with this statistical series that it may appear superfluous to single it out for
comment here. However, there is good reason for calling attention to it, since
most critics disregard this aspect of the Reports and confuse the perspective
by criticizing them for not being something which they were never intended
to be.

One of the most frequent criticisms, a reproach that the Reports do not
give a full picture of criminality in this country, is easily countered by the
simple recognition of the fact that police statistics alone are never intended
as a complete description of criminality. In fact, criminologists, rather than
the police, are the ones who have extolled the significance of police statistics
as an index of criminality. At the base of this claim lies the famous dictum
of Professor Sellin that the value of crime statistics for index purposes decreases as the distance between the statistics and the criminal act increases in
terms of steps in the criminal procedure; hence, the police statistics of criminality — as the earliest measure — are considered to be the best statistics for
measuring the crime situation.

The use of the Reports has not been confined to the cooperating police
departments. In fact, the data contained in the Reports have been widely
publicized by the mass media, and the FBI recognizes that these annual
compilations have become a major source of information for the general
public on the subject of criminality.

Let us now turn to the analysis of the function of the police statistics as
a source of information about crime. Two major issues should be singled out
for clarification: the extent to which information about criminal activity
reaches the police, and the extent to which information that reaches the
police is suitable for forming the public's knowledge about criminality. The
first issue concerning information being reported to the police may be divided into two categories. One of these categories is the extent to which the
victims of criminal violations are supposed to be brought to the attention of
the police, since there are other law-enforcement channels.

For a variety of reasons not all criminal acts are reported to the police.
Some criminal offenses are not reported because they involve such minor
losses that the victims do not feel it worth their effort to bother reporting
them; to a certain extent, of course, the law-enforcement systems themselves
discourage complaints based upon such minor violations. The old Roman

principle *de minima non curat praetor* generally applies. Another reason for failure to report such acts may be the low expectancy of securing any help, and kind of satisfaction, or any result in general. Still another reason for remaining silent in certain situations is the victim's own involvement in the offense or his reluctance to publicize the fact that he was victimized, as in the case of confidence games and certain sex offenses. In all of these cases the extent of non-reporting can be estimated only through intensive research of sample situations. It is difficult to evaluate this factor properly, but it can distort the meaning of the reported figures as reflected in the statistics.

The second category of reasons why certain offenses do not appear in police statistics is that these offenses are such that they are not channeled through the police. Offenses reported to the federal and state regulatory commissions, offenses reported directly to the prosecuting attorney's office, such as embezzlement, federal violations reported to United States Commissioners, Marshals, and Prosecutors, and crimes by military personnel that are handled by the law enforcement system of the Department of Defense are not reflected in the police statistics. The so-called "white-collar crime" is often claimed to be flagrantly under-reported to any appropriate agency. To the extent the total picture of crime depends on consideration of the criminal activities of the kinds just mentioned, our present police statistics are decidedly not the sole measure of criminality.

With respect to the extent to which police statistics, and therefore also the Reports, with all the qualifications mentioned above, may serve as a meaningful index of criminality, the generally accepted position of American criminologists, as expressed in Sellin's formula, is quite clear. However, it would seem that the nature of the law enforcement process should lead one to the acceptance of judicial statistics as the most appropriate measure of criminality, because until a court has rendered its decision on whether a crime has been committed and who the criminal is, strictly speaking there is no basis for a final listing of crimes or offenders. Apparently because of some idiosyncrasy of the law enforcement process in this country, the criminologists do not agree with this logical position. They seem to feel that too many offenses which are actually committed disappear without being reflected in a final court disposition establishing them as crimes.

It appears that criminologists are willing to take the assertions of complaining victims as being closer to reality than the dispositions of the courts. The numerous ways in which offenses "disappear" in the course of the criminal procedure are usually given as the reason for their position. Subsidence of a victim's willingness to prosecute and testify, the well-known practice of accepting a plea of guilty to a lesser offense, prosecution on only one of a few counts as long as conviction of the criminal can be obtained, and withdrawal of a large number of additional counts may serve as a few examples of the kind of practices alluded to in this connection.

The question is often asked why the compilers of the Reports should not resort to a sampling procedure instead of striving for the universe of offenses known to the police and of arrests in the United States. The Consultant Committee on Uniform Crime Reporting addressed itself to this issue in considerable detail in 1958 and decided in favor of a recommendation to continue the present practice of collecting all of the information rather than resorting to a sampling technique. The primary argument in favor of the present procedure is probably the interest of the cooperating police departments in having their data appear alongside the similar data of other jurisdictions, so that comparisons can be made. Such comparisons with other communities and departments can presumably be more detailed and therefore more meaningful than comparisons with national statistics arrived at as the result of samples.

The second reason for maintaining the current method of gathering data is that the Reports have by now achieved practically complete coverage. Typically, one of the main arguments in favor of sampling procedures is the impossibility of achieving the universe of data. However, this problem has been largely overcome by the compilers of the Reports through continued expansion of the area covered and continued improvement in the uniformity of the reporting procedures.

Finally, as a third justification for the present methodology, it should be noted that the principal device for developing uniformity of categories and procedures and for improving the quality of reporting has been to involve all police departments of the nation in the reporting system. Refusal by the FBI to accept and publish reports which fail to satisfy the minimum standards of quality has served as a major influence in improving the work of the police departments over a third of a century.

Another issue that has often been raised with regard to the Reports is the reporting of multiple offenses. It has been asserted for instance by Marvin E. Wolfgang that the current practice of reporting only the most serious offense of a group of offenses committed in the course of a single criminal exploit is inadequate. This writer is not particularly inclined either to defend or to criticize the current practice of the Reports. It should be kept in mind that the problem of reporting multiple offenses has not been solved in the general theory of criminal statistics; there is simply no generally accepted point of view or practice.

The alternative of listing all the offenses also presents considerable difficulties. The following hypothetical case should illustrate the problems. On suspicion that a certain car has been stolen, the police give chase to the driver and catch him. However, in the process of the apprehension, the driver goes right through fifteen red lights, exceeds the speed limit in five different speed zones, makes five unauthorized left turns, and fails to signal turns at ten intersections. Although such itemized accounts are occasionally presented by the police in court, it is highly questionable whether thirty-five moving traffic violations should be reported. It would appear that neither the extreme of reporting only one offense nor the extreme of reporting every offense committed in the course of a single criminal undertaking is altogether desirable.

Another topic of current interest is the development and publication in the Reports of a Crime Index. The Index was instituted in 1958 as a result of recommendations offered by the Consultant Committee on Uniform Crime Reporting.

The purpose of an index of crime, as in the case of any index, is to select a few categories of events, rather than utilizing the entire universe, in order to provide information that is being sought with regard to temporal changes in crime. Many criminologists have thought that the use of the fluctuations in a limited number of offenses may more adequately characterize the fluctuations in the total area of crime than would be possible by the presentation of the total volume of criminality itself.

It is obvious, of course, that the crucial criterion in selecting the offenses for a crime index is the purpose of the index. In the case of the Reports, this purpose is to give the police a concise picture of criminal activities and, in the same context, some data for evaluating police activities in the area of these offenses.

With respect to the question of whether to weight the offenses within the Index, it should be observed that an ingeniously composed weighted index may be quite useful for some specific purposes. There is nothing, however to prevent anyone who is skeptical of the unweighted totals of the Index from using separately the offenses contained therein or from actually weighting them. The fact remains, however, that the more elaborate an index becomes, the more narrow must be its purpose and applicability. Moreover, if the FBI were to adopt such a specialized index, it would be satisfying some interests while not serving others.

Among other issues brought up in connection with the methods employed by the FBI in the Reports, one might mention a question raised with reference to the category of automobile theft, which is an important offense in the United States and which is included in the Crime Index. It has been suggested for some time that the offenses listed in that category actually fall into two distinct types: thefts which have as their purpose the permanent appropriation of the car, or its sale or stripping for profit, and thefts committed exclusively for the purpose of what is called joyriding, usually by juvenile or youthful offenders.

It would seem generally advantageous and justified to differentiate the two offenses and list them separately. This writer has strongly advocated such a differentiation, but the Committee on Uniform Crime Records of the IACP has consistently rejected this recommendation, primarily, it appears, on the ground that separating the offense of joyriding from auto theft would diminish the deterrent effect on potential violators.

There is another type of criticism that is often directed at the Reports —

the reproach that they point out increases in criminality without at the same time explaining the reasons for the increase.

First, the increase in criminal activity is a fact; from the point of view of the volume of work thereby created for the police, the explanation for the increase is irrelevant. The police function must be performed regardless of the cause underlying recent trends, and thus the information is of importance to the police. Second, it cannot be denied that this information in general represents a valid criminal statistic, and there is no reason why it should not be reported.

This analysis makes it clear that the interpretations, for the absence of which the Reports are being criticized, should be provided not by the Uniform Crime Reporting program — which is intended to be a program of police statistics — but rather by some national crime research institute or academy of criminology. Thus, given the present rationale of the Reports, most of the criticisms of this type must be considered misdirected.

Beginning with the 1963 Reports, the FBI undertook a new venture in reporting crime statistics, which departs, at least to a certain extent, from strict police-data reporting and enters into the area of general crime statistics. This recent development is the "Careers in Crime" series.

The development of such criminal career statistics or criminal career records is extremely difficult in the United States, primarily because of the lack of centralization of the law enforcement and correctional systems. Securing information on the arrests, convictions, placements on probation, violations of probation, imprisonment in both local and state institutions, releases on parole, revocations of parole, and escapes of an offender who operates in a major metropolitan area located at the juncture of several states, each of which has completely independent law enforcement and correctional systems, is a problem that has not been solved.

The best approximation to the criminal career records that this country has can be found in the police records — in the identification files of offenders who from the point of view of law enforcement warrant such attention. The information concerning these offenders is secured by the police departments through ad hoc investigations, which frequently extend beyond the boundaries of the jurisdiction of their own law enforcement system. Nevertheless, although some of these identification files are excellent, they do not, of course, provide a true statistical criminal career report of all criminals.

PERSISTENT PROBLEMS OF CRIME STATISTICS *

ROLAND J. CHILTON

This brief discussion of the problems of crime statistics is essentially an argument for the establishment of a national center with responsibility for developing a comprehensive system of crime statistics. The suggestion is not new; it has been proposed in various forms for a number of years. But the discussion which follows attempts to identify specific contributions which such an agency might make to the solution of some of the most persistent problems of crime statistics. The discussion is purposely selective and no attempt is made to show that such an agency would solve all of the problems which have been identified in a number of very thorough critical examinations of current crime reporting systems. Instead of such a procedure, a limited number of problems are identified and discussed and what a number of people have thought to be a plausible solution is presented.

In selecting a sub-set of problems which impede the development of adequate statistics, we have attempted to concentrate on the most persistent limitations of the present systems and to examine those limitations in the light of the current uses of crime statistics. If crime statistics were used primarily by social scientists it might be argued that the problems selected do not require costly changes in the system. In the same way, if the uses were primarily local and administrative in nature, problems of accuracy, representativeness, uniformity, and interpretation would not justify extensive changes. But crime statistics are used more extensively and there are increasing indications that they affect important public and private decisions.

The use of crime statistics in politics and journalism has resulted in increased public concern about crime and its control, and it may be generating sufficient public alarm to alter the living habits of large numbers of Americans. Such use appears to have prompted greater public expenditure and occasionally to have led to suggestions for major changes in the system of justice. If crime statistics are to be used to justify such changes, they should obviously be as accurate and informative as possible.

* Presented at the 1966 meeting of the American Sociological Association in Miami and prepared as part of a larger study of crime statistics for The President's Commission on Law Enforcement and Administration of Justice. I am indebted to Lloyd Ohlin, James Vorenberg, and David Burnham for their critical comments on an earlier version.

Despite the periodic use of crime statistics in politics and journalism and the potential impact of these uses on the administration of justice in criminal cases, one of the problems which impedes the development of criminal statistics is the lack of general utility of such information. There appears to be no commercial market for crime statistics and no consistent demand for such information. Unlike Census information and some other official statistics, the demand for crime figures seems to be extremely limited. Although various specialists charged with the administration of justice in criminal cases make some administrative use of official information, it is probably more often used to justify budget requests and to provide people with periodic information on crime in their community.

This limited demand has sometimes made it difficult to justify the collection and publication of some kinds of crime statistics and it also made it difficult to assign responsibility for collecting and publishing such information.

National judicial criminal statistics, and to a lesser extent national prisoner statistics, may be cited as reporting systems which suffered from this lack of utility. Apparently both systems were also retarded by problems of limited cooperation and lack of uniformity. But part of the justification for the discontinuation of the judicial series was their lack of general utility. The national prisoner statistics program has survived but there were several years when no reports were produced or where the lag between collection and dissemination was as long as five years. Clearly, the problem of limited utility and lack of demand must be ranked as a principal barrier to the development of adequate crime statistics.

Perhaps an even more difficult problem with crime statistics is their potential as measures of effectiveness. Official figures when published constitute a form of self-evaluation in that the information which is published is, in effect, used as a measure of effectiveness of the agencies which provide it. If a police agency conscientiously keeps and reports offense and arrest information, those in charge of the agency may find themselves criticized for poor performance or their communities may be described as dangerous places to live. The personnel of many agencies may find it more expedient to keep official crime reports down to an acceptable level than to record and report all of the information which comes to their attention.

This problem may be more important for some agencies than others, but its potential effect is obvious in every area of the system of justice. Court statistics may be used to evaluate the activities of judges, prosecutors, and defense counsel. Parole and probation outcome figures may be used to judge the effectiveness of such programs. And crimes which occur in a community may be used to measure police effectiveness. Without accepting crime statistics as desirable or useful measures of effectiveness, it is clear that their use in this way creates some pressure for the persons supplying the information to withhold or to modify it in such a way as to limit its impact.

There are numerous examples of the results of this pressure in the history of police statistics despite vigorous efforts by the FBI over a number of years, but the issue is less clear in judicial and correctional statistics. The fact that more examples exist in police statistics than in the other series may be a result of the level of development of police statistics relative to judicial and correctional statistics or it may simply be historical accident. In any case, the pressures of self-evaluation — or more accurately the pressures inherent in the provision of information to others which will be used to score one's own performance — are probably as important to judges, lawyers, and correctional workers as they are to the police. These pressures can be expected to work against the accuracy and utility of any system of statistics and constitute a major problem which must be overcome if the information is used to support important changes in the system of justice.

Another persistent problem with crime statistics has been the general lack of reasoned interpretation of such figures and the difficulty of independent interpretation inherent in the format and presentation of the basic data. Some have argued that the purpose of those gathering the data imposes on them only a limited obligation to interpret it and that more detailed analyses are more properly the province of sociologists or criminologists. It is still a matter of debate as to just where the responsibility for interpretation should be lodged. But this controversy should be resolved because presentation of crime statistics without analysis and interpretation compounds the effect of fragmented effort, self evaluation, and the lack of general utility.

When analyses and interpretations are presented they frequently provide a single perspective which reflects the current interests of the agency which publishes the report. More frequently, however, no interpretation at all will be attempted and the figures will be asked to speak for themselves. Sociologists and criminologists who have attempted to re-analyze and interpret such information frequently encounter great difficulty in working with the published information and sometimes are unable to obtain more detailed information from the agencies involved because of the agencies' lack of funds or personnel. In addition, there is no clearly formulated policy on the public nature of such information and the desirability of providing basic data to any serious student of crime who requests it.

A fourth problem with crime statistics is that of uniformity and comparability and the difficulty of obtaining the cooperation of thousands of independent agencies. In spite of the great effort made by the Uniform Crime Report section of the FBI, uniformity is a constant problem of police statistics and this is true to a much greater extent for court and correctional figures. In addition, there is considerably less effort being made to obtain the cooperation of agencies working with parolees and minor offenders.

This difficulty is, in part, a result of the necessity of obtaining information from thousands of independent local agencies. If a large number of such agencies cooperate, it may then become extremely difficult to audit and check reports for uniformity and adherence to standards set down by the collecting agency. When large numbers of agencies fail to report, or different sets of agencies report at different times, comparability becomes a serious problem. These problems of comparability and uniformity plague all present statistical reporting systems but are, of course, of less importance for police statistics than court statistics. They remain important barriers to the development of better crime statistics.

The fragmented and uncoordinated nature of the present approaches to crime statistics may also be classified as a major problem of crime statistics in the United States. Perhaps the most important effect of this fragmentation is the practical impossibility of following individuals through the system to learn what happens to them at each stage in the process and why it happens. The absence of such information dooms any attempt to reconcile the statistics produced by each of the systems and makes it almost impossible to describe the operation of the larger system of justice with any accuracy. The fragmented effort has also resulted in the development of systems reflecting uneven amounts of statistical expertise. Both developments work against uniformity, comparability and the improvement of some of the separate systems.

Problems of crime statistics which are of particular importance for criminological research have not been emphasized in this review in the belief that the most persistent general problems of crime statistics are also the most serious limitations of statistics for criminological research. For example, the existing fragmented systems provide very limited information on the characteristics of persons involved in the several stages of the criminal process. This fragmentation also makes it particularly difficult to study problems of recidivism or to assess effectiveness of various treatment programs. In similar ways, the problems of interpretation, uniformity, and those resulting from self-evaluation limit the research utility of current statistics.

A number of other problems might have been selected for emphasis but the problems of general utility, self-evaluation, analysis and interpretation, uniformity and cooperation, and fragmentation are sufficiently broad to introduce a tentative solution. The solution presented here is one way in which the problems with the present system might be met. It is selected because of its potential for long-term improvement in criminal statistics, because it would seem to overcome the most frequently identified shortcomings of the present systems, and because it is not too detailed, too expensive, or too unrealistic.

The central recommendation in this solution is the establishment of what might be called a national center for crime statistics. Such an agency could reasonably be expected to work in two directions. First, it could be given sufficient resources to undertake independent internal programs to improve criminal statistics. In addition, it could be given the task of providing assistance in the development of criminal statistics to federal agencies and state and local governments when requested.

One of the agency's internal programs might involve the regular use of sample survey procedures to develop independent indicators of the volume and nature of specific kinds of criminal events. In such a procedure, victims of certain kinds of offenses would provide the information used to arrive at an estimate of the amount of crime occurring in a given area during a given period of time. If the geographic areas and the time periods were properly selected, this procedure would work to overcome the problems of self-evaluation which are inherent in the present approach to crime statistics.

Such surveys would, of course, be an expensive way to provide regular estimates of the amounts and kinds of crime occurring in the country as a whole. But use of this technique in a limited number of standard metropolitan statistical areas and in a slightly larger number of representative counties could provide an important indication of the strengths and weaknesses of current reporting procedures. It might very quickly permit the national agency to identify strong and useful reporting areas and to begin a program of registering counties as areas providing acceptable crime statistics.

Another independent indicator which might be developed, probably in cooperation with the insurance industry, would be the collection and analysis of information on losses due to crime which are covered by insurance. Experimentation with insurance data might produce a reliable indication of the amounts of certain kinds of criminal conduct. If developed in cooperation with other commercial associations this indicator might become an important index of the amount of commercial theft and might also produce some better data on the costs of this kind of crime.

In addition, such an agency might work toward the development of independent auditing procedures which would permit reasonable evaluations of the accuracy of crime figures reported by official agencies. The checks made in such a program would in effect provide another indication of the numbers and kinds of crimes and offenders encountered by the police, the courts, and correctional agencies.

Other independent programs which might be undertaken by such an agency include a periodic re-examination of official crime reports, the establishment and operation of a repository for official crime statistics, and the provision of careful and detailed interpretation of official statistics. The agency might also work with other federal agencies such as the Census Bureau in the development of the best use of demographic and economic information for criminal statistics.

These kinds of programs are closely related in several ways. A federal agency charged with the responsibility of analyzing and interpreting crime statistics could be subjected to pressures to emphasize or de-emphasize some aspects of the problem depending on their possible impact on the party in power. This pressure could probably be countered most effectively by a program which provides independent investigators with ready access to the basic statistical data. If criminal statistics gathered by federal agencies were deposited in the center and made available, at cost, to anyone who requested them, in much the same way as census information is now available, the possibility for misinterpretation would be decreased and the possibilities for re-examination greatly increased. Obviously, no information could be distributed which might identify particular individuals but information about individuals could be made available without names or identifying numbers.

The information deposited with the center might also be a valuable resource for regular and periodic re-examination and re-analysis by the center's staff to determine at a given point in time the state of development of official criminal statistics and to make suggestions for improvements which might be made in reporting programs.

In brief, work undertaken in these programs would (1) provide a basis for the development of an integrated and comprehensive system of criminal statistics, (2) provide the machinery for the development of independent indicators which would avoid the problems of self-evaluation, and (3) provide periodic analyses and interpretation of the available figures which at the same time make it possible for independent investigations to re-examine data for purposes of criminological research as well as assure the independent operation of the agency.

In addition to these internal programs, such a center might also be expected to provide assistance to other agencies and to state and local governments in the development of more complete and more accurate criminal statistics. They might, for example, provide assistance to state governments in the development of a state survey of victims program or a state auditing program. They might also work with the states to develop uniform reporting programs which could be put together to form an integrated system. And they might develop programs for training or helping state governments train persons working in state and local systems.

This assistance aspect of a statistical center's work might provide a solution to the problem resulting from a lack of uniformity and the need to obtain the cooperation of thousands of separate agencies. The center might encourage the establishment of state centers for crime statistics and could attempt to work with such centers in the development of national reporting programs, thus providing the ground-work for closing the numerous gaps in the present fragmented system.

In cooperation with state centers, a national center might develop a system which would provide information on the flow of cases from arrest to final disposition and provide some indication of the reasons for specific types of dispositions. In addition, cooperation might result in a useful set of crime indicators and improved measures of the costs and effectiveness of their agencies for social control.

No revolutionary change in the current national reporting systems is required, other than the cooperation of the national agencies in depositing copies of their data in the center, but the establishment of such a center would provide one method for solving some of the most difficult problems of criminal statistics.

The use of crime information in politics, journalism, and social science would not be impeded and might be made more rational. Use by police administrators to justify budget requests and to provide local newsmen with material would still be possible but they would have the additional advantage of having more than one index of crime in their community and would be better able to compare the situation in their community with the situation in other communities and to examine the crime situation in their community at different points in time. In this way, new or different approaches to the problem could be evaluated and something approaching cost-effectiveness studies could be made.

4 | THE RANGE OF
CRIMINAL BEHAVIOR

INTRODUCTION

Criminal behavior covers a wide range of activities which have but one characteristic in common — the violation of one or more criminal laws. Criminal violations subsume everything from murder, manslaughter, assault, and rape on the one extreme, to activities which, except for their illegality, are little different from legitimate occupations in that the focus is purely on monetary gain. Between these polar types of *expressive* (nonutilitarian) and *instrumental* forms of crime are many widely divergent varieties of offenses. One need only examine the criminal codes in any state to be impressed with the enormous range of possible illegal acts.

No single section of readings can possibly do more than illustrate this diversity of criminal behavior. The focus in this chapter will be concentrated at both poles. We will consider aggressive, assaultive, and generally violent behavior, on the one hand, and also deal with such specific orders as organized, professional, and white collar crime.

The first article, taken from an official report of the State of California on the subject, concerns a somewhat new phenomenon in American life — outlaw groups of motorcyclists who have become a serious problem to many small communities. Such groups have been implicated in many incidents of rape, assault, motorcycle theft, car theft, forgery, and other crimes in various parts of the country. Mainly, however, they specialize in activities which shock a community. The Hell's Angels Motorcycle Clubs set the patterns for many imitators. This selection describes what is known about these "disreputable" groups and their activities.

Daniel Glaser, Donald Kenefick and Vincent O'Leary are concerned with "The Violent Offender" and with developing a behavioral typology of murderers. The major types they describe include the ordinary, cultural, professional, inadequate, psychopathic, and psychotic murderers. This selection also includes a general discussion of the legal definition of violent crimes and the distinctions, for example, between murder, manslaughter, justifiable homicide, and assault.

The next selection deals with the organization and, to a lesser extent, with the activities of the Mafia and its successor, La Cosa Nostra. Both the Mafia and La Cosa Nostra have been consistently identified in various U. S. Senate investigations into the rackets as the dominant elements in syndicate crime in the United States. This article on organized crime is excerpted from the final report of the President's Commission on Law Enforcement and Administration of Justice. In this report, *The Challenge of Crime in a Free Society*, twenty-four syndicate groups or criminal cartels are identified as the core of organized crime. The nature of these twenty-four groups, known as families, is detailed. Each family is described as being headed by a boss and beneath him by an underboss. At the next level down the hierarchy are the go-betweens or *caporegime* and beneath them are the *soldati*. At the lowest level are the employees — generally the only ones subject to arrest and prosecution. The report also treats the "commission" or the highest ruling body in organized crime. This is a fascinating look into the business of crime as distinguished from crime as expressive behavior (reported in the two preceding essays).

While the syndicate criminal might be likened to the "organization man" who has a job to do and does it within the rules of the organization, the professional criminal is very much more the "entrepreneur" type. Working with others in a loosely organized framework, he is non-violent and basically capitalizes on the cupidity of his victims and his own highly polished skills. Two articles are included in this section which illustrate the deft touch and approach of the professional, and the difference between this type and others.

The first selection, "Confessions of a Master Jewel Thief," is about a professional second-story man (burglar) whose "clients" were Social Register matrons and whose working uniform was a tuxedo. There are few such specialists around any longer and old-line policemen have been known to bewail the changing patterns of criminal activity which have made fossils of men such as Barry and replaced them with less adept and often more violent operatives.

In the second contribution, Robert Louis Gasser describes the criminal activity which enjoys the highest status of all conventional criminal activity — the confidence game. According to Gasser in "The Confidence Game," the essential difference between confidence and all other forms of fraud and swindling is that only in confidence activities is there no such thing as an honest victim. As far as is known, there is no other form of crime in which the victim must, of necessity, be culpable and an accomplice in his own downfall. The article also discusses the two major types of con games, the nature of the process involved in fleecing the victim, the selection of con men, their status in the criminal world and several other interesting aspects of the business of confidence.

The last article in this section, "The Man Who Fooled Everybody," illustrates by far the most costly, least reported, most hotly debated form of crime — white collar crime. White collar crime is committed by respectable persons in the normal course of their business, professional or occupational activities. Such crimes are frequently referred to as "scandals," and they take the form of either misrepresentation or duplicity, or both. Neither the criminal nor the general public is likely to think of such depredations as real crimes. For this and other reasons, white collar crimes are usually handled outside of ordinary criminal channels further reinforcing the public's conception of such activity as almost, but not quite, criminal.

The case of Anthony "Tino" De Angelis illustrates most of the more important aspects of white collar crime — its costliness ($214 million), the respectability and high status of the perpetrator, the involved, puzzling, and difficult-to-unravel activities, the misrepresentation and duplicity, the violation of trust and faith vested in him and his position, and, finally, the differential implementation of law. One wonders how society would have reacted to a $200 million burglary or robbery. In the famous Brink's robbery the "take" was less than $2 million. The interesting aspect of all of this is that nearly everyone knows of the Brink's case or the famous train robbery in England but not one in a hundred persons is likely to have heard of Mr. De Angelis. Finally, this case is illustrative of the *tour de force* in white collar crime. The pattern exhibited in the electrical conspiracy case in which many of the most important firms were, through some of their division heads and lesser executives, rigging prices and dividing up the business, is another and perhaps even more serious form of white collar crime.

HELL'S ANGELS
MOTORCYCLE CLUBS*

On the Labor Day weekend, 1964, a large group of Hell's Angels motorcycle clubs gathered in the vicinity of Monterey and established a camp area at the seaward end of Beach Road in Marina, which is in unincorporated territory. Early on the morning of September 6, complaint was made to Sheriff's officers by the erstwhile companions of two girls, aged 14 and 15, that they had been taken away from the boyfriends by some Hell's Angels at the site of the camp. Shortly, deputies found one completely nude and another with only a small amount of clothing on her. Both alleged that they had been raped by five to ten men just prior to the arrival of the officers. They professed to be unable to identify any responsibles at that time. Some hours later, four men were arrested after being identified by the girls. Two of the men identified themselves as presidents of the North Sacramento and Richmond Hell's Angels groups, respectively.

As a result of this case, State Senator Fred S. Farr requested the Attorney General to make an investigation, and on September 18, 1964, a circular letter was sent to all district attorneys, sheriffs, and chiefs of police requesting information concerning the Hell's Angels and also soliciting any suggestions as to methods to control them.

Within the sphere of reference in the original assignment by the Attorney General, most of the information herein relates to the Hell's Angels. However, it should be stressed that there are a number of other so-called "disreputable" motorcycle groups within the State which have constituted a police problem albeit without quite as much notoriety as achieved by the Hell's Angels. Any firm estimate of numbers involved is difficult to make because active membership in the Hell's Angels groups varies from time to time. A similar situation exists in the other local clubs which have been identified and recorded by local law enforcement agencies, as well as by the California Highway Patrol.

Hell's Angels and other "disreputable" motorcycle groups are certainly not typical of the average motorcycle rider in California. As some officers pointed out, there are a number of legitimate groups of motorcyclists, many of them affiliated with the American Motorcycle Association, which hold recognized events and annual tours to various parts of the State. In several such instances the Hell's Angels have constituted a small fringe group which

* Reprinted from a report by the Bureau of Criminal Statistics, State of California, Sacramento, California, 1966, mimeographed.

sought to disrupt the events. However, they were thwarted in their attempts not only by local peace officers, but with the cooperation and assistance of members of the legitimate motorcycle groups, a number of whom were off-duty policemen.

In response to the Attorney General's letter, replies were received from 22 district attorneys, 15 sheriffs, and 67 chiefs of police. Nine district attorneys reported no contact with the motorcycle groups, while 13 submitted reference information and suggestions. Six sheriffs had no information to offer, and 9 submitted information and suggestions concerning the Hell's Angels. Thirty-eight chiefs of police submitted information for our files and suggestions concerning enforcement tactics.

Several sheriffs' offices and police departments have set up special details and/or files to maintain records concerning the Hell's Angels and other problem motorcycle groups. In addition, California Highway Patrol has, since July 12, 1962, maintained a special file in its Auto Theft Unit at Sacramento through which tactical information concerning meetings and group movements are coordinated. The assigned highway patrol officer has in turn coordinated his information with the Fraud Unit of the Bureau of Criminal Identification and Investigation, which agency has, whenever possible, furnished identification data, record transcripts, and photographs of identified subjects.

It is reported that the Hell's Angels group was originally founded in 1950 at Fontana. The San Bernardino County chapter remains the "mother" organization and issues charters to local groups which are located, for the most part, in urban areas. Some claims have been made that the Hell's Angels are affiliated with various other "outlaw" clubs organized in various parts of the State. However, it has been noted that the charters and by-laws of several Hell's Angels groups stress that anyone who is a member of another motorcycle club is not eligible for membership in Hell's Angels.

In several instances, Hell's Angels' representatives have claimed national and international membership. Reference has been made to a Hell's Angels chapter founded in New Zealand. However, to date, and on the basis of information submitted to the Department, there is no confirmation that Hell's Angels as such are organized outside of California, with the possibility of some members or clubs being located at Phoenix, Arizona, and possibly Portland, Oregon.

A description of the club's initiation rites figures in many reports. It is alleged that any new member must bring with him to the meeting a woman or a girl, termed a "sheep," willing to submit to sexual intercourse with each member of the club; in some instances it is reported that one or more members, or the initiate himself, commit cunnilingus on the woman in the presence of the group. While homosexuals seem to be attracted to Hell's Angels, no information received indicates that the Hell's Angels as a group are homosexuals. They seem primarily concerned with heterosexual contacts. Some heterosexual perversions figure in the reports, but taken in context they appear to be means of attracting attention, "being different," and performed primarily for the shock impact on others. These and other attention-attracting actions are characterized by the Angels as "showing class."

On the basis of information submitted by the California Highway Patrol and other law enforcement agencies, some 446 subjects have been *identified* in CII files as members or associate members of Hell's Angels chapters. Of the 446 identified, 250 show records of felony arrests, 151 have had felony convictions, 85 have records of commitment either to State prison or the California Youth Authority, and 8 have been patients at State hospitals. Total felony arrests for this group is 874 and felony convictions for the group as a whole total 300. Misdemeanor arrests of record amount to 1,682 with total misdemeanor convictions of 1,023.

Additionally, there were 276 subjects reported by the Highway Patrol as Hell's Angels prior to the current survey, but which are now included in CHP files only as members of "disreputable" motorcycle clubs. It is believed a large number of this group may still be considered as Hell's Angels but there was no way of definitely ascertaining their category during the present survey. If the 276 previously considered as Hell's Angels are added to the above classifications, the figures would be increased to 445 showing records of felony arrests, 284 with felony convictions, 141 with records of commitments to State prison or Youth Authority, and 12 as patients at State hospitals. Likewise the total felony arrest figure would be 1,457, total felony convictions 553, misdemeanor arrests 3,068, with total misdemeanor convictions of 1,919.

The emblem of the Hell's Angels, termed "colors," consists of an embroidered patch of a winged skull wearing a motorcycle helmet. Just below the wing of the emblem are the letters "MC." Over this is a band bearing the words "Hell's Angels." Below the emblem is another patch bearing the local chapter name, which is usually an abbreviation for the city or locality. These patches are sewn on the back of a usually sleeveless denim jacket. In addition members have been observed wearing various types of Luftwaffe insignia and reproductions of German iron crosses. Many affect beards and their hair is usually long and unkempt. Some wear a single earring in a pierced ear lobe. Frequently they have been observed to wear metal belts made of a length of polished motorcycle drive chain which can be unhooked and used as a flexible bludgeon.

In addition to the patches on the back of Hell's Angels jackets, the "One Percenters" wear a patch reading "1%-er." This badge is currently worn by members of clubs other than the Hell's Angels, including the "Coffin Cheaters" and "Satan's Slaves" in Los Angeles County and a relatively new group, "The Iron Horsemen," in the San Diego area. It is reported that they obtain the "One Percenter" badges through the Hell's Angels San Bernardino club. Another patch worn by some members bears the number "13." It is reported to represent the 13th letter of the alphabet, "M," which in turn stands for marijuana and indicates the wearer thereof is a user of the drug.

Hell's Angels have been most conspicuous when participating in group hoodlum activities at lower class bars and while engaged on a "run" to some smaller city.

On November 4, 1961, a San Francisco resident driving through Rodeo, possibly under the influence of alcohol, struck a motorcycle belonging to a Hell's Angel parked outside a bar. A group of Angels pursued the vehicle, pulled the driver from the car and attempted to demolish the rather expensive vehicle. The bartender claimed that he had seen nothing, but a cocktail waitress in the bar furnished identification to the officers concerning some of those responsible for the assault. The next day it was reported to officers that a member of the Hell's Angels gang had threatened the life of this waitress as well as another woman waitress. A male witness who definitely identified five participants in the assault including the president of the Vallejo Hell's Angels and the president of the Vallejo "Road Rats" advised officers that because of his fear of retaliation by club members he would refuse to testify to the facts he had previously furnished.

Early on the morning of April 22, 1962, a group of Hell's Angels were congregated in a bar at Rodeo when two uniformed sheriff's deputies entered to serve a warrant on one of those present. The arrestee ran out the front door followed by 15 to 20 Angels who surrounded him. One officer was knocked down, kicked and hit over the head with a partially filled beer bottle, while the other was hit with a billiard cue. A number of citizens came to the officers' assistance and the Angels ran off in all directions. Several arrests were made for assault and battery, but the deputy district attorney in charge decided not to file complaints of assault with a deadly weapon.

Early in the morning of June 2, 1962, it was reported that three Hell's Angels had seized a 19-year-old woman in a small bar in the northern part of Sacramento and while two of them held her down on the barroom floor, the third removed her outer clothing.

Several persons present in the bar at the time of the offense refused to admit to officers that they knew anything about it; the victim told investigators that she had been warned by one of the participants that if she told anyone about the incident they would "bust her up."

During the Labor Day weekend of 1963, a large group of motorcyclists consisting of Hell's Angels, "Stram Satans," "Galloping Gooses," "Comancheros," and the "Cavaliers" converged on the city of Porterville. By Saturday evening they had assembled in the center of the city where they parked their motorcycles and automobiles. Most started to drink in local bars, becoming obnoxious and vulgar. They stood in the middle of the street where they stopped vehicles, opened car doors and attempted to pet and paw female passengers in the automobiles. The women who accompanied the group lay in the middle of the street where they went through suggestive motions. At about this time, some half dozen motorcyclists invaded a bar and brutally beat an old man and attempted to abduct the barmaid. Shortly thereafter some dozen motorcyclists went to the local hospital where they pushed in every door of the hospital looking for the victim of the beating.

On July 4, 1964, at the invitation of the same bartender who had previously worked at a Hell's Angels hangout in Rodeo, the Oakland Hell's Angels made a "run" to Willits. By the afternoon of the 4th there were some 120 motorcyclists and their female companions congregating at a local bar. In addition to those from Oakland, there were Angels from Vallejo and Richmond, as well as the "Mofo" club from San Francisco. Periodic fighting between the motorcyclists and local citizens broke out with beer bottles, belts made from motorcycle drive chains, and metal beer can openers being used as weapons. It was noted that some members apparently designated as sergeants at arms did not drink, but spent their time watching the group. When police were called, these people would pick up broken bottles, pour beer on any blood remaining on the floor, and move their groups in and out of the bar to make police interrogation more difficult.

On April 2, 1964, a group of eight Hell's Angels invaded the home of an Oakland woman, forcing her male friend out of the house at gunpoint and raping the woman in the presence of her three children. Later that same morning, female companions of the Hell's Angels threatened the victim that if she cooperated with the police, she would be cut on the face with a razor. She refused to sign a complaint and stated she would not testify.

On July 15, 1964, five young males wearing Hell's Angels jackets invaded a liquor store in Sacramento and assaulted a Negro customer who was at the time reaching into the refrigerator for a bottle of soda water. The victim was punched in the face and pushed against the refrigerator with such force as to break the door. During the melee, the other Angels stole two cartons of beer and a bottle of wine, departing rapidly thereafter.

On September 19, 1964, a large group of Hell's Angels and "Satan's Slaves" converged on a bar in South Gate, parking their motorcycles and cars in the street in such a fashion as to block one half of the roadway. They told officers that three members of the club had recently been asked to stay out of the bar and that they had come to tear it down. Upon their approach the bar owner had locked the doors and turned off the lights and no entrance was made, but the group did demolish a cement block fence. On arrival of the police, members of the club were lying on the sidewalk and in the street. They were asked to leave the city, which they did reluctantly. As they left, several were heard to say that they would be back and tear down the bar.

Early on the morning of October 25, 1964, nine Hell's Angels and two of their female companions were arrested by Gardena police and sheriff's officers after a riot call had been received from a Gardena bar. Police reported the group "started ripping up the whole place" after someone had splashed a mug of beer over one of the group. The bar was left in shambles and pool tables covered with beer and urine.

Apart from general hoodlum acts, many Hell's Angels have records for other criminal offenses. The Sheriff of San Bernardino County advised that because of extensive cooperation between law enforcement agencies in his area, he had encountered no difficulties arising out of activities of large groups. His chief concern has been the criminal actions of individual members either in small groups or alone. Offenses mainly were forgery, assault, auto theft, rape and sex perversion. He pointed out that the Hell's Angels have been particularly active in the area of forgery of credit cards and the thefts of motor vehicles and motorcycles. From time to time they are very active in the altering of motor numbers and forgeries of vehicle ownership certificates. Officers report that many Angels are adept at stripping and cannibalizing motorcycles, including removal of serial numbers which are replaced with fictitious numbers.

Generally, those responding to the Attorney General's inquiry emphasized the necessity of maintaining adequate intelligence concerning activities and movement of both Hell's Angels and other outlaw motorcycle clubs. Several law enforcement administrators whose departments had successfully coped with large assemblies of Hell's Angels stressed strong enforcement techniques, utilizing an adequate number of officers and making valid arrests based on sufficient evidence. One chief stated, "It has been our experience that the only thing members of the Hell's Angels group understand is unrelenting firmness in law enforcement backed by sufficient show of strength to implement it."

The validity of this approach may be confirmed by the fact that those areas where the Hell's Angels have constituted a group or near-riot problem, the local law enforcement agency has usually been limited in manpower. It appears that in major jurisdictions where a sufficient number of officers is available, these disturbances as group activities have not occurred to any great extent.

Officers of one sheriff's department pointed out that a major difficulty in identifying stolen motorcycles is the detection of altered serial numbers when officers are making a field check. It was suggested the problem could be alleviated to a large extent by proper registration procedures. New motorcycles have frame numbers and motor numbers which usually are different. To standardize procedures and facilitate field checking, it was suggested that all vehicles, including automobiles, be registered by both engine and frame numbers in the space already provided on the certificate of registration and ownership issued by the Department of Motor Vehicles.

The examples cited illustrate some of the problems of investigating officers to obtain witnesses willing to testify in cases involving Hell's Angels. The group seeks to exploit the so-called "gangsters' code" of group loyalty and threats to persons who might appear in court against them. There have been instances of Hell's Angels punishing witnesses by physical assault. In the event the witness or victim is female, the women associates of the Angels seem willing to participate in threats to discourage testimony. A practical problem seen in various cases is that both victims and witnesses generally exist in the same environment as do the Hell's Angels. While gang rapes and forced sex perversion may have occurred, the victims and witnesses frequently are not of the higher social strata and thus are vulnerable to the mores of the "saloon society." It is believed that the only feasible approach to the solution of this problem is for investigating officers to recognize it and take all steps possible to protect witnesses both before and after trial.

A number of law enforcement officials stressed that the cooperation of prosecuting and judicial officials should be sought in assuring that appropriate charges and sentences would result from arrests of outlaw motorcyclists. In some instances, felony cases have been reduced to low misdemeanor charges. Defendants with lengthy prior records may receive suspended sentences or summary probation. Several officers expressed themselves as believing that any probation granted should be under strict supervision, a condition of which should be that the probationer refrain from riding motorcycles and associating with outlaw clubs.

As previously related, general movement activity and day-to-day operating information is now being coordinated by a specially assigned officer in the Auto Theft Unit at the Sacramento headquarters of the California Highway Patrol. This agency is the logical coordinating point by virtue of its resources for rapid communication and furnishing manpower assistance. The Bureau of Criminal Identification and Investigation has participated by making available to the Highway Patrol and other interested law enforcement agencies record transcripts and photographs of Hell's Angels and other outlaw motorcycle groups. As a result of the current investigation, this information has now been set up on punched tabulating cards to facilitate sorting and the printing of listings.

THE VIOLENT OFFENDER *

DANIEL GLASER,
DONALD KENEFICK,
AND VINCENT O'LEARY

Most prominent among the violent offenses is homicide, or the killing of human beings. The most heinous homicide is murder or the *deliberate* killing of another human being. In about 40 states murder is divided into several "degrees." First degree murder is defined as killing with premeditation and malice aforethought, while second degree murder involves murderous intent, but not premeditation. Manslaughter is a form of homicide in which, though a victim is killed, the criminal is held not to have had murderous intent. Where this is differentiated into degrees, first degree manslaughter is that in which a fatal result could reasonably be anticipated, as in a knife fight, while second degree manslaughter is one in which homicide could not so readily be anticipated, as in a fist fight or an auto accident. Sometimes another label, such as "reckless homicide," is employed for homicide due to negligence, thus giving separate treatment to most killings by automobile.

No crime is involved in an act which legally is classifiable as "justifiable homicide," such as killing someone in order to defend life or property, providing the force employed in this defense is not excessive under the circumstances. Also, no crime is involved if someone is killed from an act which is classified as "excusable homicide," which means that death resulted from some behavior which was legal and was performed with reasonable caution, but had unanticipated lethal consequences. Sometimes the defendant in a murder case has convinced himself that his act was justifiable or excusable, despite the court's finding to the contrary. The parole board must assess whether such a person is more likely to commit a crime than another prisoner who admits his guilt in a deliberate murder.

Often it is pure chance, or a lack of skill, which makes an offense definable as "assault," rather than "homicide." This implies that there was intent to kill, but the criminal was unsuccessful in his effort to carry out such an

* Reprinted from *The Violent Offender*, U.S. Department of Health, Education, and Welfare, Welfare Administration, Office of Juvenile Delinquency and Youth Development, Washington, D.C., 1966, pp. 1, 3–5, 7–9, 23–30, 32.

intent. The crime of assault may be defined legally either as a felony (with such labels as "aggravated assault," "assault to kill," and "assault to do bodily harm"), or as a misdemeanor (with labels like "simple assault," "fighting," or the catchall "disorderly conduct"). Strictly speaking, "assault" is only the attempt to do bodily injury, while actual injury has the old common law designation "battery." Again, the legal designation of a particular assaultive offense is determined not just by studying the language in the statutes; it frequently is the outcome of a bargaining process in which the accused will plead guilty to the charge carrying the least penalty, in exchange for non-prosecution of the charge most accurately describing his offense.

An important group of violent crimes involve sexual acts. One of the most serious sexual offenses, of course, is rape. Usually this consists of having sexual intercourse with a female without her consent, for example, by use of force or threat of force to secure the woman's compliance.

There are a large variety of sexual offenses which are passionate acts usually considered unnatural, but which do not generally involve violence. These include indecent exposure, peeping, and homosexuality. Those which are more likely to result in imprisonment, if prosecuted, include bigamy, incest, and child molesting. Bigamy and incest are rather rare, but child molesting is a problem persistently confronting parole boards. Usually the offender claims he merely was fondling the child, but repetition of this behavior by one individual, especially if it involves his contact with the child's sexual organs, marks it as a compulsion seriously offending our moral standards.

The term "sodomy" designates a sexual felony in many jurisdictions, but it seldom is defined precisely. It may refer to any unnatural sexual act, including homosexuality, child molesting, or sexual intercourse of a human with an animal.

Strictly speaking, "robbery" which is the taking of money or other property by force or threat of force, might also be considered a crime of violence. However, the violence here is a means to an economic end rather than an end in itself, and so robbery will not be dealt with in this report.

One of the most striking facts about homicide is that it is becoming less frequent. In an area when rising crime rates are widely deplored, the downward trend in murder rates is peculiar. The homicide rate in the United States was approximately halved in the past 30 years. Homicides have declined from nearly 10 to less than 5 per 100,00 per year, according to local health department death certificates compiled by the National Center for Health Statistics. These are believed to be the most complete figures on this offense. Both the death certificates and the police figures include some cases which courts later adjudge as noncriminal homicide (about 5 to 10 percent of the totals).

The reporting of assaults to the police, and police recording of them, has always been markedly incomplete, but the completeness of these statistics probably has increased in recent years. This increase in reporting and recording could account for the increase in assault rates, even if actual assaultive behavior did not become more prevalent. Aggravated assault rates were only about 7 times murder and nonnegligent manslaughter rates in 1933, but increased to about 20 times the homicide rates by 1963. Presumably homicide always was more completely counted than assault, although the fact that FBI rates for murder and nonnegligent manslaughter have become increasingly close to the homicide rates by death certificates suggest that police reporting has also increased in completeness on these fatal crimes.

Statistics on rape probably have always been highly incomplete, partly because publicity given this offense often adds appreciably to the long-run suffering of the victims who, therefore, frequently hide their victimization.

In summary, for the more incompletely reported offenses, it is difficult to know whether long-run increases reflect shifts in the prevalence of criminal behavior, or merely trends in the completeness with which offenses are reported to the police and are statistically tabulated by them. However, even for homicide, the presumably most completely recorded offense, and the one in which rates are declining, Wolfgang has argued that the statistical trend may not reflect any change in actual modes of criminal behavior. He argues that the decline in homicide rates may result from improvement in medical services during the past 30 years, whereby the lives of many victims of aggravated assault now are saved who previously would have died. Thus, many actions which formerly would have contributed to homicide statistics may now add only to the assault statistics.

Nevertheless, there is some basis for inferring that a decline has occurred in the United States not just in homicide, but also in most other crimes of violence. One ground for this conclusion is the fact that rates of violent crime decline with education, and the general education level of the United States has been rising. Another argument for the view that violent crimes are decreasing in the United States despite the apparent statistical increase, is the belief that crimes of violence decrease with urbanization, but that notification of police and courts when violence occurs increases with urbanization; the reaction to violence more frequently involves recourse to agents of the law in urban than in rural situations. It is quite difficult to test these ideas, but some data on the geographical distribution of crimes of violence may permit crude testing of theory on the causes of violent crimes, and may also support inferences on actual trends in the frequency of violence independently of trends in official statistics on violence.

First of all, murderers (and the "violent criminal"), as has been implied, might be thought of as falling into two roughly defined groups. They either commit a crime that:

(A)   is understandable as being an appropriate reaction, under the given circumstances, to a specific situation; and is so understood by most individuals of the same sex, ethnic group, social class, and age as the murderer;

(B) or they do not.

Let us look at some of the murderers in category (A):

(1) The "ordinary" murderer: Most often, he is a good example of a product of the "culture of violence." The murder frequently is not only excused but even expected. "Premeditation," when it exists, is usually some activity like staggering out of a barroom to find a convenient weapon. In a large number of cases, the person he murders on return is a friend. Both are drinking, both are trying to prove their masculinity, both know the survivor will not be severely condemned by the people that matter (their other friends) even if the police and the courts take a dim view of the outcome. The quick-triggered male who assaults (and kills, occasionally) is often responding to an affront to his maleness, doubly intolerable because it comes from another male.

Kept away from alcohol and threats to their self-esteem, they are relatively nonassaultive people. They may be frightened enough of their own anger after one murder or violent assault to walk very circumspectly thereafter. The probability of their nonrecidivism is highest when they can be induced to accept more of the values of lower middle class citizens or when the situations likely to trigger assaultiveness are controlled.

(2) The "cultural" murderer: Another variety of the type (A) murderer is the "cultural" murderer, i.e., a man who is compelled by social pressures to commit murder. An example is the Ku Kluxers in the Deep South, who are convinced they are preserving the fabric of a great society. Another is the occasional feuding seen among old American groups, usually of Scotch or North Irish descent. These murders are "premeditated," but are similar to the "ordinary murderer" in that the culture condones violence, in fact, insists on it, under the circumstances mentioned. They are individuals who possess, in exaggerated form, patterns of behavior condoned and supported by their environment. They are apt either to be normal or neurotic, seldom much worse.

(3) The "professional" murderer: Another variety, although relatively few in number, is the professional murderer. Of this type, there seems to be at least two subvarieties: The Mafia "soldier," who does the assigned task in line of duty and the much rarer killer, of various ethnic groups, who is on call for anyone who can afford him. We know nothing scientifically about either, though we could hazard a guess that the first is not *necessarily* any more disturbed than many, and that the second probably is pretty disturbed, indeed. The first is apt to be a model prisoner unlikely to "reform"; the second is apt to be at the dead center of any riot and probably will not change either. There is a good chance that he resembles one or another of the subjects in the following section.

We come now to category (B), to those murderers and violent criminals whose acts are not condonable by their own milieu, may not even be understood by it. All of these taken together form probably a relatively small percentage of murderers. All are most probably psychiatrically disturbed. Their individual outlook for rehabilitation varies as their psychiatric condition, and since we do not know as much as we would like about the outcome of a given psychiatric condition, prediction must be cautious.

(4) The "inadequate" murderer: [This] murderer is often the never-quite-respected, never-quite-respectable fringe member of the group. The very instabilities and infantilities that keep him peripheral, blind him to the fact that avenging the group will merely lay him open to greater hostility from it, since he is not even the official executioner. These individuals are not quite psychotic but their need for self-esteem is so pathetically great that they cannot be fed, as it were, by any action. They are bound to defeat themselves. Their outlook is poor, psychiatrically, since they usually have little insight and are frightened of getting more, since their fantasies of importance are all they have.

(5) The "psychopathic" murderer: The characteristic ways of handling some kinds of stress seem to fall into one of two large areas.

(a) The person is stimulus-bound, i.e., he has to respond to certain stimuli. These people seem to be either compulsive neurotics or brain-damaged. A few violent crimes are certainly committed by the latter, but compulsive neurotics are generally excessively law-abiding.

(b) The second way of handling stress is more difficult to describe than is impulsivity. If there is any validity to the term "psychopath," it would hold for the individuals we are about to discuss. Basically, they show a complex *pattern* of response, which is still coherent enough to be recognizable.

First of all, these are people who seem "keyed up" most of the time. This is indicated by tests of blood pressure, pulse, skin resistance, and the like — all of which rather crudely measure autonomic nervous system sensitivity. However — and this is the important point — somehow they have learned to deal with this constant jangling in a very pathologic way — they ignore it, are not really aware of it consciously at all. In other words, they are responding to stimuli more often and more vigorously than others, but are not really able to respond by appropriate means, using words and/or muscular action as "normals" do. This surface inertia gives them that appearance of blandness, of not caring, that so irritates their fellows.

(6) The "psychotic" murderer: Most murderers kill one person only, usually in the heat of passion. The more people a person kills and the more occasions on which he kills, the more it can be taken as preliminary evidence that he will be found psychotic. Psychotics are, as a general rule, more law-abiding than the normal or neurotic, but when they do murder or assault, they do so with a certain exaggeration and bizarrie that is diagnostic. The

"ordinary" murderer murders a friend or a spouse; the psychotic murders a parent or a casual stranger. This is why most murders are relatively easy for the police to solve and why a "Jack-the-Ripper" or a "Boston Strangler" is an enigma, since this type murders strangers only.

NATIONAL SCOPE OF
ORGANIZED CRIME*

In 1951 the Kefauver committee declared that a nationwide crime syndicate known as the Mafia operated in many large cities and that the leaders of the Mafia usually controlled the most lucrative rackets in their cities.

In 1957, 20 of organized crime's top leaders were convicted (later reversed on appeal) of a criminal charge arising from a meeting at Apalachin, N.Y. At the sentencing the judge stated that they had sought to corrupt and infiltrate the political mainstreams of the country, that they had led double lives of crime and respectability, and that their probation reports read "like a tale of horrors."

Today the core of organized crime in the United States consists of 24 groups operating as criminal cartels in large cities across the Nation. Their membership is exclusively Italian, they are in frequent communication with each other, and their smooth functioning is insured by a national body of overseers. To date, only the Federal Bureau of Investigation has been able to document fully the national scope of these groups, and FBI intelligence indicates that the organization as a whole has changed its name from the Mafia to La Cosa Nostra.

In 1966 J. Edgar Hoover told a House of Representatives Appropriations Subcommittee:

La Cosa Nostra is the largest organization of the criminal underworld in this country, very closely organized and strictly disciplined. They have committed almost every crime under the sun. . . .

La Cosa Nostra is a criminal fraternity whose membership is Italian either by birth or national origin, and it has been found to control major racket activities in many of our larger metropolitan areas, often working in concert with criminals representing other ethnic backgrounds. It operates on a nationwide basis, with international implications, and until recent years, it carried on its activities with almost complete secrecy. It functions as a criminal

* Reprinted from *The Challenge of Crime in a Free Society: A Report by the President's Commission on Law Enforcement and Administration of Justice* (Washington, D.C.: Government Printing Office, 1967), pp. 192–96.

cartel, adhering to its own body of "law" and "justice" and, in so doing, thwarts and usurps the authority of legally constituted judicial bodies. . . .

In individual cities, the local core group may also be known as the "outfit," the "syndicate," or the "mob." These 24 groups work and control other racket groups, whose leaders are of various ethnic derivations. In addition, the thousands of employees who perform the street-level functions of organized crime's gambling, usury, and other illegal activities represent a cross section of the Nation's population groups.

The present confederation of organized crime groups arose after Prohibition, during which Italian, German, Irish, and Jewish groups had competed with one another in racket operations. The Italian groups were successful in switching their enterprises from prostitution and bootlegging to gambling, extortion, and other illegal activities. They consolidated their power through murder and violence.

Today, members of the 24 core groups reside and are active in [many] States. The scope and effect of their criminal operations and penetration of legitimate businesses vary from area to area. The wealthiest and most influential core groups operate in States including New York, New Jersey, Illinois, Florida, Louisiana, Nevada, Michigan, and Rhode Island. [There are also] many States in which members of core groups control criminal activity even though they do not reside there. For example, a variety of illegal activities in New England is controlled from Rhode Island.

Recognition of the common ethnic tie of the 5,000 or more members of organized crime's core groups is essential to understanding the structure of these groups today. Some have been concerned that past identification of Cosa Nostra's ethnic character has reflected on Italian-Americans generally. This false implication was eloquently refuted by one of the Nation's outstanding experts on organized crime, Sgt. Ralph Salerno of the New York City Police Department. When an Italian-American racketeer complained to him, "Why does it have to be one of your own kind that hurts you?" Sgt. Salerno answered:

I'm not your kind and you're not my kind. My manners, morals, and mores are not yours. The only thing we have in common is that we both spring from an Italian heritage and culture—and you are the traitor to that heritage and culture which I am proud to be part of.

Organized crime in its totality thus consists of these 24 groups allied with other racket enterprises to form a loose confederation operating in large and small cities. In the core groups, because of their permanency of form, strength of organization and ability to control other racketeer operations resides the power that organized crime has in America today.

Each of the 24 groups is known as a "family," with membership varying from as many as 700 men to as few as 20. Most cities with organized crime have only one family; New York City has five. Each family can participate in the full range of activities in which organized crime generally is known to engage. Family organization is rationally designed with an integrated set of positions geared to maximize profits. Like any large corporation, the organization functions regardless of personnel changes, and no individual — not even the leader — is indispensable. If he dies or goes to jail, business goes on.

The hierarchical structure of the families resembles that of the Mafia groups that have operated for almost a century on the island of Sicily. Each family is headed by one man, the "boss," whose primary functions are maintaining order and maximizing profits. Subject only to the possibility of being overruled by the national advisory group, which will be discussed below, his authority in all matters relating to his family is absolute.

Beneath each boss is an "underboss," the vice president or deputy director of the family. He collects information for the boss; he relays messages to him and passes his instructions down to his own underlings. In the absence of the boss, the underboss acts for him.

On the same level as the underboss, but operating in a staff capacity, is the *consigliere,* who is a counselor, or adviser. Often an elder member of the family who has partially retired from a career in crime, he gives advice to family members, including the boss and underboss, and thereby enjoys considerable influence and power.

Below the level of the underboss are the *caporegime,* some of whom serve as buffers between the top members of the family and the lower-echelon personnel. To maintain their insulation from the police, the leaders of the hierarchy (particularly the boss) avoid direct communication with the workers. All commands, information, complaints, and money flow back and forth through a trusted go-between. A *caporegima* fulfilling this buffer capacity, however, unlike the underboss, does not make decisions or assume any of the authority of his boss.

Other *caporegime* serve as chiefs of operating units. The number of men supervised in each unit varies with the size and activities of particular families. Often the *caporegima* has one or two associates who work closely with him, carrying orders, information, and money to the men who belong to his unit. From a business standpoint the *caporegima* is analogous to plant supervisor or sales manager.

The lowest level "members" of a family are the *soldati,* the soldiers or "burron" men who report to the *caporegime.* A soldier may operate a particular illicit enterprise (e.g., a loan-sharking operation, a dice game, a lottery, a bookmaking operation, a smuggling operation, or a vending machine company) on a commission basis, or he may "own" the enterprise and pay a portion of its profit to the organization, in return for the right to operate. Partnerships are common between two or more soldiers and between soldiers and men higher up in the hierarchy. Some soldiers and most upper-echelon family members have interests in more than one business.

Beneath the soldiers in the hierarchy are large numbers of employees and commission agents who are not members of the family and not necessarily of Italian descent. These are the people who do most of the actual work in the various enterprises. They have no buffers or other insulation from law enforcement. They take bets, drive trucks, answer telephones, sell narcotics, tend the stills, work in the legitimate businesses. For example, in a major lottery business that operated in Negro neighborhoods in Chicago, the workers were Negroes; the bankers for the lottery were Japanese-Americans; but the game, including the banking operation, was licensed, for a fee, by a family member.

There are at least two aspects of organized crime that characterize it as a unique form of criminal activity. The first is the element of corruption. The second is the element of enforcement, which is necessary for the maintenance of both internal discipline and the regularity of business transactions. In the hierarchy of organized crime there are positions for people fulfilling both of these functions.

The highest ruling body of the 24 families is the "commission." This body serves as a combination legislature, supreme court, board of directors, and arbitration board; its principal functions are judicial. Family members look to the commission as the ultimate authority on organizational and jurisdictional disputes. It is composed of the bosses of the Nation's most powerful families but has authority over all 24. The composition of the commission varies from 9 to 12 men. According to current information, there are presently 9 families represented, 5 from New York City and 1 each from Philadelphia, Buffalo, Detroit, and Chicago.

The commission is not a representative legislative assembly or an elected judicial body. Members of this council do not regard each other as equals. Those with long tenure on the commission and those who head large families, or possess unusual wealth, exercise greater authority and receive utmost respect. The balance of power on this nationwide council rests with the leaders of New York's 5 families. They have always served on the commission and consider New York as at least the unofficial headquarters of the entire organization.

The leaders of the various organized crime families acquire their positions of power and maintain them with the assistance of a code of conduct that, like the hierarchical structure of the families, is very similar to the Sicilian Mafia's code — and just as effective. The code stipulates that underlings should not interfere with the leaders' interests and should not seek protection from the police. They should be "standup guys" who go to prison in order that the bosses may amass fortunes. The code gives the leaders exploitative authoritarian power over everyone in the organization. Loyalty, honor, respect, absolute obedience — these are inculcated in family members through ritualistic initiation and customs within the organization, through material rewards, and through violence. Though underlings are forbidden to "inform" to the outside world, the family boss learns of deviance within the organization through an elaborate system of internal informants. Despite prescribed mechanisms for peaceful settlement of disputes between family members, the boss himself may order the execution of any family member for any reason.

The code not only preserves leadership authority but also makes it extremely difficult for law enforcement to cultivate informants and maintain them within the organization.

Although law enforcement has uncovered the skeletal organization of organized crime families, much greater knowledge is needed about the structure and operations of these organizations. For example, very little is known about the many functions performed by the men occupying the formally established positions in the organizations. In private business, identifying a person as a "vice president" is meaningless unless one knows his duties. In addition to his formal obligations, the corporate officer may have important informal roles such as expediter or troubleshooter.

More successful law enforcement measures against the organized crime families will be possible only when the entire range of informal and formal roles for each position is ascertained. Answers to crucial questions must be found: While it is known that "money-movers" are employed to insure maximum use of family capital, how does money move from lower-echelon workers to top leaders? How is that money spread among illicit activities and into legitimate business? What are the specific methods by which public officials are corrupted? What roles do corrupted officials play? What informal rules have been devised for successful continuation of each of the illicit enterprises, such as gambling and usury? Only through the answers to questions such as these will society be able to understand precisely how organized crime maintains a coherent, efficient organization with a permanency of form that survives changes in working and leadership personnel.

CONFESSIONS OF
A MASTER JEWEL THIEF*

ROBERT WALLACE

Arthur Barry was an incomparable second-story man; even the phrase, in the age of the ranch house, must be explained to the children. Second-story men are not often in the news today, but there was

* Reprinted with permission from Robert Wallace, "Confessions of a Master Jewel Thief," *Life*, March 12, 1956, pp. 121–26. © 1956 Time Inc.

a time when they were aristocrats among thieves and when Barry himself was a king. There are elderly detectives still active today who regard him as the greatest jewel thief who ever lived. In the 1920s Barry collected a pile of loot valued somewhere between $5 and $10 million. He rarely robbed anyone who was not in the Social Register, his manners were impeccable and his working uniform was often a tuxedo. He seldom carried a gun or a knife, never indulged in violence and almost invariably left a favorable impression upon his victims, whom he called clients. In his prime he looked much like Ronald Colman; weathy matrons, awakening at night to find him puttering about their bedrooms, often failed to scream.

Barry attributes his downfall in the main to simple physiological mischance; he matured too early and was full-grown at 13. The companions he sought out were of his own size but considerably older, and in his efforts to ingratiate himself with his elders he presently found himself running errands for some sinful people. One of these was a "peteman," in the language of the trade, a master safecracker named Lowell Jack, who was then in semi-retirement and made his living by manufacturing special tools and nitro-glycerin. Lowell Jack had no difficulty making the nitroglycerin: he simply heated dynamite and water in a bucket on the kitchen stove and bottled the essence. But he needed a good delivery boy who would not drop the stuff in a public place and damage a number of bystanders. He employed young Barry, at $4 or $5 per delivery, and sent him on trains to other New England cities. Barry did just as he was told and soon became a trusted member of the small-time Worcester underworld. As he rode from city to city, a quiet, manly youngster of 14 in knickers, with his bottle of nitroglycerin in a cotton-filled suitcase between his knees, he was the perfect picture of the noble lad of whom people say, "If we only had more fine boys like this one."

Barry committed his first burglary at 15, a small job that netted him less than $100 but a thoughtful and deft one all the same. His victims were a middle-aged couple who ran a dry goods store and brought the day's receipts home with them each evening, there being no night depositories at the Worcester banks in those days. For several days before the robbery, while the couple was at work, Barry entered their house through an unlocked window and prowled about, looking for the place where, if he were a middle-aged man who ran a dry goods store, he would hide the money. Eventually he found it, an empty desk drawer that seemed to have the smell of cash lingering in it. On the night of the burglary he entered the house through the same unlocked window tiptoed directly to the drawer, removed the money and tiptoed out.

Barry committed a number of other minor burglaries during his formative years, then interrupted his career to serve in the Army in World War I. He was wounded in action and recommended for a Silver Star, but went AWOL before he could get it. After the war he settled in New York. It had never seriously occurred to him to follow any honest profession; his problem was merely to decide what sort of thief he would be. Safecracking and bank robbery did not appeal to him, and ordinary burglary and holdups struck him as unprofitable and somehow disreputable. Although he had only a high school education, Barry was a polished individual, a good conversationalist and something of a dandy. There was one specialty that seemed appropriate for him: jewel theft.

Jewel theft was attractive because of the ease with which, in the 1920s in New York, a thief could dispose of his loot. "Why," Barry says, "there were fences in those days who could have got rid of the Statue of Liberty."

Having decided what to steal, Barry had only to decide whom to steal it from. "I noticed that a lot of wealthy women who came into New York shopping used to wind up their afternoons at the casino in Central Park. So I'd go up there plenty myself to look them over. When I spotted a woman who had plenty of diamonds on her, I'd follow her out to her limousine and take the license number. Then all I had to do was go to the nearest phone, call up the police traffic bureau and say, 'This is Patrolman Schultz, badge number 465786. I've got an accident up here, and I need the name and address of Cadillac sedan, New York plate number XYZ-123.' The traffic bureau never took the time to check on Patrolman Schultz. They'd simply give me the name and address."

Barry also selected his victims from the society columns, paying particular attention to announcements of wedding and engagement parties in the estate section on the North Shore of Long Island, his favorite hunting ground. On the afternoon of a party he would drive out to the Island, park his car near the estate in question and change into formal clothes. Then he would crash the party. Lawn parties were particularly easy for him since he had only to climb unnoticed over a wall or through a hedge, pick up a drink and a canapé from a passing waiter and mingle with the guests. Thereafter it was easy for him to get into the house, wander upstairs and make a mental sketch of the floor plan. Often he was able to enter the master bedroom and locate likely hiding places for jewelry, although on such preliminary forays he never stole anything. Sometimes he unlocked a half-dozen windows in strategic spots, hoping that they would remain unlocked for a day or two, and occasionally he cut off the burglar alarm system. If he was discovered wandering about the house, he pretended to be a drunk looking for a place to lie down. No one ever challenged him. His stage presence was faultless, his taste in clothes excellent and his grammar good enough to fool the King of England — which, as a matter of fact, it did, at a time when Edward VIII was Prince of Wales.

Barry encountered the prince on an evening at a speakeasy on 59th Street and made a very favorable impression on him. They had several drinks in the course of two or three hours, during which the prince chatted gaily and perhaps a little too informatively. A few days later, early on the morning of

September 9, 1924, a thief entered the home of Mrs. Joshua Cosden at Sands Point, Long Island and made off with $150,000 worth of jewels, including some which belonged to guests of the Cosdens, the prince's cousin, Lord Louis Mountbatten, and his wife. It was almost as though someone, in the vulgar phrase, had fingered the job.

The proceeds of a $150,000 robbery could not support Barry in the style to which he was accustomed for very long. He could sell only the most valuable jewels and for only a fraction of their worth. His usual procedure was to break up the compound pieces, such as necklaces, pins and brooches, at once and throw away the gold and platinum settings and the smaller stones. The safest depository for these, he decided, was New York Bay.

Because his cash realizations were low in relation to the value of what he stole, Barry was obliged to make numerous business trips to the suburbs. After the Cosden affair he paid a call at the home of a Social Registerite named John C. Greenleaf of Hewlett Bay Park, Long Island and took $10,000 worth of jewels. He had also stopped at the residence of Mr. Harold E. Talbott, who would someday become President Eisenhower's Secretary of the Air Force, and had taken $23,000 worth.

Barry did very well during the mid-20s, averaging about half a million dollars in thefts per year. He extended his territory up into Dutchess County in New York and in that area in 1926 he performed a feat that aroused real awe in police circles. Having discovered that the master and mistress of a large estate kept their jewelry in a 150-pound safe in their bedroom closet, Barry climbed into the bedroom on a ladder, tiptoed to the closet and silently hoisted the safe on his shoulder. (Although he stands only 5 feet 8 inches, Barry was and still is a man of astonishing physical strength.) Without a sound he withdrew the way he had come.

Silence and deftness also characterized the great Hotel Plaza robbery on September 30, 1925, in which jewelry valued at $750,000 disappeared in broad daylight from the six-room suite of Mrs. James P. Donahue, daughter of F. W. Woolworth. Among the objects stolen were a 10-carat diamond ring worth more than $50,000 and a rope of pearls valued at $450,000. These were taken from a dressing table in Mrs. Donahue's bedroom while she sat in a tub in a bathroom only a few feet away. A maid was in a nearby room and a masseuse in another. No one heard a sound.

The only one of his 150 major thefts for which Barry was prosecuted, convicted and jailed was the stealing of some $100,000 in jewelry from the late Jesse Livermore, the Wall Street operator, whose summer home was in Kings Point, Long Island. It took place early in the morning of May 29, 1927 and was a double-headed operation: the Livermores had some house guests at the time and Barry robbed them too.

During the Livermore burglary, as in many others in which he could not handle all the details by himself, Barry had an accomplice, a strong-arm named "Boston Billy" Monaghan. Barry did the thinking and talking while Monaghan stood ready to take care of anyone who interrupted the proceedings.

It was not a professional blunder that brought about his arrest, but, as he supposes today, a woman. Although he was married, Barry was a formidable ladies' man. "That's where all the money went," he explains. Barry suspects that one of his girls, in a fit of monogamous jealousy, went to the police and told them that he had committed the Livermore burglary. At any rate someone did, and he was arrested by a platoon of cops at the railroad station at Ronkonkoma, Long Island, at 7:30 o'clock on a summer Sunday evening. He was sentenced to 25 years in Auburn Prison.

As he began his sentence Barry was 31 years old and might have been released on parole, if he had behaved well, at the age of 47 or 48. But he did not behave well. On July 28, 1929 he shot his way out of Auburn in one of the boldest, wildest jailbreaks in U.S. prison history.

For more than three years Barry was a successful fugitive. He made his way south to New York, then to New Jersey, where he settled in a small town not far from Flemington. His wife joined him there. He took the name of a man he had once known, James Toner, and became a salesman of windshield wipers. He committed no more burglaries, kept the peace admirably and attracted no attention. But on the night of October 22, 1932 there came the inevitable pounding on his door.

"Do you know what it was?" he says indignantly. "The Lindbergh kidnapping. The cops and the FBI had been going through every town near Flemington checking the background of every new resident. They weren't even looking for me."

For a time Barry was the prime suspect in the Lindbergh case and in a half-dozen other major crimes that had taken place during his vacation from Auburn. But after examining Barry closely, Dr. J. F. ("Jafsie") Condon, the celebrated middleman in the kidnapping, announced firmly that Barry was not the man to whom he had given the ransom money.

Barry spent the next 17 years in jail, most of them in Attica Prison in New York and five of them in solitary confinement as punishment for his escape. Upon his release in 1949 he went home to Worcester and got a job with a boyhood friend who operates a chain of four restaurants. During the period of his parole, one of his chores involved collecting the receipts from all four restaurants and carrying them unguarded to the bank. "I never thought I would live to see the day," a Worcester policeman recently remarked, "but I have seen it, and there's no doubt of it. He's an honest man." Barry is not only honorably employed but has some active extracurricular interests as well. Recently, with the members having full knowledge of his past, he was elected commander of a local veterans' organization.

THE CONFIDENCE GAME*

ROBERT LOUIS GASSER

Every year in the United States hundreds of thousands of dollars are taken from the victims of confidence schemes. We do not know how many people lose their money through such schemes nor do we have any idea how much money is lost. As a confidence man recently pointed out, there are at least two reasons for this: First, the victim does not realize he has been victimized, and second, his involvement is so direct or his humiliation so great that he fears any disclosure of the scheme.

What, then, is the nature of the practice of confidence? What distinguishes it from swindling or other types of fraud?

It is difficult to make a clear distinction between confidence games and other fraudulent practices; they seem to shade gradually into one another. There are, however, criteria which distinguish the practice of confidence from other types of fraud. The controlling factor in all true confidence schemes is the way in which the victim is involved. True confidence games always make use of the avarice and dishonesty of the victim. Their common element is showing the victim how to make money, or gain some other advantage, in a dishonest manner and then taking advantage of his dishonesty. A true confidence game leaves no innocent victim.

Among the con folk there is a saying, "You can't cheat an honest man." By this they mean an honest man cannot be brought into a true confidence scheme. And, for their part, professional con players make sure the victim is willing to enter into a dishonest scheme. This affords them a degree of protection and makes the victim a partner in the proceedings.

Confidence, then, is quite a different matter from a fraudulent or swindling scheme that cheats an innocent, unsuspecting victim. Most frauds or swindles merely misrepresent; the victim can make a protest with impunity. In a true con scheme, he cannot.

The professional confidence man (or woman) is skilled in selecting his victim. Once he becomes acquainted with the "mark," he decides how best to appeal to his sense of dishonesty. In con parlance this is called "what the mark will go for," and may run the gamut from women to cards, from horses to stocks and bonds. The weakness, or the mark's "go for," is essential to the operation of the well-conducted confidence game for several reasons, not

* Reprinted with permission from *Federal Probation,* XXVII, No. 4 (December 1963), 47–54.

the least of which is control of the mark and limiting the number of players required to bring the game to a successful fruition.

Confidence games may be roughly divided into two types: short-con games and big-con games. Short-con games require only a short time to carry out and generally are limited to the amount of money the victim has on his person or can readily produce. Big-con games may take weeks or months to accomplish and usually involve the return of the victim to his home to get a large sum of money.

It is possible to subscribe for agency services today that will furnish a con man a report on anyone, with information on his personal history, hobbies, clubs, lodges, habits, moral standards (as far as they are known), and even his mistress' name — all in 2 to 4 weeks. There is no need for today's con man to spend time getting this information on his own.

The following is the usual chronological sequence of events and the terminology used in big-con games: (1) tying into the mark; (2) telling the mark the tale; (3) initial money gaff; (4) putting the mark on the send; (5) playing the mark against the store; (6) cooling out the mark; and (7) putting the mark in the door.

Whenever possible, the con man will avoid the use of violence in carrying out a scheme, even if it means losing a score. It is generally felt that violence is beneath the dignity of the professional. It does occur, occasionally, but is an exception rather than a general practice. Bodily harm may be done to the victim under certain circumstances. For example, if he attempts to run off with the initial winnings gained with money supplied by the con men themselves, or if he attempts to call in the police. As a rule, however, violence is rare in con games.

In most con schemes, there are two essential operators. These players are called by various names such as "outside-man" and "inside-man," "roper" or "steerer" and "spieler," "catchman" and "lickman," or any of a number of other designations. Each has his specific role to play.

The function of the outside-man, or roper, usually is to put a likely victim in touch with the inside-man, or spieler. The latter player then takes over the game and carries out the scheme. Some operators prefer, or are better equipped, to play one part than the other. Sometimes their talent for their special part in a game falls little short of genius. In short-con games, the roles are usually determined by which operator brings the mark into play; and, therefore, the outside-man and inside-man often change places from game to game. Though many con men can play either part well, especially in short-con games, it is rare for men to exchange roles with other members in a big-con game, in which more specialization is the rule.

Con men usually conceal their techniques from other con men who are not their partners or who are not within their own circle. There is a rule within professional con that prohibits the revelation of techniques to anyone.

The con man must keep himself and his ideas secret. When he meets someone who knows how to keep things to himself, the con man might teach him part of the game. If things go right, he is taught more, until he learns the ropes. After that, he must develop on his own.

Generally, the score is divided evenly between the partners after the expenses of the operation have been met. It is important for a man in con to act honestly toward his partner because, if he does not, no one will want to work with him, and he may eventually be forced out of the group.

Con folk often go to the aid of each other in times of need. One old con man states that the esprit de corps is not what it was in years past, though. In the old days, he says, when a con man took a fall (was convicted of a criminal offense), his friends would get together at a party, or through solicitation, to contribute money to be used in meeting the con man's needs while in jail or prison and in trying to get him out.

Jargon is often used to identify con men among themselves, but it is never used if a potential victim is present. A true con man can be readily determined by the way he speaks and acts in the company of other professionals. There is some indication that signs are frequently used by con men among themselves. These signs convey certain meanings, such as warnings of impending danger; they are made in an inconspicuous manner and are understood only by the initiated.

In the underworld the con men consider themselves as the elite; and they are, in turn, accorded this status by the underworld in general.

While con men seem to hold themselves aloof from the rest of the underworld, they often use the services of other underworld specialists. Gamblers sometimes give aid to con men, as do forgers or other operators having special talents. For a price, a con man can always get expert help.

Con teams sometimes have working agreements with the police. One con man, in discussing his relations with law-enforcement officers, reports that there are many cities and towns in the United States in which he is permitted to operate by the local officers for a fee so long as he does not trim the local residents.

It should be noted that the "fix" is not limited to the fixing of local law-enforcement officers. While this is very often the case, i.e., operating in an area in which "the clout is in," or what is also referred to as a "juice town," this is by no means the extent of fixing. The payoff to police officers is minor compared to the expenses of bail bondsmen, attorneys, and, most important, newspaper reporters. Much of the confidence man's time is spent in determining what he will do when he is caught. Perhaps his most valuable ally is the newspaper reporter since the way the reporter writes his story will, unfortunately, influence public opinion.

Con players come from all walks of life and may enter the practice at almost any age. They may come from any legitimate profession, provided they get to know a con man who will teach them the ropes. Their techniques are developed by apprenticeship training gained through association with professionals in con *and not* by reading about it.

In general, however, recruiting may go on anywhere; but it occurs only when the recruit gets to know someone who is already in the profession. Con men are probably more frequently recruited from the ranks of persons in closely allied rackets — among pickpockets or professional gamblers, for example — than from legitimate society. Usually the recruits begin in short-con games; then the most talented move up into the big-con operations.

For those engaged in it, con is a way of life, with traditions, codes of behavior based on recognized values and beliefs, and a system of techniques known only to the initiated. Con men believe that not just anyone can become a professional, but that this takes rigorous training and experience. They feel, too, that, once a person possesses the necessary skill in con, he never need worry again about having enough money.

For a professional con man to be successful, he must have what the con folk refer to as "larceny sense." Commenting on this, one con man said that con is a business, like any other business, and that, if a man works at it and develops himself, he will be successful. In con, a man thinks in a certain way, a way geared to making money in terms of the methods he knows, just as a legitimate businessman thinks in terms of making money by methods that are familiar to him. Each must have a "feel" for the possibilities of making money in every situation as it presents itself.

While entrance into con may come at almost any age, it is rare for a man to become a professional in con before age 25. Some con men feel that a person has not had enough of life's experiences to become a professional in con as early as this.

It frequently happens that men remain active in con after age 60. Con men believe that the only things to prevent an old con man from active participation are losing his sight or losing his mind. About all that advancing age does to the con man is prevent him from traveling around as much as he once did, in which case he usually plays the inside-man for a roper or group of ropers who travel.

Some con folk maintain permanent places of residence, but this seems to depend upon methods of operation and the type of game involved. Most young con men, 25 to 30 years old, do not have permanent places of residence because this seems to hamper their work. They travel constantly and rely on "drops" to enable other con men to locate them. This is particularly true of men operating as ropers or locators of marks.

The older con men do maintain homes. Indeed, they must, for appearance's sake, when not engaged in the game itself, be above reproach! These older operators attempt to assume the role of Mr. Slightly-Above-Average-Citizen.

Confidence games appear to be as old as recorded history. The earliest descriptions of the structure of the confidence system shows it to be substantially the same as it is today; about all that differs is the name given to each position in the scheme. As we look back through history, it becomes apparent that, for more than 400 years, the art of confidence has had a continuing structure, organization, and tradition. This art seems to have been handed down from generation to generation, for it operates today in precisely the same way as it did in the 16th century, and with some of its argot surviving even to our day. In short, it has been a subculture in Western society.

THE MAN WHO FOOLED EVERYBODY*

"You have caused terrific loss to many of your fellow Americans," said the judge. The defendant, Anthony ("Tino") De Angelis, folded his hands over his paunch and shifted nervously from foot to foot. He had pleaded guilty to four federal counts of fraud and conspiracy, and last week in a Newark courtroom, the time had come for sentencing.

Federal Judge Reynier J. Wortendyke sentenced De Angelis to ten years in prison — but with a surprising twist. Invoking a new section of the federal criminal code, he turned De Angelis over to the personal custody of U.S. Attorney General Nicholas Katzenbach. FBI agents will continue to question De Angelis about his tangled affairs. In August, U.S. Director of Prisons Myrl Alexander will report to the judge and 1) affirm the sentence, 2) suggest a reduction, or 3) recommend that De Angelis be put on probation immediately. If he cooperates in answering the many riddles that remain, he could go free within three months.

Embarrassed Bankers. So climaxed the latest chapter in the incredible soybean commodities scandal — the most prodigious swindle in modern times, reaching out from the grimy waterfront of Bayonne, N.J., and involving big commodities dealers in Buenos Aires, recipients of U.S. foreign aid in Karachi, and a numbered bank account in Zurich. Sixteen companies have been bankrupted. Eleven firms controlled by De Angelis have gone under, as have two respected Wall Street brokerage houses and one subsidiary of American Express Co. Embarrassed bankers from London to San Francisco have been taken for many millions. So have De Angelis' customers, notably the Isbrandtsen Shipping Line, and such worldwide commodities dealers as Continental Grain Co. and the Bunge Corp.

The affair is far from over. The Department of Agriculture is studying measures to tighten up the easy rules for trading in grains, oils, pork bellies

* Reprinted from *Time*, June 4, 1965, pp. 20-21.

and other commodities. A wide variety of companies and individuals have filed a total of 160 damage claims contending that Tino De Angelis took them for $219 million.

Compared with that, Charles Ponzi, Lowell Birrell, Eddie Gilbert and Billie Sol Estes were pikers. Only Ivar Kreuger, the Swedish match king who in the 1920s defrauded investors of $500 million, ever topped Tino. More than that, De Angelis presents the classic example of how a man can exploit a complicated situation and use the credulity of high financiers for tremendous gain.

Gut Expert. De Angelis hardly looks the part of an international swindler. Short, fat and 50, he wears pearl grey ties and a perpetual look of hurt innocence. Although he pleaded guilty, he continues to blame his troubles on jealous competitors ("Powerful forces were working against me") and on the Department of Agriculture ("They called me a guinea bastard down there").

The son of poor Italian immigrants, De Angelis was forced to quit high school to support his parents. Starting out as a meat cutter in The Bronx, he devised a method for speedily dismembering hogs by slicing them up on a moving assembly line. That helped him get a $10,000 loan to open his own pork-packing plant. While still in his 20s, he built it into the largest such operation in the Eastern U.S. and sold copious quantities of meat to the federal school-lunch program.

De Angelis wisely saw that a shrewd operator could make a fortune out of two other Government programs: farm price supports and foreign aid. His idea: buy up the bulging soybean surplus, turn it into soybean oil, which is used for everything from salad dressing to paint, and ship the oil abroad — either privately or through the many Government aid programs. Between 1958 and 1962, De Angelis built a sprawling refinery in Bayonne and leased 139 oil storage tanks, many as tall as five-story buildings. Operating in a slippery, fiercely competitive industry, he outdid other companies by buying the most modern equipment, paying the highest wages and putting in the lowest bids for Government export contracts. By 1962, he accounted for three-quarters of the nation's exports of soybean and cottonseed oils, shipping 361 million lbs. All this required considerable capital — and that is how the swindle began.

Paper Mountain. To finance his rapid growth, Tino borrowed huge sums of money, using huge amounts of oil as collateral. But there was one hitch: he never had all that oil. What he did have was a mountain of paper — certificates attesting that he owned the oil. Although Billie Sol Estes at that very time was making headlines for having passed off similarly spurious paper for nonexistent ammonia tanks, the bankers and brokers never bothered to check up on De Angelis' warehouse receipts, because Tino had them signed by officials of American Express Co.

In a sense, American Express got mixed up with Tino in an effort to spur sales of its famous travelers' checks. Back in 1944, the company figured that it could induce bankers to push the checks by performing a service for them. A subsidiary, American Express Warehousing, would store, inspect and vouch for the oil that commodities dealers commonly used as collateral for their bank loans. It was a rewarding business — De Angelis paid American Express Warehousing up to $20,000 a week — but terribly risky. If anything went wrong, Amexco's subsidiary was responsible for making good on its warehouse certificates.

Shouting Down. De Angelis' men duped Amexco with surprising ease. Often, one of them would clamber to the top of a tank, drop in a weighted tape measure, then shout down to an Amexco inspector on the ground that the tank was 90% full. Sometimes the tanks were indeed full — with water, topped by a thin slick of oil. Usually many were empty. Moreover, the tanks were connected by a jungle of pipes; Tino's men sneaked into the casually guarded tank farm on weekends, pumped oil from one tank to another. These machinations gave him an endless supply of oil certificates — and endless borrowing power. At one time he had loans out on three times as much oil as the Bayonne tanks could hold. But Tino figured — rightly — that his various and hotly competitive creditors would never get together and compare their overlapping certificates.

1¢ Equals $12 Million. In 1962 Tino set out on a fantastic scheme to corner the entire market in soybeans. He plunged into commodities futures, a frantic market of paper and promises, where fortunes are made or lost on fluctuations of a fraction of a penny. Betting that the price of soybeans would rise, Tino bought huge contracts for future deliveries of soybeans from other speculators who in turn were betting that the market would fall. He was helped by the fact that commodities markets work on bargain-basement margins of 5% to 15% — that is, big traders need to put up as little as 5% of the purchase price.

Still, his purchases were so enormous that he needed plenty of credit. He got loans from two old-line Wall Street brokers, Ira Haupt and J. R. Williston & Beane, who also handled his futures trading and pocketed commissions totaling up to $100,000 a month. For collateral, they took De Angelis' warehouse receipts for the nonexistent oil. In turn, the brokerage houses used this paper to borrow money from such eminent banks as Chase Manhattan and Continental Illinois. What made the matter more complex was that Tino by then had grown so cocky and creative that he bypassed even the lax warehouse inspectors, forged some of his own receipts. By mid-1963, he had contracted to buy 20,000 tank cars of oil — an astonishing 1.2 billion lbs., worth about $120 million. With every 1¢ shift in price, he stood to gain or lose $12 million.

Assist from the Soviets. For a time it seemed that the gamble would pay off. The market soared, thanks to De Angelis' big buying and an assist from — of all people — the Communists. Russia was clamoring to buy U.S. wheat, and when reports hit Wall Street that the Soviets' sunflower crop had also failed, rumors flared that the Russians would soon be shopping for U.S. vegetable oil. In six weeks during the autumn of 1963, soybean oil climbed from 9.2¢ per lb. to 10.3¢.

On that day, the U.S. Senate broke off debate on the Russian wheat deal, and prospects looked dim. In the next 48 hours, soybean oil tumbled to 7.6¢. The commodities exchanges began pressuring Ira Haupt — by far the biggest broker for De Angelis — to put up another $14.1 million in margin to cover Tino's vast contracts. The Haupt brokers frantically called Tino for the money. But Tino could not make it.

Now Haupt was on the hook to the exchanges. The firm desperately undertook to cover Tino's contracts, for which it was responsible. In all, it borrowed some $30 million from U.S. and British banks. But when the soybean market failed to rise, Haupt went under.

Hundreds of Haupt's customers crowded into its 15 offices, demanding the return of the stocks that were held on account in the brokerage firm. In many cases, their stocks were held in Haupt's name, and the bankers were legally entitled to take them in payment for loans made to Haupt. The New York Stock Exchange, fearful that the scandal would shake the public's trust in the market, put up $9.5 million to pay off Haupt's anxious customers. The New York Produce Exchange halted all trading in cottonseed oil. Tino's major company, Allied Crude Vegetable Oil Refining Corp., tumbled into bankruptcy. Wall Street's Williston & Beane was obliged by a capital shortage to merge into a stronger firm, Walston & Co. Tino's dazed creditors finally began peering into those Bayonne tanks. Instead of finding 1.8 billion lbs. of oil for which they held receipts, they found scarcely 100 million lbs. — a shortage worth $130 million.

Conflict & Claims. There was no shortage of losers. Among the many firms still tied up in knots of litigation:

The banks: They have filed towering claims against American Express Warehousing, contending that it must make good the oil that its subsidiary vouched for. The Morgan Guaranty Trust Co. claims $3,273,000, the Bank of America $11.4 million, Chase Manhattan $17 million, and Continental Illinois $34 million.

The brokers: D. R. Comenzo Co., a firm that handled some of De Angelis' futures' trading, has been reorganized under the Bankruptcy Act, owes about $8,000,000 to various banks, is struggling to pay off. Hapless Ira Haupt faces claims of $38 million, has itself sued American Express for $52 million.

The oil dealers: Tino's biggest customer, Buenos Aires-based Bunge Corp., claims $18 million from American Express Warehousing. Another customer, Continental Grain, claims $5,600,000 from the same American Express subsidiary.

The warehouses: Harbor Tank Storage Co., which issued some warehouse receipts for De Angelis, has sued him and one of his cronies, Joseph

Lomuscio, for $46.5 million. Harbor Tank, in turn, faces claims from bankers and other creditors for the same amount.

By far the biggest loser stands to be American Express. Though the question of how much responsibility it has for the debts of its subsidiary is open to legal dispute, President Howard L. Clark bravely declared that the company is "morally bound to do everything it can." Claims against Amexco, filed by 43 companies, total more than $100 million. But the claimants have been squabbling among themselves over who should get how much. Lately a group of them called for a package settlement of $80 million — $60 million from Amexco and $20 million from the insurance companies covering it against fraud (American Express Warehousing was insured for $30.5 million).

The Secret. And what happened to all the money? Trustees for De Angelis' bankrupt companies have some estimates. About $40 million of it moved, quite legally, into the pockets of traders who sold soybean futures to Tino and profited when prices plummeted. Another $60 million went to bankroll the fast growth of his refining empire, cover operating losses and pay interest charged on loans. Countless millions probably stuck to the hands of his friends and cohorts. De Angelis' refinery, real estate and other assets have been sold at bankruptcy auctions for a low $3.5 million; most of these assets have since been bought by Theobold Industries, Inc., whose officers had friendly dealings with De Angelis in the past.

Tino himself drew at least $100,000 a year from Allied, boasts that he gave away perhaps $3,000,000 to pals. Now he claims that he is broke. But the court pried out of him the fact that he had $500,000 in a numbered Swiss bank account; this cache has been turned over to his bankruptcy trustees. How much more Tino may have stashed away is a secret locked in the nimble brain of the fat man who fooled everybody. If he values his freedom highly, he may, under the terms of his sentence, still tell quite a story.

5 | JUVENILE INVOLVEMENT

INTRODUCTION

Since World War II nearly every country has experienced a sharp increase in the criminal and delinquent acts of juveniles. Almost all languages in the world now include some word or phrase to designate delinquency. A few even contain a label for the middle-class delinquent such as *blousons dores* (jackets of gold) in France to differentiate them from those of lower-class origin or *blousons noirs* (black jackets). Even Israel is concerned with its *B'nei tovim* (middle-class delinquents) — a problem historically alien to Jewish life.

Whatever their local name and reputation — *stiliagyi* in Russia, *vitelloni* in Italy, *halbstarken* in Austria and Germany — and regardless of class origin, juvenile delinquents account for a substantial proportion of all major crimes. In the United States, persons under twenty-five account for no less than three-quarters of the arrests for the seven major Crime Index offenses of murder and nonnegligent manslaughter, forcible rape, robbery, aggravated assault, burglary, larceny, and auto theft. Even more to the point, according to the report of the President's Commission, *The Challenge of Crime in a Free Society,* persons under twenty-one constitute an actual majority of those arrested for the major property crimes and a sizeable minority of those arrested for the personal crimes. Most shocking of course, is that more fifteen-year-olds are arrested than persons of any other single age; the second most frequent age of arrest is sixteen. Like blight and slums, air and water pollution problems, and congestion, juvenile delinquency has become a symbol of industrial urban existence. It is, in fact, part of the penalty and price of modern existence.

Despite its prominence as a social problem, there are some critical issues which have not as yet been resolved. There is no agreement on who is delinquent, what constitutes delinquent conduct, whether delinquency should be viewed in a legal or welfare context and how to prevent and control such behavior. Equally problematic is the relationship of delinquency to the culturally induced trauma which is adolescence. No closer to solution either are the problems of how to deal with the loosening of family ties, the failures of the educational system, and the unemployment of undereducated, unskilled youth in an ever more highly technical society. The several readings which follow consider nearly all of these issues.

In the first selection, "Juvenile Delinquency: A Problem for the Modern World," William C. Kvaraceus describes the wide range of behaviors labelled as delinquent — from hawking without a license in Hong Kong to collecting cigarette butts from the street in Cairo through the more usual activities such as stealing, vandalism, truancy, and violence. Many of these activities are mediated through the "gang," a loosely used term which subsumes everything from a group of boys out on the town to a syndicate-like organization. The author finds evidence for the existence of the juvenile gang in almost every city in the world. The major part of the essay is given over to a discussion of the "causes" of this worldwide juvenile delinquency phenomenon and the measures which a community and its specialized agencies might consider in order to alleviate the problem. Special attention is focused on the school, family, police, and the world of work as the more significant areas in the re-education of the delinquent and his re-direction along socially acceptable lines.

One of the thorniest problems concerns the extent of "hidden delinquency." Almost all of our knowledge about delinquency comes from police and juvenile court records. Many criminologists are convinced that these records are totally inadequate, that they are biased according to race, class, and sex and reflect the prejudices of the community and the inadequacies of the reporting system. As a result, a variety of attempts have been made using either interview or self-reporting techniques to obtain some estimate of the "real" incidence of delinquency. Some self-reporting research studies have used ingenious approaches. The second selection, "Undetected Delinquent Behavior" by Martin Gold is an example of such a study. Although this article has been heavily edited to eliminate the more technical aspects of the problem, the difficulties in developing an accurate index of delinquency come through rather forcefully. Through interviews with 522 public and private school students and with school dropouts, Gold concludes that on two indexes of delinquency F (frequency) and S (seriousness), most delinquent acts are unknown to the police and that there is, in fact, an inverse relationship between social class and delinquent behavior. The most surprising finding is that although official records exaggerate lower-class involvement, they do nonetheless approximate more closely than expected the reality of differential class behavior in delinquency.

In a very tidy and important study, John C. Ball is concerned with "The Extent of Recidivism among Juvenile Delinquents in a Metropolitan Area." While there is a great deal of information on recidivism in large urban centers and for the country as a whole, very little is known about the juvenile delinquent repeater in the smaller, more stable community. Ball selected all 365 offenders who appeared before the Juvenile Court of Fayette County (Lexington), Kentucky in 1960. Tracing their histories through the ten-year period 1952 through 1961, he concludes that at least 20 percent of all the boys in the county will have appeared before the juvenile court by the time they reach 18 and that most of these — about 60 percent — will have been early and also persistent offenders.

For whatever comfort it may offer, juvenile gangs can be found elsewhere and everywhere. Their form and character, however, are rooted in the special characteristics of the society and culture in which they exist. Gilbert Geis in his analysis "Juvenile Gangs" examines the different types of gangs which emerge in different settings. He contrasts the *bezprizornye* of post-Revolutionary Russia with the *Vandervogel* of pre-Hitler Germany. The first, spewed up in the aftermath of World War I, were literally family-less and homeless youngsters who became a menace to society. The latter, drawn mostly from the German bourgeoisie, banded together as a form of social protest against "decadent" and "material" cultural norms and values. Geis also considers the gang problems elsewhere but he continues to focus attention on the situation in present-day Russia and the westward-looking orientation of the modern Russian delinquent.

Nathan L. Gerrard in "The Core Member of the Gang" is interested in the match or fit of the gang leaders' personalities with the needs and style of the delinquent gangs. His thesis is that delinquent gangs are characterized by malice, diversified stealing, rejection of authority, and strong internal cohesiveness. To match these roles and values, the core member's personality is marked by response-insecurity and weak self-esteem with regard to activities outside the home. The core member feels that people are hostile, fueling his own deep hostilities. The result is often the release of this hostility in acts of aggression — which, of course, is the trademark of the conflict gang. Much of this analysis is based on psychoanalytic premises. Much of it, too, derives from the impressive work of Yablonsky in his volume *The Violent Gang.* The reader should bear in mind, however, that other types of gangs than those devoted to violence select leaders with probably far different qualities than those described in this essay.

In the final analysis, the goal of all professionals in the field is the prevention of delinquency. But the translation of understanding into social action and the modification of social conditions has just begun. Most attempts at prevention have been restricted in scope and time. These programs have dealt with the more visible and superficial aspects of the problem and have all but left untouched the more fundamental issues. In a perceptive article which deals with the philosophy and character of delinquency prevention rather than with specific programs as such, John M. Martin outlines "Three Approaches to Delinquency Prevention." The first involves bringing about improvement in the quality of American life, such as the reduction of economic insecurity and social inequality. The second focuses more directly on overcoming adversities in the immediate environment through neighborhood reorganization and the extension of services to the community. The classic illustrations of this approach are the Chicago Area Project and The Mobilization for Youth Program in New York City. The third approach lies in extending and upgrading individual-centered techniques, such as probation and parole, and child guidance clinic services. Martin believes that community-centered programs, in attempting to reorganize and unify neighborhoods, are likely to make the greatest positive impact. In the long run, however, assimilation of low-status groups into the mainstream of American affluence and values seems to be the most desirable, but also the most difficult objective to obtain.

JUVENILE DELINQUENCY:
A PROBLEM FOR THE
MODERN WORLD*

WILLIAM C. KVARACEUS

Almost every language in the world now yields a phrase labelling those youngsters of many nations whose behaviour or tastes are different enough to incite suspicion if not alarm. They are the "teddy

* Reprinted with permission from *Federal Probation,* XXVIII, No. 3 (September 1964), 12–18; digest from *Juvenile Delinquency: A Problem for the Modern World* (Paris: UNESCO, 1964), 100 pp., reissued New York City: UNESCO Publications Center, 1965.

boys" in England, the "nozem" in the Netherlands, the "raggare" in Sweden, the "blousons noirs" in France, the "sotsis" in South Africa, the "bodgies" in Australia, the "halbstarken" in Austria and Germany, the "taipau" in Taiwan, the "mambo boys" or "taiyozuku" in Japan, the "tapkaroschi" in Yugoslavia, the "vitelloni" in Italy, the "hooligans" in Poland, and the "stiliagyi" in the U.S.S.R.

But it is not our right to assume that every "teddy boy" or every "blouson noir" is actively engaged in delinquency. These names often mislead people. It is unjust to assume automatically that a youngster who likes rock 'n' roll music or bizarre clothing is on his way to becoming a delinquent if he is not one already. Too often, the adult world has used the word "delinquent" to express anger or bewilderment at adolescent tastes.

Nor should every minor who breaks a rule or behaves offensively be considered a delinquent. The behaviour of young people rarely consistently conforms with the standards and expectations that adults have for them.

What are the offences and what are the penalties? The differences from country to country only indicate how divided the world is on who is a delinquent, who is not, and what should be done about it.

A widespread form of delinquency in Cairo is the collection of cigarette butts from the street. A recent survey in India, conducted in Lucknow and Kampur, indicated that the second most common juvenile offence was vagrancy. A few years ago in Hong Kong, juveniles brought before the magistrate's court reached the startling figure of more than 55,000 and yet over 90 percent of them had committed only technical breaches of the law such as hawking without a license. Information from Lagos, Nigeria, shows that a delinquent there is primarily an offender against the unwritten laws of the home: disrespect and disobedience are regarded as serious offences.

So we see that the numbers of children cited for delinquent acts can sometimes be misleading unless we are to know the nature of the offences and what particular law they violate.

Yet even when we take the most cautious attitude towards statistics on delinquency from all corners of the world, the evidence mounts. The offences are varied. They range from stealing, vandalism and property offences, petty extortion and gambling to violent behaviour, rowdiness, truancy, immoral or indecent conduct, drinking, and drug addiction.

In almost every city in the world where delinquency exists, so does the juvenile gang which looms up as a modern social institution. These gangs, innocent or evil, are an important element in the overall pattern of juvenile delinquency. Looking at delinquency in a worldwide context, one does not often see individual youngsters becoming delinquent each in his own fashion, but rather as a number of boys participating in joint activities that derive their meaning and pleasure from a set of common sentiments, loyalties, and rules.

The majority of these gangs often engage in acts which do not always bring financial gains and to the rest of the world seem almost purposeless in their malice.

In Poland, teenage gangs have damaged railroad trains and molested passengers for no apparent reason. In Saskatchewan, Canada, groups of boys have entered private homes and mutilated expensive furnishings without attempting to steal a single object. In Chiengmai, Thailand, a band of male minors, with a symbol of a white eagle tattooed on their arms, found their greatest diversion in terrorizing or injuring outsiders. In Argentina, gangs of boys have gathered in cafes or bars to insult or humiliate customers.

Some juvenile delinquents, however, have clearer goals in mind. Racketeering or petty extortion are good examples. A gang in Detroit, Michigan, which was composed of 15 boys from 13 to 16 years of age, organized a racket in which all the smaller children of the neighbourhood were forced to pay 5 cents for the insurance of not being molested on the way to and from the local cinema. A report from India indicates that gangs of young boys and girls have learned to be highly successful smugglers of illicit liquor and drugs.

In the past, tabulations on the backgrounds of a cross section of the juvenile delinquents always seemed to indicate that these children were reared in poor living conditions. A recent United Nations report, however, points to a strong change in this tendency. There are numerous and increasing indications that children from the higher-income brackets are becoming delinquents. In France, the expression "blousons dores" (jackets of gold) is a somewhat sarcastic reference to delinquents from richer families than those of the "blousons noirs."

In the United States, a recent survey revealed that a relatively large number of teenage boys admitted that they had committed serious acts of delinquency which had never become a matter of court record. These were sons of middle- and upper-income families.

Delinquent behaviour, which stems from so many combinations of factors, cannot be treated or controlled until several scientifically evolved theories about the individual offender have been checked. The boy must be considered apart from his conspirators. His life at home, his problems at school, his relationships with his parents, his own self-image, and his personality must all be carefully revealed and evaluated.

One theory says that delinquency results from severe frustrations suffered by a growing child. Another, that it is an expression of rebellion. Yet another theory suggests that juvenile delinquency is perhaps the failure of a young male to be able to identify himself with what is professionally referred to as a "male authority figure." This naturally means the child's father, the dominating and consistent male influence in his life. If there is no father, if he is rarely at home, or even if he is a dim or withdrawn figure in the child's life, a small boy may come to feel a very deep insecurity about his own image of himself as a man.

In the broadest sense, any adolescent who is unsure of himself can appease his worries — or will try to — by being aggressive. Here is where one of the rare positive statements about all delinquent behaviour can be made: it is remarkably aggressive. Aggression may be verbal, it may consist of destructive acts, it may be sexual. Aggression may be directed towards one's self, towards the world, or both.

A deep questioning in the child's mind about his own value as a human being can cripple him so that he is almost unable to make any honest or lasting attachment with other people. For if his parents have not loved and accepted him and admitted him, how can a child believe that someone else will? Children who feel they are not loved or wanted can be very severely damaged by such deprivation — real or imaginary. Maladjusted adolescents are usually those youngsters who have suffered from these feelings.

Sometimes even genuine love is not enough. In the case of a family where the mother is the head of the house, the provider, and the voice of authority, a rebellion may occur. Young boys wishing to become young men must break from this world of feminine rule, even if it means defying the mother, and assert themselves as males. When there is no man around the house on a permanent basis this becomes difficult. The boy is under a peculiar sort of stress. It is possible that because of this stress he will try to take on attributes which will symbolize to him, and to the world, an unassailable masculinity. There are a number of activities and even possessions which symbolize clear-cut and irreproachable masculinity. For example, there is ability in combat, ownership of a car or motorcycle, techniques in violence or sadism, or even a vocabulary. There are forms of dress. One has only to think of the much-publicized American juvenile delinquent who owns a motorcycle and wears a black leather jacket and blue jeans.

In most societies it is accepted and understood that adolescence is the period when a youngster forms his own identity, usually by a meaningful conflict with his parents or the older generation. Nothing in this world causes as much concern to the adolescent as this question of his own identity: how he sees himself and how he feels the rest of the world sees him. Even a negative identity — and more than one habitual delinquent child has described himself as "plain mean" — can be satisfying.

So much for the interior forces that may shape the child so crucially at the beginning of his life. There is also the outside world which begins to intrude upon his thoughts and feelings when he is very young.

For example, a young person who grows up in a deprived area learns certain kinds of behaviour as naturally and normally as the middle-class boy learns exactly the opposite. A middle-class child might be taught to fear poor marks in school, fighting, cursing, and being rude to his teacher. But the slum child, conversely, might fear doing well in school and being friendly with his teacher, for this would set him apart from the other children and possibly evoke their anger or ridicule. All too often he learns that the best way to express his aggressions is with his fists.

The child who lives in an underprivileged neighbourhood may often resent the limits that he feels society has imposed. This may be illustrated through hundreds of case histories. One example could be the boy who knows he will never make enough money to buy the car he wants. Another is the child who knows that it is impossible for him to attend college. These are frustrations that society creates and they can often be as disturbing as the frustrations that are emotionally aroused by a lack of inner security.

One of the most crucial forces, if we consider only the number of years during which it exerts an influence over the child, is the school. Together with the home it provides the basic learning experience for all children. The teacher, who is a trained observer, can detect evidence or incipient signs of personal or social problems that are affecting the child and perhaps offer the pupils some form of help and relief. He can do much to make the child aware of his own basic values and teach him to develop them.

Ideally, specialized professional personnel are needed to reinforce and augment the assistance a teacher can give to a pupil. Through timely and skillful use of auxiliary services, the school can often help a child from becoming a failure. The visiting teacher who can establish a close contact with a child's parents, the school social worker, or the psychiatric worker are all trained to evaluate and relieve the pressures that often contribute to a child's defeat in the classroom.

Delinquents, for a variety of reasons, frequently do not have an accepting or reassuring relationship with their parents. Any education programme or any counselling that the community makes available to parents, provided it is wisely presented, can often be a turning point.

Some city communities have established neighbourhood centres where informal educational activities are conducted. These activities include parent discussion groups. Through these neighbourhood centres, people of all backgrounds who have a natural ability for different kinds of leadership can be found and involved in committee or recreational work.

The importance of the police in a community with delinquency can hardly be overrated since they often represent the first official contact between the young offender and the law. The policeman or juvenile officer is the one who must frequently decide whether to let the child off with a reprimand or to refer him to a juvenile court or some other agency set up to deal with such children.

In some countries the evolution of the work of the police has given rise to more definite forms of action of a preventive nature. In Liverpool, since 1949, there has been developed a city police programme known as the Juvenile Liaison Scheme. Its object is to deal with youngsters under 17 years of age who manifest some behaviour disorders or who have already committed petty offences. The police officials try, after an interview with a child, to secure the cooperation of the individual family and school. Then they often contact appropriate officers, and family service units in order to provide suitable help.

If there are a number of boys who have left school in one particular neighbourhood with a high incidence of delinquency, most people would hope that they would find jobs instead of loitering on street corners. But it is not enough to find them jobs — any job — just to keep them out of trouble. What has to be done is to make youngsters who are vulnerable to delinquent behaviour *more* employable in addition to creating new employment opportunities for them.

One possible remedy, especially in poorer neighbourhoods, is a community-organized youth jobs centre, the function of which would be to help the young person enter the world of work. Such a centre could offer guidance and counselling, placement service, and help redirect the youngster to a training programme. The aim should be to make the boy more employable by improving his social, academic, and job skills.

In the long run, only the delinquent can solve the delinquency problem. In the past, many agencies working with the delinquent encouraged him to be passive. The professional workers tended to moralize over him, scold him, threaten him, study him, relocate him, and treat him. Today, hopefully, the emphasis in many parts of the world is to encourage the delinquent to play a much more active and decisive role in the solution of his own problems.

This must be done with considerable skill and patience. Very often, he will refuse to cooperate and refuse to help himself. Involving the delinquent can mean a multitude of things. Here is a very simple example of how one community approached it. At the suggestion of a team of professionals, a group of 34 delinquents who had previously been gang members were divided into three squads, according to age. They are encouraged to suggest or consider certain projects for their particular group with an adult adviser. A feeling of mild competition between the three squads was encouraged.

The ideal result of such a project is not to convert every delinquent into a civic-minded prude. It is to show the young delinquents that conformity need not be stifling, and that they themselves are capable of choosing and reaching socially acceptable goals.

UNDETECTED DELINQUENT BEHAVIOR*

MARTIN GOLD

Students of juvenile delinquency and practitioners who explore the research literature for help in training delinquents have found that measurements of delinquency have been grievously inadequate. A youngster generally has been labeled "delinquent" either because he has been caught by the police or because his answers to questions about himself are similar to those of youngsters caught by the police.

This article introduces an interview method designed to find out from teenagers how many delinquent acts they have committed in the recent past and to discover other pertinent information about this behavior.

We aimed to study a representative set of teenagers in Flint, Mich., an industrial city of 200,000 people. With the cooperation of the public school system, we selected at random a sample of six hundred from a list of almost all boys and girls thirteen through sixteen years old living in the school district, regardless of whether they were attending public or private schools or had dropped out of school altogether. We eventually interviewed 522 of them, or 87 per cent of those originally selected.

We elected to employ the method of personal interview for two reasons. First, we wanted to obtain detailed descriptions of delinquent acts, to find out the *who, what, when, where,* and *how* of them. Such data are too complicated to get in a self-administered questionnaire.

Second, we suspected that, given a checklist, some youngsters might admit delinquent acts which would turn out not to be offenses at all, while others might overlook actual offenses. Probing by an interviewer on the spot could winnow out the misunderstandings and identify and draw out omissions.

The interviewer questioned the youngster about those offenses he admitted committing in the last three years. If the youngster indicated he had committed any particular offense more than once in that time, he was asked about each of the two most recent offenses of that kind. A standard form administered to every respondent, elicited demographic and other data.

A central problem in this sort of research is the extent of concealment by respondents.

To study concealment we found it necessary to interview a criterion group, youngsters about whose delinquency we already had reliable information but

* Reprinted by permission from *The Journal of Research in Crime and Delinquency,* III, No. 1 (January 1966), 27–46.

who were not aware we had it. We managed eventually to interview 125 youngsters under these conditions.

Our strategy was first to contact teenagers who seemed likely to have information about the delinquency of other boys and girls. We were introduced to these potential *informants* by teachers, youth workers, other interested adults, and by some informants themselves.

Our data on concealment came from comparisons of the responses of the 125 validating respondents with what our informants had already told us they had done. We considered a youngster a *truthteller* if he told us what our relevant informant had told us, or if he told us about more recent offenses of the same type, of if he told us about more serious offenses. A respondent was considered a *concealer* if he did not confess to an offense about which an informant had told us, or to any more recent similar offense, or to any more serious offense. Youngsters were categorized as *questionables* when they told us about offenses which were similar to but did not exactly match offenses about which we already had information. In such cases we were not certain whether something was being deliberately concealed or distorted or whether the memories of informants and respondents merely differed.

Overall, 72 per cent of the youngsters seemed to tell us everything which informants had told us; 17 per cent appear to be outright concealers; the rest are *questionables*.

Measures of delinquent behavior are based on the confessions of the random sample of boys and girls, aged thirteen to sixteen, who lived in the Flint school district in 1960. Of the several indices of delinquency which have so far been constructed from these data, two — Index F and Index S — are currently employed in our analyses.

INDEX F

Index F draws data only from the detailed descriptions of delinquent acts which youngsters most seldom conceal — trespassing, assault, stealing a part of a car or gasoline, hitting father, hitting mother, drinking alcoholic beverages without parental knowledge or permission, running away from home, gang-fighting, shoplifting, larceny, and fornication. This list covers a wide range of offenses, including offenses against persons (e.g., assault) and against property (e.g., theft); offenses generally believed to be more typical of boys (stealing a car part or gasoline) and more typical of girls (shoplifting); and offenses generally thought trivial (trespassing) as well as serious (hitting mother).

The major advantage of Index F is that detailed information on the relevant offenses permitted exclusion of all those "offenses" which coders judged not to be chargeable by the police; that is, Index F includes only those offenses which in themselves would clearly have warranted police action if they had been detected.

INDEX S

This index is based on a delinquency index devised by Sellin and Wolfgang, which takes into account the *seriousness* of an offense as rated by university students, police officers, juvenile aid workers, and juvenile court judges. Each offense is weighted by some factor which reflects the seriousness with which that offense was regarded by the raters.

Our data were not collected in a way which allows precise application of the weights prescribed by Sellin and Wolfgang, for our data collection had begun before they had published their index. However, we found it possible to use an approximation of their index, assigning the weights to a set of nine offenses.

A reader familiar with social scientific data will recognize the familiar J-shape of the curves generated by the distributions of the delinquency indices. Allport has observed that this is just the shape of curve one should expect from data on deviations from recognized norms. That is, most people stick closely to the rules, and the curve drops off sharply and bottoms out at its more deviant end. In this case, most youngsters are not very delinquent, either in the frequency or seriousness of their delinquent behavior, and there are relatively few youngsters at the more delinquent ends of the curves.

These indices are highly correlated with one another as one might expect since they are both based largely on the same set of responses. However, correlations among several indices reveal that Index S, which takes into account a judgment of seriousness of the offense, stands somewhat apart from the others. Material presented later will demonstrate that the data on official records and the data collected from Negro boys turn out somewhat differently when seriousness is taken into account from when it is not. This difference makes Index S of special interest.

Our findings indicate that social status is indeed inversely related to juvenile delinquency, that more lower status youngsters commit delinquent acts more frequently than do higher status youngsters. However, the data allow us to be more specific about who among lower status youngsters are more likely to be delinquent and enable us to place important qualifications on the general statement of the relationship.

"Social status," as we use the term here, refers to the prestige hierarchy of occupations in our society. There is a great deal of agreement in the United States about the relative prestige of occupations and a great deal of stability to the prestige hierarchy. In this paper, a youngster's "status," unless otherwise qualified, refers to social status based on father's occupation.

These data demonstrate that official records exaggerate the delinquent behavior of boys from lower status homes relative to their higher status peers. Police are more likely to record officially those offenses committed by lower status youngsters, the children of semi-skilled and unskilled men. Only about 3 per cent of all the chargeable offenses reported by the youngsters in the sample resulted in police apprehension of the offender, and, if the offender came from a higher status family, police were more likely to handle the matter themselves without referring it to the court.

Some judgment by the police about the ability of a family to control its son's behavior is likely to be a major factor in determining whether official action will be taken. Lower status families as a group are judged less able to keep their sons out of trouble, so official action is more often taken.

Partly as a result of this procedure, court records in Flint demonstrate the usual relationship between delinquency and social status: greater proportions of boys are adjudged delinquent as one goes from higher to lower status categories. [Our data showing that] four to five times more lower status boys are delinquent than higher status boys, is a common ratio in the delinquency literature.

While official records are selective in a way which exaggerates the relative delinquency of lower status youngsters, they may nevertheless approximate real delinquent behavior. For example, even though most juvenile offenses do not result in the apprehension of the offender and few juvenile offenders are on record with the authorities, the more delinquent youngsters may have been detected and recorded.

It is clear from the data that the more delinquent boys are more likely to be caught by the police. Sixteen per cent of the boys report being caught at least once; but, compared with the least delinquent boys, about four times as many of the most delinquent boys on Index S are caught, and about seventeen times as many when Index F is the measure of delinquency. Since Index F emphasizes frequency of offenses, while Index S emphasizes seriousness, these data suggest that frequency of offenses is a greater determinant of being caught than their seriousness.

Furthermore, it seems that the seriousness of an offense is taken into account in the decision to book a boy. The data have shown that frequency is a greater determinant of apprehension than seriousness; that the most serious offenders, high on Index S, are about as likely to be booked as the most frequent offenders, high on Index F. Of course, most of the boys high on one index are also high on the other. But although more of the frequent offenders are caught, no more of them are booked. Seriousness of the offense enters the decision to book.

It should be borne in mind that the majority of even the most delinquent boys are unknown to the police and the courts. This comes as no surprise to the police. The point is that the one-third or less of the most delinquent boys who are caught may be a highly selected group of youngsters; and the 16 per cent of all the boys caught are not by any means equally delinquent or representative of delinquent boys. Researchers who generalize about delinquents from apprehended or adjudged delinquents should be cautioned by these data.

The data to be presented now demonstrate that there is indeed an inverse relationship between delinquent behavior and social status. However, this relationship exists only among boys.

The data reveal no reliable relationship between delinquency and social status among girls. The pattern in the data on white boys is quite different from that for the girls. The proportion of lowest status boys climbs from 8 per cent in the lowest delinquency category of Index F to 36 per cent in the highest; the proportion of highest status boys falls from 35 per cent in the lowest category to 11 per cent in the highest category. The two middle status categories of white boys occupy intermediate positions on delinquency Index F.

Among the nonwhite boys, the two delinquency indices produce somewhat different results. Neither index is correlated reliably with social status, but the range of social status among nonwhite boys is so truncated, effectively encompassing only the lowest three scores, so that any rank correlation is limited by the data themselves. Index S, which takes seriousness of the offense into account, better discriminates between higher and lower status nonwhite boys than Index F does. Index S puts the proportions of lower status boys below the proportions of higher status boys at the less delinquent end of the index and above the higher status boys at the more delinquent end.

So it seems that, in frequency of delinquency, the sons of nonwhite unskilled workers do not differ much from the sons of nonwhite, semi-skilled workers; but, in seriousness of offense — as defined by white, middle-class judges — the former commit more serious offenses than the latter.

So we have found that delinquent behavior among boys is related to social status, just as the much criticized official records have demonstrated over and over again. It seems reasonable, then, to raise the question: why not continue to employ official records, at least to explore this relationship, rather than collect more expensive data?

One reason is that the official records exaggerate the differences in delinquency among boys of different status levels. They make social status, in the sense of the breadwinner's occupation, seem more important than it really is as far as researchers and practitioners are concerned. About five times more lowest than highest status boys appear in the official records; if records were complete and unselective, we estimate that the ratio would be closer to 1.5:1.

However, there is a sense in which the actual ratio of delinquent behavior specifically among boys is closer to 5:1 than 1.5:1 against the lowest status boys; that is, the official records come closer to a valid picture than does the estimate of unselective records. The data show that three to four times more lowest status boys than highest status boys behave at the *highest* delinquency level on either index. If we consider these boys to be the ones who represent the most pressing social problem and therefore should be apprehended and given attention, then the official booking rates do not depart so far from truly representing differential delinquency among social status levels.

On the other hand, if we define the social problem to include the top two levels of delinquency, then the ratio of delinquents is only about 1.5:1 or 2:1 against the lowest status boys.

This kind of discussion exposes the greatest source of invalidity inherent in official records: youngsters are categorized as "delinquent" or not categorized at all. Some researchers have found this distinction too limiting, so they have distinguished between "sometime delinquents," who appear in the official records only once, and "repeaters." We share the view of other researchers in this field that it is more useful to think of delinquency as a continuous rather than as a discrete variable. One of the major advantages of our method of gathering data is that it permits us to measure delinquency in this way.

Our data are limited to one city. However, we suspect that, in regard to delinquency, Flint is not different from any other community encompassing a fairly broad range of social status categories. We suspect that these same findings will hold not only for other urban communities but also for rural communities.

THE EXTENT OF RECIDIVISM AMONG JUVENILE DELINQUENTS IN A METROPOLITAN AREA*

JOHN C. BALL

Eventually the various contending theories of delinquent behavior, of which many are as yet quite speculative, will have to be documented with empirical findings. When this is done, we believe it will be demonstrated that there are several quite distinct, though not unrelated, types of juvenile delinquency in the United States: for example, female, gang, rural, middle-class, and lower-class preadolescent. We also believe a careful consideration of the commencement of delinquency and the extent of recidivism within each type will materially contribute to the knowledge of deviant behavior. Indeed, such empirical studies are a prerequisite to the development of any scientific theory of delinquency and crime.

It is now established that 20 to 35 per cent of all boys in urban areas in the United States have official delinquency records before age eighteen. The further question arises as to the extent of recidivism within this population of delinquents. Are most juveniles who come before the police and courts

* Reprinted with permission from the *Journal of Research in Crime and Delinquency*, II, No. 2 (July 1965), 77–84.

early and persistent offenders, or are they one-time offenders who commit minor infractions of the law? This is the research question of the present study.

In 1960, 365 offenders appeared before the Juvenile Court of Fayette County (Lexington), Ky. Following an analysis of the incidence and prevalence of delinquency in this metropolitan area, the research problem was to delineate the extent of recidivism — repeated offenses — within the population, describe the persistent offenders and the first offenders, and distinguish between the two groups. A principal purpose of the study was to ascertain whether the records of most juvenile delinquents revealed early and persistent patterns of serious antisocial acts. Such research findings should have manifold implications for contending theories of delinquent behavior and should reveal information about patterns of life developing within the structure of American society.

The cohort of 365 delinquents was traced longitudinally, through police and court records to determine age at time of first offense, number and type of subsequent offenses, and other relevant information. In the tabulation and analysis of data, the boys were separated from the girls and recidivists were contrasted with first offenders.

The cohort includes all boys and girls who appeared in the juvenile court in 1960 whether they were first offenders or recidivists.

The incidence of delinquency increases markedly with age among the boys. Thus, the rate doubles from age eleven to age twelve. Exactly 7 per cent of the total seventeen-year-old male population in the Lexington Standard Metropolitan Statistical Area (SMSA) appeared in court during this one year.

The overall incidence of recorded delinquency for the girls was less than one-fourth of that for the boys. The peak age for delinquency among girls was fifteen, after which the rate decreased notably by more than 50 per cent — from 2.2 per cent at age fifteen to less than 1 per cent at age seventeen.

Of the 365 juveniles, 113 — or 31.1 per cent — were Negro. In the total population in 1960, non-whites represented only 14.9 per cent of those aged five through nineteen. The difference in percentage reflects in large part the higher delinquency rates found in lower socio-economic areas.

With respect to place of residence, 50.6 per cent of the cohort aged thirteen through seventeen lived in four of the twenty-eight census tracts in the SMSA. In these four high-delinquency tracts, constituting the central area of the city, the 1960 male delinquency rate — incidence of court appearances — ranged from 10.7 to 16.2 per cent of all males aged thirteen through seventeen.

The ages of the 302 boys and 63 girls at the time of first court appearance were tabulated. The mean age of boys at time of first court appearance was 13.5 years. More than one-third of the boys were delinquent by age twelve, and two-thirds by age fourteen; only 19 per cent of the boys first appeared in court after age fifteen.

A detailed search of the juvenile court records was undertaken to ascertain the number of times each of the 365 delinquents had been brought before the court. It was found that the first court appearance of the 1960 cohort occurred in 1952. All appearances from this year through 1961 were tabulated. From these data a comprehensive portrayal of the extent of recidivism within this juvenile delinquent population was afforded.

The number of times the 302 male delinquents appeared in court varied from one to fourteen. Some 60 per cent of the boys (181) were recidivists, and the mean number of juvenile court appearances for them was 4.2. Thus, most of the male delinquents repeatedly committed offenses sufficiently serious to result in juvenile court proceedings. Among these recidivists, a pattern of persistent delinquency is evident.

The extent of juvenile court recidivism among the girls is somewhat less than that found among the boys. Of the sixty-three delinquent girls, 48 per cent had had more than one court appearance, and the mean number of court appearances of the thirty recidivists was 3.2.

An analysis of the time between successive juvenile court appearances provides data as to the temporal sequence of official delinquency. The mean number of months between the first and second juvenile court appearance for the 181 male recidivists was 12.7; for the thirty female recidivists the comparable figure was 9.2 months. The time between successive court appearances decreased as the number of appearances increased: the mean number of months between the second and third court appearance was 9.9 for the boys and 5.8 for the girls; the comparable figure for the time between the third and remaining court appearances was 7.3 for the boys and 3.4 for the girls.

In order to provide an overview of the type and volume of delinquent offenses committed by the 1960 cohort during their careers, we searched available police records for additional offenses recorded over the ten years. These data were tabulated.

The male cohort committed 1,307 offenses during the ten-year period; the female cohort committed 162. These figures refer to separate offenses charged by the police as well as those resulting in official and unofficial juvenile court appearances.

The type of offense most frequently committed by the boys was stealing. Over 50 per cent of the boys' offenses consisted of larceny, burglary, and auto theft. Non-property offenses constituted a small portion of the volume of delinquent acts, with the notable exception of the "incorrigible" classification, a rubric that serves as a catchall for such disparate charges as disorderly conduct, fighting, running away, drunkenness, less serious sexual promiscuity, and similar acts.

Among the girls, incorrigibility was the predominant charge recorded.

Commonly this involves some type of sexual misconduct. The absence of a single auto theft offense by the girls indicates that each sex has a quite distinct pattern of delinquency.

When we consider the early commencement of recorded delinquency and the persistence of this pattern of antisocial behavior among most of the delinquents in this metropolitan area, a number of further questions arise. Clark and Wenninger have asked whether high delinquency rates and gang-oriented subcultures are restricted to lower-class areas of our largest cities. The present data and other studies have found that high male delinquency rates — from 20 to 35 per cent — characterize urban American society. Gang delinquency, however, appears to be endemic only to the slums of our most populous cities. There are no conflict gangs in the Lexington SMSA, and there is no present indication that such a subculture is developing. It seems likely that gang delinquency requires cultural transmission from generation to generation and that this process can occur only in the largest metropolitan slums.

Juvenile delinquency in Lexington is concentrated in the lower-class part of the city; most delinquents live in or near the central business district. The data do not afford a means of analyzing middle-class delinquency in the Lexington SMSA, but we have reason to suppose that offenses committed by boys from middle-class census tracts occur at a later age and are not as likely to be repeated.

In the measurement of recidivism in this metropolitan area, it is pertinent to note that our data underrepresent the phenomena. This is so for the following reasons: (1) families migrated to and from this jurisdiction; (2) the 1960 cohort did not include juveniles incarcerated during 1960 at the Training School; (3) offenses committed by local juveniles outside of this county were not included; (4) name changes and incompleteness of reporting occurred; (5) deaths occurred; and (6) an incomplete risk period was studied. The appropriate model for a complete enumeration of recidivism would require the compilation of offenses committed by a cohort of juveniles in all jurisdictions throughout the entire risk period designated — for instance, from ages six through seventeen. We do not know what effect these limitations have imposed upon our recidivism rates, but they have certainly lowered them to some extent.

[In conclusion] a cohort of the 365 juvenile delinquents who appeared before the Juvenile Court of Fayette County (Lexington), Ky., during 1960 was selected for a longitudinal study of recidivism. It was found that 60 per cent of the boys and 48 per cent of the girls had had two or more court appearances from 1952 through 1961. An analysis of the data revealed that the mean age of the male delinquent recidivists at time of first court appearance was 12.9 years; the comparable figure for the girls was 13.8 years.

From this study of recidivism and from our previous study of the incidence and prevalence of recorded juvenile delinquency in the Lexington Standard

Metropolitan Statistical Area, we conclude that at least 20 percent of all boys in Fayette County will be delinquent by virtue of court appearance before age eighteen and that most of these delinquents will be early and persistent offenders. The research findings substantiate the thesis that a persistent pattern of delinquency is endemic to lower-class American society and that this behavior has its inception in the preadolescent period.

JUVENILE GANGS*

GILBERT GEIS

The material that we have from foreign countries regarding delinquent and gang behavior is quite suggestive in terms of broadening our understanding of the full panorama of such activity. It also helps to provide additional clues to the cultural roots of delinquency since it is often through noting similarities and variations to the thing that interests us that we come to a clearer understanding of its generic attributes.

It is worth noting initially that the present state of gang behavior in the United States hardly indicates the total depravity of our society. Nor is it accurate to maintain that conditions today are worse than they were in the romanticized past of human history. Daniel Bell, among other social commentators, has tried to show that crime was probably appreciably higher and more brutal during America's frontier period than it is today. Bell believes that the general breakdown of social barriers between classes has brought about the myth that the country is more ridden with illegality now than earlier in its history. Previously, persons in the middle class were merely better shielded, because of communication and transportation obstacles, from evidence of violence and theft.

Throughout recorded history, individuals and groups have always failed to adhere to demands for conformity to the general dictates of their society, and they have resorted to acts which were outlawed or disapproved. It is very difficult to specify with precision those conditions which have particularly encouraged or discouraged illegal aggression or depredations in any society at any time in history. A lack of consensus regarding proper social behavior among all members of the society is, of course, virtually by definition an underlying factor in disruptive activity.

But it again needs to be emphasized that gang behavior today hardly points to a state of degeneracy and decline in contemporary civilization. Note,

* Reprinted from Section II, entitled "Gangs in Perspective," *Juvenile Gangs,* President's Committee on Juvenile Delinquency and Youth Crime (Washington, D.C.: Government Printing Office, 1965), pp. 5–16.

for instance, the following vivid portrayal of gang activity in the 18th century by William Lecky, the noted historian of bygone manners and morals:

The impunity with which outrages were committed in the ill-lit and ill-guarded streets of London during the first half of the eighteenth century can now hardly be realized. In 1712, a club of young men of the higher classes, who assumed the name of Mohocks, were accustomed nightly to sally out drunk into the streets to hunt the passers-by and to subject them in mere wantonness to the most atrocious outrages. One of their favorite amusements, called "tipping the lion," was to squeeze the nose of their victim flat upon his face and to bore out his eyes with their fingers. Among them were the "sweaters" who formed a circle round their prisoner and pricked him with their swords until he sank exhausted to the ground, the "dancing masters" so-called from their skill in making men caper by thrusting swords into their legs, the "tumblers," whose favorite amusement was to set women on their heads and to commit various indecencies and barbarities on the limbs that were exposed. Maid servants, as they opened their masters' doors, were waylaid, beaten and their faces cut. Matrons enclosed in barrels were rolled down the steep and stony incline of Snow Hill. Watchmen were beaten unmercifully and their noses slit. Country gentlemen went to the theater as if in time of war, accompanied by their armed retainers.

Such behavior makes most contemporary juvenile gangs appear by comparison to be composed of gentle and mild-mannered lads out for a playful romp. It is usually reassuring and always fruitful to try to gain a clearer perspective of current events by looking back into historical annals and archives.

The two most noteworthy parallels to American gang activity in recent European history appear in prewar Germany and in the post-revolutionary Soviet Union. Both seem to indicate a combination of social upheaval and ideological disruption as major ingredients in the emergence of juvenile gangs.

Following the Soviet revolution of 1917, large groups of youths, finding themselves in a socially disorganized society, which was still groping for political order, and also finding themselves without adequate adult supervision because of the death or dislocation of their parents and relatives, formed marauding bands, housing themselves in cellars and similar makeshift shelters in or near the large urban centers.

Attempts to incorporate these youths into the majority society after the regime had become more stabilized were unsuccessful at first, and the explanation offered, "that children who had lived for more than a year on the streets found it difficult to adapt themselves to the new life" because they had been "influenced by the picaresque life of the vagabond," has relevance to work with gangs in the United States. It suggests the importance of appreciating fully the attractions of gang existence, the camaraderie, the self-indulgence, the luxury, and the excitement of gang life that must be weighed with the disadvantages so that a better understanding is achieved of both the lures and the fears connected with gang membership.

The major stress in Soviet efforts to reform the habits of the *bezprizornye* (literally, "the neglected"), who numbered more than 524,000 by 1921, was placed upon training for factory employment. Special use was made of the honor code of the boys, a code somewhat similar to that found among members of American gangs:

In the beginning we made many mistakes, but now we know that, above all, we must teach these children by appealing to their sense of honor. Strange to say, a sense of honor is much more strongly developed amongst the *bezprizornye* than it is in normal children. Locks are of no use at all, for they can easily pick them, so we give them keys. They are really astonished that they are treated like ordinary children.

The Soviets inaugurated a rule that no questions be asked of a boy concerning his past life or record, unless he initiated the subject. They also attempted to put group pressure upon individual boys who would not abide by the rules and to instill a sense of shame through ritualized examples of disapproval:

The children have meetings every evening, and those who have not worked well, or who have done something wrong, are called to account. The unfortunate delinquent has to stand in the middle of a circle and submit to a fire of questions. The worst punishment is temporary forfeiture of the badge of the community.

The use of peers to impose sanctions, in ways similar to that described above, has traditionally been one of the most effective techniques in working with any group. This is particularly true when the peers themselves have at one time occupied the same position as those whom they are now trying to influence. But the technique also contains many subtle pitfalls and much potential for boomeranging upon a program, unless it is employed with considerable care and understanding. In fact, as we shall shortly see, despite their apparent success with the *bezprizornye*, the Soviets actually still have not resolved the problem of youthful rebellion and continue to grope for adequate methods for dealing with it.

The German adolescents, the *Vandervogel*, had a considerably more formal and formidable structure than the Russian youths and resembled in some respects the Boy Scouts in the United States. Their generally middle-class background adds a different note to the study of rebellious gangs, which usually are formed in working-class settings. The *Vandervogel*, unlike our Boy Scouts, however, were in strong opposition to the values of their parents, whom they viewed as stolid burgher types, unexciting and hardly worthy of emulation. As Becker has noted:

German youth loathed and hated the world of their elders, and were ready to follow any Pied Piper whose mystery and power held promise of a new realm where longings found fruition. Definite promises, clear-cut goals, purposeful methods were unnecessary — indeed, no small part of the revulsion against adult life was against its very planfulness, its readiness to cast aside the joys of spontaneity in favor of crafty money-getting and the ribbon to stick to the coat. It was a rebellion against flabby school routine, insincere church attendance, flatulent concerns, boring parties designed for display and climbing, repellent counsel about ways of getting on in the world — to escape making you feel that adventure was still possible.

The German *Vandervogel* groups tended to be led by individuals who have been characterized as "eternal adolescents" — unstable of purpose, diffusely emotional, dogmatically idealistic, intellectually fuzzy, and erotically fixated on leaders or followers — Becker thus describes them, and believes that "they found the gates of the adult world too high to scale or too forbidding to enter." The *Vandervogel* were also characterized by a strong homosexual tinge, a trait that may not be receiving adequate attention in studies of American gang behavior, in which personal adornment and fanciful hair styles, normally considered the province of female plumage, often represent the trademark of the gang member. The *Vandervogel*, however, were considerably more monastic than their American counterparts, which often have girl auxiliaries and extensive heterosexual involvement.

The *Vandervogel* engaged in numerous outings and camping expeditions, sometimes traveling to neighboring countries, where they acquired experience and information that later was to prove of considerable value to invading German troops during the second World War. It was during the course of the War, in fact, often as gestapo members, that *Vandervogel* initiates found a sympathetic response to their previous social protest, and it was in the gestapo that they often discovered a satisfying role to play and a niche that was able to provide them with the rewards and the recognition they desired.

The German and Russian material on gangs points consistently to the relationship between social conditions and the appearance of juvenile groups of a particular nature. The political and middle-class coloration of the German gangs and the prevalent pattern of mobility among the dispossessed Soviet youth are both adaptations different from the phenomenon of today's American urban, insular, and apolitical working-class gangs. It may be that we are soon to witness the birth of political awareness among American gangs, particularly as racial issues blaze in urban areas, and it may be that middle-class youths will revolt more pronouncedly against social pressures and gather together in defiant groups in order to render their protest more effective. If so, we will have to trace the origins of these movements to social conditions and base attempts to ameliorate them upon an understanding and interpretation of such conditions.

The lesson that might be read from the history of the German and Soviet youth movements is that there are at least two general ways of "reforming" gangs — one is to make them by one means or another conform more closely to the values of the major social system, while the other is to have that system move more closely toward their values. It would seem perhaps to be the better part of social wisdom, granting these choices, to aim for some sort of an intermediate condition: To offer to the gang member some acceptable use and outlet for his talents, feelings, and aspirations by effecting some alterations in the social system or in his ability to cope with it. In response to such widened opportunity, presumably the gang member will come to abandon some of his more unacceptable behavior.

Most countries designate delinquents and gang members by special terms, thus singling them out for the verbal attention we have mentioned earlier. It is only in the United States that a designation as awkward as *juvenile delinquent* has not yielded to a shorter and more colorful term. In England, delinquents are called *teddy boys*, and a description of some of their behavior sounds quite familiar to an American:

It is not uncommon for groups of twenty or more city boys, sometimes with girls in tow, to arm themselves with knives, bicycle chains, studded belts, and even cut-throat razors and to sally forth by bus, taxi, private car, and motor bike to dance halls fifty miles away with the express purpose of seeking out the local youth gangs and provoking a fight. On a less dramatic scale, groups of boys on foot come together and wander about the cities looking for mischief and fun, or, in their words, "kicks," wherever such opportunities are to be found.

In Japan, Melvin Belli, a San Francisco lawyer visiting there, found what he called "a modern social malignancy" in the youth gangs, or *shintaro*. Belli reported that gang members affect a wild bushy haircut and the Japanese version of the "zoot suit." In Western Germany and Austria, gangs of provocatively dressed adolescents have been labelled *halbstarke* or, in English, the "the half-strong." In Sweden, similar youths are known as the *skinnknutte* or "leather jackets," an appellation that first was applied to youth who were wont to race motorcycles through the streets. France employs the designation *blousons noirs* or "black jackets" to its delinquents. In New Zealand and Australia, we have the "mild bar cowboys" and the "bodgies" (boys) and "widgies" (girls).

Surveying the cross-cultural material, one writer has noted:

There has probably been no more dramatic discovery in recent years in the field of practical sociology than the fact that the problems of Red Hook, Brooklyn, or Manhattan's East Side cannot only be duplicated in Chicago's South Side but also in London's Notting Hill, Amsterdam's new housing projects, the Lenin Hills area of Moscow, and the crowded factory districts of Tokyo.

A newspaper report from Auckland, New Zealand, indicates in further detail some of the overseas attributes of gang behavior, and traces the source of this behavior, probably quite erroneously, to the infiltration of ideas from American motion pictures — such as "the Wild One" — and weapons and styles of dress carried to New Zealand by young British sailors:

They gather outside milk bars, the equivalent of the American drug stores, play the juke boxes and cause chaos by roaring their motorcycles in large groups through busy city streets. Late at night they ride off to the suburbs to engage in vandalism.

The male wears his hair long, with a fringe hanging down over the collar at the back, or he sweeps it up on the top of his head, with a floppy curl hanging down on the forehead.

His female companion favors vivid make-up, a tight high-necked sweater and tight toreador pants, or even tighter skirt slit up the side.

Several gangs have earned the hostility of the armed forces through a series of attacks on men in uniform found alone on unfrequented streets. Young sailors, soldiers and airmen have retaliated by moving into the favorite haunts of the gangs and ejecting them into the streets.

Several ugly brawls have started, but large reinforcements of policemen have been able to keep the feud within limits by separating the combatants and arresting the more violent of them.

This news item deserves a closer examination in terms of our understanding of gang behavior. It is particularly instructive as an indication of how the mass media represent and formulate characterization of gangs. In many ways, of course, the story is extremely superficial. It provides little more than descriptive material on a form of gang behavior. It does not indicate, for instance, how prevalent fighting gangs are in contrast to other kinds of gangs, nor does it provide us with any useful information about the origin and the purposes of gang membership and activity.

The story does, however, particularly when it is combined with numerous similar dispatches from around the world, give us an indication of at least two traits of certain kinds of gangs which seem to appear with some regularity in all settings: First, their distinctive mode of dress and second, their hostility to authority, as that authority is represented by the police, the military, or adults in general. Dress, of course, serves a basic purpose of putting on view an identity, labelling oneself in clear-cut fashion and indicating how one wants to be treated. We know from quite good experimental evidence that people do in fact respond to other individuals at least partly in terms of how those persons are dressed. A man in evening clothes usually will be granted considerably more respect than a man in working clothes.

There is, however, beyond this, the fact that there are many ways of dressing differently — why is one particular form selected over others? It is said that dress and clothing play a particularly prominent role in English gangs, and one writer, T. R. Fyvel, has suggested that the exaggerated teddy boy styles have been important in changing a basic element of the English class structure by reshaping the tastes of working-class youngsters more in accord with the fashions of the middle-class. It is important for the worker to appreciate the meaning of dress to gang members: It can function as a badge of status and identity, as a symbol of prowess and also as an emblem of disqualification — certain things will not come to or happen to boys dressed in certain ways, and in this manner they will be spared the difficulty of having to cope with things which might upset or otherwise disconcert them.

The rebellion against authority that generally marks gang members is equated in psychoanalytical theories with poor experiences in the home, particularly in relation to the father. Other writers are more inclined to see social authority — the power system of the society — as highly restrictive of the aspirations and freedom of gang members and thus truly deserving of their fervid antagonism.

The study of gang behavior throughout the world would be incomplete without careful attention to the situation in the Soviet Union, which throws into striking perspective many of the fundamental problems of rebellion and nonconformity among young people.

First, it should be realized that the Soviet Union is able, as efficiently and thoroughly as any large country is apt to be able to do so today, to propagandize its younger generation regarding the behavioral virtues it expects them to manifest. Unsatisfactory examples are quickly repressed and contradictory and alien ideas are submerged as ruthlessly as possible. Nonetheless, all reports indicate the presence of large youth movements in the Soviet Union that strongly resemble gang behavior as we find it in the United States. It is toward America, in fact, that much of the enthusiasm of the Russian teen-age deviants appears to be directed.

A newspaper reporter, who had previously studied gangs in New York City, has noted that Russian adolescents insist on calling Moscow's Gorky Street *Brudvay*. Russian youths are said to engage in the same kind of "nihilistic revolt as that of their coevals in the west":

Party agitators exhort them. Komsomol bully squads rout them out of the restaurants and cafes and send them home. Photographs of them are plastered on billboards under headings: "Parasites, Get Out." They are shipped to virgin lands or the reconstruction sites in Siberia.

But nothing that the party has been able to devise wins back the loyalty or enthusiasm of the bored, nihilistic and disoriented generation.

"This is our greatest defeat," a middle-aged party man conceded. "The young people have deserted the cause. I do not know how we are going to get them back."

The number of internal rebels are great. They can be seen everywhere. They dance to Western music. They wear Western-style clothes. They act as much like Westerners as they are able.

In a play by Ivan Kupriyanov, a rude young man, a complete delinquent, is asked what he wants in life:

"My golden desire? Well, nobody wants a heart attack. What do I want? Drink . . . restaurants . . . jazz . . . money . . . women . . . a Volga (a Soviet car) . . . a country cottage . . . you know, the complete gentleman's selection."

In provincial towns and Moscow's sprawling industrial suburbs the picture of the "young generation" is hardly attractive. The boys organize in tough gangs that often terrorize people on the streets. The newspapers constantly report that bands of hooligans in various cities have taken control of the streets and ordinary citizens hardly dare venture out at night. The gangs amuse themselves by attacking police posts and beating up militia police officers.

This kind of behavior baffles the older generation. As a party chief accurately declares in one Moscow theater play:

"I cannot understand our young people. They have some kind of kink. They are growing up without ideals. They have lost their ideals."

But the reply is: "What kind of ideals were they—that they were so easy to lose?"

A recent study, Soviet Youth Program: Regimentation and Rebellion, reemphasizes the note sounded in the foregoing newspaper report. Many young persons in the Soviet Union, called derogatorily the *bezdelnichestvo* ("idlers"), are said to reject the production ethic, to refuse to work in remote countryside areas or to labor at monotonous jobs for minimal reward. The Soviet regime has attempted to link the social misbehavior of the idlers and that of delinquents (*stiliagyi*) with political disloyalty by charging it to the impact of western culture and considering it a form of espionage. Attempts to deal with the disaffiliation of youths are concentrating on reductions of the salary gap between manual workers and persons holding white-collar jobs or performing more glamorous tasks. There is also a long-range plan to establish boarding schools for virtually the entire school-age population in the Soviet Union in order to reinvigorate the indoctrination of the youth.

The relative intransigency of the problem to date in the Soviet Union, however, sheds considerable light on the parallel concerns in the United States. In fact, one of the most intriguing theses concerning gang behavior in the United States as contrasted to that in the Soviet Union suggests that by the very rigor of its demand upon youth for rigid conformity the Soviet Union may be creating a hard-core group of intractable rebels, since it requires a particularly strong will to resist the pressing demands of the government. On the contrary, it has been hypothesized, the more laissez-faire and permissive attitude in the United States may in terms of its very flexibility be pushing young people into making commitments to one or another of the diverse groups in the society so that they can come to feel more secure. These commitments may then become strong levers for the further inculcation of conforming behavior. Whether or not this tentative speculation is valid, the general conclusion regarding the present situation in the Soviet Union has direct applicability to understanding juvenile gangs in the United States:

> In spite of all the resources at its command, in spite of its monopolistic advantage, in spite of the unprecedentedly vigorous efforts to indoctrinate entire generations, the youth program does not work well when it is undermined by the actual conditions of the larger society. The program's central image — the valor and glory of service to the state through self-sacrificing labor — thorough and persistent though it may be, cannot compete with the more compelling influence of hard reality.

THE CORE MEMBER OF THE GANG*

NATHAN L. GERRARD

The personality of the core member of the delinquent contraculture is depicted as marked by a generalised feeling that others are hostile or indifferent to his welfare, plus inferiority feelings with regard to conventional activities outside the home. It is hypothesized that (1) child-rearing practices fostering the development of these personality traits are most likely to be found in urban slums; (2) there is a strong congeniality between these personality traits and the salient traits of the delinquent contraculture; (3) there is a significant relationship between the personality traits and the intense but fragile quality of gang cohesion.

The core member of the gang with a delinquent contraculture characterized by wholesale malice, diversified stealing and sectarianism is not the average gang member but the member "who needs the gang more than anything else . . . and who is always working to keep the gang together and in action." He is the totally committed gang member whose contacts with law-breaking groups since childhood have been more intimate and frequent than with conventional groups (differential association). He is likely to pursue, at great personal cost, an adult criminal career while his former "partners in crime" have long abandoned their delinquent ways and associations and are enacting conventional occupational and family roles. In him, the distinctiveness of the delinquent style of life is made clear, and without him the delinquent contraculture would probably lack viability.

* Reprinted with permission from *The British Journal of Criminology*, IV, No. 4 (April 1964), 361–70.

The structure of the core member's personality is marked by two elements: (1) response-insecurity; (2) inferiority feelings (weak self-esteem) with regard to conventional activities outside the home.

Response-insecurity is a generalised feeling that others are hostile or indifferent to one's welfare. Because of this feeling, the core member has relatively little capacity for sympathy, and relatively little anxiety that his anti-social behavior is forfeiting the affection and good will of others. Response-insecurity is developed where the boy has continuously felt that his parents, instead of being responsive to his needs, are hostile or indifferent to his welfare.

Inferiority feelings with regard to conventional activities outside the home are likely to develop where the boy's efforts to acquire conventional skills, for example manners and school skills, have not been guided and rewarded by his parents. Inferiority feelings and response-insecurity do not necessarily exist in the same personality structure — for example, the excessively modest but compliant boy, or his opposite, the "temperamental genius." Where both are present, however, as in the case of the personality structure of the core member, each is intensified by the other, and the instigation to engage in anti-social behavior in a wide range of social situations is particularly strong.

It is not surprising that many slum parents rear their children not according to a system of social beliefs, but according to the mood and expediency of the moment, relieving tensions accumulated in the non-parental roles by employing child-rearing practices that damage the response-security of the small child. They rationalise free use of the whip or fist, and callous neglect as "old-fashioned" discipline. But in the rural communities of their childhood or of their parents' childhood, corporal punishment was employed only in situations specifically defined by custom, and the severity with which it was administered was restrained effectively by public opinion. The practice of leaving the small child to his own resources as soon as he was able to walk also had different consequences for his personality development in a rural setting, in a community of relatives and life-long neighbors.

Wholesale malice and negativism are manifest not only in the stealing and destruction of property which cannot be used, but in many other activities such as gang wars, driving conventional children from playgrounds for which the gang itself may have no use, the flouting of school rules that goes beyond mere evasion, and other forms of hoodlum behavior.

His response-security rubbed raw in the family, and his self-esteem in conventional roles, the core member is marked by an all-pervading hostility. Fantasies of retribution in which his sufferings are wiped out by the suffering of others develop a tendency to take advantage of any opportunity that may come his way to express his feelings in acts of aggression.

During the excitement of successful gang exploits, the core member experiences the magical feeling of omnipotence which, according to the psychiatrists, is characteristic of infancy when parents are viewed as instruments completely at one's beck and call. In his case, the need to feel omnipotent, i.e., to feel that others are at his mercy and are objects of contempt, is particularly strong because of the generalised feeling that others are hostile and contemptuous.

Like the rest of us, the American slum adolescent is constantly stimulated by images of conspicuous consumption to desire and achieve pecuniary success. Where self-esteem is strong, as in the case of the slum "college boy," persistent, strenuous and self-disciplined efforts along conventional lines are made to overcome long-run goals. Where self-esteem is relatively weak but response-aspirations are downgraded, substitute gratifications are sought in the congeniality of friends and family. Where both self-esteem and response-security are weak, as in the case of the core member, the hunger for at least the simulacrum of success (e.g., expensive automobiles and expensive women) is particularly great — for, in fantasy, only the manipulation of pecuniary wealth can win deference and response, and immunity against humiliation and rejection. His unrelieved feelings of worthlessness pressure him toward a short-cut solution: sudden riches, the "big score" or "haul."

Moreover, since he is burdened with strong inferiority feelings with regard to winning recognition in conventional groups, he finds it easier to demonstrate "smartness" in delinquent groups through stealing, making up in daring what he lacks in conventional knowledge and skills. It is easy to exaggerate the number and quality of skills involved in delinquent activities. It takes much more skill, for example, for a 17-year-old conventional boy to repair a 1940 model automobile which he purchased for $25 than for a 17-year-old delinquent to break into a 1963 automobile and drive it away.

The vicissitudes of small predatory groups of adolescents are many, even in those slum areas where opportunities for relatively immune illegitimate enterprises are available (older, more experienced gangs, fences, corrupt politicians, shady lawyers and the like). There is always the danger of official detection and punishment. Strong pressures also are exerted on the delinquent by conventional primary groups to give up his delinquent activities and associations. The exigencies of sheer survival require that the delinquent gang develop social norms assuring insulation against the demands of conventional groups, and mutual assistance and loyalty. The delinquent contraculture accordingly prescribes:

A. No sentimental interest or trust in social authority, and no intimate contact with conventional boys.
B. Mutual assistance and loyalty in all matters involving members as individuals.

In the case of the core member, the internalisation of "A" is effected with relatively little difficulty. The hatred for social authority is deeply imbedded in his character structure. The psychological support of the gang does not create the hatred, but intensifies and consolidates it, and fosters its untrammeled expression. The original hatred is also reinforced by the negative sanctions with which social authority responds to delinquent behavior; a vicious circle is established which can be broken only under very special "antiseptic conditions," to use Fritz Redl's simile.

The delinquent contraculture represents a rebellion against conventional society, but, to borrow from Lindner's terminology, it is rebellion without a cause. Accordingly, the social norms prescribing delinquency lack moral validity for the participants in the delinquent contraculture themselves. As one 19-year-old member of a delinquent group remarked in the writer's presence: "Sure it isn't right to steal. The world would go to hell if everybody stole." This is not to say that the social norms are not binding as a condition of participation in the delinquent contraculture, but that the commitment is on the basis of expediency rather than moral validity. This suits the core member fine, for he is suspicious of all social ties that are not established on a strictly *quid pro quo* basis, since the first and perhaps the most important bond in his life, that between himself and his parents, was repeatedly violated, first by his parents in their hostility or callous indifference to his welfare, and then by himself in self-defense and spite.

His feeling that others would not hesitate very long to violate the delinquent code prescribing mutual assistance and loyalty were it to their advantage to do so makes it relatively easy for him to do the same. The feeling of solidarity in successful defense or attacks against a hostile world is undoubtedly exhilarating, and mob activity has a strong appeal to the core member. But when the gang is defeated and scattered, or when the core member comes in conflict with other members of the gang, it takes relatively little provocation for him to feel that the other members are essentially hostile or indifferent to his welfare. Under these circumstances — and they occur frequently — it is relatively easy for his gangster's superego to be circumvented through projection and rationalisation.

In other words, the intense but fragile ties that unite the members of the gang are established through social processes in which out-group hostility is an important element and in-group altruism relatively unimportant. What is viable is the delinquent contraculture, not the gang that is its carrier. Gangs are constantly dissolving and regrouping with new personnel.

[In sum] dominant roles in delinquent contracultures marked by wholesale malice, diversified stealing, and sectarianism are enacted by boys with response-insecurity and inferiority feelings with regard to conventional activities outside the home. The life style of the contraculture is matched by the personality style of the core member.

THREE APPROACHES
TO DELINQUENCY PREVENTION:
A CRITIQUE*

JOHN M. MARTIN

Aside from punishment and strict repression, delinquency prevention is usually defined in these three different ways:

1. Delinquency prevention is the sum total of all activities that contribute to the adjustment of children and to healthy personalities in children.

2. Delinquency prevention is the attempt to deal with particular environmental conditions that are believed to contribute to delinquency.

3. Delinquency prevention consists of specific preventive services provided to individual children or groups of children.

The logic underlying preventive activities of the first type is disarmingly simple: anything that contributes to the adjustment of children and to their healthy personality development prevents delinquency. Basically this approach links delinquency prevention with general improvements in the institutional fabric of our society, particularly as these affect child welfare. In large part this approach rests on a continuation and extension of measures, now commonplace on the American scene, which are designed to reduce the economic inequities of our social system. Such activities include procedures for raising the income levels of poverty stricken families, better low-rent housing, improving job tenure and work arrangements, and other means for reducing the rigors of poverty and economic insecurity. The approach also embraces attempts to reduce prejudice and discrimination against minority group people, increase the educational achievements of oncoming generations, improve marital relations by premarital counseling and family social work, and increase the impact of religious doctrines on both adults and children.

Preventive activities of the second type, by and large, aim to overcome factors in the immediate environment of children that seem to contribute to their delinquency. Such activities include attempts at community organization, such as the Chicago Area Projects (to be discussed later in this article); work by "coordinating councils" for harmonizing the efforts of welfare and child care agencies in delinquency prevention; the work of recreational and character-building agencies of all types; and attempts to reduce the com-

* Adapted from John M. Martin, *Juvenile Vandalism: A Study of Its Nature and Prevention* (Springfield, Ill.: Charles C Thomas, 1961), and reprinted with permission.

mercial activities of adults which are clearly illegal and detrimental to the welfare of children who may get caught up in such traffic as, for example, the sale of liquor to minors, dope peddling, and receiving stolen goods.

Preventive activities of the third type include probation and parole services to children and youths, the programs of residential institutions and special schools for delinquents, child guidance clinics insofar as they are concerned with the diagnosis and treatment of delinquents, direct work with antisocial street gangs, and a variety of other services whose principal purpose is the adjustment of individual children or groups of children.

In the main it is correct to conclude that improvement in the collective welfare, particularly in the welfare of depressed minority people, will reduce delinquency. In areas such as metropolitan New York the reduction of juvenile delinquency is most intimately linked with the successful assimilation of low-status groups, in particular the ever increasing number of migrants and uprooted Negroes and Puerto Ricans. Whatever contributes to the welfare and assimilation of these people reduces the delinquency rate among their children and, correspondingly, in the communities in which they live; conversely, whatever impedes their progress inflates the delinquency rate in those areas.

The relationship between delinquency, at least in terms of official statistics, and poverty and poor housing has, of course, long been noted by students of social problems. However, it is erroneous to conclude that the abolishment of these living conditions will also abolish delinquency among low-status children. As Bernard Lander pointed out in his study of differential juvenile delinquency rates by census tracts in Baltimore, delinquency appears to be fundamentally related to social instability or *anomie* and not basically to poverty and poor housing.

Emphasis upon *anomie* or social disorganization as a basic contributing factor to the high delinquency rates characteristic of some urban areas, with a concomitant de-emphasis of the obvious poverty of these areas as the underlying factor in their high delinquency rates, would then appear to be of cardinal importance for understanding and preventing delinquency in such places.

Similarly, practitioners of such techniques as social casework and related psychological-psychiatric services work toward individual adjustment, not social change. Seldom do they try to reduce the delinquency-producing features of the delinquent's environment, especially his extrafamilial environment; instead they emphasize adjustment to prevailing environmental conditions. For most delinquents, who are generally without emotional disturbance and who reflect the patterned deviancy so often found in their lower-class neighborhoods, this means that they are expected to make a non-delinquent adjustment to a highly delinquent life situation. Our recidivism rates testify that at best this adjustment is precarious. Furthermore — and this is perhaps the more basic point — because such efforts fail to come to grips with the underlying social and cultural conditions giving rise to delinquency, they do little to prevent the outcropping of delinquency in the first instance. Most try to take hold only after maladjustment, even delinquency itself, has become manifest in the lives of the youngsters they seek to help.

We must not be so carried away by our desire to rehabilitate delinquents that we fail to see individual treatment in a proper perspective, lose sight of its limitations, and ignore the fundamental proposition that *the prevention of delinquency should include both individual treatment and general or social prevention.* Unfortunately this is just what has happened. To a truly remarkable degree public and private delinquency-prevention agencies have spent comparatively little money or energy on community-centered programs of social prevention. For decades most of these agencies have put their effort into establishing various kinds of facilities for rehabilitating delinquents on a case-by-case basis, with the "model" and most prestigeful approach in recent years being that of the psychiatrically oriented child guidance clinic.

Basically, the problem of delinquency prevention is a problem of social organization or reorganization, and other approaches have merit only to the degree that they contribute to such reorganization.

Unfortunately we have no rich arsenal of tried and proven techniques for accomplishing such change. Much needs to be learned and many innovations need to be developed toward this end. Despite these difficulties, however, we do know much about stimulating change in delinquency areas. The framework within which the reorganization of such neighborhoods can be accomplished has been well described by Frederic M. Thrasher in his outline of a proposal for coordinating neighborhood activity for delinquency prevention.

This proposal envisions that any attempt to prevent delinquency in local areas must fix responsibility for social change at the neighborhood level where such changes can be implemented by local community leaders assisted by experts. Implicit in this approach is the assumption that in even the most delinquency-prone neighborhoods not all the residents are criminals or delinquents, and that in such areas there is actually a duality of conduct norms — one favoring law-abiding behavior, the other favoring delinquency.

Fundamentally the difference between the kind of plan outlined by Thrasher and traditional social work proposals for community organization is that in the former the real work is done by local residents who, banded together in a committee or council, act to (1) get the facts about delinquents and delinquency in their neighborhood; (2) organize existing preventive forces serving their neighborhood; (3) stimulate the development of new programs and services as required; and (4) in cooperation with professional agencies, look to the adjustment of their own delinquents, organize the leisure-time activities of their own children and young people, and improve the neighborhood environment, particularly by encouraging the enforcement of laws outlawing the activities of "slum landlords," petty racketeers, and other adults that are clearly detrimental to the welfare of their neighborhood and their children.

The inclusion of children and youths in neighborhood organizations for delinquency prevention is most vital. Too often they are simply left out of the planning and management phases of such activity. As a result, the isolation of their adolescence is compounded, and a real opportunity for establishing closer ties between the generations is overlooked.

Perhaps the best known of the relatively few delinquency-prevention programs predicated on local community organization that are actually in operation are the Chicago Area Projects developed by Clifford R. Shaw and his associates. Basically these projects aim at producing internal cohesiveness and conventional behavior in delinquency areas through the development of *indigenous leadership.* Outside professional leadership is minimal. Chiefly it is used to interest and develop local talent. Program activities are not ends in themselves but are used to achieve local unity. Some direct work is done with children and adolescents on a one-to-one counseling basis, and psychiatric and other types of referrals are made when needed. But the central aim is to draw local youngsters into various project activities so that they will identify with conventional rather than with delinquent groups and cultural patterns.

Outside leaders have a definite but limited role. This approach to area reorganization places principal emphasis on the role of natural community leaders who are carriers of conventional conduct norms. Not only do such leaders serve as nondelinquent models for emulation by youngsters attracted to programs offered by projects of this type, but because these indigenous leaders have prestige in the local area, they easily attract adults, as well as children and youths, to project programs in the first instance. It is around natural community leaders, then, that legitimate social structures can be germinated and multiplied in delinquency-prone areas. And it is in relationship with such leaders and within such structures that youngsters can develop the close and intimate attachments with conventional models, achieve the satisfactions, and acquire the sense of personal worth and purpose necessary to counter the drift toward delinquency characteristic of their life situations.

Students of delinquency are becoming increasingly aware of the necessity of reaching out beyond the child and his family in their efforts at prevention. It is submitted that the most efficacious approach for modifying the operating milieu of the bulk of our delinquents is through the widespread establishment of community-centered programs of prevention. Supported by continued improvement in the collective welfare — particularly in terms of the successful assimilation of low-status groups — and incorporating the best of "corrections" and individual treatment, the community-centered approach offers the most hope for reducing law-violation by our children and adolescents.

MAJOR DEVIATIONS
RELATED TO CRIME

INTRODUCTION

One of the more important trends in American legal thought and in the field of criminology, following the lead of many European countries, is the decriminalization of many kinds of behavior which heretofore were punished as felonies or misdemeanors. Spurred by greater psychiatric and sociological insight, it is becoming ever more clear that some expressive forms of deviancy and especially those with a strong compulsive overtone are not properly criminal in character. To be criminal, the actor or perpetrator must wilfully commit an act in violation of the law. The act committed must also be harmful or injurious. In short, a competent perpetrator must injure or in some way harm an innocent victim. The difficulty comes in what some criminologists call "affiliated" crime problems such as drunkenness and alcoholism, vagrancy and homelessness, narcotic addiction and other drug abuse, homosexuality and gambling. In some of these illegal activities, the perpetrator may be unable or incompetent to control his behavior and/or there may be no harm or injury to any but the deviant himself.

Indicative of this decriminalization process, England and the State of Illinois have recently eliminated homosexuality as a crime if the activity takes place between consenting adults in private. In practice, if not by law, many other communities do the same thing. Also, as a rule, Western European countries neither consider nor punish narcotic addiction as criminal. In the United States, New York and California have led the way in specifying civil commitment (treatment) rather than incarceration for drug users. There is even the possibility that maintenance on a mild synthetic narcotic under medical auspices may be considered quite legitimate in the future. Similarly, the Driver and Easter case decisions handed down by higher courts in the early part of 1966, portend the end of incarceration as a means of dealing with public drunkenness by excessive drinkers and alcoholics. Said the court in the Easter case, "We hold . . . that the public intoxication of a chronic alcoholic lacks the essential element of criminality; and to convict such a person of that crime would also offend the Eighth Amendment." The implications of this trend are clear: treatment instead of punishment; medical and psychiatric (rather than legal and criminal) definition of the problems of the compulsive and addictive offender. There is, of course, one major exception to this decriminalization movement. Legislators at all levels — municipal, state and Federal — have shown great willingness to criminalize the possession and use of hallucinogens, particularly LSD. It is likely, however, that the furor over the use of hallucinogens will not appreciably retard the decriminalization of other "affiliated" crime problems.

In the first contribution, Judge John M. Murtagh expresses concern over the treatment, or rather the lack of treatment, accorded the half million or more skid row derelicts in the United States. His main theme is that, as a judge, he is fully cognizant of the utter futility of traditional sentencing policies applied to the alcoholic who has lost all control and ends up on skid row. He insists that the only reasonable approach is therapeutic — not penal. His prescription for the present — and until better methods become available — is the public shelter facility where derelicts can be detained for a short period before being released back on the street.

The President's Commission on Law Enforcement and Administration of Justice was also very concerned with the drunkenness problem and with perfectly good reason. One in every three arrests in this country — about 2,000,000 a year in all — are for the offense of public drunkenness. The report is critical of present methods of handling intoxicated persons and approvingly cites the practice in St. Louis where arrests for drunkenness, disorderly conduct and vagrancy accounted for about 19 percent of all arrests compared to 77 percent of all arrests in cities of comparable size such as Atlanta and Washington, D.C. The Commission recommends the establishment of detoxification centers and aftercare services as alternate and preferable means of handling the problem.

Despite the far more numerous and intense problems, criminal and social, associated with alcohol, Americans seem considerably more interested in the relatively uncommon problem of drug addiction and abuse. Perhaps the very rarity of the addict, and the total inexperience of most persons with narcotic drugs accounts for this concern. Whatever the reasons, drug abuse has been disproportionately discussed and agonized over compared to alcohol abuse. In the first of two contributions on drugs, Daniel Glaser and Vincent O'Leary describe the various substances which are considered dangerous or wholly illegal drugs, or both. These include: opium, heroin, marihuana, the barbiturates, cocaine, and the amphetamines. Their article, "The Control and Treatment of Narcotic Use," also examines seven major trends in drug usage since World War II. These new features of the problem are the different demographic characteristics of present-day drug users and the changed geographic pattern of addiction.

In the second contribution on drugs, Roland Fischer, a pioneering researcher in the area, discusses "The Realities of Hallucinogenic Drugs: A Compendium." The article describes the accidental discovery of the hallucinogenic properties of LSD, the mode of action of the hallucinogenic compounds, the legal status of the hallucinogens as far as Federal law is concerned, the psychotomimetic character of these drugs, and related matters, including the social context of drug experience.

Two papers discuss different aspects of the dilemma of homosexuality. Maurice Leznoff and William A. Westley are interested in the organization of the homosexual community and its constituent social groups. They single out two major types of groups — the secret and the overt — and discuss the characteristics of each and the points at which they intersect one another. Like other kinds of deviants, the homosexual has great need for the identification, acceptance, and social support provided by specific homosexual groups and by the larger homosexual community.

"The Female Homosexual" emphasizes a number of aspects of the problem which are often overlooked. George L. Kirkham presents data to indicate that the prevalence of female homosexuality is quite great — perhaps even rivaling that of male sexual inversion. Lesbians, however, are considerably more secretive than male homosexuals thereby accounting for the seemingly low rates of female involvement. Further, the social definitions and roles of women also tend to make lesbian manifestations not nearly as detectable. There is even some doubt whether the legal statutes on homosexuality are applicable to the female. Certainly law enforcement policy is to avoid confronting the issue whenever possible. The article also stresses the relationship of homosexuality in the female to a variety of other illegal and deviant activities, including prostitution and drunkenness.

The last selection in this section on the range of crime-linked or affiliated problems is an informative article on "Apprenticeships in Prostitution." Prostitution in the United States, while still reasonably commonplace, has certainly undergone a major transformation in the past quarter-century. The changing sex norms and codes, early marriage, and the increasing opportunities for women in legitimate employment generally have drastically reduced *organized* prostitution in this country. Present-day practitioners in the field are more likely to operate independently of houses of prostitution, red-light districts, and syndicate control. Call-girl prostitution reflects these changes. Operating quietly and discreetly in contracting her services, customers (clients) are sought by telephone and via the recommendation of former patrons. The induction and apprenticeship of the call-girl prostitute and her relationships with other "working girls," her trainer, and customers are also described. This article is particularly valuable in directing attention to prostitution as an occupation rather than as a form of psychopathology and as an expression of deviant sexual needs.

THE DERELICTS OF SKID ROW*

JOHN M. MURTAGH

There are at least half a million derelicts throughout the United States. Yes, there is a skid row in your home town, be it West Madison Street in Chicago, Mission Street in San Francisco, the Bowery in New York, the Tenderloin in Philadelphia, Congress Street in Houston, Main Street in Kansas, the freight yard on the outskirts of town, or the blighted alley up the street from the village theater.

My skid row is New York City's Bowery. For more than a century the Bowery has been a kind of magnet for the miserable, for men and women seeking a dark place of escape. It is dotted with scores of moldering tan, red-brick, and blackened-frame flophouses, some dating back a hundred years. On its lonely beat live thousands of grimy unfortunates in almost every stage of decay.

A goodly portion of the drunks currently arrested in New York City are arraigned in night court, held since 1940 in the modern Criminal Courts Building in lower Manhattan, a little to the south and west of the Bowery,

* Reprinted from *Proceedings of The Ninety-Fifth Annual Congress of Correction of The American Correctional Association*, 1965, pp. 201–209, by permission of the American Correctional Association. Copyright 1966.

and within a stone's throw of the historic Five Points area. Court is conducted in an imposing, mahogany-walled, air-conditioned courtroom.

Almost of necessity I had followed the traditional sentencing policy that if a drunk is not too seedy and says he has a job, he is given a suspended sentence; otherwise, he may be given fifteen or thirty days, depending on his condition. When I finished imposing the sentences, it occurred to me that most of them would be back again in a matter of days or weeks after their release.

Night court is truly the dismal dumping ground for the also-rans of society. The faces that had stood before the bench at night haunted me in the days that followed. Not fully appreciating the enigmatic nature of the problem, I vowed, somewhat naively, not only to do something about it but to do it quickly.

Nelson and McCoy, the arresting officers, were known to the Bowery habitués as "ragpickers." Their daily assignment was the rounding up of derelicts along the Bowery from Chatham Square to Cooper Square, the most miserable mile in the United States. Accompanying them on a tour of duty a week later made more vivid the tragic picture I had witnessed in night court.

Nelson was a tall, lean man in his fifties, with closely cropped brown hair, a sallow face, and amiable brown eyes. He wore a gray suit on the job and was always chewing gum. McCoy, a small, stocky man in his forties, was the pugilist of the pair. They worked from a patrol wagon known as the "pie wagon." Nelson, the more gregarious, did most of the talking.

"There's one," said Nelson. We were proceeding up the Bowery and approaching Rivington Street. We pulled over to the curb and parked. A man lay sprawled on the sidewalk. Nelson and I went over to him. McCoy went to have a look up the street.

The derelict was a huge man. He was only about forty-two, but grime, malnutrition, and a graying stubble on his sunken cheeks made him look much older. An unlabeled pint bottle containing a pinkish fluid lay at his side. He had no socks, and his bare feet protruded through holes in the soles of his shoes, his big toes sticking out of the uppers. A zephyr of alcohol confirmed an already obvious diagnosis.

"Well," Nelson said, "darned if it isn't Andy. He's been around for years. Let's go for a ride, fella." He pointed to the man's hands. "See the pink stains between the fingers? Canned heat."

Since that time, I have tried to fathom the enigma that is the Bowery mile of misery. I have visited social agencies and missions in and near the Bowery. I have made the acquaintance of many of those whose lives are dedicated to helping the unfortunate. I have become fascinated by Alcoholics Anonymous, which has helped many whose problem is primarily alcoholism. I have been inspired by the spiritual zeal of men such as the Right Reverend Monsignor Charles B. Brennan, who for years conducted the Holy Name

Center for Homeless Men on Bleeker Street. I have become acquainted with the personnel of the Department of Welfare, who operate the Muni (public shelter) and who conduct Camp La Guardia in Orange County, a rest home for the aged and infirm. I have come to realize that, as inadequate as the city's program may be, it is properly regarded by the experts as "probably the most highly developed community program for the care of the homeless" in the United States.

Why do cities other than New York persist in an inhumane and un-Christian approach to the skid-row derelict? Can we properly bear malice in our hearts for the poorest among us — empty, bewildered souls, born in the image of God — whose degradation our society and our culture helped create?

Incarceration never cured a derelict, and never will. The problem of the skid-row derelict is basically social, medical, and spiritual in nature. Whether the derelict is a true alcoholic or merely a problem drinker, he usually has a much more deep-seated pathology, an emotional disturbance, if you will, that is an enigma to all of the disciplines. The penal approach to his problem is at best but a feeble attempt to repair damage done in early childhood.

Why, then, do judges go right on sentencing men and women through an endlessly revolving door? Don't they know the folly and futility of it all? Of course they do. But they say, "This is what the public wants. It wants these bums punished." But why? What drives people toward the urge for punishment? Ask them, if you will. Tell them how useless jails have been historically when it comes to reforming derelicts. And they will ask you, "How can you let such men go unpunished?" You might ask, "Are they hurting you? Are you being threatened? When they overindulge, who are the losers, except themselves?" After you have made your most persuasive arguments, they will look you in the eye and reply, "It's justice."

Psychiatrists who have studied the motivations of the urge to punish say this talk of impersonal justice is more often than not an outlet for people's repressed aggressiveness. It is never he who is without sin who casts the first stone. Is it not likely that people cast their own sins, their own miseries, guilts, and hatreds along with the stones they throw? This is not to say that the derelict, abandoning all that is sacred and leading a life of utter degradation, is attractive or nice. But what right do the rest of us have to become so furious with him? Those who wish to see him treated as a menace to society ought to look into their souls and gauge their reasons.

So should the law. It is time to put the hostile public in its proper place and to stop dignifying its thirst for vengeance and instinct for hate. It is time the police and the judiciary, instead of following in the wake of a misguided public, assumed the responsibility of providing leadership toward understanding.

We can help some derelicts by a modern therapeutic program. Alcoholics Anonymous does have the answer for some others. We can help all of them by a more humane program of day-to-day care and relief. But we must seek the fundamental and ultimate answer in an improved society, a society that will produce fewer misfits, fewer inadequate human beings. We will neither solve nor ameliorate the problem by more vigorous police enforcement or sterner justice.

"Would you then continue to permit the derelict to lie in the gutter?" The answer is simple. I would arrest the unfortunate who is a menace to the community, such as the derelict who is loud and boisterous or assaultive. I would have the police escort others for their own safety to a public shelter, to the Muni, as Officer Nelson suggested, there to remain, perhaps, for the cooling-off period of six hours. But there is no moral justification for the present program of wholesale arrests that takes place throughout the United States. Its only function is to keep depravity from becoming too assertively public.

Once we appreciate these almost self-evident truths, we must realize how farcical our primitive justice is and has been over the years. Today we recoil at the manner in which past generations used burning and whipping to curb crime. It is not likely that future generations will read of our imprisonment of drunken derelicts with a similar sense of shock and outrage?

DRUNKENNESS OFFENSES*

Two million arrests in 1965 — one of every three arrests in America — were for the offense of public drunkenness. The great volume of these arrests places an extremely heavy load on the operations of the criminal justice system. It burdens police, clogs lower criminal courts and crowds penal institutions throughout the United States.

Because of the sheer size of the problem and because of doubts that have recently been raised about the efficacy of handling drunkenness within the system of criminal justice, the Commission sought to reexamine present methods of treating drunkenness offenders and to explore promising alternatives. It was not in a position to undertake a comprehensive study of the complex medical, social, and public health problems of drunkenness.

Drunkenness Laws. Drunkenness is punishable under a variety of laws, generally describing the offense as being "drunk in a public place," often

* Reprinted from *The Challenge of Crime in a Free Society: A Report by the President's Commission on Law Enforcement and Administration of Justice* (Washington, D.C.: Government Printing Office, 1967), chap. 9.

without providing a precise definition of drunkenness itself. Some laws include as a condition that the offender is "unable to care for his own safety."

In some jurisdictions there are no laws prohibiting drunkenness, but any drunkenness that causes a breach of the peace is punishable. In Georgia and Alabama, for example, drunkenness that is manifested by boisterous or indecent conduct, or loud and profane discourse, is a crime. Other jurisdictions apply disorderly conduct statutes to those who are drunk in public. In Chicago, for example, the police, having no drunkenness law to enforce, use a disorderly conduct statute to arrest nondisorderly inebriates. Some jurisdictions permit police to make public drunkenness arrests under both State laws and local ordinances.

The laws provide maximum jail sentences ranging from 5 days to 6 months; the most common maximum sentence is 30 days. In some States an offender convicted of "habitual drunkenness" may be punished by a 2-year sentence of imprisonment.

The Offenders. The two million arrests for drunkenness each year involve sporadic and regular drinkers. Among the number are a wide variety of offenders — the rowdy college boy; the weekend inebriate; the homeless, often unemployed single man. How many offenders fall into these and other categories is not known. Neither is it known how many of the offenders are alcoholics in the medical sense of being dependent on alcohol. There is strong evidence, however, that a large number of those who are arrested have a lengthy history of prior drunkenness arrests, and that a disproportionate number involve poor persons who live in slums. In 1964 in the city of Los Angeles about one-fifth of all persons arrested for drunkenness accounted for two-thirds of the total number of arrests for that offense. Some of the repeaters were arrested as many as 18 times in that year.

The police do not arrest everyone who is under the influence of alcohol. Sometimes they will help an inebriate home. It is when he appears to have no home or family ties that he is most likely to be arrested and taken to the local jail.

Drunkenness arrest practices vary from place to place. Some police departments strictly enforce drunkenness statutes, while other departments are known to be more tolerant. In fact, the number of arrests in a city may be related less to the amount of public drunkenness than to police policy. Some of the wide variations in police practices can be seen in the table below that compares drunkenness arrests by two police departments known to be guided by policies of strict enforcement (Atlanta, Ga., and Washington, D.C.) to arrests by a department that is considered more tolerant (St. Louis, Mo.).

In some large and medium-size cities, police departments have "bum squads" that cruise skid rows and border areas to apprehend inebriates who appear unable to care for their own safety, or who are likely to annoy others. Such wholesale arrests sometimes include homeless people who are not intoxicated.

Comparison of Drunkenness Arrests
in Three Cities

| Population (1965) Estimates | Arrests (1965) | | | % of Arrests Accounted for by: | |
	Drunkenness arrests	Disorderly conduct and vagrancy arrests	All arrests	Drunk arrests	Drunk disorderly and vagrancy arrests
Washington, D.C. 802,000	44,792	21,338	86,464	51.8	76.5
St. Louis, Mo. 699,000	2,445	5,994	44,701	5.5	18.9
Atlanta, Ga. 522,000	48,835	22,379	92,965	52.5	76.6

Operation of the Criminal System after Arrest. Following arrest, the drunk is usually placed in a barren cell called a "tank" where he is detained for at least a few hours. The tanks in some cities can hold as many as 200 people, while others hold only 1 or 2. One report described the conditions found in a tank in this way:

Although he may have been picked up for his own protection, the offender is placed in a cell, which may frequently hold as many as 40-50 men where there is no room to sit or lie down, where sanitary facilities and ventilation are inadequate and a stench of vomit and urine is prevalent. The drunken behavior of some of the inmates is an added hazard. It is questionable whether greater safety is achieved for the individual who is arrested for his safe-keeping.

The chronic alcoholic offender generally suffers from a variety of ailments and is often in danger of serious medical complications, but medical care is rarely provided in the tank; and it is difficult to detect or to diagnose serious illness since it often resembles intoxication. Occasionally, chronic offenders become ill during pretrial detention and die without having received adequate medical attention.

If the offender can afford bail, he usually obtains release after he sobers up. In many jurisdictions an offender is permitted to forfeit bail routinely by not appearing in court. Thus, if the arrested person has the few dollars required, he can avoid prosecution; if he has no money, as is usually the case, he must appear in court.

Drunkenness offenders are generally brought before a judge the morning after their arrest, sometimes appearing in groups of 15 or 20. Rarely are the normal procedural or due process safeguards applied to these cases. Usually defendants are processed through the court system with haste and either released or sentenced to several days or weeks in jail. In some cities only those offenders who request it are jailed. In others chronic offenders, who are likely to be alcoholics, are generally sent to jail.

Effect on the Offender. The criminal justice system appears ineffective to deter drunkenness or to meet the problems of the chronic alcoholic offender. What the system usually does accomplish is to remove the drunk from public view, detoxify him, and provide him with food, shelter, emergency medical service, and a brief period of forced sobriety. As presently constituted, the system is not in a position to meet his underlying medical and social problems.

Effect on the System of Criminal Justice. Including drunkenness within the system of criminal justice seriously burdens and distorts its operations. Because the police often do not arrest the intoxicated person who has a home, there is in arrest practices an inherent discrimination against the homeless and the poor. Due process safeguards are often considered unnecessary or futile. The defendant may not be warned of his rights or permitted to make a telephone call. And although coordination, breath, or blood tests to determine intoxication are common practice in "driving-while-intoxicated" cases, they are virtually nonexistent in common drunk cases. Yet, without the use of such chemical tests, it is often difficult to determine whether the individual is intoxicated or suffering from a serious illness that has symptoms similar to intoxication.

The handling of drunkenness cases in court hardly reflects the standards of fairness that are the basis of our system of criminal justice. One major reason is that counsel is rarely present. Drunkenness cases often involve complex factual and medical issues. Cross-examination could be conducted on "observations" of a police officer such as "bloodshot" and "glassy" eyes, "staggering gait," "odor" of alcohol on defendant's breath. The testimony of an expert medical witness on behalf of the defendant could be elicited.

The extent of police time allotted to handling drunkenness offenders varies from city to city and from precinct to precinct. In most cities a great deal of time is spent. The inebriate must be taken into custody, transported to jail, booked, detained, clothed, fed, sheltered, and transported to court. In some jurisdictions, police officers must wait, often for hours, to testify in court.

There is a commensurate burden on the urban courts. Notwithstanding the fact that an overwhelming caseload often leads judges to dispose of scores of drunkenness cases in minutes, they represent a significant drain on court time which is needed for felony and serious misdemeanor cases. More subtly, drunkenness cases impair the dignity of the criminal process in lower courts, which are forced to handle defendants so casually and to apply criminal sanctions with so little apparent effect.

In correctional systems, too, resources are diverted from serious offenders. After court appearance, some offenders are sent to short-term penal institutions, many of which are already overcrowded. Correctional authorities estimate that one-half the entire misdemeanant population is comprised of drunkenness offenders. In one city it was reported that 95 percent of short-term prisoners were drunkenness offenders.

Treating Drunkenness as Noncriminal. The Commission seriously doubts that drunkenness alone (as distinguished from disorderly conduct) should continue to be treated as a crime. Most of the experts with whom the Commission discussed this matter, including many in law enforcement, thought that it should not be a crime. The application of disorderly conduct statutes would be sufficient to protect the public against criminal behavior stemming from intoxication. This was the view of the President's Commission on Crime in the District of Columbia, which recommended that the District of Columbia drunkenness law "be amended to require specific kinds of offensive conduct in addition to drunkenness."

Perhaps the strongest barrier to making such a change is that there presently are no clear alternatives for taking into custody and treating those who are now arrested as drunks. The commission believes that current efforts to find such alternatives to treatment within the criminal system should be expanded. For example, if adequate public health facilities for detoxification are developed, civil legislation could be enacted authorizing the police to pick up those drunks who refuse to or are unable to cooperate — if, indeed, such specific authorization is necessary. Such legislation could expressly sanction a period of detention and allow the individual to be released from a public health facility only when he is sober.

Drunkenness should not in itself be a criminal offense. Disorderly and other criminal conduct accompanied by drunkenness should remain punishable as separate crimes. The implementation of this recommendation requires the development of adequate civil detoxification procedures.

An alternate approach to present methods of handling drunkenness offenders after arrest and a prerequisite to taking drunkenness out of the criminal system is the establishment of civil detoxification centers. The detoxification center would replace the police station as an initial detention unit for inebriates. Under the authority of civil legislation the inebriate would be brought to this public health facility by the police and detained there until sober. Thereafter, the decision to continue treatment should be left to the individual. Experience in New York and Boston indicates that some alcoholics may be willing to accept treatment beyond the initial "sobering up" period. The center should include such medical services as physical examinations, an emergency-care unit for the treatment of acutely intoxicated persons, and transportation to a hospital, if advanced medical care seems necessary.

The Commission recommends:

1. Communities should establish detoxification units as part of comprehensive treatment programs.

2. Communities should coordinate and extend aftercare resources, including supportive residential housing.

3. Research by private and governmental agencies into alcoholism, the problems of alcoholics, and methods of treatment should be expanded.

THE CONTROL AND TREATMENT OF NARCOTIC USE*

DANIEL GLASER AND VINCENT O'LEARY

Perhaps the most adequately confirmed knowledge available on the drug problem pertains to the physiological effects of the drugs. The chemicals classified as narcotics fall into two main categories in terms of their effects on the human body. Those most commonly involved in illegal use are "depressants," so called because, if taken in sufficient quantity, they affect the central nervous system in such a way as to slow up bodily functions and lower body temperatures. The principal depressants are opium and its derivatives (such as morphine, heroin, and codeine), marihuana, and the barbiturates. Alcohol and tobacco also are physiological depressants. The other category of narcotic drugs consists of the stimulants, which raise the body's nervous and muscular tone and keep one awake. Cocaine and benzedrine are the principal stimulants among drugs involved in illegal use. Coffee and tea are also stimulants to a much lesser degree.

Opium in its original form consists of the seed capsules of the Oriental poppy plant. These have been smoked or eaten for their depressant effects, particularly in the Orient, since ancient times. Morphine, a chemical derived from opium, was first isolated in 1804 and has been invaluable in medicine as a pain killer. In recent years morphine has been replaced in medicinal usage by synthetic opiate drugs, notably demerol, which has fewer toxic side effects than morphine. Codeine is a morphine derivative commonly used in cough syrups.

Heroin is a morphine derivative used by over 90 percent of the persons convicted of felonious drug usage in the United States in recent decades. Because of this association of heroin with illegal narcotic usage, and because it has no advantage over other available drugs in medical treatment, the manufacture and distribution of heroin is not permitted for medical purposes. Heroin generally is used by drug addicts in a mixture of about 2 percent

* Reprinted from *The Control and Treatment of Narcotic Use,* U.S. Department of Health, Education, and Welfare, Welfare Administration, Office of Juvenile Delinquency and Youth Development, Washington, D.C., 1966, pp. 1–3, 5–6, 7–9, 11–13, 15, 18–19.

heroin and 98 percent lactose (milk sugar). The addict dissolves this mixture in a spoonful of water, heats it slightly, and injects it into his veins. It may also be sniffed in through the nostrils in powdered form. Especially when injected, it has unusually rapid and pronounced effects.

Marihuana is prepared from the flowers and leaves of several varieties of hemp plant. An Oriental variety, known as hashish, has been smoked since the dawn of history and is mentioned in the Bible. These plants grow wild in most of the United States, although a large proportion of marihuana prepared for smoking is illegally imported from Mexico. It generally is used as a cigarette. Its effects are reported to be much like those of alcohol. One cigarette deeply inhaled, in the special manner favored by this drug's users, is said to be comparable in effect to one "shot" of whiskey.

The barbiturates are a relatively recent source of addiction, and it is only within the last 15 or 20 years that barbituratism has been recognized as a "true addiction." Barbiturates are salts of barbituric acid and were first prepared in 1903 by Fischer and Von Mering. The most common barbiturates today have special names (coined by the manufacturers) ending in al to show their relationship to barbital.

Barbiturates are commonly prescribed as sleeping pills and are useful depressants of the central nervous system. Taken in small amounts under direction of a physician, they produce no ill effects, but, when taken in large and uncontrolled amounts, they become dangerous and intoxicating drugs. Barbiturates differ from the other addicting drugs in that they are comparatively easy to obtain, while other drugs in nonmedical use are dispensed primarily through underworld sources.

More deaths are caused by overdoses of barbiturates — taken either accidentally or with suicidal intent — than by any other poison except carbon monoxide. How many persons take these drugs habitually is not known, but, in 1955, 864,000 pounds were manufactured in the United States alone, amounting to approximately 26 doses for every man, woman, and child in the population. Even where sale is restricted to prescription only, it is possible, and not unusual, for addicts to obtain prescriptions from more than one physician in the same city or different towns.

Cocaine comes from the South American coca tree. It was first produced in 1853, and its use in medical practice increased tremendously toward the end of the 19th century. Classed in the stimulant or excitant group of drugs because of its effect upon the nervous system, cocaine is used principally in medicine as a local anesthetic. It desensitizes sensory nerve endings, but because of the effects of continued use — mental deterioration, nausea, digestive disorders, sleeplessness, loss of appetite, emaciation, and tremors — it has been replaced in medicine by procaine and novocain.

Cocaine, because of its toxicity, is rarely used hypodermically; addicts prefer to sniff the cocaine powder, commonly known as snow, through the mucous membranes of the nose. Frequently, the addict prefers the "speed-ball," or a mixture of cocaine and heroin, which blends the shock power of cocaine with the extended afterglow of heroin and permits the experienced addict to "go fast slow." Cocaine addiction is very rare today inasmuch as the drug is so scarce on the illicit market. International movement of coca leaves is strictly controlled, and Peru, formerly the primary source of the drug, has closed all cocaine factories.

The more recent chemical discoveries, amphetamines, desoxyphedrines, and related drugs, manufactured under various trade names, are considered potentially harmful by Federal authorities, as well as by representatives of pharmaceutical groups and medical experts. Some are actually classified under the Federal Food, Drug, and Cosmetic Act as dangerous.

Amphetamines, unlike the opiate drugs, do not produce physical dependence or withdrawal illness, but prolonged use leads to a more or less permanent state of nervousness and often causes emotional dependence. Intoxication from some actually produces hallucinations and delusions similar to those brought on by cocaine intoxication.

Many other substances are employed as narcotics or quasi-narcotics. Their variety has become so great, and the rate of innovation so rapid, that it is hard to define them all legally and to impose restrictions which will affect only their improper distribution or use. Indeed, even the most ordinary and useful drugs, such as aspirin, sometimes are taken in excess to produce a peculiar sensation, and they may even be fatal. Also, many substances not generally considered drugs, such as plastic glues from model airplane kits, paint thinners, and various spices and herbs, are sniffed, eaten, smoked, or injected to induce peculiar moods or sensations, sometimes with unhealthy or deadly consequences.

The psychological and social effects of narcotic drugs probably are more important than the physiological effects in accounting for their post-release use by individuals whom parole boards face. Persons who return to narcotics after being imprisoned or hospitalized long enough to be in good health when released clearly are not physically dependent upon the drug. If they resume narcotics usage, it is not as a relief from withdrawal effects. They clearly crave the drug for some other reason. Similarly, the difficulty which many people have in giving up the use of alcohol, tobacco, or coffee, where there definitely is not a clear physiological dependence, suggests that the term "habit-forming" may be quite descriptive of factors other than physiological dependence involved in drug usage. Additional factors in much of this persistent drug usage are social. This will be described later.

While most of the narcotic drugs can seriously injure a person or kill him if taken in an overdose, it is not clear that a regular but limited dosage shortens life or has other pronounced ill effects. This, of course, can also be said of alcohol, and until the recent statistical correlations of tobacco smoking with lung cancer, it was also said of tobacco. Certainly, there are many people who live to an old age smoking and drinking daily, and conversely many have serious illness and an early death from excessive regular use of alcohol. Dr. Laurence Kold, former head of the U.S. Public Health Service, reports a case of an 84-year-old physician who claimed to have taken a daily injection of morphine for 62 years. Before World War I, when there was no restriction on the sale of opiates in the United States, there was much addiction among Civil War veterans who, when wounded, had been issued morphine to administer to themselves.

In Europe throughout this century, and in the United States before the 1940's, most drug addiction occurred among middle-aged and older persons who were not of the lowest economic status. A major portion of the addicts were alleged to have been introduced to the drug habit through medical sources. These users included many nurses, pharmacists, and physicians, as well as some individuals for whom drugs originally were prescribed for medical purposes, but who remained addicts after their ailments were cured. There was also a cult of artists of various sorts using narcotic drugs experimentally, in search of unique experiences. These included prominent writers, painters, and musicians. Also, throughout the 20th century, drug use has been associated with professional playing of jazz music.

Seven distinctive features of drug usage in the United States since the start of World War II are noteworthy. One of these is the increase in drug use by younger persons.

A second trend is an increase in the extent to which drugs are used by persons of the lowest economic status. Related to this is a third trend, the concentration of drug usage in persons of minority racial and national groups. In the large cities of Northeastern United States, especially New York and Chicago, Negroes have comprised over 90 percent of those arrested for narcotics, and the usage has been concentrated in the poorest sections of the Negro slums. In Southwestern United States, in the Los Angeles area, those apprehended for narcotics use are more ethnically diverse than in most other large cities; they include large proportions of whites, Negroes, and persons of Mexican descent. The concentration in large cities appears to be a fourth trend of the midcentury decades. Most commitments to U.S. Public Health Hospitals for addiction in the 1930's were from Southern States, from rural areas and small towns, whereas a majority now are from New York City.

A fifth postwar development has been the widespread linkage of different types of drug use. Apparently, smoking marihuana was spread in minority groups in the 1930's, and around the end of that decade a pattern of progressing from marihuana to heroin was common. Both of these drugs are distributed exclusively through criminal channels, whereas in the 1930's and earlier, narcotics used by older addicts of higher social and economic status were more often drugs illegally diverted from their normal distribution for medical use. There still are many who use marihuana but never try opiates, and an appreciable fraction of opiate addicts have never used marihuana.

A sixth trend in the 1940's and 1950's was the increased association of drug addiction with other types of criminality. Not only did most persons arrested for drug use have a record of other types of delinquency before they became involved with drugs, but the high cost of the drugs and their low incomes made it necessary for them to support the narcotic habit by procuring a criminal income. The fact that heroin was imported and distributed completely through criminal channels, and was highly profitable, apparently led to the distributors soliciting sales in the slums, where they were in contact with delinquents and other criminals.

A seventh trend, especially prominent in the 1960's, was use of new types of drugs. Notable here are use of a large variety of pills, including several new and dangerous drugs, LSD and other "hallucinogenic" drugs, and the glue-sniffing fad among juveniles.

The process of introduction to drug use has been vividly described by several researchers. Becker notes that persons become habituated to the use of marihuana only through: (1) meeting people who will teach them how to use it by deep inhalation, rather than by ordinary smoking, to produce marked physiological effects; (2) using it in a social situation where these physiological effects are interpreted by others as evidence that the user is "high" and is supposed to feel happy, even though the physiological effects may often include dizziness and nausea; (3) defining the overall effects of the total experience, including the social situation, as pleasurable.

As Becker also has pointed out, the illegality of narcotics has social consequences which may promote persistence in drug use. First of all, to get the drugs the user must become familiar enough with persons already using them, or selling them, to win their confidence. Secondly, because their use is criminal, drug-taking must be concealed from nonusers; it is generally done only when or where conventional persons are not likely to observe it, so that users create a social world increasingly out of contact with nonusers. Thirdly, since use of the drug generally is defined as immoral, the user has to develop a special rationalization to justify its use to himself.

Drug users frequently rationalize their habit to themselves by denying that there is anything evil in the drug, finding immorality and hypocrisy in conventional persons, and thinking of themselves as having an unusual aesthetic experience which "squares" are incapable of appreciating. Another important feature of the rationalization is to insist to themselves and to others that they are "not really hooked," but could give it up if they wished. A fourth factor in the social involvement of the narcotics initiate with other users is the fact that his first drugs generally are received as a gift from a more experienced user. This creates an obligation to reciprocate, which means that the initiate must maintain this contact, or make new contacts, to purchase his own supply.

In talking with drug users, whom they interviewed at Chicago's Institute of Juvenile Research in the early 1950's, Kobrin and Finestone distinguished three stages of involvement in heroin addiction. The first they called the "joy popper," where the individual has had an occasional small dose and has not experienced marked withdrawal effects. The second state they called the "frantic junkie," where the offender has taken sufficient drugs to have very clear withdrawal effects, but has not established a regular pattern of drug procurement. These are the only opiate addicts at all likely to commit desperate and violent crimes to procure money for drugs, or to seize drugs.

The third state is the "stale addict," who takes a regular dosage, usually has an adequate supply on hand to last him over periods when he may not be in contact with his source of drugs, and generally has several alternative sources. Such an individual is likely to spend from $50 to $200 a week for his drugs, and the lethargic state which this use promotes impairs what legitimate income-earning ability he may have.

Although some upper class persons, as well as musicians and entertainers, have enough legal income to support stable opiate addiction, most stable addicts must also be professional criminals. Their crimes generally are nonviolent offenses, yielding small sums each time, but pursued regularly enough to support their habit. These offenses including shoplifting, stealing from parked cars ("car clouting" or "boosting"), picking pockets, pandering, and prostitution. The sale of narcotic drugs sometimes becomes a source of income for advanced addicts, who are able to buy the drugs in large quantities at relatively low prices; they then regain funds for further purchases by selling a portion at a profit to less advanced addicts. It is alleged that the "higher ups," the importers and wholesalers in the criminal distribution of drugs, generally are not addicts, but that at least two-thirds of the retailers, those who sell directly to users, are addicts themselves.

It is widely held that addicts are of a distinct personality type, usually described as inadequate, immature, passive, and dependent. Unfortunately, these are not precise terms, and the characteristics which they describe are matters of degree, in which different ranges shade into each other. Indeed, it is probable that both addicts and all other human beings vary considerably in these traits. While the average addict may be more passive, inadequate, or immature than the average nonaddict, some addicts do not have these traits pronouncedly and they are found in many persons who are not addicts.

The fact that many persons with the types of personalities described do not become addicts, and that addicts are highly concentrated in the slum areas of our large cities, and in minority groups, suggests that more than personality is involved in the acquisition of a drug habit. However, the fact that most minority youth reared in the highest drug-rate neighborhoods do not become addicts also suggests that more than neighborhood conditions is involved. Apparently both neighborhood and personality influence complex selection processes, in which only certain segments of our population have much contact with opportunities or inducements for drug use, but only certain personalities in these segments of the population find the drugs particularly adjustive. Chein describes this selection process in the slum areas as follows:

In the adolescent state (roughly under the age of 18) the street culture favors "acting out" on a gang basis. Rumbles, fights, hell-raising, competitive sports are an appropriate expression for this age. Even if the gang includes a large proportion of anxious, inadequately functioning boys (of the type we would consider prone to drug use), the activities of the gang offer a measure of shared status, a measure of security, and a sense of belonging. The boys do not have to face life alone—the group protects them. Escape into drugs is not necessary as yet.

But as the group grows older, two things happen. Sports, hell-raising, and gang fights become "kid stuff" and are given up. In the normal course of events, the youthful preoccupations are replaced by more individual concerns about work, future, a "steady" girl, and so on. If most of the gang members are healthy enough to face these new personal needs and engage in the new activities appropriate for their age, the availability of drugs will not attract their interest.

But for those gang members who are too disturbed emotionally to face the future as adults, the passing of adolescent hell-raising leaves emptiness. boredom, apathy, and restless anxiety. In a gang where there are many such disturbed members, the lone user will soon find companions, and cliques of users will grow quickly. Enmeshed in the pattern of activities revolving around the purchase, sale, and use of drugs and the delinquent efforts to get money to meet the exorbitant cost of heroin, the young users can comfortably forget about girls, careers, status, and recognition in the society at large. Their sexual drive is diminished, they maintain a sense of belonging in the limited world of the addict, they remain children forever.

Cloward and Ohlin suggest that young drug addicts commonly are "double failures." They have a history of failure in conventional pursuits, school and employment, and failure to achieve success and status in groups pursuing delinquency and crime. It is conceivable that such failures would include a disproportionate number of inadequate personalities, as well as a disproportionate number of persons handicapped by membership in minority groups. However, still another possibility is that part of the reported personality inadequacy or weak ego is an erroneous diagnosis. Such errors could reflect a bias of successful middle class observers, especially those not from minority groups, who may fail to appreciate the normal differences between their own past career outlook and the goals and expectations of most slum and minority youth. Large-scale research on various aspects of delinquency now underway in several cities may result in more precise knowledge in this area.

THE REALITIES OF
HALLUCINOGENIC DRUGS:
A COMPENDIUM*

ROLAND L. FISCHER

The four "divinatory" plants of Mexico at the time
of its conquest were *picietl* yielding *nicotiana rustica L,* a sister species to our
ordinary tobacco; *peyotl* or "mescal buttons" from the Mexican cactus *Lopho-
phora williamsii* containing, among other alkaloids, mescaline; *Teonanácatl*
(God's flesh) from *Psilocybe Mexicana Heim,* the sacred mushroom containing psilocybin; and *Ololiuhqui* from the seeds of *Rivea corymbosa* containing
a lysergic acid derivative, d-lysergic acid amide, of which d-lysergic acid di-
ethylamide (LSD) is a further derivative belonging to the family of ergot
alkaloids. The discovery of the latter compounds in morning glory seeds
(*Ipomoea violacea*) is of recent origin.

These drugs, referred to as phantastica, psychotica, hallucinogens and
psychotomimetics or psychodysleptics, produce "a flight of the soul from the
body" or *ekstasis* in Greek. The late Aldous Huxley believed that under the
influence of these drugs, particularly mescaline, we can enter the "Other
World which the natural visionary can enter at will." Others disclaim the
similarity between the two types of mystical experiences. Such a disagreement is reasonable to expect since there is a certain proportion of eidetic
(from *eidos* = image, in Greek) subjects in every population including drug-
takers; eidetic people have an unusually acute visual memory and thus a
"visionary gift" which is enhanced under the influence of these drugs. In
general, the drugs accentuate the already existing personality; visionaries
become more visionary and bores more boring.

For a North American Indian of the Rio Grande Valley, the eating of
Peyote buttons under the proper ritual conditions is part of a sacramental
act comparable to the Christian consuming the sacramental bread and wine.
An unfriendly or hostile environment or even a plainly unstructured situation, on the other hand, may adversely effect the drug experience. It is,
therefore, not the drug alone but also the individual's personality and the
total context which shape "the variety of drug experience."

There is an interesting parallelism between the two main types of divinatory drugs used by peoples of Mexico and those used by the ancient Arabs:

* Reprinted by permission from *Criminologica,* IV, No.
3 (November 1966), 2–7, 12 & 13.

in Mexico there were the two excitatory drugs Peyote — containing mescaline — and Teonanácatl — containing psilocybin — and one sedative, *Ololiuhqui*, whereas the Arabs had the excitatory hashish (from cannnabis sativa L) and the strongly sedating drug "Bendsch" containing scopolamin.

The discovery of hallucinogenic properties of LSD in 1938 by A. Hofmann, a research chemist in the Sandoz Research Laboratories in Basel, Switzerland, started with the observation that such small amounts as 100 µg (1 kg = 1000 gm; 1 gm = 1000 mg; 1 mg = 1000 µg) can considerably but reversibly alter normal human behavior for approximately 12 hours. It changed the religious significance formerly attached to these drugs and has given way to an interest in the similarity of their chemical structure to that of neurohumors: substances that chemically transmit impulses across synapses between two neurons or nerve cells, or between a neuron and an effector such as a muscle cell. Acetylcholine and the catechol amines, pinephrine and norepinephrine as well as serotonin are such neurohumors.

It is instructive to recall the discovery of the hallucinogenic properties of LSD. This was a discovery by serendipity: Hofmann planned to combine in a new compound the uterus contracting properties of "ergobasine," a synthetically modified natural ergot alkaloid of lysergic acid structure from fungus infected rye and nikethamide, an analeptic, i.e., a central nervous system stimulant. Indeed, he synthesized LSD which displays the desired characteristics, but, in addition, has turned out to be the most potent hallucinogen to date.

In Hofmann's own words, this is how it happened.

Being a cautious man, I started my experiment by taking 0.25 mg of d-lysergic acid-diethylamide tartrate thinking that such an extremely small dose would surely be harmless, considering that the natural ergot alkaloids produce toxic symptoms in man only with doses exceeding several milligrams.

After 40 minutes I noted in my laboratory journal: slight giddiness, restlessness, difficulty in concentration, visual disturbances, laughing.

At this point the laboratory protocol ends. The last words are hardly legible and were written down only with greatest difficulty. It was now obvious that LSD was responsible for the earlier intoxication. I requested my laboratory technician to accompany me home. Since it was war time and no car was available, we went by bicycle. This trip is about four miles and I had the feeling of not getting ahead, whereas my escort stated that we were rolling along at a good speed. I lost all control of time. I noticed with dismay that my environment was undergoing progressive changes. My visual field wavered and everything appeared deformed as in a faulty mirror. Space and time became more and more disorganized and I was overcome by a fear that I was going crazy. The worst part of it being, that I was clearly aware of my condition. The mind and power of observation were unimpaired. I was not, however, capable, by any act of will, of preventing the breakdown of the world around me. At home the physician was called.

At the height of the experience, the following symptoms were most marked:

Visual disturbances, everything appearing in impossible colours, objects out of proportion. At times the floor seemed to bend and the walls to undulate. The faces of the persons present changed into colorful grimaces. Marked motor restlessness alternating with paralysis. Limbs and head felt heavy as if filled with lead and were without sensation. Occasionally I felt as if I were out of my body. I thought I had died. My Ego seemed suspended somewhere in space, whereas I saw my dead body lying on the sofa.

When the physician arrived, approximately 2½ hours after I took the drug, he reported that my cardiac function was normal, pulse good, blood pressure normal, respiration deep and regular.

In the course of the evening the symptoms subsided gradually and then disappeared completely. Only the visual disturbances persisted somewhat longer. It was particularly striking how acoustic perceptions, such as the noise of water gushing from a tap or the spoken word, were transformed into optical illusions. Then I fell asleep and awakened next morning somewhat tired but otherwise feeling perfectly well.

That was the first experiment with LSD and rather a dramatic one. In spite of my caution, I had chosen a dose that was five to ten times too high.

The mode of action of the hallucinogenic compounds, which also include harmine and the piperidylbenzylates, as well as other experimental compounds, is not yet elucidated. It is assumed, however, that mescaline, LSD, and psilocybin have a common mechanism of action, i.e., they converge on the same circuitry which means that they elicit a similar chain of events by shifting the precarious balance of neurohumors in the organism. One needs to ingest orally approximately 400 to 500 mg of mescaline or 80 to 150 μg of LSD or 10 to 15 mg of psilocybin in order to experience comparable changes in behavior, changes which can be described as the excitation syndrome. The latter consists of a set of symptoms including rise in body temperature, metabolic rate, blood sugar, and rate of heart beat, pupilary dilation, facilitation of monosynaptic reflexes such as the knee jerk reflex and increased sensitivity to sensory stimulation. This central sympathetic excitation syndrome is interwoven with a psychological state of exaltation.

Taking any one of these drugs repeatedly, in the above-mentioned dosage, produces tolerance to them. For instance, the daily intake of 100 μg of LSD during three consecutive days results in a gradually diminishing experience as if the subject would have taken 50 and 25 μg on the second and third days respectively. A similar tolerance develops if LSD, mescaline, and psilocybin are taken interchangeably in comparable dosages.

By intensity of experience it is meant that the ordinary level of sensory stimulation through light, sound, taste, etc., is more intense to subjects under the influence of the drug; in other words, perceptual acuity is increased. The expression "increase in data content" aptly characterizes the experience, with the fast-flowing imagery moving along curved space. This spatial transformation is due to the fact that nearby objects appear closer and larger whereas far away objects appear farther and smaller than under ordinary conditions. It is in this space that objects and subjects suddenly emerge much larger and in more rapid succession. The experience of a faster flowing time is a manifestation of the increased sensory data content squeezed into each chronological time span. This experience of time contraction is illustrated by subjects who describe "the torrential flood of inner sensation" as the peak of the drug experience: "A hundred years would not suffice to describe the fullness of experience contained in a single minute," an observation quite in agreement with Hofmann's impression of "not getting ahead" (on the bicycle) "whereas my escort stated that we were rolling along at a good speed." Objective scientific experimentation has also substantiated the initial subjective descriptions: nearby space, as exemplified by handwriting size, increases with the drug-produced excitation as contrasted by a decrease under drug-produced tranquilization; finger-tapping rate, a measure of time contraction, critical flicker-fusion and frequency of small involuntary eye movements are also increased during excitation.

It is important to distinguish between the proper use of these drugs in a therapeutic, experimental or educational setting and their indiscriminate use and abuse by thrill seekers, "lunatic fringe," and drug addicts. More dangers seem likely for the unstable character who takes the drug for "kicks," curiosity, or to escape reality and responsibility than someone taking the drug for the therapeutic reasons under strict medical aegis and supervision. For this reason, the plea to curb the growing illicit traffic in psychotomimetic drugs, especially among the more unstable and fringe elements of society, is of the utmost importance.

Couldn't it be, however, that certain characteristics of a society are themselves instrumental in shaping the quality and quantity of "thrill seekers." It could be argued that the brightest and most sensitive of college youths are among those who are examining the values of our Western World and are finding them wanting. There is an upsurge of interest in introspection, Zen Buddhism and the realm of subjective experience. This concern with subjective experience parallels the increasing mechanization and objectification of our culture. The interest of many students in drug experience, therefore, should not be dismissed simply as a sign of delinquency, rebelliousness or psychological pathology. It represents a search and indicates needs and desires that American society and education apparently do not now meet or fill. The interest in drug experience reveals that our social milieu is lacking in the richness of life; the most shiny gadgets being no substitute for meaningful subjective experience.

THE HOMOSEXUAL COMMUNITY*

MAURICE LEZNOFF AND
WILLIAM A. WESTLEY

The significance of homosexuality in our society has been minimized and obscured by the force of social taboo. Yet there is evidence that homosexuals are distributed throughout all geographical areas and socio-economic strata. Furthermore, the subjection of homosexuals to legal punishments and social condemnation has produced a complex structure of concealed social relations which merit sociological investigation. The psychological isolation of the homosexual from society, his dependence upon other deviants for the satisfaction of sexual needs and self-expression, the crystallization of social roles and behavior patterns within the deviant group, the reciprocal obligations and demands within the homosexual community, and their significance for the larger society in which they occur, are but a few of the areas of theoretical interest to the sociologist.

In this paper we shall confine our discussion to the social organization of one homosexual community and its constituent social groups: their function, etiology, and interrelationships.

The report is based upon an intensive study of 60 homosexuals in a large Canadian city. The data consist of four-hour interviews with 40 homosexuals and briefer interviews with 20 others. In addition, the data include information based on the observation of many homosexual parties and gatherings in bars and restaurants, and a series of 30 letters written by one homosexual to another.

The primary function of the homosexual group is psychological in that it provides a social context within which the homosexual can find acceptance as a homosexual and collective support for his deviant tendencies. Most homosexuals fear detection and are often insecure and anxious because of this.

To relieve this anxiety the deviant seeks collective support and social acceptance. Since the homosexual group provides the only social context in which homosexuality is normal, deviant practices moral, and homosexual responses rewarded, the homosexual develops a deep emotional involvement with his group, tending toward a ready acceptance of its norms and dictates, and subjection to its behavior patterns.

Within these groups the narration of sexual experiences and gossip about

* Reprinted with permission from *Social Problems*, III, No. 4 (April 1956), 257–63.

sexual exploits of others is a major form of recreation. The narration of sexual experiences functions to allocate prestige among the members because of the high evaluation placed upon physical attraction and sexual prowess. Yet it creates hostility and sexual rivalry.

An additional function is the provision of a social situation in which the members can dramatize their adherence to homosexual values. Thus, the gossip about sex, the adoption and exaggeration of feminine behavior, and the affectation of speech, represent a way of affirming that homosexuality is frankly accepted and has the collective support of the group.

In our society, homosexuality is defined both legally and socially as a criminal and depraved practice and the homosexual is threatened by powerful legal and social sanctions such as imprisonment, physical violence, social and occupational ostracism, and ridicule. Therefore, all homosexuals face the problem of evading social controls. They do this in two predominant ways.

Some pass for heterosexuals on the job and in most of their social relationships. They mix regularly with heterosexuals for business, entertainment, and other social activities. They avoid situations and persons publicly recognized as homosexual for they fear that discovery will threaten their career and expose them to sanctions. Others openly admit and practice homosexuality. They usually work in occupations where the homosexual is tolerated, withdraw from uncompromising heterosexual groups, and confine most of their social life to homosexual circles.

The chief distinctions between homosexual groups correspond to the differences in the general modes of evading social controls which homosexuals have developed. Thus, secret and overt homosexuals form distinctive groups. The distinctions between these groups are maintained by the secret homosexuals who fear identification and refuse to associate with overt homosexuals. As a result of this social distance a certain amount of reciprocal hostility has developed between the members of secret and overt groups. This hostility helps maintain the social distance and distinctions between these groups.

The secret homosexuals form groups which consist of a loose amalgamation of small cliques. Interaction within the cliques is frequent, with members meeting at each other's homes and in bars and restaurants. The clique's structure is a product of the diverse interests and occupations and of the desire to limit homosexual contacts which characterize secret homosexuals. The clique unites its several members in common specialized interests apart from the larger group. A secret homosexual group is generally characterized by: (a) informal standards of admission; (b) discretion in the manner in which homosexuality is practiced; (c) an attempt at concealment; (d) partial rather than complete involvement in the homosexual world.

Overt homosexuals gather in cohesive social groups which become the dominant focus of their lives. These groups are openly homosexual in character. The members make little effort to conceal their deviation, spend almost all their free time with the group, and tend to regard their other activities as peripheral. These groups generally draw their members from persons of low socioeconomic status who have jobs where concealment is not a prerequisite.

The members of (one overt) group met daily either at a bar, a restaurant, or at the house of the acknowledged leader or "queen." They spent their time in endless gossip about the sexual affairs of the members or other homosexuals known to them. Often they would go to bars and restaurants in the attempt to make a "pick-up," or spend the evening "cruising" individually or in groups of two's and three's.

The queen seems to characterize only "overt" groups. Functionally, the role of the queen is very important in the life of these groups. He provides a place where the group may gather and where its individual members may have their "affairs." He helps finance members in distress, functions as an intermediary in making sexual contacts, partially controls the entrance of new members, and warns the members of hoodlums who would prey upon them. Generally the queen is an older homosexual who has had wide experience in the homosexual world.

Overt groups are characterized by: (a) no particular standards of admission; (b) unself-conscious and unrestrained practice of homosexuality; (c) little or no concealment; (d) high degree of social isolation with little involvement in heterosexual activities; (e) little concern with identification as a status threat or the sanctions of heterosexual society.

The diverse secret and overt homosexuals are linked together either through bonds of sex or of friendship. Within the primary group, the emphasis upon friendship rather than sex serves to eliminate excessive sexual competition and preserves group unity. However, this creates a sexual interdependency upon those outside the group with important social consequences. In the first place, it forces the secret homosexual out into the open in an attempt to solicit sexual partners. He thus frequents the known homosexual meeting places within the city such as specific bars, hotel lobbies, street corners, and lavatories. These activities make him an increasingly familiar figure within the homosexual world. Secondly, this solicitation leads to the interaction of secret and overt homosexuals on a sexual as opposed to a social basis. While these contacts occur in a spirit of anonymity, an approach to the other often requires an exchange of confidences. Thirdly, this sexual interdependency increases the anxiety of secret homosexuals since it forces them to contact the overt ones whom they fear as a threat to their security. Thus, it is the casual and promiscuous sexual contacts between the members of different categories of evasion (i.e., the secret and the overt) which weld the city's homosexuals into a community.

The homosexual community thus consists of a large number of distinctive groups within which friendship binds the members together in a strong and relatively enduring bond and between which the members are linked by tenuous but repeated sexual contacts. The result is that homosexuals within the city tend to know or know of each other, to recognize a number of common interests and common moral norms, and to interact on the basis of antagonistic cooperation. This community is in turn linked with other homosexual communities in Canada and the United States, chiefly through the geographical mobility of its members.

THE FEMALE HOMOSEXUAL*

GEORGE L. KIRKHAM

Female sexual inversion, or "lesbianism" as the phenomenon has long been called, runs like a thread along the time continuum stretching from antiquity to the present. At times the thread is difficult to follow as a consequence of society's tendency to minimize the importance of female homosexuality, yet it is always present.

The earliest record of "lesbianism" is to be found in a perusal of the history of early Greece. Sappho, a poetess living in a village on the island of Lesbos (from whence the term "lesbian" is derived), is reputed to have founded a cult dedicated to homosexual love around the year 590 B.C. Gathering about her a group of disciples, Sappho devoted her life to the cultivation of music, poetry, dancing, and woman's love for her own sex. Legend has it that she was indeed attractive to the opposite sex, but spurned the advances of any and all suitors because of the hostility she harbored for her three brothers who dominated the life of her beloved mother.

While female homosexuality has traditionally been accorded less attention by writers than male sexual aberration, one finds the lesbian theme in the literature of both past and present: "The Well of Loneliness," by Radclyff Hall; "Diana" by Diana Fredericks; "The Girl with the Golden Eyes," by Pere Goriot; "The Children's Hour," by Lillian Hellman (a book [sic] recently made into a popular motion-picture) — all of these to a greater or lesser extent deal with the theme of female homosexuality.

It is indeed a formidable task to accurately estimate the incidence of female homosexuality in our own or other societies. Lesbianism, by its very nature, is less flagrant than male homosexuality, and consequently more apt to be overlooked by society. As Katherine Davis has observed, intimacies between women tend to be more or less "taken for granted." While any form of physical contact between men, other than shaking hands is apt to arouse suspicion, our society thinks nothing of women embracing, dancing together, even kiss-

* Reprinted with permission from *The Female Offender,* J. C. Esselstyn, ed. (San Jose, Calif.: The Spartan Book Store, San Jose College, 1966), pp. 62–69.

191 | GEORGE L. KIRKHAM

ing. We invariably perceive such behavior on the part of women as an expression of emotion and assign no special sexual significance to it.

Alfred Kinsey reported that about 25 percent of his sample of American women ". . . had recognized erotic responses to other females" by the age of 30 and that by the age of 40, 19 percent of the total sample ". . . had had some physical contact which was deliberately and consciously, at least on the part of one of the partners, intended to be sexual." The duration of these contacts varied. Of those with homosexual experiences, half were limited to a year or less, one quarter continued for two or three years, and one quarter lasted for more than three years. The number of partners with whom homosexuality was experienced tended to be limited. Half had limited their homosexual episodes to one partner. About a fifth had two partners. Thirty percent of this group had three or more partners and only four percent had more than ten.

Edmund Bergler is dissatisfied with these reported frequencies. He states that Kinsey's failure to realize the motives which led his homosexual group to submit to interviews, and his failure to interview a representative economic, social and regional sample of women has produced deflated figures for female homosexuality and inflated figures for male homosexuality. Bergler states that "male homosexuals habitually overplay, female homosexuals habitually underplay the perversion." In contrast to Kinsey's finding, Bergler points to the estimates of Hirshfeld and Ellis which suggest that there are twice as many female as male homosexuals. Stearn also suggests that lesbianism is quite possibly as "rampant as male homosexuality, only far more secretive."

Any study of the legislation and enforcement of laws pertaining to female sex inversion is necessarily a study in the differential treatment of male and female homosexuals. There exists in most societies, as in our own, a dearth of law relating specifically to female homosexuality.

The status of female homosexuality is at present a moot point in four states: Arkansas, Colorado, Iowa, and Nebraska. While the sex statutes in forty-six states would seem to be clearly applicable to female as well as male homosexuality, almost all prosecution is directed exclusively against offending males.

Kinsey's recent review of the enforcement of New York's sex statutes over a ten-year period reveals only three arrests of females in the past ten years, but all of those cases were dismissed, although there were some tens of thousands of arrests and convictions of males charged with homosexual activity in that same period of time. With regard to the attitude of law enforcement officials and legislators toward feminine homosexuality, it is further interesting to note that in those states in which sodomy includes fellatio but not cunnilingus, an act of oral-genital copulation performed upon a female by a male is a crime, but the same act performed by a female on another female is not perceived as a crime.

This invidious differential perception of male and female homosexuality is also reflected in the behavior of most police departments. Many police agencies, like the Los Angeles Police Department (which has launched a vigorous program against male homosexuals, employing a squad of under-cover agents who frequent male homosexual hangouts in the hope of making arrests) press constantly for arrest and conviction of male homosexuals, yet display attitudes of indifference toward female homosexuality.

Stearn relates the rather humorous case of a female homosexual in San Francisco who actually tried to get herself jailed after a row with her girl-friend which left her feeling jilted. Walking up to a policeman in the street, she threw herself at him, shouting "Arrest me, I'm a lesbian." Regarding her with an air of indifference, the officer replied "Go home and sleep it off," and then strolled off — leaving her to think of some other way to pun-ish her erstwhile girl friend. Seldom are lesbian bars and known hangouts raided by the police, though male "gay bars" are closed by officials with astonishing efficiency and regularity. Such is the impunity accorded female homosexuals that they are even able to organize publicly in a number that would surely spell arrest and imprisonment for their male counterparts. Thus, the "Daughters of Bilitis" (an avowed lesbian organization) was able to hold its 1960 national convention at a prominent Los Angeles hotel — in full sight of God, the public, and the Los Angeles Police Department without incident.

It should be added that while the police are often reluctant to arrest fe-males for behavior comparable to that which would result in the arrest of males, lesbians are generally much more difficult to observe engaging in legally proscribed behavior. While most arrests of male homosexuals are made in parks, bars, public rest rooms, and well-known "cruise" areas, female homo-sexuals simply do not usually frequent such places. They are neither as promiscuous, nor as open, in the homosexual relationships as males are. We have already observed how the slightest suggestion of physical contact be-tween males is apt to arouse suspicion, whereas the sight of two women holding hands, embracing or even kissing, is nothing extraordinary — cer-tainly no grounds on which to attempt an arrest in our society.

The legal leniency shown the female homosexual is understandable in light of the long-standing social and legal status of women in our society. Being regarded as of far less social importance than men, the private activities of women have traditionally been ignored and regarded as of little moment. Only where another man was involved in such activities was there concern — and here the issue was the violation of the property rights of one party, for woman was regarded as the chattel of man.

Society's leniency toward female homosexuality is reflected throughout the history of Judaic-Christian law and religion. The ancient Hittite code, for example, vigorously condemned male homosexuality yet made no mention of homosexual activity among females. Both the Bible and the Talmud pre-scribe severe penalties for males discovered in homosexuality (most often calling for death), yet female homosexuality is rarely mentioned. Even where it is cursorily alluded to, no severe penalties are set forth. European history provides us with numerous accounts of cases where males were put to death for homosexuality, yet there are few cases where punitive sanctions were imposed on homosexual women.

While the list of crimes which are clearly and directly related to female sexual inversion would indeed be a short and empirically unsubstantial one, it is possible to discuss several forms of female criminality which bear a more oblique, subtle relation to homosexuality.

We have earlier suggested that there often exists an intimate nexus between prostitution and female homosexuality. Prostitution is often entered because the promiscuity which it necessarily involves affords a woman with repressed homosexual proclivities evidence that she is "normal" in her sexual behavior, even though she may be strongly attracted to members of her own sex. Such "pseudoheterosexuality" often serves as a "front" for herself and others.

If female homosexuality is related to prostitution, it is also related to those crimes which are so often concomitants of prostitution. Many prostitutes cater to a masochistic clientele — a service which necessarily involves the crime of battery.

Prostitution and involvement with narcotics sales or usage go together like the proverbial "horse and carriage." Female homosexuals with no prior narcotics history may well be introduced to the world of drugs once they become prostitutes.

The crime of blackmail (extortion) may likewise come about as a consequence of female homosexuality. The lesbian may be relatively safe from the arm of the law, but like the male homosexual, she always faces the possibility of being "blackmailed" if her sexual deviance is discovered. A great many lesbians occupy positions (such as social workers, teachers and probation officers) in which the revelation of their homosexuality would prove catastrophic — a factor which renders many of them actual or potential victims of extortion.

Murder and suicide may also follow in the wake of a lesbianic relationship. Lesbians, perhaps even more so than male homosexuals, tend to be extremely jealous of their sexual partners. This often leads to a fierce possessiveness in which the slightest sign of infidelity on the part of a partner may produce assaultive — and sometimes homicidal behavior. The strong emotional and affectional components involved in female homosexual liaisons, when combined with jealousy and insecurity, may spell injury or death for one or both partners. Actual or attempted suicide, of the type intended by women to hurt those whom they love, may follow the dissolution of a long-standing homosexual "marriage" between two women.

Sexual assaults by females on other females are not unknown. While "rape" is usually legally defined in terms of "penetration," a definition which (by virtue of her physiology) categorically excludes females from the commission of this crime, male-female sexual assaults committed by women are similar to what we think of as rape. Ellis reports the case of an older working woman who "raped" a young girl who was held down by two other women. A friend of Ellis' reports to him from Guadalupe that sexual assaults by women on colored girls between the ages of 12-14 occurred very frequently there, whereas similar attacks by boys or men were rare. Hirschfeld refers to a masseuse in Berlin who tried to "rape" a female client during a massage, as well as the case of a certain Katherine Veress who was in the habit of luring young girls to her apartment under promise of employment, and then forcibly "raping" them. He goes on to observe that "of twenty-five women sentenced at Turin for immoral acts, nine had attempted sexual intercourse with immature girls."

A suggestion that female crimes of arson and theft may also be linked to sexual aberration comes from Chideckel. While not all women who steal are kleptomaniacs, he observes that many women who are well educated wives and mothers often engage in the theft of objects for which they have no use, or for which they could have paid anyway. For such women, the theft of objects represents a symbolic attempt to steal love. Chideckel observes that both stealing and setting fires (pyromania), by virtue of the fact that they are forbidden acts, serve to enhance sexual enjoyment. He cites the case of an otherwise sexually frigid woman who constantly relapsed into the theft of objects, experiencing an orgasm each time she succeeded in the theft. Whether or not such women, as a result of their frequent heterosexual frigidity and the embarrassment of being repeatedly caught in acts of theft, ever turn to other women for sexual satisfaction is a question which Chideckel does not pursue.

We have earlier alluded to the role of alcohol in some cases of female homosexuality. While drunkenness, per se, is not a crime in most countries, when combined with disorderly conduct it often constitutes a breach of the peace. As we have observed earlier, many women indulge in homosexuality only as a result of the lowered inhibitions which follow intoxication. While doubtless most of the annual female arrest rate for drunk and disorderly conduct has nothing to do with homosexuality, many cases of female homosexuality are probably hidden in police blotters under the label "drunk and disorderly."

APPRENTICESHIPS IN PROSTITUTION*

JAMES H. BRYAN

This paper provides some detailed, albeit preliminary, information concerning induction and training in a particular type of deviant career: prostitution, at the call girl level. It describes the order of events, and their surrounding structure, which future call girls experience in entering their occupation.

The respondents in this study were 33 prostitutes, all currently or previously working in the Los Angeles area. They ranged in age from 18 to 32, most being in their mid-twenties. None of the interviewees were obtained through official law enforcement agencies, but seven were found within the context of a neuropsychiatric hospital. The remaining respondents were gathered primarily through individual referrals from previous participants in the study. There were no obvious differences between the "psychiatric sample" and the other interviewees on the data to be reported.

All subjects in the sample were call girls. That is, they typically obtained their clients by individual referrals, primarily by telephone, and enacted the sexual contract in their own or their clients' place of residence or employment. They did not initiate contact with their customers in bars, streets, or houses of prostitution, although they might meet their customers at any number of locations by pre-arrangement. The minimum fee charged per sexual encounter was $20.00. As an adjunct to the call girl interviews, three pimps and two "call boys" were interviewed as well.

Approximately two-thirds of the sample were what are sometimes known as "outlaw broads"; that is, they were not under the supervision of a pimp when interviewed. There is evidence that the majority of pimps who were aware of the study prohibited the girls under their direction from participating in it. It should be noted that many members of the sample belonged to one or another clique; their individually expressed opinions may not be independent.

The interviews strongly suggest that there are marked idiosyncrasies from one geographical area to another in such practices as fee-splitting, involvement with peripheral occupations (e.g., cabbies), and so forth. For example, there appears to be little direct involvement of peripheral occupations with

* Reprinted by permission from *Social Problems*, XII, No. 3 (Winter 1965), 287–97.

call girl activities in the Los Angeles area, while it has been estimated that up to 10% of the population of Las Vegas is directly involved in activities of prostitutes. What may be typical for a call girl in the Los Angeles area is not necessarily typical for a girl in New York, Chicago, Las Vegas, or Miami.

Immediately prior to entrance into the occupation, all but one girl had personal contact with someone professionally involved in call girl activities (pimps or other call girls). The one exception had contact with a customer of call girls. While various occupational groups (e.g., photographers) seem to be peripherally involved, often unwittingly, with the call girl, there was no report of individuals involved in such occupations being contacts for new recruits. The novice's initial contact is someone at the level at which she will eventually enter the occupation: not a street-walker, but a call girl; not a pimp who manages girls out of a house of prostitution, but a pimp who manages call girls.

Approximately half of the girls reported that their initial contact for entrance into the profession was another "working girl." The nature of these relationships is quite variable. In some cases, the girls have been long standing friends. Other initial contacts involved sexual relationships between a Lesbian and the novice. Most, however, had known each other less than a year, and did not appear to have a very close relationship, either in the sense of time spent together or of biographical information exchanged. The relationship may begin with the aspiring call girl soliciting the contact. That is, if a professional is known to others as a call girl, she will be sought out and approached by females who are strangers.

Whatever their relationship, whenever the professional agrees to aid the beginner, she also, it appears, implicitly assumes responsibility for training her. This is evidenced by the fact that only one such female contact referred the aspirant to another girl for any type of help. Data are not available as to the reason for this unusual referral.

If the original contact was not another call girl but a pimp, a much different relationship is developed and the career follows a somewhat different course. The relationship between pimp and girl is typically one of lovers, not friends. Occasionally, however, a strictly business relationship will be formed.

Whether the relationship is love or business, the pimp solicits the new girl. It is usually agreed that the male will have an important managerial role in the course of the girl's career, and that both will enjoy the gains from the girl's activities for an indefinite period.

Once the girl agrees to function as a call girl, the male, like his female counterpart, undertakes the training of the girl, or refers the girl to another call girl for training. Either course seems equally probable. Referrals, when employed, are typically to friends and, in some cases, wives or ex-wives.

Although the data are limited, it appears that the pimp retains his dominance over the trainee even when the latter is being trained by a call girl. The girl trainer remains deferential to the pimp's wishes regarding the novice.

Once a contact is acquired and the decision to become a call girl is made, the recruit moves to the next stage in the career sequence: the apprenticeship period. The structure of the apprenticeship will be described, followed by a description of the content most frequently communicated during this period.

The apprenticeship is typically served under the direction of another call girl, but may occasionally be supervised by a pimp. Twenty-four girls in the sample initially worked under the supervision of other girls. The classroom is, like the future place of work, an apartment. The apprentice typically serves in the trainer's apartment, either temporarily residing with the trainer or commuting there almost daily. The novice rarely serves her apprenticeship in such places as a house of prostitution, motel, or on the street. It is also infrequent that the girl is transported out of her own city to serve an apprenticeship. Although the data are not extensive, the number of girls being trained simultaneously by a particular trainer has rarely been reported to be greater than three. Girls sometimes report spending up to eight months in training, but the average stay seems to be two or three months. The trainer controls all referrals and appointments, novices seemingly not having much control over the type of sexual contract made or the circumstances surrounding the enactment of the contract.

The structure of training under the direction of a pimp seems similar, though information is more limited. The girls are trained in an apartment in the city they intend to work and for a short period of time. There is some evidence that the pimp and the novice often do not share the same apartment as might the novice and the girl trainer. There appear to be two reasons for the separation of pimp and girl. First, it is not uncommonly thought that cues which suggest the presence of other men displease the girl's customers. Secondly, the legal repercussions are much greater, of course, for the pimp who lives with his girl than for two girls rooming together.

Because of the convenience in separation of housing, it is quite likely that the pimp is less directly involved with the day-to-day training of the girls than the call girl trainer.

The content of the training period seems to consist of two broad, interrelated dimensions, one philosophical, the other interpersonal. The former refers to the imparting of a value structure, the latter to "do's" and "don'ts" of relating to customers and secondarily, to other "working girls" and pimps.

Insofar as a value structure is transmitted it is that of maximizing gains while minimizing effort, even if this requires transgressions of either a legal or moral nature. Frequently, it is postulated that people, particularly men, are corrupt or easily corruptible, that all social relationships are but a reflection of a "con," and that prostitution is simply a more honest or at least no more dishonest act than the everyday behavior of "squares." Furthermore, not only are "johns" basically exploitative, but they are easily exploited; hence they are, in some respects, stupid.

The general assumption that man is corrupt is empirically confirmed when the married male betrays his wife, when the moralist, secular or religious, betrays his publicly stated values, or when the "john" "stiffs" (cheats) the girl.

Values such as fairness with other working girls, or fidelity to a pimp, may occasionally be taught.

It should be noted, however, that behavior based on enlightened self-interest with concomitant exploitation is not limited to customer relationships. Interviewees frequently mentioned a pervasive feeling of distrust between trainer and trainee, and such incidents as thefts or betrayal of confidences are occasionally reported and chronically guarded against.

It seems reasonable to assume that the value structure serves, in general, to create in-group solidarity and to alienate the girl from "square" society, and that this structure serves the political advantage of the trainer and the economic gains of the trainee more than it allays the personal anxieties of either. In fact, failure to adopt these values at the outset does not appear to be correlated with much personal distress. Good empirical evidence, however, concerning the functions and effectiveness of this value structure with regard to subjective comfort is lacking.

A series of deductions derived from the premises indicated above serve to provide, in part, the "rules" of inter-personal contact with the customer. Each customer is to be seen as a "mark," and "pitches" are to be made.

Any unnecessary interaction with the customer is typically frowned upon, and the trainee will receive exhortations to be quick about her business. Other content taught concerns specific information about specific customers.

Training may also include proprieties concerning consuming alcohol and drugs, when and how to obtain the fee, how to converse with the customers and, occasionally, physical and sexual hygiene.

Interestingly, the specific act of telephoning a client is often distressing to the novice and is of importance in her training. Unfortunately for the girl, it is an act she must perform with regularity as she does considerable soliciting. One suspects that such behavior is embarrassing for her because it is an unaccustomed role for her to play — she has so recently come from a culture where young women do *not* telephone men for dates. Inappropriate sex-role behavior seems to produce greater personal distress than does appropriate sex-role behavior even when it is morally reprehensible.

It should be stressed that, if the girls originally accepted such instructions and values, many of them, at least at the time of interviewing, verbalized a rejection of these values and reported behavior which departed considerably from the interpersonal rules stipulated as "correct" by their trainers. Some show considerable affect toward "johns," others remain drunk or "high" throughout the contact. While there seems to be general agreement as to what the rules of interpersonal conduct are, there appears to be considerable variation in the adoption of such rules.

A variety of methods are employed to communicate the content described above. The trainer may arrange to eavesdrop on the interactions of girl and client and then discuss the interaction with her. One trainer, for example, listened through a closed door to the interaction of a new girl with a customer, then immediately after he left, discussed, in a rather heated way, methods by which his exit may have been facilitated. Direct teaching, however, seems to be uncommon. The bulk of whatever learning takes place seems to take place through observation.

To summarize, the structure of the apprenticeship period seems quite standard. The novice receives her training either from a pimp or from another more experienced call girl, more often the latter. She serves her initial two to eight months of work under the trainer's supervision and often serves this period in the trainer's apartment. The trainer assumes responsibility for arranging contacts and negotiating the type and place of the sexual encounter.

The content of the training pertains both to a general philosophical stance and to some specifics (usually not sexual) of interpersonal behavior with customers and colleagues. The philosophy is one of exploiting the exploiters (customers) by whatever means necessary and defining the colleagues of the call girl as being intelligent, self-interested and, in certain important respects, basically honest individuals. The interpersonal techniques addressed during the learning period consist primarily of "pitches," telephone conversations, personal and occasionally sexual hygiene, prohibitions against alcohol and dope while with a "john," how and when to obtain the fee, and specifics concerning the sexual habits of particular customers. Specific sexual techniques are very rarely taught. The current sample included a considerable number of girls who, although capable of articulating this value structure, were not particularly inclined to adopt it.

While the imparting of ideologies and proprieties to the prospective call girl is emphasized during the apprenticeship period, it appears that the primary function of the apprenticeship, at least for the trainee, is building a clientele. Since this latter function limits the degree of occupational socialization, the process of developing the clientele and the arrangements made between trainer and trainee will be discussed.

Lists ("books") with the names and telephone numbers of customers are available for purchase from other call girls or pimps, but such books are often considered unreliable. While it is also true that an occasional pimp will refer customers to girls, this does not appear to be a frequent practice. The most frequent method of obtaining such names seems to be through contacts developed during the apprenticeship. The trainer refers customers to the apprentice and oversees the latter in terms of her responsibility and adequacy in dealing with the customer. For referring the customer, the trainer receives forty to fifty per cent of the total price agreed upon in the contract negotiated by the trainer and customer. The trainer and trainees further agree, most often explicitly, on the apprentice's "right" to obtain and to use, on further occasions, information necessary for arranging another sexual contract with the "john" without the obligation of further "kick-back" to the trainer. That is, if she can obtain the name and telephone number of the customer, she can negotiate another contract without fee-splitting. During this period, then, the girl is not only introduced to other working colleagues (pimps and girls alike) but also develops a clientele.

A final word is needed regarding the position of the pimp vis-à-vis the call girl during the apprenticeship period. While some pimps assume the responsibility for training the girl personally, as indicated above, as many send the novice to another girl. The most apparent reason for such referral is that it facilitates the development of the "book." Purposes of training appear to be secondary for two reasons: (1) The pimp often lacks direct contact with the customers, so he personally cannot aid directly in the development of the girl's clientele; (2) When the pimp withdraws his girl from the training context, it is rarely because she has obtained adequate knowledge of the profession. This is not to say that all pimps are totally unconcerned with the type of knowledge being imparted to the girl. Rather, the primary concern of the pimp is the girl's developing a clientele, not learning the techniques of sex or conversation.

The apprenticeship period usually ends abruptly, not smoothly. Its termination may be but a reflection of interpersonal difficulties between trainer and trainee, novice and pimp, or between two novices. Occasionally termination of training is brought about through the novice's discovery and subsequent theft of the trainer's "book." Quite frequently, the termination is due to the novice's developing a sufficient trade or other business opportunities. The point is, however, that no respondent has reported that the final disruption of the apprenticeship was the result of the completion of adequate training. While disruptions of this relationship may be due to personal or impersonal events, termination is not directly due to the development of sufficient skills.

7 | Focus on the Victim

INTRODUCTION

Not in one thousand years has society shown as much concern for and about the victims of crimes as has been evidenced in the last few years. Almost completely neglected in the criminal law and by the police, prosecutor, judge, and correctional worker, the victim has traditionally been the forgotten man except insofar as he is a complainant and witness in a given case. It seems rather peculiar, to say the very least, that the emphasis on the perpetrator and his punishment, as well as on the deterrence of other would-be violators, has relegated the hopeless victim to the status of a cipher in modern criminal law and its administration. Recently, however, a combination of historical events has reintroduced the victim into the proceedings. He is "in," so to speak, and it is likely that some of the previous concern with the perpetrator will devolve on the victim. As a result, a more balanced approach to the crime problem seems certain to follow. The focus on the victim has led to several distinct concerns. First, the new field of victimology has emerged. A post-World War II development, victimology has sought to determine the attributes of the victim-prone person. It has also attempted to show that the criminal act against a person is frequently the outcome of the relationship of victim and perpetrator. The victim, in his behavior and demeanor, may well play an unwitting but critical role in invoking the act against himself. In a real sense, the sufferer may be partly responsible for his own victimization. The nice clean break demanded by the law between the total guilt of the perpetrator and the total innocence of his "victim" may thus fail to reflect the reality. Second, there are offenses in which the victim and perpetrator are one and the same or, put differently, there are crimes devoid of victims. The drug addict, the alcoholic, the homosexual, the woman seeking an illegal abortion — all, at the very least, are willing victims, and the addict and alcoholic are perpetrators as well. The question then is: how should the victim as perpetrator be viewed? As victim (psychiatric view) or as perpetrator (legal conception)? Moreover, the very concept of crime without victims is a difficult one to integrate into any conventional conception of criminality.

Third, and most important, the reemergence of the victim as an entity worthy of study has led to demands that society do something to compensate him for the injury which he may have suffered. If society can spend a considerable amount of its resources in apprehending, convicting and incarcerating perpetrators, why should it not also be responsible for the losses sustained by innocent victims. The movement to some type of victim compensation scheme for victims of violent offenses is sweeping the country and much of the world. It is not unlikely that many states will have enacted some type of compensation law in the near future. The nature of such victim compensation systems and the problems raised by this issue are discussed in the articles which follow.

In an exceptionally provocative essay, Michael Fooner takes a look at some of the basic issues (and future controversies) arising out of the recent and publicly popular proposals for compensating the victims of violent crimes. In considering victim-compensation proposals, is compassion for the victim to be the basic guideline or the principle that a victim has a moral and legal "right" to compensation? Who is to be compensated — all victims or only those in financial need? If the latter, how is such need to be assessed? Finally, should the offender be obligated to help share or fully pay the compensation? Victim compensation proposals also raise some additional and equally vexing problems. What if the victim instigates the crime against himself? Who, then is responsible? Suppose, also, that a severely injured person reports a mugging, robbery or aggravated assault and the police cannot find a suspect or be certain that the man was, in fact, a victim of a crime. Is he entitled to compensation? Finally, will a system of victim compensation materially increase the temptation opportunity pattern in victim behavior comparable to carelessness in property crimes? These are indisputably questions of substance and the author's treatment of them makes "Victim-induced Criminality" a timely and important paper.

The second selection, "Compensation to Victims of Crimes of Personal Violence," addresses itself to the solutions offered to many of the questions posed in the Fooner article. J. Ll. J. Edwards compares and contrasts the two pioneering schemes of victim compensation as they function in New Zealand and Great Britain. The operation of these laws is discussed in terms of the types of criminal acts for which compensation may be given, the degree of responsibility attributable to the victim, the basis of the compensation awardable, the characteristics of the victims in Britain whose cases came before the compensation agency, and the procedures in determining compensation eligibility and recovery from the offender.

In the final selection, "The Correctional Rejuvenation of Restitution to Victims of Crime," Stephen Schafer is concerned not only with making the victim "whole again" through compensation but also in using restitution as a method for the reformation of the offender.

The essay briefly reviews the divergence of civil and criminal law on the matters of punishment and restitution. In tracing the history of "composition," the medieval ancestor of the idea of restitution to victim, the point is made that "composition" was deflected into our system of fines, particularly in minor offenses, rather than into compensation for the victim. In the criminal law itself, despite this early principle of compensation, the victim continues to be habitually forgotten.

Modern compensation proposals are seen as largely unsatisfactory, though an improvement over the present state of affairs. They are unsatisfactory because the state and not the perpetrator retains responsibility for repairing the damage intentionally caused the victim. Instead, compensation systems should include some consideration of the correctional value in having the offender make restitution to his victim. The essay considers the problems involved in implementing this principle of restitution as a vehicle for reformation and correction. Schafer concludes that one possible way to serve both needs — the compensation to the victim and the reformation of the offender — would be to compel the offender to make restitution as an integral part of the sentence.

VICTIM-INDUCED CRIMINALITY*

MICHAEL FOONER

Proposals for compensating victims of violent crime are gaining widespread support in the United States, but studies analyzing the behavior of victims suggest that legislators should be alert to the possibilities that some compensation schemes may contribute to the growth of crime and add unwarranted complications to the administration of criminal justice.

The history of crime and punishment in the whole civilized world reveals a steadily increasing concern with the treatment of the criminal, and a virtual blackout of attention to the situation of the victim. For more than 1000 years prior to the mid-20th century, the victim of crime in our society — and in the administration of justice — has been ignored.

In the past decade, however, a new line of interest has opened up. The victim has been "discovered," and there are signs of change. Victims, it is being said, are also human; they bleed and suffer; their children and spouses may be deprived of the breadwinner's support.

New Zealand, Britain, California, and New York City have already installed victim-compensation systems and are paying out public money. Many other jurisdictions here and abroad are drafting such legislation.

Most people approve the humanitarian motivation of victim-compensation proposals. But there is a serious degree of uncertainty — even a degree of confusion in some quarters — about the specific objectives and proper functioning of the compensation-for-victims concept.

Whereas Britain seems to emphasize loss of earnings, California emphasizes need, plus young dependent children. Although hailed as a "pioneer" in concern for unfortunate victims of violent crime, California makes them ineligible for compensation if they are unmarried individuals, childless married couples, elderly people, or individuals unable to pass a public-welfare needs test.

Uncertainty about objectives is matched by uncertainty about costs. Legislators thus far seem not to have concentrated on this aspect of the matter. Notable generosity sometimes is advocated by public officials, but usually with reference to particular cases that receive extensive publicity.

* Reprinted with permission from Michael Fooner, "Victim-Induced Criminality," Science, CLIII (September 1966), 1080–1083. Copyright 1966 by the American Association for the Advancement of Science.

The California legislature, however, disposed of this uncertainty through the simple expedient of setting a ceiling — a maximum of $100,000 for claims in the first half year. Meanwhile, the British Criminal Injuries Compensation Board reported it had made 282 awards totaling $232,000 in its first 11 months of activity. The first award made under a New York City law was $4200 per year to a murder victim's widow; with her life expectancy assumed to be 50 years, this represents over $200,000 to one person.

It seems evident that evaluation of proposals for victim compensation will require consideration of a rather wide spectrum of questions, and that legislators at present have little information on which to base answers. Probably, considerable research is needed on the following points. Is one to be guided solely by considerations of compassion, or does the victim have a "right" to compensation? Should all victims receive compensation, or only those who are in financial straits? How is a victim's financial need to be measured? If a victim is to be compensated, should the offender in some way have, or share, the obligation to pay?

For example, from certain points of view compensation might be regarded as a moral and even legal right of the victim. This might be based on the "state duty" theory, which holds that society has a duty to protect its citizens from crime, that occurrence of a crime represents society's failure in the performance of that duty, and that this failure entitles the victim of the crime to a compensatory payment, usually in money.

Moral and legal right might also be established on the "wheel of fortune" theory, based on the assertion that crime is an inherent hazard of our society; that it inevitably falls upon someone, though the particular victim may be "selected" by chance; and that the individual, as victim, should not have to bear his misfortune alone. Under this theory, compensation is a mechanism by which lucky members of society "make it up" to the ones who are unlucky.

If the social insurance route is chosen, government declares by fiat that crime, like unemployment and old age, is an "insurable hazard" of its citizens; it would collect contributions from them through its taxing powers, and devise a scale of benefits.

In contrast to the "right to compensation" concept is the "social welfare" theory, which holds that society ameliorates the distress of its members not as a "right" but as "social policy," if they become widowed, orphaned, or indigent. Victims of crime would be added to the lists of individuals eligible for relief payments under existing state or local welfare systems.

Another approach is more specialized, providing compensation for those harmed when attempting to protect their fellow citizens from criminals, or when cooperating with police. For example, the New York City law which grew out of the strongly publicized case of a man killed when going to the aid of two women being molested in the subway provides a pension for the widow similar to that given one whose husband was a policeman killed in the line of duty.

There are, of course, certain philosophical issues, such as that raised by G. O. W. Mueller when he suggests, by way of illustration, that compensation for the family of a murdered man is not socially defensible unless society at the same time provides compensation for a family whose breadwinner is killed by lightning.

Would the administration of criminal justice be seriously affected by proposed systems of victim compensation? If there were no cases other than those in which the victim is clearly an innocent recipient of injury or death at the hands of a criminal, the matter would be simple. But in crimes where there is conflicting testimony, or where there is no credible witness or no apprehended suspect, how should the victim's claim for compensation be adjudicated? How can it be decided whether the injury was caused by an assault, or by an argument, or by a fall due to drunkenness? How can the victim's trial testimony be evaluated if victim compensation is a factor in the case? Standards will have to be developed after careful criminological research.

In summary, there are certain issues that need to be dealt with if a coherent system of victim compensation is to be created.

1) Is the victim's entitlement to compensation qualified by his behavior in connection with the crime?
2) Is the victim's entitlement to compensation on the basis of indigency to be qualified by the requirement that an offender be apprehended and his guilt determined by a court?
3) To what extent will a particular proposal for victim compensation contribute to a temptation-opportunity pattern in victim behavior?

It would seem, therefore, that we can draw the following conclusions:

(1) If "society should assume some responsibility for making the victim whole," it should also require victim behavior that will diminish the number of temptation-opportunity situations for offenders. Such behavior could be encouraged through educational programs on citizen defenses against criminality, plus legislative provisions which make victim compensation contingent upon the victim's actions not being contributory to the crime. Similar standards of behavior might be studied for adaptation to casualty insurance practices. The new practices would either be adopted voluntarily or imposed through legislation.

(2) The experience of insurance companies probably offers considerable material for study of the victim-compensation problem. Among other things, there is a seeming paradox: if the beneficiary of a life insurance policy causes the death of the insured the claim will not be paid, but with burglary insurance an individual can be careless or imprudent to the point of "inviting" theft and still be compensated for a loss. "Insured" thefts seem to be a law-

enforcement problem of growing significance. The relationships between compensation and carelessness and between carelessness and criminal incentives need to be studied for guidance in creating a workable victim-compensation system.

(3) Provisions for compensation of the citizen injured while assisting a law officer or while, on his own initiative, restraining an offender can be administered effectively only if standards of citizen behavior are carefully defined. Payment of compensation must be on such a basis as to discourage the vigilante and the busybody. A large-scale educational effort would have to be conducted, so that citizens would know their obligations and rights.

COMPENSATION TO VICTIMS OF CRIMES OF PERSONAL VIOLENCE*

J. Ll. J. EDWARDS

In its first Report to Parliament, tabled in October 1965, the British Criminal Injuries Commission Board declared: "The need in the modern state for a scheme for the compensation of victims of crimes of violence has been well shown even during the few months of the running of this scheme. It is true that many of the applications submitted relate to comparatively minor injuries and the compensation paid is correspondingly small. But no one who is called to deal with those cases in which a blameless victim has been seriously disabled, sometimes for life, or with those cases in which the elderly and infirm have suffered injury and shock, can fail to feel deeply what a worthwhile part is played in the full administration of justice by the power to award compensation."

The current surge of concern for the innocent victim of a violent crime, which is evident in the various studies that have been set in motion in recent months in New York, New Jersey, Michigan, Pennsylvania, Maryland and other parts of the United States is, in itself, an interesting phenomenon. Not for the first time in the field of social legislation, New Zealand has shown the way and provided the necessary leadership by drawing attention to the yawning gap in the law of nearly every civilised country so far as providing some form of compensation for the victims of crime is concerned. In some ways our Anglo-Saxon forbears were more advanced in their laws than our

* Reprinted with permission from *Federal Probation*, XXX, No. 2 (June 1966), 3–10.

modern criminal legislation, providing as they did appropriate forms of sanction for wrongdoing by the exaction of bot and wergild in the form of monetary compensation to the victim or his family. Hebrew law, as reflected in the Book of Exodus, and the Salic law of the Franks, provide additional testimony as to the wide resort in early Western culture to the notion of crime compensation.

Basic to each of these early precedents was the requirement that the offender himself should make reparation to the victim of his misdeeds, a principle that modern states have been all too prone to ignore in the development of their penal systems. Such a requirement represents one of the more notable differences between the British and New Zealand schemes as originally formulated. It is significant, however, that in the British Government's most recent White Paper on "The Adult Offender" the view is reiterated that an eventual solution to the problem of providing work for prisoners "may be a system under which prisoners received normal wages, out of which they contribute to their own support and that of their families, and perhaps also to the cost of compensating their victims."

The accumulative body of experience that has been gained in Britain and New Zealand in administering their respective schemes may be of value to those states which are contemplating a similar development in their own jurisdictions. It is proposed, therefore, to consider the important issues underlying a state system of victim compensation by examining the statutory and administrative principles applied in these two countries and adopted by many other jurisdictions that have revealed their own legislative proposals.

1. Boundaries of criminal acts within which compensation may be awarded.

Although much of the theoretical discussion in the United States during the past few years has centered on the astronomical costs of compensating victims for damage to property, it is important to note that neither of the existing schemes in New Zealand and Britain makes any provision for reparation in such circumstances. Two notable aspects, however, distinguish the approach adopted by the respective countries. First, New Zealand law provides for compensation in the event of a person being killed by any act or omission of another person which falls within a list of crimes enumerated in a schedule to the Criminal Injuries Compensation Act, 1963. The British scheme is more flexible and makes no reference to any specified crimes. Instead, it provides the simple criterion that compensation is recoverable where personal injury is directly attributable to a criminal offence. Secondly, the British scheme makes an important extension to the customary doctrine of victim compensation by also providing reparation to any person who suffers personal injury (1) in the course of arresting or attempting to arrest a suspected offender, (2) in the course of preventing or attempting to prevent an offence from being committed, or (3) in giving help to a police officer who is engaged in arresting an offender or in preventing the commission of an offence. No power exists to reward a public spirited citizen simply for assisting the police, but if he is injured in doing so then the state assumes an obligation to compensate him for any loss that he might sustain as a result of his volunteering help to maintain law and order.

2. Relevance of the victim's own behaviour in contributing to the injuries inflicted upon him.

The extent to which victims of crimes of violence contribute to the situation by their own actions or words has already proved to be a fruitful area of criminological research. Recognition of this kind of situation, by no means unknown to the criminal courts, is made explicit in both schemes. Thus, the New Zealand statute requires its Compensation Tribunal, when determining whether to make an award and also in deciding the amount to be awarded, to have regard to any behaviour of the victim which directly or indirectly contributed to his injury or death. The British scheme adopts the same approach and requires the Board to reduce the amount of compensation, or to reject the claim altogether, in accordance with its assessment of the degree of responsibility attributable to the victim.

3. Basis of the compensation awardable.

The British scheme, it is important to notice, enables the Compensation Board to make an award to a victim whether or not the offender has been brought to justice. What is required is that the circumstances of the injury shall have been reported to the police without delay or have been the subject of criminal proceedings in the courts. The award of compensation is not made dependent on a finding of guilt. This is surely right, if only in view of the technicalities of the criminal law and the underlying philosophy of the entire scheme which is to compensate for the injury suffered provided the bona fide nature of the claim is established. An additional safeguard is the requirement that an applicant must be prepared to submit to such medical examination as the Compensation Board may require. Apart from these general safeguards the only prerequisite condition is the necessity of establishing that the degree of injury suffered was "appreciable." This is interpreted to mean an injury that results in at least 3 weeks loss of earnings or an injury for which $150 would be the minimum amount of compensation.

The New Zealand Criminal Injuries Compensation Act, 1963, follows much the same lines. In particular, section 17(6) states that the Tribunal may make an award "whether or not any person is prosecuted for, or convicted of, any offence arising out of the (criminal) act or omission." The standard of proof in establishing that the injury resulted from a criminal act is the "balance of probabilities" criterion, familiar to litigants who bring their cases before the civil courts. Unlike the British scheme, the New Zealand legislation spells out the matters which are compensatable. These include: (a) expenses actually and reasonably incurred, (b) pecuniary loss to the victim as a result of total or partial incapacity for work, or pecuniary loss to the dependents of a victim who is killed, (c) pain and suffering, and (d) any other expenses which, in the opinion of the Tribunal, it is reasonable to incur.

4. Amount of compensation payable.

It is interesting to note that upper limits of compensation are laid down in the New Zealand legislation, in sharp contrast to the British scheme which places no restrictions on the discretionary powers of the Compensation Board. During the first year's operation of the New Zealand legislation seven applications only were received by the Crimes Compensation Tribunal. Of these, three cases concerned women who were attacked by an intruder when alone at home, the remainder being male victims of criminal attacks. The total amount awarded as compensation for the first full year was 9,600 dollars composed, in each case, of lump payments. This mode of payment is discretionary, the other procedure envisaged by the New Zealand Act, where there has been total or partial incapacity for work, is the making of periodical payments up to a maximum period of 6 years. Additional sums are provided for the wife of a victim and any dependent children up to 18 years who are engaged in a full-time course of education or training. For any other pecuniary loss or expenses the ceiling is set at $3,000, and up to an additional $1,500 may be awarded for pain and suffering.

Compensation, under the British scheme, is expressly assessed on the basis of common law damages for personal injuries and, other than in exceptional circumstances, a lump sum payment is made. The principle of a periodical pension, as provided for in the New Zealand system is not recognised in Britain, but more than one payment may be made, for example, where only a provisional medical assessment can be given at the time of the original application.

The first report of the British Criminal Injuries Compensation Board contains a great deal of interesting information on the working of the experimental scheme, which has already established itself as an essential part of the country's machinery of criminal justice. "So far" says the Report "we have had very few claims indeed which give rise to a suspicion of fraud." Of the 2,216 cases dealt with up to December 31, 1965, compensation has been awarded in 890 cases. Applications were disallowed in 138 cases and an additional 19 applicants withdrew or abandoned their claims. The remainder are still being processed. The vast majority of awards did not exceed $600 in individual cases, though a few reached a figure falling within the range $6,000 to $9,000. In only one case did the compensation exceed $15,000. This was a Scottish case in which the widow of a man stabbed to death in the street received $3,000, and his four children a total of $13,500.

During the period covered by the Board's first report, viz., the 8 months from September 1964 to April 1965, a total of just over $100,000 was paid out in compensation. This modest sum was explained as being attributable to the high proportion of straightforward cases involving comparatively minor injuries, which could be processed quickly. As an informed guess the British Board estimates that its payments of compensation during 1965–1966 may be in the region of $1,500,000.

Around 1,500 completed applications are expected in the current year, a steady rise being noticeable once the existence of the scheme became known to the public. The Board's policy of issuing monthly press releases, including case summaries of some of the successful and unsuccessful applications, has served a variety of useful purposes. It has generated a considerable number of informal editorials and newspaper articles, it has served to convince the sceptics of the justice of the scheme, and, perhaps above all, it has brought home to the general public that long overlooked side of the enforcement of the criminal law, namely, the fate of the victim after sentence has been passed on the offender and the drama of the trial is over. In the latest press release which brings the Board's experience up to December 31, 1965, the expected increase in the number of applications, and the total compensation paid, is strikingly evidenced. The total figure of $100,000 in compensation noted at the end of April 1965 had risen to $913,000 by the end of the year.

5. Characteristics of the victims of crimes of violence.

In preparing this article, an analysis was carried out of a sample of 391 cases drawn from the cases reported by the British Criminal Injuries Compensation Board during the first 17 months of its operation. Some of the findings may be of particular interest to those contemplating the introduction of legislation along the lines of the British scheme.

Sex and age of victims. — Males comprised 78.5 percent of the sample, females representing the balance of 21.5 percent.

The following table shows the percentage of victims falling within specified age groups:

Under 16	9.2%
17–30	35.8%
31–40	17.7%
41–50	15.1%
51–60	12.8%
61–87	9.0%

Place where the attack or injury occurred. — In about one-fifth of the cases reported, the place where the offence occurred was not reported. The remaining cases display the following pattern:

In the street	30.0%
Other public places, e.g., parks, shops, restaurants, car parks	11.7%
Place of employment	9.0%
Licensed premises or immediately outside	7.4%

Private premises	5.8%
On vehicle or premises of public transportation	5.4%
In victim's own home	5.1%
In social club or adjoining premises	1.8%
In an automobile	1.8%
On the highway	1.3%

Occupation of the victims. — It appears as if the occupation of the victim was noted in the Board's press releases in those instances only where the vulnerability of the offender was increased by reason of the nature of his employment. Thus, the occupations most frequently mentioned are as follows:

Police	7.9%
Public transport worker	3.1%
Service station attendant	2.0%
Post Office employee	1.8%
Caretaker, security guard	1.3%
Barman	1.0%
Lorry driver	.8%
Taxi driver	.8%

Special categories of victims. — Attention should be drawn to four special categories of victims, in view of the expanded nature of the British scheme to include those who are injured in the course of assisting in the task of law enforcement:

(a) Those who went to the assistance of other victims or potential victims and in the process were themselves injured. There were three cases of this kind in the sample and they received, respectively, compensation amounting to $850, $1,050, and $10,500.

(b) Those who were injured when attempting to arrest single-handedly. This group comprised three persons, the levels of compensation ranging from $220 to $800.

(c) Those who went to the assistance of the police. So far there appears to have been only one case of this kind, and he was awarded $3,450.

(d) Where the victim was a member of the police force, a category that could easily be overlooked when examining the theoretical framework of a scheme for victim compensation. At least 31 policemen have been awarded sums ranging from $100 to $11,000 with respect to injuries suffered in the execution of their duty.

6. The Compensation Board and its procedure.

Here again, a distinct difference in approach is manifest between the British and New Zealand schemes. In New Zealand, the Tribunal ranks as a Commission of Inquiry and is required to sit in public unless there are considerations, e.g., affecting the interests of public morality or the interests of the victim of an alleged sexual offence, which justify the hearing being conducted in private. The applicant can appear in person or be represented by his counsel or solicitor. Moreover, in every case the Tribunal is required to state the reasons for its decision.

Informality, on the other hand, may be said to be the key feature of the British scheme. Applications are sifted initially by the staff of the Compensation Board. In addition to describing the incident in which he was injured and the extent of his injuries and loss, the victim is required to sign an authority for the Board to obtain a copy of any statement he made to the police, medical reports from the hospital and the doctor from whom he received treatment, details of payments from his employers and public funds such as sickness or injury benefit. The initial decision whether to allow or dismiss the application and, if necessary, what amount of compensation should be payable, rests in the hands of a single member of the five-member Board. If not satisfied with the decision, the applicant can appeal and he is entitled to a hearing before three members of the Board, excluding the one who made the initial decision. The hearing is informal and in private. There are no set rules of procedure, the rules of evidence do not apply, and the victim is allowed to bring a friend or his legal adviser to assist him in putting his case.

In both Britain and New Zealand the administrative tribunal is entirely responsible for deciding what compensation should be paid in individual cases and their decisions are not subject to appeal or to Ministerial review. All five members of the British Board are legally qualified, but in New Zealand only the chairman is required to be a lawyer.

7. Recovery from the offender.

Earlier in this paper attention was drawn to the principle of personal reparation by the offender to the victim which was the foundation of early law. With the passage of time, however, the criminal law has been transformed to the point where the state assumes a pervasive role in every aspect of law enforcement, criminal adjudication, and in the subsequent handling of offenders. The victim occupies a prominent role only during the trial as an essential part of the prosecution's case against the accused. With the handing over of the offender to the state's appointed officials for administering its penal institutions and correctional services the victim's existence and problems are quickly forgotten. The time has come to seriously re-examine modern correctional philosophy in the light of the age-old theory of expiation by the criminal. Effective correctional handling of the offender may well be significantly advanced if the interests of the victim are accorded a more prominent place in the ultimate objective of changing the prisoner's attitude towards his neighbours in society. In the words of the notable White Paper "Penal Practice in a Changing Society":

It may well be that our penal system would not only provide a more effective deterrent to crime, but would also find a greater moral value, if the concept of personal reparation to the victim were added to the concepts of deterrence by punishment and of reform by training. It is also possible to hold that the redemptive value of punishment to the individual offender would be greater if it were made to include a realisation of the injury he had done to his victim as well as to the order of society, and the need to make personal reparation of that injury.

THE CORRECTIONAL REJUVENATION OF RESTITUTION TO VICTIMS OF CRIME*

STEPHEN SCHAFER

The conventional and obvious argument for restitution to victims of crime rests on the recognition of an obligation of compensation for some harm, injury or other disadvantage, caused by a criminal offense: an obligation of the offender who committed the wrong, and also perhaps another obligation of the society which failed to provide protection against the crime. A common misconception, based more or less on pity for the victim, suggests an understanding of restitution as virtually confined to the sphere of these obligations; this approach calls only for helping the victim to the reparation or remedy of the disadvantages which he suffered as a result of the offender's wrongdoing. This approach to restitution to victims of crime reduces its understanding to the concept of damages.

If one looks at the legal systems of different countries, one seeks in vain a country where a victim of crime enjoys a certain expectation of full restitution for his harm or injury. In the rare cases where there is any compensation system, it is either not fully effective, or it does not work at all; where there is no system of compensation, the victim is, in general, faced with the insufficient remedies offered by civil procedure and civil execution. While the punishment of crime is regarded as the concern of the state and thus receives official and public support, the crime as a damage to the victim is regarded almost as a private matter and, therefore nothing is done — an attitude reflecting official parsimony and public unconcern.

Apart from very rare attempts, the victim is excluded from the settlement

* Reprinted with permission from *Interdisciplinary Problems in Criminology: Papers of the American Society of Criminology*, 1964, edited by Walter C. Reckless and Charles L. Newman, Publication Service, The College of Commerce and Administration, The Ohio State University, Columbus, Ohio, 1965, pp. 156–67.

of the criminal case, although even in the presently practiced retributive penal systems his compensation could be a justified part of the punishment. Criminal justice applies punishment not only to deter the criminals of the future, but, in addition, in attempting the restoration of law and order to conciliate the disturbed society by the state's "bloodless" punishment of the guilty party. The individual victim is a part of the society, and for that reason criminal proceedings ought to be, in the last analysis, applied in the interest of this individual victim as well as in the interest of society as a whole. However, at present, the only satisfaction the individual victim may get from criminal justice is knowledge of the punishment inflicted upon the criminal.

The bridge leading to the emergence of state criminal law had as a support the system of "composition" that is the last stronghold of the private criminal law. The settlement of the amount of composition to be paid by periodic tribal assemblies provides an early example of judicial proceedings. There is more than a germ of truth in the suggestion that the "composition," the Medieval ancestor of the present-day restitution to victims of crime, was one of the fertilizers of the state criminal law; it soon was emasculated by that very law by being expelled from the penal system and left to the field of civil law. First, the monetary satisfaction was owed entirely to the victim or his family, and served as a requital of the injury, but as the central power in a community grew stronger, this financial satisfaction had to be shared with the official state (or overlord or king) as a commission for the "trouble in bringing about a reconciliation between the parties." This share gradually increased in favor of the community power, and finally, as the state fully monopolized the institution of punishment, so the rights of the injured were slowly separated from the penal law. Thus, composition, as the obligation to pay damages, became divorced from the criminal law and had to enter a special field in civil law. The victim then became the Cinderella of the criminal procedure.

If the state power sets a norm of conduct, it should, besides punishing breaches of this norm, see to it that where it is transgressed, a resulting injury is repaired. That restitution to victims of crime deserves a place in the settlement of the criminal case should be evident if only because, without the crime which is being tried, the victim would not have suffered the damage for which he seeks restitution.

To require the offender to pay money as a punishment is not something new and, in this sense, would not be strange to the administrators of criminal justice; after all, the origin of the present-day fine is the restitution or better, its ancestor, the composition. The only difference is that while the main point of composition was based on the enrichment of the victim and the community, which interposed itself between the wrongdoer and the vengeance of the victim, fines serve as a source of income for the state. As

Margery Fry pointed out: "To the offender's pocket it makes no difference whether what he has to pay is a fine, costs or compensation. But to his understanding of the nature of justice it may make a great deal."

Such considerations have led to the idea of state compensation based on fines. The ultimate aim of state compensation would be to guarantee that the victim gets his restitution. [But such a conception of] restitution would not aid the possible reform of the criminal; moreover it would perhaps exempt him beforehand and at state expense from an obligation which he ought to discharge.

In terms of a correctional rejuvenation of restitution to victims of crime, the offender should understand that he injured not only the state and law and order, but also the victim; in fact, primarily the victim and through this injury the abstract values of society. If so, the institution of restitution would not only make good, within limits, the injury or loss of the victim, but at the same time, help in the correction, reform and rehabilitation of the offender.

Research has been conducted in the State of Florida on an inmate population of 819 of those who were sentenced for criminal homicide (1st and 2nd degree murder), aggravated or other assault, or theft with violence (robbery or burglary), and were received in any Florida prison, prison camp or correctional institute in the period from July 1, 1962 to June 30, 1963. In none of the 819 cases was restitution or compensation made by the offender, and only in 88 cases were the inmates' positive or negative restitutive attitudes indicated; namely, in 19 criminal homicide, 22 aggravated assault and 47 violent theft cases.

[The Florida data] indicate that the overwhelming majority of those who committed a form of criminal homicide wish they could make some reparation of the wrong they committed. Among those who were sentenced for aggravated assault, a much smaller proportion (slightly over half), feel obliged to do something for their victim while the others suggested that their debt was only to the state. Among those who committed robbery or burglary, similarly only [slightly] more than half of the offenders accepted a sort of obligation to the victim of their crime, and the rest of them could not perceive any legal, moral, ethical or social link with other than the prison staff.

Some hold the view that punitive or correctional restitution should, in certain cases, completely replace punishment. One reason for this is that it would relieve the state of the burden of supporting in penal or correctional institutes those sentenced for minor offenses. Secondly, such a reduction in the number of inmates would enable individual methods to be used to better advantage on those committed to these institutes. To relieve the crowded state of penal institutions by substituting restitution for punishment, however, may lead to evading the problem of crime. While it appears to be reasonable to use correctional restitution as one method of the socialization of criminals, if that were to be the only sentenced consequence available for crime, it

217 | STEPHEN SCHAFER

217 | STEPHEN SCHAFER

might weaken the sense of wrongdoing attached to that crime, besides reducing the degree of socio-ethical reproach that the wrongdoer should feel. Also, it could lead to social injustice in that while the wealthy, possibly professional, criminal could buy his liberty, the financially poor, occasional criminal might eventually serve a longer term of punishment for a minor offense. If restitution could be substituted for punishment, or in any way make it possible to buy off correctional consequences with money, it might well have a reverse effect from that intended.

Correctional restitution may be distinguished from civil damages on this very point, that, while the latter are subject to compromise and are not in every case satisfied by the wrongdoer himself, restitution, like punishment, should always be the subject of judicial consideration in the criminal procedure. Correctional restitution is a part of the personal performance of the wrongdoer, and should even then be equally burdensome, reformative, and just for all criminals, irrespective of their means and crimes, whether they be millionaires or laborers, murderers or shoplifters.

The proposal that the offender should compensate by his own work for the damage he has caused, has been made more than once. Herbert Spencer suggested that prison work and the prisoner's income should be the means of making restitution, keeping the offender in prison until the damage was repaired. Garofalo suggested that where the offender was solvent, his property should be confiscated and restitution made therefrom by order of the court; while if he were insolvent, he should be made a state workman.

Yet another proposal tried to balance the burden of fines and restitution between the rich and poor. According to this proposal, a poor man would pay in days of work, a rich man by an equal number of days' income or salary. If $2.00 represented the value of a day's work, and the poor man were sentenced to pay $2.00, he would be discharged by giving one day's labor to the victim. The rich man, instead of being sentenced to give so many days of labor, would pay an equal number of days' income or salary, and if this represented, say $200 a day, he would have to pay accordingly.

However, if the offender were at liberty after he had served his punishment, but had to make restitution to his victim through his personal work, restitution would retain its reformative-corrective character, and could be regarded not as an extension but a part of the sentence.

8 | PROBLEMS OF LAW ENFORCEMENT

INTRODUCTION

The present turmoil concerning law enforcement and the operation of the criminal courts is so apparent that it needs little elaboration. The police accuse the public of apathy and the courts of interference with legitimate law enforcement procedures. Police spokesmen have been very outspoken about the "Warren Court" which, they contend, is more concerned with "protecting" the rights of criminals than of law-abiding citizens. On the other hand, minority groups claim that the police discriminate against them, support the status quo rather than law and order, and charge that the police often use needless force and brutality in making arrests. The poor police image, they contend, is well deserved. The conflict is sharply focused in such issues as civilian review boards to investigate complaints made against police, in the unwillingness of many Negroes to join the police force for fear of being labeled as "Uncle Toms," in the treatment of the police in the Negro press, and in police attitudes towards the lower-class Negro community. Almost any incident or even rumored incident is often sufficient to trigger the release of this hostility. It is ironic that a car bumper sticker which says "Support the Police" has become the symbol of this conflict between a substantial part of the public and the police.

The difficulties experienced by the police, their poor image, low salaries, problems in recruitment, concerns about professionalization, and relations with the courts are hardly new. The difference is perhaps one of degree, not kind. Americans have been inherently suspicious and fearful of police power and the disrespect for law enforcement is traditional in this country. Unlike firemen, who are viewed as helpful in times of dire stress, and other public servants, the public's contact with the police is almost always restricted to instances when the citizen has violated some sort of legal code. The performance of the police function irritates the violator and causes him to define the policeman as the enemy. It is therefore doubtful that the negative public image of the police can be totally reversed. Surely, however, it can and must be improved.

The courts, particularly the lower courts, are also in trouble. Dockets are long, procedure is cumbersome, and the setting hardly inspires confidence. To the indigent and friendless defendant, the procedure seems confusing, clumsy, and heartless. The "due process" guarantee is one thing in theory and another in practice. Every part of the procedure — from initial judicial appearance after arrest, the granting and setting of bail, the formal charge, arraignment, preparation for trial, the trial itself, and the imposition of sentence represents a hopelessly complicated and maze-like affair to the uninitiated. It is easy to become cowed by the procedure itself. On the other hand, the defendant of substance, well represented by counsel, is insulated against the more negative aspects of this experience. The system, because of its very complexity, can be legitimately used to delay, to bargain, and to move toward a more favorable outcome.

At the higher-court levels, recent decisions emphasizing and protecting the rights of the individual have come precisely at a time when the police and lower courts are already in trouble. The Escobedo, Gideon, and Miranda Supreme Court decisions have made the police and the lower courts even more defensive about their role, status, and operations.

The contributions in this chapter cover the area of law enforcement both in generalities and in specifics; analytically and polemically. In the first article, "The Social Control Role of the Police in Changing Urban Communities," Robert L. Derbyshire examines the problem of policing the inner city. Derbyshire argues that children in the slums are made aware of the policeman before they know the role of the teacher. For this reason, the policeman can be a critically positive influence in the neighborhood. The article concludes with six positive suggestions to lessen Negro-police conflict and to make the police more effective, and persuasive, agents of social control. The battle, he suggests, will be won when a middle-class mother is moved to say with pride, "My son the policeman."

On the same matter of police-Negro conflict, George Edwards, former Police Commissioner in Detroit and currently a Federal judge, offers some very concrete suggestions for reducing the hostility and improving the law-enforcement image and function in urban slum areas. Judge Edwards in "Order and Civil Liberties: A Complex Role for the Police," traces the policing problem to four sources — urbanization, recent Supreme Court decisions, the mass migration of Negroes, and the effect of the civil rights movement. Drawing on his own experience, he suggests fifteen measures — from the abolition of the "alley court," to ending investigative arrests, to the integration of police teams — as means of achieving impartial law enforcement and the deescalation of police-Negro hostility and conflict.

In an impassioned piece, "Improving the Law Enforcement Image," Michael J. Murphy lashes out at the apathy and uncooperativeness of the general public. In turn, this public apathy and the poor reputation of the police are traced to various distortions and smears of policemen and their role. Quite correctly, Murphy points out that police selection and training have markedly improved of late, especially in the large metropolitan areas. This upgrading, now and in the future, is vital if the policeman is to cope with the myriad of diverse problems — some old, many new — which daily confront him. Finally, and fundamentally, the population must be convinced that police authority is being wielded for the welfare and protection of the entire community.

The President's Commission on Law Enforcement and Administration of Justice was understandably concerned with the police and courts. Based on extensive research and expert testimony, the Commission offered a number of recommendations in all areas of the criminal and legal process. Two selected sets of recommendations — one concerning the police and the other the courts — are presented. Most of these recommendations are sensible and should be implemented as quickly as possible. A few, such as the policing proposal and one on the use of firearms by an officer, are worthy of very special consideration.

The recommendations concerning both substantive and, especially, procedural law hold few surprises. Of special importance, however, are the proposals for the unification of felony and misdemeanor courts, bail reform legislation, witness immunity statutes, the reexamination of sentencing provisions in state penal codes, the addition of court probation services when lacking, and the creation of assigned counsel and defender systems on a regular and statewide basis.

Stuart S. Nagel in "The Tipped Scales of American Justice" documents the disparities by social class, race, age, rural-urban location, and section of the country in the procedural steps from arrest through sentence. It is precisely these discrepancies which the recommendations of the President's Commission seek to minimize. The analysis is based on 1,949 state and 981 federal cases from all fifty states in 1962–63, in which the defendant was charged with either assault or larceny. The findings are particularly impressive with regard to how indigents and non-indigents fare for the same offense of either assault or larceny. Proportionately more indigents remained in jail by reason of failure to raise bail; their trials were delayed longer; they were less likely to have a grand jury indictment; and they were found guilty more often than the non-indigents. They were also less likely to be recommended for, or to receive, probation or a suspended sentence. This inferior treatment and outcome reflects inferior legal help. Providing skilled counsel is one way to even the scales. Clearly, in the legal realm, as elsewhere, differential life chances are associated with differential class and racial status. It is no easier to eradicate these inequities in the procedural legal system than in other social institutions.

The translation of the need for legal aid for those who cannot afford representation into some sort of system through which counsel can be obtained is the subject of the contribution by Junius L. Allison. In "Legal Aid for the Indigent Accused of Crime," Allison discusses legal-aid services in both the federal and state courts. There is an exposition of the strengths and weaknesses of the four principal methods — case-by-case court assignment, privately financed defenders, public defenders, and a mixed public-private system — used by the various jurisdictions in providing lawyers for indigent defendants. There is also some emphasis on the minimum standards to be met by the defender system of every state. Whatever the exact dimensions of the system which emerges, representation for the poor will surely improve in the future. The next major effort then, will be to insure that counsel will be "experienced, competent, and zealous" and have the investigatory facilities to conduct a complete defense.

The final selection, "Standards Relating to Fair Trial and Free Press," deals with two opposing and very important rights — of a free press to gather and disseminate news, and of a defendant to receive a fair, impartial and unprejudiced hearing of his case. Complete freedom in the news realm may jeopardize a fair trial; curtailment of press freedom may lead to star chamber proceedings and worse. There are good men and excellent arguments on both sides of the issue. Such, indeed, is the nature of social controversy. In this specific article, defense lawyers were questioned about the role of the press in creating a significant problem for the defendant. Most had handled cases in which such was the case. Press coverage given crimes in twenty metropolitan areas was analyzed for content. The results indicated that the pre-arrest, arrest-to-trial, during-trial, and after-verdict stages all had special problems in regard to press coverage. Most frequently it was the police spokesman or prosecutor whose injudicious statements to the press tended to weaken the defendant's case. In other words, the press was merely reporting what was said. Presumably, less loquacious officials might well prevent retrials and public prejudice in many cases. To balance the picture, the article concludes with a paean to the press for its potential and actual contributions at each step in the legal process.

THE SOCIAL CONTROL ROLE OF THE POLICE IN CHANGING URBAN COMMUNITIES*

ROBERT L. DERBYSHIRE

Public criticism of police and their tactics is a favorite American pastime. The validity of most police criticism is analogous to reprimanding a physician for not saving the life of one whose heart has been punctured by a bullet. In the case of the physician, there are biological and physiological forces determining the patient's expiration, over which the physician has little or no control. Similarly, policemen are exposed, in their battle against deviancy, to cultural, social, and psychological forces over which they have little or no control. Generally, these social forces are the political structure of the community, including the efficiency and reliability of elected and appointed officials; the patterns of coercion, leadership, and responsibility of and between police officials and political leaders; the capabilities, training and experience of policemen; the attitudes and behavior of citizens toward the police; and the particular conditions or set of circumstances under which these forces interact.

The urban condition is complex. Reciprocal relations between community and police present myriad problems. Police systems operate at an efficiency level commensurate with their ability and training, their status and salary and the community's attitude toward its own responsibility for social control. More recent problems illustrated by urban conflict in Northern cities during the summer of 1964 require a re-evaluation and re-examination of the social control role of police systems in these centers of culturally excluded citizens.

Social control among Homo sapiens is based upon custom. The system of social control consists of those mechanisms and techniques used to regulate the behavior of persons to meet societal goals and needs. All cultures provide adequate control over behavior. Controls are initiated either formally or informally. Informal controls usually start in the family and consist of orders, rebukes, criticisms, reprimands, ridicule, blame, gossip, praise, rewards, etc.

* Reprinted from *Excerpta Criminologica*, VI, No. 3 (May–June 1966), 315–21. By permission of the Excerpta Criminologica Foundation.

How an individual responds to informal and formal social control in the community frequently depends upon the consistency and certainty of these controls in his family experience while growing up. Most frequently, informal controls are used by primary groups. Primary affiliations require emotional reciprocity, therefore they are more subject to informal control.

Formal controls are those sanctions instituted by the body politic and its agencies. Since emotional attachment is seldom a part of secondary associations, laws, sanctions, and punishments are explicitly stated and theoretically apply to everyone, no matter what his position in the social structure. Schools, hospitals, welfare agencies, and the police are examples of secondary socializing agencies who use formal social control methods.

Social control systems operate most effectively and efficiently, the police notwithstanding, where there is constant and unified, both overt and covert, cultural and social support from all social control agencies. This support must be unambiguously stated in the value systems of families, community and the greater society of which the individual is a functional part.

Urban centers, particularly inner city areas, are the most difficult places to maintain overt behavior at a level acceptable to middle class standards. Frontier and farm towns need a sheriff more because of the transients than the town-folk. Sheriffs had the most trouble with the out-of-towners who lacked integration with the local community and who, with their anonymity, used Friday and Saturday nights as moral holidays. As towns became larger and centers for attracting transients, segments of the community became notorious for harboring persons with little integration in community life. Although most of the nation's population is essentially urban, the urban attitude is most pronounced in the inner city. The inner city or slum areas exemplify excessive amounts of personal, social, political, religious, family, and economic instability. A disproportionate amount of time is spent policing inner city areas.

Summer riots in Northern cities were not led by communists or any other organization, nor were they racial in nature, states the Federal Bureau of Investigation. Although these riots predominantly involved Negroes they were a product of conflicts in values and norms.

The ghettoized lower class Negro exists in a contra-culture, prone to deviancy from middle class values. Absent father households with matrifocal structures, insufficient skills for adequate employment opportunities, over-representation as welfare recipients, over-crowded and deteriorated inner city ghettos, education significantly lower and crime rates significantly higher than comparable white populations, ten times more out-of-wedlock births than whites and twice the Caucasian infant mortality rate, are social facts related to being a lower class Negro in the urban United States. There is a reciprocal relationship between these social facts, urban conflict and problems of the United States Negro's acceptance and assimilation into American culture.

Lack of social cohesion and integration is a major problem in areas of high mobility. Cohesion and integration are major social control devices. Secondary socializing agencies are most effective when cohesion and integration have existed, but for some reason have suddenly broken down. Evidence supports the fact that the police, social workers, courts and other secondary socializing agencies do their most effective work with persons who temporarily lack integration with the prevailing society, while they help the least those individuals who have rarely or never experienced cohesive and integrated community life.

Norm and social role conflicts are rampant in the inner city. Next door to a law abiding citizen who maintains conventional sexual and moral behavior, may live a sexually promiscuous person who has little respect for law, officials, property or others. Tremendous variations exist in religious beliefs, family systems and means of achieving and satisfying human relationships.

The increased impersonality of city life fosters individual freedom. This individualism is a peculiar type. Most inner city or slum persons pay lip service to their own individuality while simultaneously conforming to the expected behavior of those persons or segments of their associations applying the most pressure at any particular time. With these persons frequently there is a lack of intimacy, yet a need to conform to perceived wishes; this type of man has been termed by David Riesman as "other directed."

Primary socializing agencies are the immediate family, relatives by blood and marriage, age and sex peers, neighbors and others who aid persons, usually on a long term, face-to-face basis, with intimate contact, to learn culturally approved ways of controlling one's behavior. On the basis of present knowledge, it appears that social control is most effective when it is practiced at this level.

Secondary socializing agencies are those whose specific purpose is to aid in socialization or to re-socialize individuals whose primary agencies have for some reason become ineffective. The presently established secondary agents of social control are most effective as re-integrators and are less effective as substitutes for primary agents of social control.

The police, particularly for the inner city urban community, is the most important agency of social control. Historically police systems have been primarily concerned with coercive control. Coercive control which emanates from law and government agencies is accomplished by force or threat of force.

Power and authority are vested in the symbols of the uniform and badge and, if that is not enough, the spontoon, side arm and handcuffs take on functional elements of legal authority. Pillars of the middle class community feel safe with the knowledge that this type of control protects their neighborhoods, while lower class persons more frequently view the coercive powers of the police as a threat. There is every reason to believe that the coercive powers of the police are most effective with persons who have internalized controls over their behavior. In other words, coercive control is most effective with those who need it the least.

Coercive control is a necessary function for all police systems, but more important, particularly in urban centers, is the need for persuasive control functions of the police. Middle class youth who have the advantage of intact homes and adequate supervision seldom see a policeman except possibly directing traffic. Middle class citizens learn in school that "we should obey the laws" and "the policeman is our friend," but direct contact with him is seldom encountered. Little firsthand knowledge of behavior patterns associated with the police role exists in middle class culture.

On the other hand, in the inner city many youngsters observe the police more frequently than their own fathers or other important relatives. These same children lack much of the informal social controls taught by and expected of the middle class. Young persons in lower class communities see policemen breaking up family fights, taking drunks and derelicts off the street, raiding a prostitute's flat or a gambling house, picking up some of the local boys for interrogation, knocking on the door because a disturbance had been reported, breaking up a game of pitching coins or shooting dice on the street, checking locked doors of merchant neighbors, evicting slum residents, asking questions pertaining to rat control, transporting patients to mental hospitals, beating others and being beaten, taking bribes and arresting bribers, and numerous other behaviors associated with most police systems. It is within this context that the growing lower class child forms his impressions and develops attitudes toward the police. These attitudes are then transferred toward the larger adult world and its system of social control. Within this environment he gains his most purposive information about law, rights, duties, privileges, loyalties and many other items necessary for adulthood. Many of these are developed from impressions received from the policeman, one of the few representatives of the social control system with whom he has had direct contact.

In the lower class community the function of the police is integrated into the child's knowledge before he knows the role of teachers. More important for the policeman in inner city crime control is the role of persuasive control. Lower class youngsters need a stable, steady, friendly person with whom to identify, to help them understand that controlling their behavior is most effective and appropriate when it is controlled because one wants to do what significant persons in his life wish him to do and not because he is afraid of force if he doesn't control his behavior.

Effective persuasive control emanates from a particular type of policeman who has the personality, motivation, interest, time, training and the fortitude to work closely with slum families and other human beings. He should be specifically and adequately trained for this role and commensurately rewarded. An emulative image must be presented consistently so that children, adolescents, young and old adults alike will look to him for guidance in areas other than crime control.

Cities and states must pay adequate salaries, extend fringe benefits and provide professional pride and status to the degree that police departments can hire the type of men and women necessary to fulfill the role of future policemen. This new role should place greater emphasis upon crime prevention. Excellent persuasive control is good crime prevention. Certainly, knowledge of riot control and police tactics is essential to stopping riots and criminal activity after they start; this is a necessary coercive function of the policeman's social role. But, more important than stopping a crime is its prevention.

A number of suggestions for more effective social control over urban conflict during a period of rapid social change are: (1) More important than placing Negro policemen in Negro communities is to rid the police hiring procedures of discrimination. Hiring a man on the basis of his ability to meet specific criteria does more to increase the social status and image of the police in all Negro areas than "tokenism" as it has been practiced in the past. (2) The most highly educated and motivated, and those persons whose character is beyond reproach should be placed in inner city areas. These persons should seek out and identify indigenous leadership. Also, they should learn to communicate effectively with persons in the community. Knowledge of potential ignitors of tension and conflict is a necessary part of the police role. After identification of such persons, the policeman's duty is to seek a change in attitudes, to call in appropriate resocializing aid when necessary or at least to see that those persons who are potential agitators are immobilized during periods of high tension. In an area where stability is seldom evident, the policeman should be emotionally stable and a pattern of social stability must exist, in that turn-over of men on these assignments must be minimized. Inner city dwellers need some source of a stable predictable relationship; this the police can provide. (3) Raise the social status of the police by increasing the quality of men hired and requesting improvement programs for those who are already on the force. Education programs sponsored and promoted by law enforcement agencies in collaboration with behavioral scientists in universities [are] indispensable. State and local officials and police organizations must stop paying lip service to the need for responsible, educated policemen. Responsible, emotionally stable, well educated policemen will make more lasting contributions to crime prevention and control than many other measures already requested by responsible politicians. (4) The police image must be changed to such a degree that middle class mothers will say with pride, "my son the policeman." (5) Each policeman involved in learning this role must be aided to live with himself. That is, the dichotomy between persuasion and coercion is great, and frequently appears incompatible, therefore each law enforcement officer must learn to integrate both roles with as little discomfort as possible. (6) Discrimination toward Negroes and other minorities in areas of employment, housing, in fact in all areas, must cease. As long as it exists institutionally or socially, the American lower class ghettoized Negro is a potential for urban conflict. He is in this conflict-producing situation partly because he is Negro, but more, because he has the same American aspirations for achievement and success, but the social structure restricts this American's ability to obtain his goal.

ORDER AND CIVIL LIBERTIES: A COMPLEX ROLE FOR THE POLICE*

GEORGE EDWARDS

Judge Edwards' suggestions were put forth in 1965. Two years later Detroit, among other American cities, experienced severe racial disturbances. One wonders, naturally, whether putting his recommendations into practice might have averted the riots in Detroit and other cities, or whether their causes may not lie in other more profound inadequacies of our society's treatment of the Negro.—Eds.

The police function is in trouble in every section of our nation. This fact may be attributed to the impact of four historic trends: the increasing urbanization of our country; the increasing insistence of the United States Supreme Court on strict compliance by the police with the principles of the Bill of Rights; the vast and continuing migration of millions of Negro citizens, principally from southern rural areas to the great metropolitan centers; and the civil rights revolution of the 1960's which is seeking to establish within this decade full freedom and equality for all Negro citizens. I do not decry any of these trends, but it is quite evident that each of them imposes certain problems upon the metropolitan police function.

Social order has always been the basic function of every organized government. However, our American government, while plainly designed to preserve order, has also made the signal contribution to history of avowing as a governmental objective the achieving of individual liberty for its citizens. Thus, the policeman has the responsibility of reconciling these two objectives of order and freedom; in a large city, this is a complex task.

Freedom in a metropolitan area is entirely different from the freedom that was once enjoyed on the frontier. In relation to the man of the frontier, liberty could almost be defined as the right to do what one wished without hindrance. In a big city, however, liberty might be more accurately referred to as the maximum freedom of choice consistent with the maintenance of similar freedom for the other members of society.

* Reprinted with permission from *The Michigan Law Review*, LXIV, No. 1 (November 1965), 47–62.

At least partly from necessity — and frequently without recognizing what we have done — we have turned over to the police officers of our big cities many functions which used to be among the most important duties of the individual and the family. A modern policeman's tour of duty is full of radio runs which require him to correct the conduct of children, to mediate family quarrels to determine the right of way between over-eager drivers, to care for the injured on the streets, and to protect our homes at night and our persons in the daytime. All this is expected to be done with the concern of a social worker, the wisdom of a Solomon, and the prompt courage of a combat soldier. It is interesting to note that in our day when the parable of the Good Samaritan is re-enacted on a city street, almost invariably the modern Good Samaritan wears a blue coat.

For over a decade our Supreme Court has been engaged in leading this country toward making more effective the high ideals of our American Constitution. It has been setting ever higher standards of law enforcement; it has told us that equality before the law and the equal protection of the laws must be made realities of everyday life; it has told us that deprivation of human liberty is essentially a decision for the judiciary; it has told us that as far as the Constitution is concerned in the absence of probable cause or a judicial warrant, there is no such thing as a lawful arrest for investigation only; and it has told us that forced confessions are anathema to American law and that a citizen has a right to counsel in all felony prosecutions. Thus, it seems clear that the Constitution and the Supreme Court have ruled out of our system of law such old-fashioned police measures as dragnet arrests, detention for investigation only, and third-degree procurement of confessions. However, no matter how much we approve in general of the objectives just outlined, it must be recognized that they demand more intensive police training and increased police manpower.

The third tremendous change which has taken place in this nation and which has had a concomitant impact on law enforcement and social order has been the redistribution of millions of Negro citizens who have departed from the rural areas in the South. To some degree, this movement is still continuing. The problems which confront American cities as a result of this human migration were well summarized by one recent writer:

The solution is not, as so many assume, to bring the wandering middle class back from the suburbs. The large city . . . cannot import a middle class; it must manufacture its own. . . . Bringing people from society's backwaters into the mainstream of American life has always been the principal business, and the principal glory, of the American city. . . . It isn't any longer; the city is in trouble today because it isn't dealing successfully with its newcomers. They are still pouring in—not from County Cork, or Bavaria, or Sicily, or Galicia, but from Jackson, Mississippi, and Memphis, Tennessee, and a host of towns and hamlets with names like Sunflower, Rolling Fork, and Dyersburg. The new immigrants are distinguished from the older residents not by religion or national origin, but by color. Between 1950 and 1960 the twelve largest U. S. cities lost over two million white residents; they gained nearly two million Negro residents.

It is the explosive growth of their Negro populations, in fact, that constitutes the large cities' principal problem and concern.

In every one of our large cities, there are two other factors which should be obvious to any who will look. First, it is clear that the portion of our society with the greatest stake in effective, vigilant, and vigorous law enforcement is the Negro community. Although more crimes are committed by Negroes than whites in the core areas of our cities, Negroes also constitute a higher percentage of the victims than do whites. For example, eighty-four per cent of the assault victims in Washington, D.C., are Negroes. A study conducted in one of Detroit's precincts heavily populated with Negroes disclosed that although seventy-eight per cent of the identified assault offenders were Negroes, seventy-six per cent of the victims were also Negroes. Similarly, a 1963 survey undertaken in Dallas revealed that sixty-eight per cent of the persons arrested on suspicion of homicide were Negroes and that sixty-nine per cent of the victims were likewise of Negro extraction. Finally, in Philadelphia a five-year study of homicides indicated that all but 6.6 per cent of the crimes were committed by offenders belonging to the same race as the victim. With respect to the small number of interracial homicides, 2.7 per cent were committed by whites and 3.9 per cent by Negroes. Thus, it can be seen that, contrary to widely held beliefs about the nature of crime in the United States, Negroes are much more likely to be victims of crimes involving violence than are whites.

The second factor that deserves emphasis is that just as it is true that it is easy to police the better sections of the white-occupied portions of any city, so it is also far easier to police the better sections which are occupied by Negro residents. A good example of this exists in Detroit, where for approximately forty years a particular neighborhood has attracted Negro businessmen, lawyers, doctors, and skilled craftsmen, who have built homes and reared their children in a pleasant residential atmosphere. Indeed, this neighborhood — Conant Gardens — is known as one of the quietest areas in the entire city of Detroit. Thus, it should be evident that the notion that crime is a race problem is totally false. But wherever there has been discrimination, impoverishment, and denial of rights, automatically there will also be built-in problems in relation to social order.

The foregoing observations provide a background for a discussion of the fourth major influence upon the law enforcement function — the civil rights revolution of the 1960's. The local police should always be the representatives of the law; it is, therefore, a tragedy to have their energies diverted to defiance of the law, the Constitution, and the courts. It requires condemnation from every law-abiding citizen in this country. Episodes like those experienced in Birmingham and Selma, Alabama, and in Oxford and Neshoba County, Mississippi, add to the police problems in every section of the country. These episodes represent the most futile exhibitions of this century. There is no real question about whether such fundamental constitutional rights as equal education and equal voting will be granted to all citizens in this country; it is only a question as to when and how this result will be achieved. Equal treatment with respect to these essential rights is required by the basic religious concepts of the American people and is mandated by every aspect of our constitutional law.

Conflict between the police and the Negro people is deep-rooted in our history. The Negro citizen sees the police officer in blue coat, with a white face, as the representative of the white man's law, who for nearly 300 years has enforced the laws — first of slavery and more recently of legally sanctioned segregation. Similarly, the bitterness that has been demonstrated by Negro rioters may be the product of a long series of unforgettable personal experiences. For example, in the 1930's if a teenage Negro boy met a white police officer in the late afternoon on the streets of a town in eastern Texas near where I grew up, his first contact with the law would probably be the command: "Nigger, don't let the sun set on you in this town!" Thirty years later in a large northern city, the bitterness engendered by that memory could turn a Saturday night party that has become loud enough for a police call into a dangerous melee.

Feelings of hostility also exist on the other side of the conflict. Police officers have grown up in a tradition in which part of their historic function assigned by the community has been "keeping the Negro in his place." This history produces current attitudes which are illustrated by the great number of present-day police officers who invariably use the hated term "nigger" in talking about (and sometimes to) Negro citizens.

While I was Police Commissioner of Detroit during 1962 and 1963, we formulated a policy for the police department which was specifically designed to achieve these three goals. It provided: "We seek: (1) More law enforcement and more vigorous law enforcement. (2) Equal protection of the law for all law-abiding citizens; equal enforcement of the law against all law violators. (3) The support of law-abiding citizens for law enforcement." We posted this policy statement above the admitting desk in each of the precinct stations. I always thought that the mere statement of these very general principles was of real value, because they were read by both the men on the force and the general public. However, awareness of such a policy is only the initial phase; the real problem relates to the method of implementation. That is, how does one actually guarantee equal and effective law enforcement? The answer to this question is crucial to the task of ending the feelings of hostility, fear, and distrust which currently affect a major portion of the people in American cities. The following guidelines are offered as a means to this vital end.

First, it is essential to find the facts and face them. Unfortunately, this has not always been the practice. "The police officer is always right" is a familiar slogan in precinct station houses, and the temptation, regardless of the facts, to defend police conduct which violates the book of procedure and the law is a temptation to which many police officers are, by social pressure of their own ranks, quite inclined to yield.

However, facts are frequently misstated against the police as well as in their favor. The criminal arrested on the street almost invariably wants to find something on the policeman. The fact that he would lie to achieve this should surprise nobody. Therefore, some suspicion is justified in relation to almost anything that such a person may offer in mitigation or expiation of his conduct.

The second means suggested to achieve impartial and effective law enforcement involves knowing the community. The administrative branch of every police department should open and maintain lines of communication between the department and all sections of the community it serves. Particularly in this decade meaningful communication with the Negro community and its leaders is essential. Police administrators should always be available to meet with them, to exchange information, and to try earnestly to resolve problems. Furthermore, if the administrators are conscious of a problem, they should themselves initiate the discussion instead of waiting for someone else to call.

The administration of every police department should also make it known that it will not tolerate the institution commonly referred to in police circles as "alley court." No legal concept or constitutional theory sanctions the use of such disciplinary devices. Nevertheless, a few police officers are sincerely convinced that they are unable to maintain peace and order unless they are allowed to bolster their authority in the streets by the use of a fist or billy when they feel it is necessary. Our total society prohibits "alley court." Punishment is not the function of the police; their function is to detect and apprehend and bring into court for punishment.

"Alley court" is ordinarily used against minority groups. It is easy to see how such a practice can inflame the attitude of such a group — in this case the Negro population. It produces cries of "police brutality," and it deprives the police department of its most important weapon against crime — the support of the law-abiding populace residing in the core areas of our big cities. There are relatively few police officers who believe in "alley court"; they cannot be allowed to perpetuate an utterly indefensible institution.

The remaining suggestions designed to achieve impartial law enforcement do not require elaboration; I have therefore incorporated them into the following checklist:

1. Identify police troublemakers on the force and transfer them to non-critical jobs.

2. Ban "trigger words" in police action.

3. Enforce politeness in the giving of traffic tickets.
4. End investigative arrests.
5. Increase law enforcement in high-crime precincts.
6. Drive out organized crime and pay particular attention to its manifestations in the core areas.
7. Make certain that equal opportunity exists in all phases of department operation — recruitment, assignments, and promotion.
8. Ban the use of police dogs in core areas. A dog companion for a single patrolman on a lonely beat may be useful, but that same dog at a racial demonstration is a symbol of race hatred.
9. Integrate police teams — particularly details employed at racial demonstrations and "ready forces" employed to respond to street conflicts.
10. Seek more police officers.
11. Seek better training for police officers.
12. Seek better pay for police officers.

IMPROVING THE
LAW ENFORCEMENT IMAGE*

MICHAEL J. MURPHY

Improving the law enforcement image is a matter which, despite its Madison Avenue overtones, is of basic and vital concern in our nation today. It is not primarily the District Attorney's concern, it is not only the obligation of the courts. It is basically the obligation of the citizens of the community, collectively and individually.

Unfortunately, the true image of law enforcement — particularly as it applies to police in our nation — is being unfairly distorted and smeared today as never before in our history. At a time when the need for justice under law was never more apparent or necessary, those who enforce and administer the law find themselves the targets of ridicule and contempt. The serious consequences of this type of attack cannot be overestimated. It strikes at the very foundation of our democratic process and could, if successful, so weaken the structure of our government that the rights of all citizens to the pursuit of life and liberty would be jeopardized.

Although part of the distortion is being created by certain groups determined to weaken the democratic process, a greater proportion unconsciously

* Reprinted by special permission from *The Journal of Criminal Law, Criminology, and Police Science*, copyright © 1965 by Northwestern University School of Law, LVI, No. 1 (March 1965), 105–108.

emanates from a lack of knowledge of the role and attitude of law enforcement officers. In a way we are to blame for the latter, for a failure to drive home our message that the vast majority of men in the police and law enforcement professions are honest and devoted public servants, dedicated only to the public welfare.

The distortions become the smears. Sadly enough, those who are responsible for providing the material for the smears are the small number of men within the police ranks who have betrayed their trust out of greed, unconcern for their oath of office and the public welfare, and with cynical disregard for the fine records established by thousands and thousands of devoted police officers.

In these days we hear more and more reference to "the police image." This is but another term for the police reputation. The "image" is the outer reflection of the standing of the department based on its performance and service. It is the reaction which emanates from the public and which is based on the public's expression of confidence and respect in a police department or a lack of such confidence and respect.

To most people the policeman is part of the scenery; they see him but seldom have any dealings with him. Occasionally, a citizen is shocked by the intrusion of a policeman into what he regards as his private life — an intrusion he deeply resents — when stopped for jay walking or when given a summons for a traffic violation. For the most part, however, even at this point the policeman is regarded as a necessary but annoying part of the modern municipal picture.

Most conceptions, and misconceptions, of law enforcement are derived from motion pictures, television shows, and mystery stories. There have been many times, certainly, when law enforcement officials have gritted their teeth at the televised inadequacies of Mr. Hamilton Burger. Because of these fictional portrayals, the best thing any person can do is to forget what he has seen and heard and just start afresh. It should be pointed out that the Keystone Kop was just the figment of a film director's imagination; that the loud-mouthed, red-faced, fat bully in uniform — if he ever existed is a thing of the past. Even on the constructive side, the new, cleancut, clever sleuth of the television crime series is a streamlined and over-simplified portrayal of the modern detective. Yet the myths persist, and the over-dramatized portrayal of the past, plus the few misfits of the present, have succeeded in cruelly smearing the ordinary policeman, in fact the entire police service. The misdeeds of one policeman stains all policemen. No other group in civil service or industry carries the shame of a member longer and strives so earnestly to win back the loss in public confidence such an act causes.

The accent in the New York Police Department and in most departments throughout the United States, has been more and more on selection and training. To become a policeman in this city involves much more than merely passing a physical and civil service mental examination. It means surviving one of the most intensive character investigations given by any governmental agency, an investigation which generally takes at least three months and which probes the police applicant's background from the date of his birth through his last position. It is in this process that most men deemed unqualified to become New York policemen are dropped. The department accepts about one man in twelve, and this is one of the reasons for the recruitment problem which constantly faces the Police Department. But despite this, the standards of this department will not be lowered.

Once accepted, the police rookie undergoes a thorough training at the Police Academy which is of four months' duration, and which earns him ten college credits towards a degree in Police Science. After graduation and through the program conducted jointly with the Baruch School of City College, he can continue his college education when not on duty. His courses are geared so as not to conflict with his working hours. At least 552 men have earned associate, bachelors, and masters degrees and about 1,200 others are now attending such courses. This is all part of the department's program to bring a professional viewpoint to police work. During his Academy training period, the recruit learns more than merely the police rules and regulations. He is drilled in the law, in civil rights, and in human relations. He is taught to understand people for he deals only in people, and he cannot help but wonder why people do not understand him.

The policeman of today is confronted with scores of new problems; problems his police ancestors never heard of, and were not trained to handle. The police officer of fifty years ago had little vehicle traffic to contend with, never heard of juvenile delinquency or narcotics, knew nothing about demonstrations, and would be shocked at the disrespect and flouting of the law which is so prevalent these days, not only in New York but throughout the nation.

The foot patrolman is responsible for all conditions on his beat, and only a few are listed to try to give an idea as to the extent of his responsibility. He must keep an eye out for known criminals, for known gamblers, for suspicious persons, for lost and mentally ill persons, for truants, for wayward minors, for youth gangs, for youths on bridges or highways or railroad overpasses, for loiterers, known degenerates, prostitutes, and dissolute persons. He must keep his other eye on fire alarm boxes to prevent false alarms; on areaways and alleys; on business places after closing hours; on vacant lots; on sidewalks and gutters to see that they are clean and that snow is removed; on banks, particularly at opening and closing hours; on schools to prevent vandalism; and on playgrounds where conflicts might occur. He must be on the lookout for dangerous conditions, such as holes in the streets; abandoned refrigerators; for dangerous or weakened signs of building cornices; for street lights, to see that they are working; for parking meters, to see whether they have been damaged or broken. He is also responsible for enforcing the laws against unnecessary noise, on the ordinances pertaining to air pollution and violations of the Health and Administrative Codes. He must notify the station house if there are any dead animals on his post or any abandoned automobiles. And he is responsible for enforcement of all traffic regulations. In between times, he must be aware of everything else that is going on in his area and be ever alert for a call for help.

He does this all within his eight-hour day, with an hour off for lunch, and he does it around the clock. For this, he starts at $6,355 a year and gets $7,806 after three years. Even when off duty, he is still held accountable as a policeman, both in his own behavior and in his official capacity. He is required to take action when off duty if he sees a crime committed and must carry his revolver whenever he leaves his house. He is, in effect, on duty twenty-four hours a day.

THE POLICE:
SELECTED RECOMMENDATIONS*

The police should formally participate in community planning in all cities.

Police departments in all large communities should have community-relations machinery consisting of a headquarters unit that plans and supervises the department's community-relations programs. It should also have precinct units, responsible to the precinct commander, that carry out the programs. Community relations must be both a staff and a line function. Such machinery is a matter of the greatest importance in any community that has a substantial minority population.

In each police precinct in a minority-group neighborhood there should be a citizens' advisory committee that meets regularly with police officials to work out solutions to problems of conflict between the police and the community. It is crucial that the committees be broadly representative of the community as a whole, including those elements who are critical or aggrieved.

It should be a high-priority objective of all departments in communities with a substantial minority population to recruit minority-group officers, and to deploy and promote them fairly. Every officer in such departments should receive thorough grounding in community-relations subjects. His performance in the field of community relations should be periodically reviewed and evaluated.

* Reprinted from *The Challenge of Crime in a Free Society: A Report by the President's Commission on Law Enforcement and Administration of Justice* (Washington, D.C.: Government Printing Office, 1967), pp. 99–122.

Every jurisdiction should provide adequate procedures for full and fair processing of all citizen grievances and complaints about the conduct of any public officer or employee.

Basic police functions, especially in large and medium sized urban departments, should be divided among three kinds of officers, here termed the "community service officer," the "police officer," and the "police agents."

Police departments should recruit far more actively than they now do, with special attention to college campuses and inner city neighborhoods.

The ultimate aim of all police departments should be that all personnel with general enforcement powers have baccalaureate degrees.

Police departments and civil service commissions should reexamine and, if necessary, modify present recruitment standards on age, height, weight, visual acuity, and prior residence. The appointing authority should place primary emphasis on the education, background, character and personality of a candidate for police service.

Police salaries must be raised, particularly by increasing maximums. In order to attract college graduates to police service, starting and maximum salaries must be competitive with other professions and occupations that seek the same graduates.

Promotion eligibility requirements should stress ability above seniority. Promotion "lists" should be compiled on the basis not only of scores on technical examinations but on prior performance, character, educational achievement and leadership potential.

Formal police training programs for recruits in all departments, large and small, should consist of an absolute minimum of 400 hours of classroom work spread over a 4- to 6-month period so that it can be combined with carefully selected and supervised field training.

Every general enforcement officer should have at least 1 week of intensive inservice training a year. Every officer should be given incentives to continue his general education or acquire special skills outside his department.

Each State, through its commission on police standards, should provide financial and technical assistance to departments to conduct surveys and make recommendations for improvement and modernization of their organization, management, and operations.

Police departments should commence experimentation with a team policing concept that envisions those with patrol and investigative duties combining under unified command with flexible assignments to deal with the crime problems in a defined sector.

A comprehensive regulation should be formulated by every chief administrator to reflect the basic policy that firearms may be used only when the officer believes his life or the life of another is in imminent danger, or when other reasonable means of apprehension have failed to prevent the escape of a felony suspect whom the officer believes presents a serious danger to others.

Specialized personnel from State or metropolitan departments should assist smaller departments in each metropolitan area on major investigations and in specialized law enforcement functions.

THE COURTS:
SELECTED RECOMMENDATIONS*

Felony and misdemeanor courts and their ancillary agencies — prosecutors, defenders, and probation services — should be unified.

As an immediate step to meet the needs of the lower courts, the judicial manpower of these courts should be increased and their physical facilities should be improved so that these courts will be able to cope with the volume of cases coming before them in a dignified and deliberate way.

Prosecutors, probation officers, and defense counsel should be provided in courts where these officers are not found, or their numbers are insufficient.

The States and Federal Government should enact legislation to abolish or overhaul the justice of the peace and U.S. commissioner systems.

Each State should enact comprehensive bail reform legislation after the pattern set by the Federal Bail Reform Act of 1966.

Each community should establish procedures to enable and encourage police departments to release, in appropriate classes of cases, as many arrested persons as possible promptly after arrest upon issuance of a citation or summons requiring subsequent appearance.

Prosecutors should endeavor to make discriminating charge decisions, assuring that offenders who merit criminal sanctions are not released and that other offenders are either released or diverted to noncriminal methods of treatment and control by:

Establishment of explicit policies for the dismissal or informal disposition of the cases of certain marginal offenders.

Early identification and diversion to other community resources of those offenders in need of treatment, for whom full criminal disposition does not appear required.

Police, prosecutors, bar associations, and courts should issue regulations and standards as to the kinds of information that properly may be released to the news media about pending criminal cases by police officers, prosecutors,

* Reprinted from *The Challenge of Crime in a Free Society: A Report by the President's Commission on Law Enforcement and Administration of Justice* (Washington, D.C.: Government Printing Office, 1967), pp. 129–57.

and defense counsel. These regulations and standards should be designed to minimize prejudicial statements by the media before or during trial, while safeguarding legitimate reporting on matters of public interest.

A general witness immunity statute should be enacted at Federal and State levels, providing immunity sufficiently broad to assure compulsion of testimony. Immunity should be granted only with the prior approval of the jurisdiction's chief prosecuting officer. Efforts to coordinate Federal, State, and local immunity grants should be made to prevent interference with concurrent investigations.

States should reexamine the sentencing provisions of their penal codes with a view to simplifying the grading of offenses, and to removing mandatory minimum prison terms, long maximum prison terms, and ineligibility for probation and parole. In cases of persistent habitual offenders or dangerous criminals, judges should have express authority to impose extended prison terms. Sentencing codes should include criteria designed to help judges exercise their discretion in accordance with clearly stated standards.

The question whether capital punishment is an appropriate sanction is a policy decision to be made by each State. Where it is retained, the types of offenses for which it is available should be strictly limited, and the law should be enforced in an evenhanded and nondiscriminatory manner, with procedures for review of death sentences that are fair and expeditious. When a State finds that it cannot administer the penalty in such a manner, or that the death penalty is being imposed but not carried into effect, the penalty should be abandoned.

All courts, felony and misdemeanor, should have probation services. Standards for the recruitment and training of probation officers should be set by the States, and the funds necessary to implement this recommendation should be provided by the States to those local courts that cannot finance probation services for themselves. All courts should require presentence reports for all offenders, whether those reports result from full field investigations by probation officers or, in the case of minor offenders, from the use of short forms.

Every State should organize and finance regular judicial institutes or conferences at which judges meet with other judges and with correctional authorities to discuss sentencing standards and learn about available correctional programs and facilities.

Jury sentencing in noncapital cases should be abolished.

Judicial tenure in major trial courts should be for a term of 10 years or more, with appropriate provisions to facilitate retirement of judges at a predetermined age.

Localities should revise salary structures so that district attorneys and assistants devote full time to their office without outside practice. The effort should be to raise the quality of the office so that highly talented lawyers will seek it. In smaller jurisdictions, where the caseload does not justify a full-time criminal prosecutor, consideration should be given to use of prosecutors representing larger districts, in place of county or town attorneys. Assistants should be hired on a nonpartisan basis.

The Federal Government, States, and district attorneys' offices, with assistance from law schools and professional organizations, should develop curricula and programs for the preservice and inservice training of prosecutors and should require the broadest possible participation in such programs by prosecutors.

The objective to be met as quickly as possible is to provide counsel to every criminal defendant who faces a significant penalty, if he cannot afford to provide counsel himself. This should apply to cases classified as misdemeanors as well as to those classified as felonies. Counsel should be provided early in the proceedings and certainly no later than the first judicial appearance. The services of counsel should be available after conviction through appeal, and in collateral attack proceedings when the issues are not frivolous. The immediate minimum, until it becomes possible to provide the foregoing, is that all criminal defendants who are in danger of substantial loss of liberty shall be provided with counsel.

All jurisdictions that have not already done so should move from random assignment of defense counsel by judges to a coordinated assigned counsel system or a defender system.

Each State should finance assigned counsel and defender systems on a regular and statewide basis.

States should provide for clear administrative responsibility within courts and should ensure that professional court administrators are available to assist the judges in their management functions.

The Federal and State Governments should improve physical facilities and compensation for witnesses and jurors, expand the use of scheduling and witness call systems to reduce unnecessary appearances and waiting, and, except in cases where there is to be an immediate hearing on the arrest or charge, substitute sworn statements for the appearance of the arresting police officer at the initial court appearance.

States should reexamine their court structure and organization and create a single, unified system of courts subject to central administrative management within the judiciary. The Commission urges States that have not yet reformed their court systems to draw upon the experience of those States and organizations that have made advances in this area. Central administration within the judiciary should have the power to make rules and shift manpower to meet changing requirements.

Universities and colleges should, with governmental and private participation and support, develop more courses and launch more research studies and projects on the problems of contemporary corrections.

THE TIPPED SCALES
OF AMERICAN JUSTICE*

STUART S. NAGEL

The Supreme Court, in an opinion in 1956, stated that "there can be no equal justice where the kind of trial a man gets depends on the amount of money he has." The Attorney General's Committee on Poverty and the Administration of Federal Criminal Justice, headed by Professor Francis A. Allen, then of the University of Michigan Law School, in its 1963 report documented the charge that the poor suffer in the courts because of their poverty. The committee recommended reforms in the bail system, in legal representation, in appeals, and at other steps in the long ladder from arrest to release or conviction.

Disparities in justice may appear at any stage of the criminal process — and most groups suffer both apparent advantages and disadvantages from them. Let us examine these stages briefly, and see what safeguards at each level can mean to an accused.

Preliminary Hearing. The preliminary hearing is the first stage on which data are available. The main purpose of a preliminary hearing is to allow the presiding official (police magistrate, justice of the peace, or judge) to decide whether there is enough evidence against the accused to justify further action. If he decides there is not, then an innocent person may be spared considerable humiliation, expense, delay, and inconvenience. The hearing is preliminary to the prosecutor's formal accusation or to a grand jury indictment, which it can prevent. The preliminary hearing also has other advantages for an accused: (1) it deters the use of the third-degree; (2) it allows counsel to appear and plead for the accused, particularly with regard to bail; (3) and it reveals the fact that the accused has been arrested and detained, so that *habeas corpus* (which can bring about immediate release), right to a copy of the complaint, and other guarantees can be secured. In short, the preliminary hearing is a safeguard for the rights of the accused; and its denial is a limitation to those rights.

Bail. The next important protection for a defendant is the right, or the ability, to be released on bail. Bail reduces his hardship, especially if he is innocent, and gives him a better chance to investigate and prepare his case.

Defense Counsel. Lawyers generally concede that few persons (including

* Reprinted with permission from *Trans-action* Magazine (May/June 1966), pp. 3–9, Washington University, St. Louis, Missouri.

lawyers) are capable of properly preparing and arguing their own cases — especially when confined. Having a lawyer, preferably of your own choice, is therefore a fundamental right. Under the Supreme Court ruling in the famous case of *Gideon versus Wainwright,* decided in 1963, all indigent state defendants must hereafter be assigned counsel for any felony.

A lawyer is considered essential for investigation, negotiation with the prosecutor, examination of witnesses, and the presentation of legal and factual arguments to judge and jury. A court-appointed lawyer is better than none, and often better than some, but he can easily suffer from lack of experience, sympathy, enthusiasm, and especially finances and time, since he will probably be appointed late, and may have to take much expense money out of his own pocket.

Grand Jury. What percentage of cases went before a grand jury? Like the preliminary hearing (and the trial) the grand jury process is designed mainly to protect and to minimize the harm done to the innocent. The alternative is to let the prosecutor alone judge whether the accused should be held for trial.

Delay. The American Law Institute Code of Criminal Procedure provides that if a defendant is held for more than three months without trial due to no fault of his own, then he must be set free without danger of rearrest for the same crime, except for extremely extenuating circumstances. A long delay before trial, especially in jail, can penalize the innocent or over-punish the guilty, as well as make witnesses less available and reliable.

Trial by Jury. Generally, there is less chance that twelve jurors will agree unanimously on conviction than one judge (especially a so-called "hanging judge"). Therefore a defendant usually has a greater chance of acquittal before a jury. In addition, if he is a member of a disadvantaged group (uneducated, working-class, or Negro) he stands a much better chance of encountering somebody like himself on a jury than on the bench.

On the other hand, our data show that seeking a jury trial may mean greater delay. It may also mean that if the defendant is found guilty, he is less likely to get probation than if he only had a bench trial. (The stiffer penalties for those convicted by juries may reflect the possibility that the more severe cases come before juries.) But on balance, the chance at a trial by "a jury of his peers" is a strong safeguard of the rights of a defendant.

Nevertheless, in the state data, 63 percent of those cases going to trial did so without a jury; 48 percent of federal trials were held without juries.

Conviction and Sentencing. About four of every five tried defendants, state and local, are found, or plead, guilty. The approximately 20 percent found not guilty, of course, had been put to the expense and anxiety of criminal proceedings. Of those considered guilty, 83 percent pleaded guilty — 25 percent to lesser offenses than the original charge, possibly after negotiating with the prosecutor. Almost half the defendants found guilty were given suspended sentences or probation. Slightly more than half of those convicted and sentenced received sentences of more than one year.

Let us examine some of these disparities.

Economic Class. In the pre-sentencing stages, 34 percent of indigents up for felonious assault in state courts did not get preliminary hearings — compared to 21 percent of non-indigents. This was also true, if not as markedly, in state grand larceny cases. Bail, since it requires the ability to raise money, shows the greatest disparity between those who have money and those who do not. About three-quarters of all indigent state cases did not raise bail and stayed locked up, with all this means in unearned punishment and inability to prepare for trial, while 79 percent of non-indigent assault cases, and 69 percent of larceny, did raise bail and got out.

In *having a lawyer,* an interesting reversal occurs. In most states one must be poor to have assigned lawyers, the rich hire their own, and it is the middle group that may be the most apt to be undefended.

In the state cases, the indigent were delayed in a jail awaiting trial more than the non-indigent. This, obviously, is related to their relative inability to raise bail.

The federal data show that the indigent are much less likely to have a grand jury indictment than the non-indigent.

About 90 percent of all indigents studied were found guilty. Though the percentage of non-indigents found guilty was also high, it was consistently lower (averaging about 80 percent). The greatest disparity was in the federal cases, where all indigents had court-appointed lawyers, and this may indicate that poorer representation had something to do with the higher rate of conviction.

Not only are the indigent found guilty more often, but they are much less likely to be recommended for probation by the probation officer, or be granted probation or suspended sentences by the judge. Of the defendants on whom we had data in this study, a sizeable majority of indigents stayed in jail both before and after trial, unlike non-indigents.

Most Negroes are poor. A great many poor people are Negroes. So the figures about indigency and race must overlap. But they are not identical, and the differences are important. Generally, the poor suffer even more discrimination than Negroes in criminal justice; and Negroes may suffer more from lack of money than from race.

For instance, a Negro is more likely to get a preliminary hearing than a poor man. He is not as likely as the white defendant to be released on bail, but much more likely to be released than the indigent defendant. Since many Negro defendants are also indigent, the Negro is slightly more likely to have a lawyer than a white defendant, given the indigency prerequisite for receiving a court-appointed lawyer.

The Negro is much less likely than the white to have a grand jury indictment in either federal assault or larceny cases. If he goes to trial he is even more unlikely to have a jury trial. Indeed, 86 percent of the Negroes in federal assault cases failed to receive a jury trial, contrasted to a 26 percent figure for white defendants. It appears that the constitutional rights of a grand jury indictment and of trial by jury are mainly for white men. Perhaps Negroes believe white juries to be more discriminatory than white judges. But it is also possible that Negroes commit the less severe larcenies and assaults, and so do not as often require grand or petit juries.

Negroes, compared to whites, are particularly discriminated against when it comes to probation or suspended sentences. This is evident in the assault convictions, but is more dramatic for larceny; 74 percent of guilty Negroes were imprisoned in state larceny cases, against only 49 percent of guilty whites; in federal larceny cases the score is 54 percent to 40 percent. With prior record held constant, the disparity still holds up.

Generally, and surprisingly, discrimination against the Negro in criminal proceedings was only slightly greater in the South than in the North. It was, however, consistently greater in the South at all stages, pre-trial, trial, and sentencing. Discrimination in the South, predictably, was also greater at the state level than the federal level, possibly because federal judges are more independent of local pressures than state judges.

Younger defendants (below 21 in the state data, 22 in federal) generally are less likely to receive the safeguards the older defendants do, but are more likely to get lighter sentences.

Younger defendants are more likely to be recommended for probation, more likely to get it (or suspended sentences), and those few who do go to prison generally receive shorter sentences.

In preliminary hearing and bail, urban-rural differences were small and inconclusive, but North-South differences were large and consistent — and not to the credit of the North. Thus 38 percent of Northern assaults had no preliminary hearing in spite of laws providing for them, compared to only 10 percent in the South. The South is more traditional toward law and custom, perhaps. The bail difference may also be due to the fact that more Northern defendants were classified as indigents.

Not having any lawyer at all was disproportionately rural and Southern; of the eleven Southern states, eight did not have laws providing for compensated counsel. (Gideon vs. Wainwright originated in a Southern state, Florida, and the South will now have to change its ways.)

The urban and Northern courts are more congested; defendants wait longer for trial. In the state assault cases, 56 percent of urban defendants sat in jail for more than two months, contrasted to 31 percent of rural defendants, and there is a similar 25 percent spread for federal larceny cases. Much has been written about congestion and delay in urban civil cases, but delay in criminal cases also needs attention, especially in the Northern cities.

LEGAL AID FOR THE INDIGENT ACCUSED OF CRIME*

JUNIUS L. ALLISON

Legal Aid, the organized method of providing legal advice or representation in both civil and criminal matters for indigent clients, reduces the gap between justice for those who can afford lawyers and justice for the impoverished.

In this article, "legal aid" will be limited to a discussion of the service relating to indigent defendants in criminal matters.

Legal Aid in the Federal Courts (prior to 1964)

The Sixth Amendment of the Constitution provides that "In all criminal prosecutions, the accused shall enjoy the right . . . to have the assistance of counsel for his defence." The Supreme Court has interpreted this to mean that if the defendant is poor, the court must appoint counsel for him — unless he intelligently waives such: "Counsel must be assigned to the accused if he is unable to employ one and is incapable adequately of making his defense." Even stronger words were used by Justice Black in the Johnson case: "The Sixth Amendment withholds from the federal courts, in all criminal proceedings, the power and the authority to deprive an accused of his life or liberty unless he has or waives the assistance of counsel."

Rule 44 of the Federal Rules of Criminal Procedure implements this right by providing:

If the defendant appears in court without counsel, the court shall advise him of his right to counsel and assign counsel to represent him at every stage of the proceeding unless he elects to proceed without counsel or is able to obtain counsel.

However, there are no public defenders for the federal courts and no money to compensate the lawyers appointed to represent the indigent defendants, despite the ringing pronouncements by the Supreme Court concerning the right to have counsel. [Note: the federal Criminal Justice Act of 1964 requires judges to assign counsel and to pay limited fees and expenses.]

The practice generally followed in the federal courts is to assign as counsel

* Abstract of an article printed in *Federal Probation*, XXVII, No. 1 (March 1963), 46–51, reprinted with permission of the author and publisher.

to indigent defendants members of the bar on any basis that seems appropriate to the trial judge. Some judges have called upon young lawyers, on those whose practice was not large, or on any lawyer who might be in the courtroom at the time. A few judges have considered the entire local bar to be available and some judges have made it a practice to designate the ablest and most experienced lawyer available, especially in capital cases.

This haphazard system may be effective in capital cases where more attention is paid to the appointment; it has worked in other cases in the less populated areas. But in the large urbanized centers, where the volume of criminal cases is great, the system has been tragically unfair to the defendant in many cases, has imposed a needless burden on the court, and has been a hardship on the lawyers appointed.

Since funds are [were] not available to compensate lawyers for their services or out-of-pocket expenses, or for investigations of the facts, the acceptance of this responsibility may be said to represent the noblest tradition of the bar. But only a small percentage of lawyers have accepted the responsibility to appear in criminal cases in the federal courts. In practice, therefore, the burden is spread among a relatively few members of the profession.

In an attempt to provide more competent representation, and on a more organized basis, a few bar associations have developed volunteer panels from which the court can make assignments.

By Congressional action, the Legal Aid Agency for the District of Columbia was created in 1960. Even though the initial appropriation was small ($75,000 annually), a highly competent director was obtained and the office is performing a remarkable service in the District Court.

Legal Aid in the State Courts (prior to 1963)

In criminal cases tried in the state courts, the right of counsel depends upon state constitutions, statutes or rules of court — except as modified by the application of the "due process" clause of the Fourteenth Amendment of the United States Constitution. There are [were] five states (Alabama, Florida, Mississippi, Pennsylvania, South Carolina) that limit mandatory assignment of counsel to capital cases. Texas was on this list, but later (1959) a statute requiring the appointment of counsel in a felony case was enacted. Assignment is not mandatory (in cases other than capital) except on request of the defendant or in the discretion of the court in the following states: Georgia, Kentucky, Louisiana, New Jersey, New York, North Carolina, Tennessee, Utah, Iowa, Oregon, California, Colorado, Delaware, Idaho, Maine, Maryland, Michigan, Minnesota, Montana, Nevada, New Hampshire, North Dakota, Oklahoma, South Dakota, Vermont, Washington, Wisconsin, Wyoming. In the first 11 states named, no (or only nominal) compensation is allowed where counsel is appointed.

Even though the Sixth Amendment applies only to the federal courts, the Supreme Court has stated that under the due process clause of the

Fourteenth Amendment, there is a right to have counsel (appointed, if necessary) in all capital cases in the state courts: The right to the aid of counsel is one of those "fundamental principles of liberty and justice which lie at the base of all our civil and political institutions." [The U.S. Supreme Court held that counsel is required in all serious cases in state courts. Therefore the states have had to make changes in their practice to meet Constitutional requirements.]

The four principal methods used to provide lawyers for indigent defendants in state courts are:

1. Assignment by the court on a case-by-case basis,
2. Privately financed defenders,
3. Public defenders,
4. The mixed public-private system.

Assigned Counsel System

Some have said the assigned counsel system is preferable because it spreads the duties among the bar generally and offers opportunity for each lawyer to fulfill his professional responsibility to the indigent. No doubt, as was pointed out before, the system may work reasonably well in many smaller communities, although in fairness to both lawyer and client, compensation should be paid. In the areas of larger populations, however, many are convinced that it does not and cannot operate satisfactorily. The reasons most frequently given bear repeating:

1. The volume of cases is too great.
2. A relatively small group of lawyers practice in the criminal courts.
3. If compensation is adequate, there may be criticism of assignment to "friends"—and the total cost would be prohibitive, or at least more expensive than a defender. For example: the cost per case in 1955 in Boston (voluntary defender) was $28; in Alameda County, California (public defender) it was $42; in St. Louis (public defender) $30; New Orleans (voluntary defender) $22.50.
4. With the advancement in crime detection and investigation, the prosecuting attorney has become such a specialist that the average practitioner is at a disadvantage.
5. Assignment is usually late—at arraignment.

The Public Defender

There are 92 [185 in 1967] public defender offices in the United States. They are distributed among 13 states and the District of Columbia, with 54 [64 in 1967] of the offices being in California and Illinois.

The public defender is a public official, selected through a civil service procedure, appointed by the judges or appropriate local officials, or elected. The office is financed by public funds and the public defender is usually required to submit an annual budget to the body making the appropriation.

The offices vary in size from the large one in Los Angeles (56 [166 in 1967] lawyers; 9 [15] investigators; 13 [35] clerical; expenditures $748,469 [$2.5 million]; engaging in 2,455 trials, 1960–61 [43,820 cases in 1965–66]) to part-time offices where an attorney in private practice is paid a small retainer to handle certain assigned cases.

The Private Defender System

The private defender system differs from the public defender system in that its financial support is derived from nongovernmental sources, such as the United Fund (or Community Chest) or contributions from lawyers and donations from other private individuals and sometimes from corporations. Also this form of organized service is privately controlled, in that there is an independent governing board that sets the general administrative policies.

As of June 1962, there were eleven private defender offices: New Orleans, Cambridge, New York City, Akron, Cincinnati, Allentown, Norristown, Philadelphia, Pittsburgh, Williamsport, and York. Five of these operate as divisions of incorporated legal aid societies: New Orleans, New York City (which receives a small appropriation from tax funds), Akron, Cincinnati, Pittsburgh. The services in Allentown, Williamsport, and York are attached to the bar associations. The Defender Association of Philadelphia is independent and has its own board of directors.

The Public-Private System

This is a somewhat unique arrangement whereby public money is used by a private charitable organization to finance a defender plan. There are seven [forty-one in 1966] such organizations which are located in Long Beach, Buffalo, Rochester (N.Y.), Cleveland, Columbus (Ohio), Toledo, and San Juan, Puerto Rico. These are established in connection with the legal aid societies, and with the exception of Cleveland and San Juan, they handle only misdemeanor cases.

Conclusion

With the courts declaring that to meet the "due process" requirements every defendant must have counsel (unless such is intelligently waived and except as limited by *Betts v. Brady*) a serious administrative problem faces the judicial branch of our government. Lawyers cannot escape their obligation in this area — neither can other responsible citizens. A workable solution to provide counsel for the poor must be found.

STANDARDS RELATING TO
FAIR TRIAL AND
FREE PRESS*

The questions confronting the Committee, though difficult of resolution, can be simply stated: (1) In what ways may the reporting of criminal matters endanger the proper functioning of the criminal process and, in particular, jeopardize the right of the accused and his accusers to a fair and impartial trial? (2) To the extent that such dangers appear to exist, can steps be taken which will reduce or eliminate them without curtailing the benefits to be obtained from informing the public and without in any way abridging freedom of speech and of the press?

In view of the development of competing forms of communication and the increased attention given to national and international affairs, as well as the rising incidence of crime in an expanding population, it may well be that news of a particular crime does not tend to saturate a community as often as it once did. On the other hand, recent decades have seen an unparalleled recognition of the basic rights of the individual who finds himself subjected to the criminal process. One corollary of this recognition is a greater likelihood that illtimed public statements will convey information to the future triers of fact that was obtained in violation of those rights and that therefore cannot constitutionally be used to establish guilt in a court of law. Moreover, the wider distribution of information, which now quite commonly occurs on a statewide or nationwide basis, may often serve to render useless one of the principal remedies — change of venue — designed to protect an accused who has been the subject of potentially prejudicial news coverage. And finally, there has been an increasing tendency on the part of all courts, including the Supreme Court of the United States, to insist that conditions at the time of trial be such that the individual juror conform as closely as possible to the ideal; to be "indifferent as he stands unsworne."

The Committee's analysis of press coverage in 20 metropolitan centers indicates that in approximately 50% of those cases which are reported in the news media, the crime and the arrest are initially reported on the same

* Reprinted with permission from a tentative draft, *American Bar Association Project on Minimum Standards for Criminal Justice*, recommended by the Advisory Committee on Fair Trial and Free Press, Paul C. Reardon, Chairman, David L. Shapiro, Reporter, December 1966, pp. 20–51. Copyright 1966 American Bar Association.

news day. This leaves a substantial number of cases in which reporting of the crime occurs prior to an arrest or formal charge.

As is true throughout the criminal process, the principal source of potentially prejudicial statements during this period is the public official, whose words have the ring of authority and authenticity. The statement from a police official or prosecutor may simply identify a person as a "prime suspect" or one who had a "definite part" in the murder.

Also infrequently, but with occasionally unfortunate results, the news media themselves will conduct a campaign to obtain an indictment and, in doing so, may well arouse the community to a fever pitch in which an impartial trial is most unlikely. One example is the famous case of the "Trenton Six," in which the local newspaper editorially deplored the idleness of the electric chair, spurring on a police campaign to solve a particular murder "through one means or another." Shortly after, six Negroes were arrested and convicted, four of whom were acquitted at a second trial. Another example, perhaps the most prominent in recent years, is the case of Dr. Sheppard, in which one newspaperman stated that the conduct of the Cleveland papers "beggars description and challenges belief." The following stories were among those appearing in the Cleveland newspapers prior to Dr. Sheppard's indictment:

WHY DON'T POLICE QUIZ TOP SUSPECT?
An editorial

You can bet your last dollar the Sheppard murder would be cleaned up long ago if it had involved "average people." . . . They'd have Sam Sheppard brought in, grill him at Police Headquarters, like the chief suspect in any murder case. . . . Now proved under oath to be a liar, . . . Sam Sheppard still hasn't been taken to headquarters.

WHY ISN'T SAM SHEPPARD IN JAIL?
QUIT STALLING—BRING HIM IN
TIME TO BRING BAY SLAYING INTO OPEN

. . . We are forced to take note that Dr. Samuel Sheppard, husband of the victim, has rejected suggestions of both lie detector and truth serum tests, and his submitting to questioning only when his family and lawyer have agreed he might.

Once an arrest has been made or a formal charge has been filed, public statements and reporting focus on the defendant himself, and the likelihood of potentially prejudicial material increases substantially. Although most of the reporting centers at the point of arrest, and trials generally do not occur for several months, the information may be repeated at the time of preliminary hearing and on the eve of trial. As the Committee's content analysis shows, the overwhelming preponderance of information during this period, except for reports of pretrial judicial proceedings, emanates from police sources.

During the one-month period in which 20 metropolitan newspapers were studied by the Committee, these newspapers contained 120 reports of confessions or statements by defendants; the substantial majority of these reports were inculpatory in nature, and 79 of them went into some detail as to content; all but six of the reports were obtained from police sources.

The Committee's one-month content analysis of 20 newspapers shows 80 instances in which a record of prior convictions, arrests, or indictments was disseminated during the period from arrest to trial, and in all but seven of those instances, the source of information was the local police department. Indeed, in most of these instances, although information as to convictions (but not arrests) may have been theoretically available in court files, it probably would not have been obtained as a practical matter except from the police.

In the one-month study of 20 newspapers, there were four instances in which a police representative commented on the character of the defendant and 11 in which a police representative expressed a firm opinion on the merits of the case. Such action goes beyond what is necessary to report the arrest and to reassure the community, and carries with it the stamp of authority that may well lead to a climate of substantial prejudice. Moreover, it blurs the distinction, so vital to our system of criminal justice, between a charge of crime and a determination of guilt. During the one-month period studied by the Committee, the 20 newspapers analyzed contained 115 reports of evidence seized at arrest, all but one of which appear to have been derived from police sources. Thus it is significant that during the one-month period studied in 20 cities, there were 29 pretrial reports of identification of the accused by witnesses derived from police sources. In addition, there were 36 reported interviews with the victim or other witnesses conducted directly by the news media. In many of these latter instances, of course, the interview related to the crime and not to the identity or character of the defendant.

In the one-month period studied by the Committee, there were in 20 metropolitan newspapers a total of 342 reports of pretrial judicial hearings; 71 of these went into some detail as to the evidence presented; and 11 included reports of confessions, prior records, or test results.

The Committee's content analysis indicates that the occasions on which potentially prejudicial material appears are considerably smaller in number during the trial than before. This is, in part, due to the number of cases, disposed of without trial as well as to the fact that trials appear to be considered less newsworthy than arrests. The decline in frequency, however, may be more than matched by the increase in the hazards. Information reported well in advance of trial may be forgotten; information appearing during the trial seems far more likely to remain in the mind of the trier of fact if he is exposed to it. Further, he may be more inclined to seek out this information when he is personally involved in the case.

One significant difference between the pretrial and trial stages is that the source of potentially prejudicial information is more often the prosecutor and very seldom the police official. This, of course, reflects the shift in the control of the matter on the government side.

With respect to the news media themselves, the content analysis indicates that characterization of the evidence introduced — in some cases by such phrases as "weakened the prosecution's case" or "destroyed the defendant's contention" — is not at all uncommon. On a few occasions, though evidently with less frequency in recent years, media representatives may go out of their way to make plainly editorial observations in their news stories or columns during the course of the trial.

Once the trial has been completed, and the verdict of the jury has been rendered, the volume of news coverage declines substantially, as does the danger of potential prejudice. Indeed, aside from reports on sentencing, which are often coupled with information as to prior records, and occasional reports of appeals or other post-conviction proceedings, the Committee's content analysis revealed virtually no news coverage of criminal cases during this period.

Research discloses, however, that significant problems do occasionally arise in connection with post-conviction reporting. Perhaps inevitable, but nevertheless troublesome, is a report of a prior trial when the defendant is just about to be retried for the same offense. A related problem arises when jurors are interviewed about their opinions or collective deliberations, particularly if sentence has not yet been imposed or if the jury was unable to agree and another trial is imminent.

Finally, there have been times when news media have taken a strong editorial stand on the sentence to be imposed, or on a proposal for commutation of a death sentence, for pardon, or for parole. There is, of course, a thin line between a reasonable and sincere expression of views and calculated intimidation, and it is true that the dangers of prejudice do diminish after the jury has completed its task. Moreover, it may be both necessary and desirable to leave many matters to the discretion of those who are expressing their views. But it does seem plain that there are occasions when that discretion has been sorely abused.

For purposes of analysis, it may again be helpful to divide the criminal process into the four stages discussed in the prior section: pre-arrest, arrest to trial, during trial, and after verdict. It seems clear, if this division is made, that the most significant and most frequent contributions resulting from the dissemination of information occur before an arrest is made or a formal charge is brought. In addition to the evident value of publicity in aiding in the apprehension of a suspect, and cautioning the public with respect to the dangers he may present, there are numerous occasions on which the media have taken the lead in uncovering the existence of crime and seeing to it that wrong-doers are duly prosecuted.

In the period from the arrest or the filing of formal charges to the beginning of trial, there are a number of contributions the news media can make. First, and perhaps most important, reports of the arrest and of the nature of the charge can serve to assure the community that law enforcement officers have been doing their job and that there is probably cause to believe that the man apprehended did commit the offense. Particularly in cases that have aroused or frightened the community, this news can be of great value. Second, by publishing the facts of arrest, and by following the case to make sure that the accused is not simply left in jail without being taken to a magistrate, the media can help guard against unlawful or unnecessary arrests and detentions as well as other abuses of the rights of those in custody. Thus one newspaper won a public service award for its report on the death of a derelict alcoholic in police custody; another exposed the frequent practice of holding persons for periods of up to forty-eight hours "on suspicion"; still another is reported to have discovered that a man had been "lost" in a jail for months without any knowledge on the part of the police of the charge against him.

A third contribution during this period, though one that seems relatively infrequent, is the production of evidence that either supports the prosecution or helps to establish the innocence of the person accused. This can be accomplished through the coming forward of a witness who read of the case or as a result of personal investigation by the reporter himself. An example of the former is a case in which an attorney successfully appealed in the press for corroboration of the defendant's alibi. Examples of the latter include several cases in which a reporter's investigation contributed to a confession by another or to the gathering of other evidence that resulted in the freeing of the accused.

During the trial, there are several important contributions the news media can make. First, informed and intelligent reporting can educate the public — many of whom have never been in a courtroom — on the workings of the criminal process. Second, such reporting can help to ensure that the conduct of those who participate in the trial — judges, lawyers, and witnesses — lives up to the standards that our system of justice demands. Finally, as in the case of reports of arrests and requests for evidence, reporting of the trial may evoke evidence that will aid in convicting or exonerating the accused.

After the trial, constructive criticism of the conduct of the participants, including the judge and the jury, can serve to improve the administration of justice. Moreover, since appeals from convictions and the exhaustion of other remedies may take an extended time, such criticism may be unwarranted; it may be designed to harass those whose conduct has been honest and courageous, but this seems a fair price to pay for a truly open society.

And there are times when the value of such discussion is immediately manifest, as when widespread dissatisfaction with the existence of racial bias in the selection and operation of juries leads to legislation designed to eliminate that bias. Also, publicity can help to expose the unfairness, and even the absurdity, of many of our laws, which of course are in constant need of improvement and correction.

There are also instances when unhappiness with the result has led individual reporters to continue their search and ultimately to come up with evidence establishing the innocence of a man wrongfully convicted. The value of such contributions in human terms cannot be overstated.

PUNISHMENT AND CORRECTIONAL SUBSTITUTES

INTRODUCTION

Not since the middle of the 18th century, when imprisonment began to be accepted as a legitimate substitute for executing and corporally punishing offenders, has there been so much ferment in the field of corrections. All sorts of ideas for reforming and improving the system are seriously offered and discussed. There is almost total agreement that the correctional system is in dire need of overhaul if only because no system can be neglected for so long without requiring updating and reevaluation.

Incredibly, the largely invisible and long forgotten correctional institutions contain about 1.3 million offenders on any given day, process nearly 2.5 million persons a year, and have a total operating budget of at least a billion dollars annually. The problem is that this vast correctional establishment often does not correct. Many of the 342,000 misdemeanants, 348,000 juveniles, and 591,000 felons in correctional settings on any given day are quite likely to be incarcerated again. Additionally, there are not enough skilled professionals attracted to the field, making the manpower situation almost critical, the facilities are aging and deteriorating, and public support for rehabilitation programs — especially at the adult level — is only lukewarm at best.

Despite the accumulated lag and neglect in corrections, change is clearly in the offing. New institutions — smaller, more specialized and better staffed — are emerging. Better programs are being formulated, introduced and implemented. More emphasis is being placed on training and reformation and less on mere confinement. Ever-increasing attention is being devoted to developing efficacious substitutes for, and alternatives to, imprisonment. Community-based corrections activities reflected in probation and parole services, halfway houses, work-release programs, detoxification centers, and mental health centers are gaining public and professional support. Prevention programs in the schools and communities with multi-problem families and street-corner gangs are now reasonably commonplace. There is now a liveliness and spirit of change and movement — if not yet accomplishment — that was hardly present even a decade ago.

The readings in this chapter are necessarily limited to only a few of the many aspects of the punishment and corrections picture. In the first selection, Shlomo Shoham, an Israeli authority, examines the historical justifications for punishment — vengeance, expiation, societal protection, deterrence, and reformation — and concludes that the traditional means of repression are now largely inadequate. His article, "Two Sides of the Barricade," considers not only a scheme of social defense against crime but also the offenders' view of society and the functional nature of crime. Society, we are told, needs its criminals for its own cohesion, as a legitimate outlet for aggression, and as a means of assuaging the guilt feelings of respectable people. The "two sides" in the title thus refer to the effect of punishment on the control of crime and on crime as functional for society. Society needs crime and needs to control it — a dilemma which may well account for part, at least, of the conflict over just about every aspect of the crime problem.

In the second article, Norval Morris is concerned about the various "Impediments to Penal Reform." Four major obstacles to penal reform are cited: the argument over the deterrent effect of punishment; the principle of "less eligibility," which means that the treatment of the criminal must never be better than that of the poorest "honest" folk; the swing of the pendulum to the rehabilitative ideal; and the absence of research on treatment and related problems. In each of these obstacle areas, Morris attempts to pinpoint the problems and offer positive alternatives.

In "The Status of Capital Punishment: A World Perspective," Clarence H. Patrick presents data on the use or non-use of capital punishment in 128 countries and the various states in the United States. He distinguishes the smaller number of nations that are wholly abolitionist *de jure* from those which are wholly or partially abolitionist in practices. He finds no worldwide sentiment for the enactment of total abolition laws. Instead, the trend is toward fewer executions in practice in those countries retaining the death penalty and for the reduction in the number of capital offenses. Although 109 crimes still carry the death penalty somewhere in the world, the principal capital offenses are murder and treason. Espionage, arson, homicide accompanied by another serious crime, rape, robbery, rebellion, and sabotage constitute the bulk of the remaining offenses in which the death penalty is most often imposed. Finally, 89 countries with the death penalty together averaged over 500 executions annually in the period 1958–62. This is a remarkably small number considering that in the past various individual countries executed that many persons, or more, yearly.

Moving from matters of punishment to corrections, the "National Profile of Correction" taken from *Correction in the United States: A Survey for the President's Commission on Law Enforcement and Administration of Justice,* describes the extent, cost, and manpower aspects of the correctional system in the United States. Beyond this description, several general categories of correctional needs are outlined including the strengthening of probation and parole services and the increased coordination of all correctional services. In addition, various specific issues involving diagnostic services, detention, presentence reports, and research, among others, are set forth. There is also a discussion of the role of the Federal government as a partner with the states in initiating and financing new and improved programs in corrections. These recommendations are based on a comprehensive survey of correctional agencies and institutions throughout the United States and reflect the best thinking in the field. It is, therefore, likely that these concerns will be translated into public policy and updated correctional practices soon.

Some of the more important innovations in the correctional system mosaic are the subject matter of the article "Correctional Institutions in a Great Society." In it, Daniel Glaser focuses principally on the emergence of new types of correctional agencies. Badly needed are new facilities partway between total confinement and outright release or even parole. The halfway house is designed to fill this void. In it, and through it, inmates can gradually be prepared for life as free men. Also designed for this purpose are various work-release programs to help the inmate adjust to the responsibilities of work and the competition in the labor market. Halfway houses and prerelease guidance centers will of necessity have to be located in urban centers and will consequently be, and look different from, the traditional prison. In other words, community treatment programs are likely to play a major role in the correctional system of the future. So will research which will feed back data to the system on the effectiveness of various practices.

While the preceding selection is oriented more to the future, the article by Harold V. Langlois, "Personnel Problems in Corrections," describes the actual implementation of the community emphasis in Great Britain. The first illustration is of a prerelease center in one of England's oldest prisons — Wormwood Scrubs. Here inmates have their own rooms and are totally free until 10:45 P.M. In six years' experience with this program, only 17 of 174 men have failed to make good after release. A second illustration of an innovation in treatment of discharged prisoners is a social center and club, the purpose of which is to reintegrate former inmates into the community. Finally, the article describes a Youth Correctional Facility (Borstal) which is so heavily staffed that an inmate subculture cannot develop to frustrate the rehabilitative efforts of the institution. The success rate in this setting reverses the dismal picture of recidivism characteristic of other Borstals.

The final contribution to this chapter is a report by Daniel Glaser on the *Effectiveness of a Prison and Parole System.* Five Federal prisons were studied — Leavenworth, Terre Haute, Milan, Chillicothe, and Ashland — which represent most of the spectrum of Federal prisons. While the results naturally focus on the recidivism of the offenders, a number of other conclusions pertaining to life in the institution, the influence of inmates on one another, prison isolation and disciplinary penalties, prerelease arrangements and postrelease adjustment are set forth. The tone of these conclusions is quite optimistic. Despite the fact that prisons are receiving more difficult inmates than before because other programs are draining off the better risks, the recidivism rate of released prisoners was found to be far lower than expected. Considering the nature of the task of rehabilitating men in prison, the optimistic note sounded in this report is certainly most welcome.

TWO SIDES OF THE BARRICADE*

SHLOMO SHOHAM

Beccaria in his famous treatise, *Dei Delitti e Delle Pene,* elucidated the idea, which was quite revolutionary at the time, that the ultimate objective of penal methods is to defend society against offenders and their offenses; this objective is based on the axiomatic necessity for the orderly existence of society.

The defense of society might be achieved by controlling and preventing crime with the ultimate, and to be sure, quite Utopian aim of eliminating crime altogether. This ultimate aim is utilitarian in the sense that it excludes the purposes of punishment which are not means to the end of social defense; these being retribution and expiation.

Social defense was not always deemed to be the ultimate aim of criminal

* Reprinted with permission from "Two Sides of the Barricade," *Police* (November–December 1964), pp. 28–35, Charles C Thomas, publisher.

law and criminal policy. The ancient response to an injury was vengeance by the victim (if he was strong enough to take revenge). Historically, the Wergild and other monetary restitutions took the place of private vengeance because the latter were considered as a breach of the peace of the sovereign, who forced the adversaries to settle their disputes (for valid consideration, of course, because a handsome chunk of the Wergild flowed to the treasury of the sovereign). The essence of the Wergild is embodied in the cry of the avenger to the aggressor: "Buy off the spear or bear it." It might be erroneous to impute public indignation in these ancient times against offenders because violence and atrocities in ancient society were everyday phenomena. The intervention of society through its sovereign in cases of injuries to individuals and their property was done for the preservation of "the king's peace," i.e., public order and tranquility which would be naturally disturbed by feuds and skirmishes resulting from private vengeance. However, there is a marked consensus of opinion among penal philosophers that the origin of legal punishment is the spontaneous retribution of the injured directed against the individual who injured or attacked him. This private vengeance turned in the course of time into the more orderly and formalized retribution of the courts of law against offenders who stand trial before them.

The ideas of retribution and expiation did play (and in many respects still do) a prominent role in criminal policy. The so-called classic school of penology relied on these premises when postulating that the penalty must be wholly determined by the objective severity of the offense and the actual damage caused by it. The whole concept of criminal responsibility is based on the Judeo-Christian doctrine of free will because the offender *chose* to do wrong he should receive his just dessert, i.e., punishment.

A whole school of penal reform has been established in Europe, its main purpose being to devise means and ways of defending society against crime. This "Social Defense" movement, although originating between the two World Wars, has fully developed only in the last ten years. The Social Defense Movement, as many other scientific schools of thought, displays internal divergencies of ideas which border sometimes on basic controversies. Some of this movement's exponents still advocate, for instance, a dual system of penal measures, i.e., repressive measures (peines) which are based *inter alia* on notions of retribution, expiation and the indeterministic concept of moral responsibility to be employed side by side with so-called measures of social defense, the purpose of which is reformative and preventive and which should be employed against offenders on the sole criterion of the danger (*état dangereux*) which they afford to society.

There is unanimity among those who are professionally engaged in prevention of crime and treatment of offenders in opposing retributive punishment in its classic or expiatory aspects. These are quite obviously outdated in the second half of the 20th century. The last traces of talionic concepts are gradually disappearing, and those few who are still fighting against a "retributive criminal policy" seem to brandish their Quixotic swords against a practically non-existent windmill.

The following resolution of the Fourth International Congress of Social Defense that:

. . . "the traditional means of repression seem to be inadequate. The necessary remedy is a series of measures designed to correct or prevent social maladjustment and to remove the cause of criminal acts and recidivism"

may be regarded as representing the predominant trend.

A very common argument is that reformative and preventive measures are incompatible with the defense of society against crime. We hold that this is not necessarily true. Reformation and prevention as conceived by modern penal philosophy are two aspects of one objective of punishment graded into a continuum. As far as it is possible and expedient, punishment is directed toward the reformation of the offender. However, where past experience or other factors indicate that the chances of reformation are meager, preventive measures, i.e., isolation of the offender from society, should be resorted to.

There is no proof whatsoever that deterrence ever served the defense of society against crime better than reformation and prevention. We have already mentioned that the real efficacy of deterrence has never been proved and on many types of offenders it has been proved of no effect. We do know that the presumable effectiveness of deterrence is not directly proportional to the severity of punishment.

Retribution *per se* never helped the cause of social defense. It might have helped, however, to fill the offender with spite and hatred and induced him to strike back with more malice and force. It might even well be that the modern largely Sisyphean efforts and meager achievement of practical penology are due to the scorn and abysmal hate felt by law enforcement officers towards offenders.

Reformation and prevention may, therefore, serve the defense of society against crime presumably better than either deterrence or retribution or both.

The schema of social defense against crime may, therefore, be divided according to the following chronological stages: (1) Criminal prophylaxis, which is concerned with the diagnosis, prognosis and treatment of potential delinquents and offenders. (2) If the first stage proved to be a losing battle we continue our war by sentencing the offender. Our next field of interest is, therefore, the sentencing policy of criminal courts which deals with the application of the various penal measures by the courts, and [the] study [of] the interrelation of factors concerning the offense and offender in the sentencing policy taken as a whole. (3) If the offender is found guilty and sentenced, we must consider the execution of the sentence, which is carried out by various administrative authorities. These authorities are, as the case may be, prisons, closed penal institutions, open ones, and bodies who administer other methods of treating offenders. (4) The last part is naturally the "after-care" stage. The offender has served his term of imprisonment or undergone the prescribed penal treatment, but the task of social defense is not finished yet. It has to see to it that the offender's first crucial steps in freedom shall not lead to a relapse into more crime. It has to try to ease the offender's re-adaptation to society and help him to lead a law-abiding life.

Many offenders share the prevailing attitude of many members of legitimate society that the latter is obviously acquisitive, lucrative, "cut-throat" competitive, morally confused and patently dishonest, a racket of "the status seekers" operated by "the hidden persuaders" and by "the organization man" for the good and glory of "the power elite." The express or implied reaction of the offender to the staff's moralizing righteousness is: "Why do you want to make a saint out of me? What about the hordes of 'fixers,' politicians, business-men and other white collar criminals who get away with it because they have the right connections and nobody really gives two hoots today for the law, all they care for is not being caught. They are the same as me, only bigger thieves and a lot smarter so they don't get caught."

Another defense mechanism of offenders against society, which is more subterranean but not less profound or real is the claim voiced by many that society needs its criminal both materially and emotionally. From time immemorial the criminals helped to fill the treasury. The "Bot," "Wite," "Freudus" and "Wergild" were wholly or partly paid into the medieval Seigneur's purse and the sentencing policy of Elizabethan courts in England was strongly influenced by the need of galley slaves in Her Majesty's warships.

But society needs its criminals for less lucrative but more important reasons. It needs them for its cohesion, inner security and as a legitimate outlet for aggression. It is also a source of pleasure, and the utilitarians who saw everything from the pain-pleasure point of view cherished the pleasure of punishing the criminal by identifying with the feelings of the victim.

More conspicuous is the release of pent-up aggression by the act of punishment. This release of aggression was possible in the public hangings and floggings and in modern times by the enormous publicity given to crimes and punishments by the press, radio and television. Here we have a striking similarity between the fights of Roman gladiators, bull-fights and prize-fights and the interest of the public in criminal trials. The fight which takes place between the defense and prosecution and the tense and exciting atmosphere of the courtroom, especially in sensational cases, turn the whole thing into a festivity where repressed aggression, perverse curiosity and sometimes latent or overt sadism are oozing from their hosts.

Punishing the criminal also helps to ease the guilt feelings of respectable citizens. Man's life is riddled with endless normative proscriptions, moral, social and legal. The constant inner struggle and especially the desire to act against these morals and laws create guilt feelings which are eased by righteously punishing the criminal. The retributive penalty inflicted on the criminal who committed acts which we secretly wish to do expiates subconsciously and symbolically our guilt for day (or night) dreaming the exploits of a Joe Adonis, a James Moran or a Lucky Luciano.

The criminal and his punishment also help the respectable and law-abiding citizen to remain respectable and law-abiding, because if the criminal is not punished properly the "squares" are going to say: "Why should I fight my natural tendencies to commit an immoral (and sometimes criminal) act when those who don't give two hoots for the law and get things which I secretly desire, get off lightly. There should be a law! And there should be heavy penalties!" This explains why the first stones are very rarely cast by those who are without sin. The stronger one's anti-social tendencies, the fiercer is his righteous demand to punish offenders. The most ardent moralizers are also the strongest subconscious sympathizers with the immoral deeds.

The criminal, his detection, apprehension and punishment help, therefore, the "legit" society to check its multiple aggressions, curb its latent criminal tendencies and ease its guilt feelings.

Last but not least, the denunciation of an out-group (the criminals) always helps the cohesion of the ingroup. There is nothing better to arouse solidarity in a citizens' action committee than the vivid description of a crime wave which threatens to engulf us. The most potent part of a norm is the sanction for not complying with it, and using this sanction on violators strengthens the force of the norm and everybody sees that the law is not an empty word but a whip with a stinging lash.

IMPEDIMENTS TO PENAL REFORM*

NORVAL MORRIS

Penal reform must stretch beyond its traditional humanitarian purposes to achieve a larger social protection from crime and recidivism. There are obstacles to this effort; I propose to consider certain of them under the following four headings: deterrence; less eligibility; the limits of the rehabilitative ideal; and the ethics and strategy of research.

I. DETERRENCE

The deterrence argument is more frequently implicit than expressed; the debate more frequently polarized than the subject of a balanced discussion.

* Reprinted with permission from *The University of Chicago Law Review*, XXXIII, No. 4 (Summer 1966), 627–56. Copyright 1966 by the University of Chicago.

When I listen to the dialogue between the punishers and the treaters, I hear the punishers making propositions based on the assumption that our penal sanctions deter others who are like-minded from committing crime. And I hear the treaters making propositions concerning the best treatment for a given offender or class of offenders which are based on the assumption that our penal sanctions do not at all deter. There is rarely any meeting of the minds on the issue central to the discourse.

European criminologists draw a distinction between special and general deterrence which is helpful to our purposes. By special deterrence they refer to the threat of further punishment of one who has already been convicted and punished for crime; it may be the same medicine that is threatened as a method of dissuading him from recidivism or it may be a threat of a larger or different dose. Special deterrence thus considers punishment in the microcosm of the group of convicted criminals. General deterrence looks to the macrocosm of society as a whole (including convicted criminals). It would seem hard to deny that for some types of crime and for some types of people, the individual superego is reinforced and to a certain extent conditioned by the existence of formal punishments imposed by society, and that we are influenced by the educative and stigmatizing functions of the criminal law.

Perhaps the capital punishment controversy has produced the most reliable information we have on the general deterrent effects of a criminal sanction. It seems to me well established, as well established as almost any other proposition in the social sciences, that the existence or non-existence of capital punishment as a sanction alternative to protracted imprisonment for convicted murderers, makes no difference to the murder rate or the attempted murder rate. Suppose this is true; there is a temptation to extrapolate such a proposition to other crimes. This temptation should be resisted for it is quite easy to demonstrate contrary situations for other crimes where increased sanctions (maintaining stable reporting, detection, arrest, and conviction rates) lead to reduced incidence of the proscribed behavior. For example, by way of extreme contrast to murder, parking offenses can indeed be reduced by an increased severity of sanctions if one is determined about the matter.

And I conclude, on this topic, as I hope you do, that those who would pin their larger faith to deterrence are unwise; and that those who deny its operative relevance in many mundane and smaller areas of behavioral control are likewise unwise. What we need are some soundings in deterrence, some tracings of this shore, so that we shall begin to know where the flatness of the human personality is relevant and where the roundness; for what purpose this particular world is flat and for what purposes round. Given these insights, a massive impediment to penal reform would be cast aside.

II. LESS ELIGIBILITY

The principle of "less eligibility" is the reverse side of the coin of deterrence. Sidney and Beatrice Webb defined this principle, in relation to the

19th century Poor Laws in England, as follows: "The principle of less eligibility demanded that the conditions of existence afforded by the relief (of the pauper) should be less eligible to the applicant than those of the lowest grade of independent labourers." When applied to penal sanctions, and certainly to prisons and reformatory institutions, it means that the conditions of the convicted criminal should be "less eligible" than those of any other section of the community. Jeremy Bentham, in his *Panopticon,* adopted this principle: "The ordinary condition of a convict . . . ought not to be made more eligible than that of the poorest class of subjects in a state of innocence and liberty."

The principle of less eligibility has, as you see, an attractive simplicity. If the conditions of the convicted criminal are to be better than those of any other group in the community, then that group, when they know of this fact, will hurry to join their more fortunate brethren — and the gates lie open via crime. Far from being deterred, they will be attracted.

The truth is that at all levels of cultural development we seem to accept that compulsory treatment, with the stigma of crime, and pursuant to a judicial sentence, is not likely to be positively attractive to other than those who by long institutionalization have been habituated to it.

Thus, though the principle of less eligibility remains a rationalization for the punitive emotions of men, it is not at present a serious bar to penal reform. There is, however, one other aspect of this principle of less eligibility that may merit a passing glance. Assume that to keep a prisoner costs the community about $2,500 a year. It may be cheaper if our prediction instruments were at all reliable, to leave him at large and by weekly subsidy of $40 to reward his virtuous avoidance of crime; like a reverse income tax, a reverse crime contribution. It may be cheaper, but it won't soon happen. We may doubt the deterrent efficacy of a sanction but we had better, for the time being, not make our punishments positively attractive.

III. The Limits of the Rehabilitative Ideal

A new but nevertheless serious impediment to penal reform is our growing skepticism about the wisdom of indulging in practice our desire better to treat convicted criminals by mobilizing for that purpose the developing skills of the relevant social sciences. We have come to fear that by so doing we will sacrifice many of the traditional and important values of justice under law. The rehabilitative ideal is seen to import unfettered discretion. Whereas the treaters seem convinced of the benevolence of their treatment methods, those being treated take a different view, and we, the observers, share their doubts. The jailer in a white coat and with a doctorate remains a jailer—but with larger powers over his fellows. It is clear that [in the absence of a precise] definition of the proper limits of the rehabilitative ideal, this lawyer-like skepticism of ours is a serious theoretical and practical impediment to penal reform.

The dangers of abuse of the rehabilitative ideal are real, but they must not tempt us to inaction; we must not let our skepticism of the reformer's simplistic enthusiasm lead us to a flat and unproductive opposition. Throughout all developed legal systems the rehabilitative ideal sweeps steadily over the jurisprudence of the criminal law and it is regrettable for lawyers to oppose it.

I do not seek to rebut the thesis that the rehabilitative ideal can be abused and has frequently been abused; it seems to me proper to look with suspicion on those who seek power over the lives of others, including the criminal and the juvenile delinquent, on the ground that it will be exercised for their own good and hence for the larger social good.

In sum, I would suggest that there is a clear difference between the medical, social welfare, psychiatric, and child care functions of the state and its police and correctional functions. There is too much confusion of purposes and too frequently a sacrifice of justice when we combine the several justifications the state may have for taking power over a citizen's life and in so doing expunge or attenuate the existing limitations and controls of power that each has developed. This confusion, productive of injustice, is frequently to be observed. I saw it first ten years ago in a most virulent form in the institution for defective delinquents in Bridgewater, Massachusetts (I hear it has much improved since then) where men were held for a combination of crime and retardation much longer and in grossly less attractive circumstances than they would have been had these labels not been combined. In the sexual psychopath laws of this country the mental health power has infested the judicial power over criminals with like result. The juvenile court suffers a similar and needless confusion of heads of authority. And many plans advanced to meet the problem of narcotic addiction, not the least being recent so-called Civil Commitment Legislation in New York, suffer pathologically from this unjust cumulative mixture of state powers. I am not preaching a sterile separation of powers which would impede penal reform. The rehabilitative ideal has luxuriant opportunity to contribute to human welfare and the diminution of individual suffering without arrogating to itself such extra power.

Let me go beyond defense of this principle of punitive ceiling and try to take the matter one step further by offering an outline of another process which seems to me to bear on our agreed aim of rehabilitation without tyranny. Perhaps, as one method of avoiding the injustice of the unfettered benevolence of the rehabilitative ideal, we should make more use of administrative controls of punishing-treating processes rather than to pursue only the separation of powers theme I have advanced.

IV. Ethics and Strategy of Research

It has recently become fashionable to stress our lack of knowledge of the relative efficacy of our various treatment methods and I do not wish on this occasion to retrace that melancholy story. The central question eludes us:

which treatment methods are effective for which types of offenders and for how long should they be applied for optimum effect? Criminological research has been unwisely concentrated on the search for that will-o-the-wisp, the causes of crime, glossing over the likelihood that crime is not a unity capable of aetiological study. "What are the causes of disease?" is surely as hopelessly wide and methodologically inappropriate a question as is the question "what are the causes of crime?" At last, however, there is widespread verbal agreement (if not action) that we must critically test our developing armamentarium of prevention and treatment methods, and that to do so requires testing by means of controlled clinical trials. Follow-up studies, association analysis, predictive attributes analysis — no matter how sophisticated other research techniques we apply, we cannot escape the need for direct evaluative research by means of clinical trials.

In medical and pharmacological research the clinical trial is well established and has proved of great value in the development of therapeutic methods. Where there is genuine doubt as to the choice between two or more treatments for a given condition, efficient experimentation requires that the competing methods be tested on matched groups of patients. Of course, the analogy between the doctor's "treatment" and the court's or penal administrator's "treatment" is imperfect. Both the subject of medical diagnosis and the criteria of successful treatment are better defined, and the patient consents to treatment while the criminal does not. Problems of abuse of human rights thus obtrude when it is sought to apply the clinical trial to correctional practice. It is justifiable to impose a criminal sanction guided by the necessities of research and not the felt necessities of the case?

It is my view that the ethical argument against clinical trials is not convincing and that, given certain safeguards, it is entirely appropriate, indeed essential, for evaluative research projects of this type to be built into all new correctional developments. The two safeguards that I have in mind may not in perpetuity solve the problem, but they do at least provide sufficient protection of human rights for many decades of correctional research.

First, we do not have to apply such research techniques at the stage of judicial sentencing; they can well operate within the sentence that the judge has determined to be the just and appropriate sentence. Secondly, by applying a principle which might be called the principle of "less severity," abuse of human rights can be minimized.

In conclusion, let me say that it is my position that the ethical difficulties in empirical evaluation research are so slight as not to constitute a serious impediment to it.

Putting the ethical obstacles aside, I come to one last but serious strategic impediment to the immediate potentiality of empirical evaluative research to lighten our ignorance of treatment methods. It is peculiarly difficult to organize an effective evaluative program from outside the penal system itself. It may be that only from within the administration can effective and continuing research programs be mounted; and it is certain that it cannot be mounted from without unless there is enthusiastic and strong support for it from within. Thus, California is now producing more meaningful evaluative research than any other state or country in the world. One reason is that the Adult and Youth Authorities in that state have built their research programs deeply into their administrative structures. The same thing is in very small part true in the United Kingdom and to some degree in the federal systems and some of the more progressive states; but it is the rare exception and certainly not the rule.

THE STATUS OF CAPITAL PUNISHMENT: A WORLD PERSPECTIVE*

CLARENCE H. PATRICK

Data were obtained on 128 of 146 countries (largely the most populous ones) selected for this study. It is virtually impossible to divide all the countries of the world into two groups — those having the death penalty and those not having the death penalty. A number of problems are encountered in attempting to assign many countries to one or the other category. For example, the question must be approached from the viewpoint of both the provisions found in the law and the actual practice of the various jurisdictions. There are countries that are abolitionist *de jure* while on the other hand there are countries that are abolitionist *de facto*. Tabulating those that are known to be completely abolitionist *de jure* presents no difficulties. In 1962 there were eighteen such countries as well as the Federal Government and twenty-five of twenty-nine states of Mexico, one state (Queensland) in Australia, and five states (Alaska, Hawaii, Maine, Minnesota, and Wisconsin) of the United States. (Michigan became completely abolitionist in 1963.)

Although having the provision for capital punishment the small country of Liechtenstein has not had an execution since 1798. Thus there is no doubt that some countries may be categorized as having abolished the death penalty *de facto*. However, establishing criteria for determining which countries should be listed as having abolished capital punishment *de facto* involves a number of significant questions. Some of the questions that must be considered are the following: What about countries that occasionally sentence

* Reprinted by special permission from *The Journal of Criminal Law, Criminology and Police Science*, copyright © 1965 by Northwestern University School of Law, LVI, No. 4 (1965), 397–411.

persons to death and then subsequently commute their sentences? It is possible that they reason that retaining the legal provision and passing the sentence of death without intending to execute it may have some salutary effect? In such situations are some of the significant elements of the capital punishment complex retained? If such is not the case then why have the death penalty laws not been repealed where no one is actually executed? It is hardly conceivable that such important and dramatic statutes could have been overlooked. Or, may it be reasoned that some countries retain the provision for the death sentence with the idea of possibly using it should some most heinous crime be perpetrated? Also, how much time without an execution must elapse before a country may appropriately be designated as having abolition *de facto*? Except for what Sellin calls one "accident" after World War II, Belgium has not had an execution since 1867. However, occasional death sentences are pronounced in Belgium, but they are customarily commuted to life sentences. Thirty-six of eighty-nine countries with capital punishment reported that they had no executions for the five-year period 1958–1962. Also during that period there were no executions in the United States by the Federal Government, the District of Columbia and nine states. May all, any, or none of these countries and jurisdictions be regarded as having abolition *de facto*? Because of the problems involved in definition the author has not attempted to list those countries that have abolished the death penalty in practice.

There are thirteen countries and two states of the United States that have legally limited the use of the death penalty. They provide the penalty only for unusual crimes such as treason, espionage, and murder of the chief of state, or crimes committed under unusual circumstances such as wartime. Most of these countries have frequently been designated as not having capital punishment. The author of this study does not list any country as having abolition if it has any provision for the death sentence.

In striking contrast to earlier times, only a small number of crimes may now carry the death penalty in the various countries of the world. At some periods in the past the number of capital crimes was virtually limitless, but at present the average number is about six in countries having the death penalty. In about fifty percent of the countries four or fewer crimes are so defined. For example, in Great Britain today, only four crimes (murder, treason, piracy with violence, and arson in H.M. dockyards and ships) are punishable by death, as compared with over 200 in the eighteenth century. Also, although the aggregate of capital crimes in all countries of the modern world is large it does not compare with the number that was obtained in single countries in the past. There are 109 crimes that may carry the death penalty in the 106 countries which reported having provisions for capital punishment. Because of some difficulties of gathering that type of data on a world-wide scale the list is probably not completely exhaustive, although nearly so. Some of the problems encountered in collecting such data are as follows: terminological difficulties, as mentioned earlier; the fact that criminal laws of many countries and states have not been codified completely, if at all; some countries operating under both written and unwritten laws or customs; and the fact that a few countries may prescribe the death sentence by analogy. It seems that a complete list of capital crimes embracing all the fifty states of the United States has not been compiled.

Murder and treason are the offenses most frequently defined as capital crimes in the world today. Each is so defined in 97 of the 106 reporting countries having the death penalty. The next in frequency of definition as capital crimes are espionage, arson, homicide accompanied by another serious crime, rape, robbery, insurrection or rebellion, patricide, and sabotage.

It is also significant to note that over fifty percent of the 109 capital offenses listed are applicable to only one of the various countries. Several reasons seem to account for that fact. Some of the listed capital crimes may be no more than anachronisms that have been overlooked in the revision of criminal statutes in some countries, some are actually capital crimes in other countries but covered by more broadly defined offenses, and others are occasionally found probably because the acts are regarded as being exceptionally odious due to peculiar national customs, attitudes and values. An example of the latter may be observed in the state of Georgia in the United States, which prescribes the death penalty for the desecration of a grave with intent to rob or molest the human remains, and in Saudi Arabia, where adultery by women is a capital crime.

At the present time considerably over fifty pecent of the countries of the world have no executions for capital crimes during the course of a year. Equally significant, is the fact that 54 (51 percent) of the 107 countries for which data were obtained on the question reported that they had not had an execution in five years. Eighteen of those countries had no provision for the death penalty. However, 36 (40 percent) of the reporting countries having provisions for the death penalty had no executions during the five-year period. In thirteen of the countries which had executions during that period the average for each was less than one per year.

The average of the combined number of executions annually (1958-1962) in the 89 countries with capital punishment that reported on the question was 535.3. Although that number may appear large, it represents a phenomenal decline when compared with the number of executions in earlier years. Actually the yearly total of executions in the world today appears to be less than the number which took place in some single countries at an earlier time. For example in England during the reign of the Tudors criminal law was administered with extreme severity. It has been estimated that the number of executions in London and Middlesex county alone was an average of 560 yearly during the reign of Edward VI. During the last thirty years the average number of executions per year in the United States has decreased from over 150 to less than 50.

With few exceptions, most countries of the present day have reduced the act of execution in capital cases to the deprivation of life only, having eliminated intended torture and prolonged suffering. This is in contrast to earlier years when a limitless variety of drawn out and painful methods of execution were employed. Nowadays in virtually all countries the immediate objective in the act of execution is to induce death by what seems to be the quickest, most painless, and most practical method. There is, however, a considerable amount of speculation and difference of opinion from country to country as to which of several methods of execution is the most satisfactory on the basis of those criteria.

Six methods of execution are in use in the world today. In no single country are all six methods employed. Many countries have two methods for carrying out the death sentence, one for cases having been tried in ordinary courts and the other for cases having been heard in military courts (violations of military codes, treason during war time, etc.).

Hanging is the most widespread method of execution. It is used in 57 (56 percent) of the reporting countries where the death penalty obtains. Traditionally hanging has been the method of execution in the United Kingdom, generally throughout the Commonwealth and in most of the territories and possessions that were formerly British. It has also long been the method used in many non-British countries. Shooting is the second most widespread method of execution in use today. It is the principal or only method used in 33 (34 percent) of the reporting countries.

Four other methods of execution are used to a lesser extent. Beheading is used in carrying out the death sentence in eight countries. This is the method France has used for ordinary crimes since the Revolution of 1789. Decapitation, however, has not been limited to France or French influenced countries. Electrocution is the method used in the Philippines and twenty-four states of the United States. Executions in Spain are carried out by strangulation (*garrote vil*). Although beheading is the principal method used in Saudi Arabia, it may be replaced by stoning to death in the case of a woman guilty of adultery or other offenses forbidden by the Quran.

The vast majority of countries provide by statute a minimum age (age at the time the crime was committed) below which no sentence of death may be passed. The offender must be at least eighteen years of age in 81 percent of the 91 countries which reported a specified minimum age in capital cases. In five of the reporting countries the legal minimum age in death cases is below sixteen years, ranging from seven to fifteen years of age. However, it again must be recognized that what is possible by law may be highly improbable by custom or practice. It also may be noted that eight countries reported they had no minimum age relative to the death sentence. More information is needed before any conclusion may be reached regarding their actual practice on the question.

From a world view the provisions and practices with respect to minimum age in capital cases is again in sharp contrast to those of former times. In the eighteenth century and later it was not uncommon for children, some as young as eight or nine years of age, to be executed, oftentimes for crimes which now would be defined as relatively minor offenses.

Public attendance at executions for capital crimes is legally forbidden in the vast majority of countries today. Executions are closed to the public in 81 or about 81 percent of the 99 countries which reported on the subject. This situation represents a vast change from the time when hangings and administrations of the death sentence by other methods were public spectacles. Until relatively recent years in numerous countries it was not uncommon for large crowds, often numbering several thousand men, women, and children, to attend public executions. A general assumption during those times was that observing an offender pay with his life for his crime would have a deterrent effect on potential criminals among the observers and in the public at large.

The practice of having public executions continues to exist in a few countries. In nine of the countries reporting on the question, executions are open to the public, and in nine other countries they may be open to the public under certain circumstances or if so ordered by the proper authorities. The following are countries that have open executions: Cambodia, Cameroun, Central African Republic, Ethiopia, Haiti, Iran, Laos, Nicaragua, and Paraguay.

At the present time there seems to be no world-wide trend toward complete abolition of the death penalty. During the past twenty-five years about as many countries have reinstated capital punishment as have abolished it. The countries that recently [date in brackets] have abolished the death sentence are Bolivia (1962), Federal Republic of Germany (1949), Greenland (1954), Honduras (1957), Italy (1954), and Monaco (1962). Those that have reinstated the death penalty are Ceylon (1959), the state of Delaware of the United States (1961), Union of Soviet Socialist Republics (1950), Somali (1960), and several European countries which reinstated it on a limited basis during and after World War II.

In the questionnaire used in this study the question was asked of each country "Are there any trends toward abolition or reinstatement of the death penalty?" Admittedly the question involved, at least to some degree, a subjective answer on the part of the respondent. Needless to say, his answer probably had to depend on what he thought were the trends as reflected by public discussion or proposed legislation. From countries having capital punishment seventy-two respondents stated there were no trends toward abolition and twenty stated there were some abolitionist trends. From the eighteen countries where capital punishment does not legally exist all respondents reported there were no trends toward reinstatement.

THE NATIONAL PROFILE
OF CORRECTION*

On any one day in the U.S., about 1¼ million persons are under the jurisdiction of state and local correctional agencies and institutions. In addition, many thousands more are serving from a few days to a few weeks in a variety of local lockups and jails not included in this survey.

Of the total volume reported, 28 per cent are juveniles and 72 per cent are adults (according to the definitions of each category, which vary from state to state). The number of adults under probation and parole supervision and in correctional institutions (876,412) is more than the number of enlisted personnel (846,684) reported in the U.S. Army for 1965.

One-third (more than 400,000) of all offenders reported, juvenile and adult, were found in institutions; two-thirds (over 800,000) were in communities under probation or parole supervision. However, about 20 per cent of the latter are on either parole or aftercare status, having first served time in an institution. Judges and juries evidently place a high degree of reliance on institutional commitment.

Agencies and institutions receive, during the course of a year, more than 2.5 million persons, whose status as inmate, probationer, or parolee directly affects, in addition, 5,825,000 members of their families. One may well speculate on the number affected over a 10 or 20-year period and the percentage of the entire population this would represent.

The question of where an offender is — in the community (on probation or parole) or in an institution — makes a profound difference to his family's economic condition and the welfare resources of his community. Although the total commitment rate for the nation cannot be estimated accurately, it would appear that (excluding those sentenced to fines) about two-thirds of all offenders are committed to institutions. That the commitment rate can be lowered has been demonstrated by the Saginaw Project, which, in addition, offered evidence of the comparatively greater success achieved with offenders through increased use of effective probation. A lower commitment rate produces enormous savings not only in manpower but also in taxes.

The estimated cost of operating state and local correctional services in 1965 was almost $1 billion ($940,467,494).

* Reprinted with permission from "The National Profile of Correction," *Correction in the United States, Crime and Delinquency* (January 1967), pp. 229–60, by the National Council on Crime and Delinquency.

About 80 per cent of the total operating cost is allocated for institutions. Of that allocation, more than half goes to support state adult correctional institutions. Local institutions and jails account for about 16 per cent of all expenditures; juvenile detention accounts for about 6 per cent of the total. Only 14.4 per cent of correctional costs are allocated for probation services, including supervision of offenders and preparation of social studies to aid courts in making dispositions.

Of the total cost, one-third ($314,569,795) is for juvenile detention, institutions, and aftercare.

Costs for local services for misdemeanant offenders account for 18.7 per cent of the total, with only 3 per cent going for probation services and 15.7 per cent on confinement of misdemeanants.

The figures for per capita cost of all correctional expenditures according to per capita income are not available for all states, but they undoubtedly would show a wide variation, with some of the poorer states paying proportionately more than some of the wealthier states.

There are wide variations in per capita expenditure for these services in the ten largest states, where the average is $2.95 but the range is from $1.75 to $5.31. The average total expenditure is 0.10 per cent of per capita income, but the range extends from 0.06 per cent to 0.17 per cent.

In some states that now expend a disproportionate share of income for correctional services, improvement of services may require even further disparity unless subsidy is obtained from some outside source.

The overall daily cost for a juvenile in an institution is 10 times more than the cost of juvenile probation or aftercare. For adults, state institutional cost is about six times that of parole and about 14 times that of probation.

The low cost of probation can be attributed in part to excessively heavy caseloads and low salaries. The average cost per case should be more than doubled to enable probation nationally to become more effective.

The "half-starved" condition of probation services may be one reason why commitment rates are so high. Many judges interviewed during the course of NCCD's state and community surveys report their reluctance to add more offenders to the burdens of an already overburdened probation service. On the other hand, where probation services has been improved, judges have made greater use of them.

If one-third of the prisoners were transferred to probation along with their share of the expenditures, they could be placed in caseloads of ten or less. As has been demonstrated by the California Community Treatment Project, this move would be a more effective disposition and use of public funds.

The overall distribution of personnel in correction is featured by disparity; specifically, a disproportionate allocation to institutions. The ratio of institutional personnel to probation and parole personnel is 4:1 in juvenile correction and 10:1 in adult correction. Institutional personnel make up almost 90 per cent of the entire correctional force. State institution personnel alone constitute 42 per cent of all correctional personnel.

Within the institutions themselves, 62.7 per cent of all employees are custodial staff. Treatment staff, including caseworkers, psychologists, and psychiatrists, are only 3.6 per cent; educational staff, including both academic and vocational teachers, account for 5.9 per cent. All other personnel account for 27.8 per cent.

Caseload sizes of field personnel also vary according to systems. Generally, parole officers and juvenile aftercare workers carry smaller caseloads than probation officers. Since caseloads are frequently mixed — combinations of probation and parole, or aftercare and juvenile probation, or juvenile probation and child neglect, etc. — the survey asked for the total average caseload being carried by correctional personnel.

More than three-fourths of the persons on misdemeanant probation and more than two-thirds of those under felony probation supervision are in caseloads of over 100. Since personnel in these two systems are responsible also for presentence investigations (each counted as equivalent to five supervision units) a caseload of "over 100" is several times larger than the 50-unit caseload recommended by the standard. Not quite 1 per cent of the misdemeanants, only 3 per cent of adult probationers, and only 8 per cent of parolees were found in supervision loads of 50 or under. The situation is a little better in the two other services: about 12 per cent of juvenile probationers and 28 per cent of juveniles under aftercare supervision are in caseloads of 50 or less. The median caseload range is 61–70 in juvenile aftercare and parole, and 71–80 in juvenile probation. As noted above, the median caseload range in both misdemeanant and adult probation is "over 100." The majority of offenders under supervision, taken as a whole (420,903 or 51.5 per cent) are in caseloads above 90.

The extreme differences in caseload percentages between services as a whole — for example, between caseloads in juvenile aftercare compared with caseloads in misdemeanant probation — very often occur in the same community and may be attributed to differences in philosophy, availability of funds, personnel, and public support, and, most certainly, to the absence of coordinated administrative direction referred to above.

Addition of 16,583 field and institutional personnel (excluding detention) to the staff now employed is needed to bring ratios of professional, social and psychological treatment services up to recommended standards. Of the total additional force, 12,532 are required in probation and parole and 4,051 in institutions.

Juvenile institutions reported more innovative programs than any other state agency; parole agencies reported the fewest.

Of the programs reported by all agencies, the most prevalent type was group counseling and group therapy for offenders or their parents. Other popular projects included special vocational counseling or training, special education, work release, and special projects for alcoholics and for narcotics law violators.

Perhaps the limited number of new and existing projects can be explained by the widespread deficiencies in basic services. Administrators are not encouraged to establish new programs when their energies are directed primarily toward securing basic program needs. Nevertheless, new programs must be evaluated and the results must be communicated to correctional executives so that what is worthwhile will become widely known and what is proved to be ineffective will not be duplicated.

Any attempt to understand the needs, problems, and possibilities of correction in the United States would be incomplete without knowledge of the opinions, attitudes, and hopes of those who operate the correctional agencies and are concerned with the problems of correction in states and communities day by day.

To tap this huge reservoir of experience, NCCD issued invitations to key correctional officials and others familiar with correctional problems in each state to attend a one-day meeting as part of the survey process.

Seven broad categories of correctional issues emerge as an overall characteristic of the state meetings:

1. The need for across-the-board strengthening of probation and parole. — Basic services such as probation and parole, which have proven effective, are still undersupported, both quantitatively and qualitatively.

2. The need for greater, broader funding of correctional services. — Correctional personnel salaries are low; correctional programs, with few exceptions, must get along on shoestring budgets, untrained personnel, overcrowding, and few treatment programs. Insufficient financing has become almost a fact of life to which some correctional people have made a resigned adjustment.

3. The need for a clearer correctional philosophy. — The nation must decide what it wants done about offenders. One meeting called this a need to define the national attitude toward offenders: "Do we wish to punish or to cure?" Many felt that the field of correction itself is torn by ideological conflicts, has failed to develop a workable philosophy on how best to control crime, and has not achieved a shared body of knowledge and skills.

4. The need for better public understanding of the correctional task. — Correctional work is hampered by public ignorance, and many correctional officials are expending much of their energy in interpreting their roles — energy that should be used with offenders and clients.

5. The need for more manpower with which to handle crime and delinquency. — The growing manpower need greatly exceeds the supply of qualified personnel.

6. The need for increased state-level coordination of correctional services. — This issue was related to funding, deployment of personnel, programing, physical facilities, provision of specialized services, and training and recruitment of personnel.

7. The need for general improvement in the administration of justice. —

The machinery of justice, on which correction is dependent, was seen as needing repair. References were made to the large number of felons in local jails, unserved misdemeanants, skewed sentencing practices, abridgment of constitutional rights of juveniles, bail bond problems, and undue response to political influences.

On the other hand, several other well-defined problems are regarded as capable of solution now or in the near future. There was hope that, in some manner, current national efforts would help ameliorate some of these specific correctional problems now.

1. Training and Education. — Though the correctional field acknowledges quite frankly that it needs more knowledge and skills, the question remains — where are they to be obtained? In-service training emerged as a top priority. Some participants called for a national academy for correction, others for regional workshops. Many expressed interest in programs that would provide opportunities for graduate and undergraduate education, though admittedly much current training seems to be unrelated to any specific correctional rationale. Some agencies have small budgets for training; many have no funds at all for this purpose. Some meetings suggested that the federal government should support correctional education as it does mental health, teacher training, medical training, etc.

2. Diagnostic Services. — The number of professional personnel available for testing, evaluation, and psychiatric and psychological consultation to courts, parole agencies, and institutions is insufficient: Diagnostic services need to be accompanied by expanded treatment resources.

3. Detention. — The conferences generalized a need for more and better juvenile detention centers. Many children are still jailed; where detention homes exist, there is often a lack of adequate programing, with undue emphasis on custody. This was consistently traced to lack of funds and trained staff. Detention centers frequently are not constructed according to modern standards; few are available regionally. Several groups shared the view that federal funds should be made available for regional detention programs and construction, but such construction should not be based on present high rates of detention.

4. Special Services. — All meetings voiced the need for more alternatives for control and treatment of the offender. Most frequently mentioned were vocational rehabilitation, group services, halfway houses, foster homes, work release, and camps — all of them well publicized but few of them available for the mass of offenders.

5. Diversification. — The groups pointed up the need for special kinds of physical facilities and programs to meet different needs. The retarded or marginally defective offender and the criminally insane were most frequently mentioned in this regard. Many participants reported that in their states retarded delinquents are held in jails and detention homes because the facilities where they should be placed are overcrowded or nonexistent.

6. Statistical System. — There was general agreement that more coordinated, centralized statistical programs are needed for accurate information on volume, costs, personnel, etc., for planning and interpretation.

7. Regionalization. — Many of the administrators deplored the location of correctional facilities in isolated rural communities, often built and retained there because of political influences. A number of participants argued that state institutions should be relocated to serve regional and local needs better.

8. Presentence Reports. — The meetings reported that many decisions affecting offenders are being made without benefit of social-psychological data, because of an insufficient number of probation staff, no staff at all, untrained staff, or an attitude that such reports are not important. It was generally thought that more and better use of presentence and diagnostic reports would be an important step toward a more effective system of correction.

9. Research. — Generally, the groups called for more research on causes of deviant behavior and on ways to measure the effectiveness of existing as well as experimental treatment programs. A strong role was seen for the federal government in meeting this kind of need.

10. Adult Services. — Additional issues related to adult programs only included (a) legislation and services needed for the misdemeanant offender; (b) disparities in sentencing practices; (c) broader development of services for addicts and alcoholics; (d) increased need for jail standards relative to construction, maintenance, and program.

11. Miscellaneous. — Among other matters considered important but not mentioned as frequently as those noted above are the following: (a) the need for more uniformity in legal codes; (b) creation of family district courts; (c) creation of youth authorities modeled on the California plan and similar plans; (d) legislation permitting youthful offender programs; (e) establishing and improving police juvenile bureaus; (f) elimination of political influences in appointments; (g) creation of commissions for planning in adult correction; and (h) state citizen action programs to bring nonpartisan interest to bear on planning.

As viewed by the more than 700 persons at the state conferences, the federal role is to prompt and initiate the plans and provide the means to carry them out; the state role is to design and execute the plans. The state meetings suggested the following as most appropriate to the federal role:

1. Education and Training. — The federal government should subsidize formal and informal education for correction — long-term graduate and undergraduate education and short-term in-service training.

2. Leadership. — Federal leadership is required in setting standards, encouraging growth, providing opportunities, assessing needs, etc.

3. Research. — The federal role here stems from the conviction that the kinds of special skills required are not generally available at the local level.

4. Statistical System. — A uniform national statistical system is suggested.

5. Grantsmanship Information. — Local leaders need authoritative advice and information on how to qualify for federal grants.

6. Permanency and Coordination of Federal Programs. — The Neighborhood Youth Corps, the Job Corps, and other similar federal programs related to delinquency prevention should become permanent and should be coordinated in a centralized structure including all federal agencies concerned with crime and delinquency. Models exist in such well-established structures as Vocational Rehabilitation, the National Institute of Mental Health, and the Hill-Burton Act.

7. Construction Subsidies. — Through the Hill-Burton Act, the federal government should provide the means for construction of detention homes, diagnostic centers, halfway houses, and facilities for group living.

CORRECTIONAL INSTITUTIONS IN A GREAT SOCIETY*

DANIEL GLASER

The most relevant aspect of the rapid social change for this audience is the probable growth of new types of correctional agencies. These will be correctional institutions in the city, replacing the present predominance of prisons and training schools in rural areas. This will be a consequence of the growing movement to graduate the release process, and to increase the contact of institutionalized offenders with beneficial persons in their home communities.

If a released offender is to obtain success in a noncriminal social life, and in legitimate occupational pursuits, he must achieve this success outside of the institution. It must be a success which he can maintain in the community to which he will be released. Obviously, with social needs, income needs and expense management problems all extreme, and all confronting a released offender at once, his chances of success would appear to be less than they would be were he able to face these problems one at a time, or to face them all gradually. Therefore, the first distinctive feature of the correctional institution of the future is that release from it will be gradual, even more gradual than by current types of parole. In this way, the offender can gain experience in pursuing a social life among noncriminal persons and in earning a living on temporary or part-time release, while he still has both

* Reprinted with permission from "Correctional Institutions in a Great Society," *Criminologica*, III, Nos. 2–3 (August–November 1965), 5–7.

some constraints, and some guarantee of subsistence in case he is unsuccessful in earning his own needs. This means a half-way house or work-release type of institution. This also makes counselling available immediately when a releasee encounters problems in the post-release world, rather than just at an institution far in advance of his post-release experience, or at a parole office appointment weeks or months after difficulties occur in the community.

It seems obvious that institutions which achieve this will be institutions geographically close to the release destinations of most of their inmates. This will, in most cases, be in large cities, since this is where the vast majority of offenders come from. If inmates are to be released from them to pursue lives as free individuals for part of the day, they must be institutions in which men have the clothing and other paraphernalia, including pocket money, necessary for ordinary life in the free community.

Correctional institutions in the future are foreshadowed by the growing number and variety of half-way houses. These new institutions will be a transition between the traditional places of long confinement and outright parole. The distinctive American contribution to corrections I suggest, though not by any means absent from experience in other countries, may well be the pre-release guidance agencies that the Federal Bureau of Prisons is pioneering, and which several other American correctional systems have also developed, notably California. Since these institutions must blend into the community, it seems obvious that they will be small establishments. They will be in conventional residential type structures such as apartment houses, family type residences or even segments of large low-price hotels.

Simply having thesse small structures will not necessarily suffice to prepare every kind of offender for success in the free community. It seems obvious that many men need a long period of intensive work and academic training before they are likely to be capable of successfully competing for a legitimate income. Many may also need an appreciable period in which to become isolated and alienated from the associates with whom they have had success in crime and delinquency. Only in this way can they develop a new experience of success and gratification in non-criminal pursuits. For the latter type of experience they will need to be in close rapport with individuals who can bring them this type of successful experience, but are not so different in background as to be incapable of gaining rapport with them. This can occur in an institution that is like the typical institution of today only in being removed geographically from the large cities where most of the offenders reside. Indeed, because of our investment in the huge prisons, these new kinds of programs may be in traditional penal edifices. However, the staff at such institutions may include successfully rehabilitated ex-prisoners. Pioneering in this kind of operation are a variety of experimental institutions in California, North Carolina and Alabama, where parolees or even discharged prisoners have been voluntarily or on an employment basis engaged as counsellors in prison education and guidance programs. These institutions will also take advantage of what we are learning from the current vast amount of research and experimentation on new ways of teaching, particularly programmed instruction, for persons who have been long-term failures in traditional schools.

However, most significant will be the extent to which institutional treatment is entirely replaced by new kinds of community treatment. This will be community treatment with almost as high a staff to subject ratio as current institutional treatment — perhaps one staff member to every six cases — but without the subsistence and overhead costs of institutions, and with much more effectiveness. It will also involve markedly different styles of treatment for different types of offenders. All this is foreshadowed by the dramatic success of the California Youth Authority's Community Treatment Centers, which have so successfully treated after an immediate parole 75 per cent of the boys and 92 per cent of the girls from a random half of all those committed to institutions from Sacramento and Stockton. The future pattern for most of the country probably is indicated by the California Youth Authority's plan to build small regional reception centers pimarily for diagnosis, and to serve as bases from which diagnosis probably will be followed, for most cases, by immediate parole and intensive community treatment.

Another development which seems to be emerging is the tremendous growth of research as a routine operation of correctional agencies. Just as manufacturing became rationalized, as the economists say, by the introduction of modern cost accounting and quality control, so crime control is likely to be guided increasingly by statistical feedback on the effectiveness of its various policies and practices. We are seeing the day when new practices are not merely innovations; instead they are introduced as controlled experiments, to a randomly selected treatment group, so that the post-release records of those receiving a new program can be compared with the records of a fully comparable group that did not receive it. Increasingly, the operating records of correctional agencies are likely to be standardized, and designed for more efficiency, both to improve their value to operations and to make them amenable to statistical analysis for research purposes.

Finally, research is pushing into new areas that were previously insulated from objective study. I refer particularly to research on the police and on the courts. The selection processes, which they control, determine who is defined as a criminal in our society, and they greatly influence the consequences of this definition. The process of convicting and sentencing a man has increasingly been recognized, through cooperation of sociologists and lawyers in research, as something quite different from what the lawyers study in statutes and in the opinions of appellate courts. Research emphasizes the informal settlement of cases as their predominant solution. This emphasis directs attention to the "station adjustment" activities of the police, and to the bargaining process of the courts; these processes replace or predetermine the formal procedures in court in a major portion of criminal litigation.

We are learning that in treatment institutions much of what seems like success is simply an adaptation of the inmate to institutional life. The hard evidence of success is absence of post-release criminality, which American correctional officials have been notably lax in tabulating. While much of this laxity is due to the inaccessibility of FBI fingerprint records for research purposes, a tremendously important body of knowledge on the effectiveness of correctional practices is possible simply from tabulation of the correlates of recommitment within a state's correctional system, and of the state prison's notifications when one of their releasees is imprisoned elsewhere. All of these are likely to become the basis for profit-and-loss statements in future correctional bookkeeping.

PERSONNEL PROBLEMS IN CORRECTIONS*

HAROLD V. LANGLOIS

Education and vocational training exist traditionally in many institutions but I ask — in what manner and to what degree? Oh sure, the pedagogy of the classroom in its traditional approach can be found in many institutions. The existence of work shops to "teach a trade" can be found the length and breadth of the land. Where do we find special courses and programs for poor and slow readers? Where do we find community education tie-ins with colleges and universities on a permanent continuing basis not only to help the prisoner but to develop within our schools and universities knowledgeable people to teach and others to explore through research many of the things we do not now know? Where do we find a true relationship of prison shops to true vocational training? Isn't it almost self-evident the work made available to the inmate population is either of a self-serving nature to the institutional needs or a manufacturing shop that produces goods year in and year out at a profit but the nature of the work is such that few or no jobs exist in the community calling for the kind of work experience gained? How many correctional work programs are based on results of surveys made in surrounding communities for needed skills and programs developed within the correctional setting of neighboring institutions to satisfy community needs?

We talk a great deal about half-way houses, pre-release centers, sabbatical

* Reprinted from *Proceedings of The Ninety-Fifth Annual Congress of Correction of The American Correctional Association*, 1965, pp. 36–43, by permission of the American Correctional Association. Copyright 1966.

leaves, inter-state exchange of prisoners, community resources available to the ex-offender, education and educational programs for the incarcerated and released, and many other things germane to the correctional process. Let us not think of a big financial grab bag alone to provide the answers. I was in Europe earlier this year and visited juvenile and adult institutional and community correctional programs in several localities. Pre-Release Centers? I visited, talked with and studied England's experience with a pre-release center that had just completed its sixth full year of operation. Inmates live in a separate section of one of the oldest prisons in London — Wormwood Scrubs. Inmates must have served four years of their sentence to be eligible for selection to enter the pre-release program and once selected are removed from the general population of whatever penitentiary to which they may be assigned and are located in an old building in a corner section of this prison. Each man is assigned his own room, given a key to its door and has the usual degree of privacy that goes with one's room. His breakfast and evening meal may be had at the institutional facility. It is seldom, however, the man eats his evening meal at the pre-release center. All men assigned to the unit, with the exception of the inmate employed as the cook (who, by the way, has a position as cook awaiting him when he is released from the institution), leave the prison early in the morning entirely on their own. They either go to work, go to look for employment or go on interviews for a job. They are totally free until 10:45 at night. When a prisoner finishes his day's work in the community he may go to his home and visit with his wife and children, his girl friend, his parents or friends, or take in a movie or the like. He must return in a condition of sobriety by 10:45 P.M. This, together with his continued noninvolvement in a career of crime, are the pre-requisites and the mandates for successful continuance in the pre-release center. One hundred and seventy-four (174) men have passed through this program in the past six years and only seventeen have failed. Fifteen of these were single men. It is significant, I believe, to note that only two married men failed in this program. It would appear that married men represent a greater potential for success and responsibility to assume the marital ties binding him closer to a sense of carrying out his responsibilities. Each prisoner must experience six months of this type of social restraint before he may be considered for outright release to the community.

A second type of program novel to me was to observe a community private agency project again in London known as the Circle Trust. This is a social center for discharged prisoners. It opens seven days a week — weekdays from 6:00 P.M. to 11:00 P.M. and on Saturdays and Sundays from 2:00 P.M. to 11:00 P.M. Admission is through referral through the secretary of social work by one of the recognized after-care agencies existing in England. Membership is subject to a preliminary interview and those accepted are required to pay a modest annual subscription fee. The purpose of the club for the ex-offender is to provide an atmosphere where the members will feel free and be able to relax in a free atmosphere to help them to understand themselves and their problems through group discussion and to provide a social place where spare time can be enjoyed. The overall purpose is to develop in the men an awareness of their responsibilities toward society and through voluntary work to integrate them slowly into the community. By one helping another and by one's interest in another there develops inner strength and sensitivity. The Center employs two trained social workers, on a part-time basis, both of whom are women. It has been their experience that men respond best to women social workers and initial contact by way of confidence and trust becomes somewhat more expedited in this way.

In still another section of England, I observed a Borstal or Youth Correctional Facility now in its third year of experimentation. Here at Hunter Combe, located just outside of Oxford, the Governor and the entire staff are trying to reverse the figures they use nationally of 30% success, 70% failure in the Borstal system. The initial and constant technique utilized is staff saturation to each and every inmate by way of constant contact. They claim inmate culture cannot and has not developed. I was informed that for the first time in their country they had achieved the absence of peer groups, the absence of inmate leaders, an absence of negativistic influences within the school such as the stigma of "anti-administration," fink, punk, screw, head-shrinker, etc. The total experience has been aimed at a fostering and development of self-reliance and programs geared toward the inmate thinking for himself. The desired effect, of course, is to develop self-reliance and confidence. This experiment should be closely followed as it has some interesting possibilities.

There is no room in the correctional field today for the opinionated individualist who knows it all. The day of such expressions uttered with pride about "my institution," our "herd," "what's your count," etc., has gone. The remnants may remain but make no mistake it has departed. Today we face problems of population shift, population decline, population growth, growing budgets of staggering proportions, changes in the philosophy of handling offenders, recognition of certain kinds of offender groups as more socio-legal in nature, more socio-economic or socio-psychological or again more socio-medical, each and all of which must be considered so one may properly determine a course of action with respect to the development of new physical facilities, modification or extension of existing physical facilities and the development of staff training such as may be the case and in which direction this too should go. For example, the jail or short-term lock-up institutions throughout the United States can no longer merely provide a clean home with good food. They must be more than holding institutions. Their problem is the community's problem and the community must be part of it. A jail, a house of correction or a prison cannot be isolated from the community as a thing apart. Its programs must be geared to community needs, community acceptance of programs and community ability to pay for and maintain.

The socio-legal approach calls for using the combined talents, specialties and energies of the police, the prosecution, the defense and the correctional personnel, both community and institutional, to bring about protection of society's interests which embrace concern and safety for the taxpayer and his property together with preserving the integrity of the family of the accused, indicted, convicted or sentenced, and providing that kind of program and supervision for the convicted that will be flexible enough to allow for quick and ready change when basic character and motivated change is observed in the offender of a positive kind, as well as to permit for the removal from a free society of a person on a parole or similar release status who again is exhibiting the danger signals of non-conformism and pre-delinquent behavior without the necessity of a new serious crime having been committed.

I do not say any one kind of correctional system is better than any other. I do say some kind of a central planning body consisting of continuing membership of certain members to afford a continuum of professional experience representing all interests in the jail, house of correction, reformatory or penitentiary field, together with representation from probation, parole, and where geographical elements permit the training schools must exist independent from any other body within the State Government and must be integrated, identified and established as a Department of Corrections. Today some thirty-five states in the United States have their Correctional Services so constructed.

As we look ahead we must *firmly believe in the integrity and uniqueness of professional practice and performance as Correctional Professional personnel.* We must look to our own areas of job experimentation — our own research and study activities — our own performance on the correctional field measured by correctional standards. Only in this way and through such exercise can we measure our growth and development.

EFFECTIVENESS OF A PRISON AND PAROLE SYSTEM*

DANIEL GLASER

Over two million Americans become prisoners each year in jails, police stations, institutions for juvenile delinquents, and prisons. We know that 99 per cent are released, most of them within a year, but no

* From *The Effectiveness of a Prison and Parole System* (pp. 3-4, 504-13, 529-31) by Daniel Glaser, copyright © 1964, by The Bobbs-Merrill Company, Inc., reprinted by permission of the publishers and author.

one knows how many are confined again or how soon the average rearrest occurs. What is more important, no one has adequate evidence as to what can be done to reduce the probability that those released will commit crime again.

There are about a quarter of a million inmates in the prisons administered by state and federal governments in the United States. These prisoners generally were convicted of the most serious offenses. Nine-tenths also had a crime or juvenile delinquency record before the law-breaking which led to their current incarceration. Indeed, about half previously served at least one other term in such a prison. Around 115,000 are released from these institutions each year, but they are replaced by an even larger number of new prisoners.

The adult male prisoners in these federal and state prisons will be the principal concern of this volume. They are men whose prior failures suggest poor prospects for the future. Yet, many are known to pursue legitimate and successful lives after prison. How can the frequency of such success be increased? This is the question we seek to answer.

The number of persons received by all agencies dealing with criminals is mounting. This growth is partly explained by the rise in our birth rate during the 1940's. The fecundity that has crowded American colleges in the 1960's also crowds American prisons with young adults. What is their future? The answer is especially ominous because greater use of probation and other alternatives to imprisonment means that the average new prisoner now has a more extensive record of prior criminality than the average prisoner of former years.

There have been many responses to this problem. New prisons, costing ten to fifteen thousand dollars for each inmate, are regularly constructed. New psychological, psychiatric, and other treatment facilities are added to prison services, so that the annual cost of operating a prison system now reaches two thousand dollars per inmate — more than twice this amount at some specialized institutions. Unfortunately, there is no convincing evidence that this investment reduces what criminologists call "recidivism," the offender's return to crime. However, since there is little knowledge on overall rates of return to crime, how can we know at all precisely the effects on recidivism of specific prison and parole practices?

For the benefit of readers of this report who are not familiar with the five federal prisons in which we did our research, the following is a brief description of each institution as of 1959, when our interviews were conducted:

Leavenworth is a high-security penitentiary housing about 2500 inmates. Established in 1895, it has somewhat diverse buildings of various ages and a high masonry wall. Most of the inmate housing is of the inside cellblock variety connected together in a huge main building which forms part of the wall. The institution is used predominantly for advanced offenders believed to be tractable but requiring secure custody. Average sentence is over nine years and average age is thirty-nine, with a large range around these averages. With Atlanta, this represents the highest security level in the federal system apart from the small "super-security" institution at Alcatraz.[1] Over a third of the inmates are employed in five large prison industry installations (shoes, brushes, furniture, clothing, and printing). These are very efficiently operated, on a production-line basis, as is indicated by their net profit of over a million dollars per year. It also has a large farm, and an inmate school provides many correspondence and evening courses.

Terre Haute is a medium-security penitentiary completed in 1940 and generally housing somewhat over 1300 inmates. Its buildings, mostly two-story, are connected together in a symmetrical telephone-pole design. It has inside and outside cell structures with over 600 single cells, and the rest of the population having dormitory housing. The entire plant, except for some farm and maintenance buildings, is surrounded by a high double security fence. Sentences are very diverse, with the average about five years. Over 300 men are employed in industry, notably in a large textile mill and a furniture renovation shop, and it has varied other work and training programs, including a large farm.

Milan is one of the small prisons which the federal system calls a "correctional institution." It consists primarily of a square two-story building so constructed as to enclose completely a square inside courtyard. A small two-story inside cellblock juts into the courtyard on one side, with the rest of the inmates housed in ten small dormitory rooms in the main structure. In these rooms, a wire mesh interior wall parallel with the outer wall of the building creates a corridor from which the interior of the rooms may be observed. The institution population generally is just under 700, and two-thirds Negro. A majority of the latter serve narcotics offense sentences which range from two to five years in length, and from which parole is prohibited. However, a fifth of the population has sentences of a year or less, and over a quarter have sentences of under two years. About 150 inmates are employed in industry, at metal work. It also has a farm and varied education and vocational training programs.

Chillicothe,[2] the federal response to the reformatory movement, was built in 1925, in the "bigger-the-better" era. It holds about 1300 inmates in somewhat diverse separate structures strung out in a line about a quarter-mile long. These are set in the middle of a rectangular compound of seventy-two acres, which provides extensive grounds for athletics within the surrounding security fence. A separately fenced adjoining compound holds industry, powerhouse, and vocational training buildings. The average sentence is about three and one-half years, but a third have Youth Correction Act sentences, which permit parole between sixty days and four years. The average age of

---

[1] Now closed.

[2] No longer operated by the federal system but is now leased to the prison system of the State of Ohio.

the inmates is about twenty, with over 90 per cent under twenty-five. About two-thirds are committed for interstate transportation of stolen autos. Inmate housing is in four cellblocks and six dormitory structures, which provide five gradations of custody ranging from maximum security to an honor unit where officers usually are not present. About 300 men work in prison industry, which operates a large chair factory and a foundry. The prisoners also operate a large farm and there is an extensive academic and vocational school program, notably an airplane mechanics school from which some inmates leave as Civil Aeronautics Authority licensed mechanics.

Ashland is a correctional institution opened in 1940, but designated as a youth center in 1954, upon implementation of the Federal Youth Correction Act. It houses about 500 inmates in an approximately telephone-pole arrangement of one- and two-story buildings. Housing is mostly of two types: long dormitory buildings with no major interior walls, and outside cell houses in which the cells have been converted to rooms with solid doors, generally unlocked. All the main buildings are in one compound, enclosed in a double security fence. The average age of the inmates is about eighteen, with none over twenty-one and four-fifths under twenty. About three-fourths of the inmates have Youth Correction Act sentences, and most of the remainder have Federal Juvenile Delinquency Act sentences. The latter generally started their minority term in the National Training School. Parolees from Ashland who violate are rarely returned to Ashland. About three-quarters of the inmates were committed for interstate transportation of stolen automobiles. Ashland has the highest concentration of treatment staff in relation to population of any of the prisons studied, including a full-time psychiatrist, a full-time psychologist, and a large education staff for this number of inmates. A furniture factory provides industrial employment and there is also a farm.

The statements that follow [selected from a substantially larger list] may be considered the principal conclusions from our research and may be of potential value in the guidance of prison and parole programs. These propositions were not necessarily first conceived in our project, but for most of them we have presented more conclusive evidence than has generally accompanied assertion of such ideas. Nevertheless, any of the statements may appropriately be considered as hypotheses for further research by correctional staff themselves. These conclusions are:

In the first two to five years after their release, only about a third of all the men released from an entire prison system are returned to prison.
The proportion of releasees returned to prison tends to be higher:
    a. where probation is used extensively, so that only the worst risks go to prison, although this use of probation may make the long-run recidivism of all felons lower;
    b. where parole is used extensively, so that many poor risk parolees are released on a trial basis;

   c. where a large proportion of parolees are returned to prison when they have violated parole regulations but have not been charged with or convicted of new felonies;

   d. where there is a high overall crime rate in the communities to which prisoners are released, so that there is high prospect of the releasee coming from and going to highly criminogenic circumstances.

The older a man is when released from prison, the less likely he is to return to crime.

The younger a prisoner was when first arrested, convicted, or confined for any crime, the more likely he is to continue in crime.

The earlier an offender of any age left home, the more likely he is to continue in crime.

Felony offenses fall into three broad rankings of recidivism, as follows:

   a. The most recidivistic category consists of economic offenses not involving violence (larceny, burglary, auto theft, and forgery), and the most recidivistic single type of felony is auto theft.

   b. Consistently intermediate in recidivism rate are several common but diverse types of crime, such as narcotics offenses, robbery, and kidnapping.

   c. The lowest recidivism occurs with those offenses most associated with unusual circumstances in the offender's life rather than with offenses pursued as vocations; notable here are murder, rape, and embezzlement.

The extent of the offender's prior record and the likelihood of his becoming a recidivist are directly correlated.

A predominant interest of prison inmates is to adjust to the expectations of their keepers in order to stay "out of trouble" while confined.

Most prison inmates maintain strong noncriminal interests, including vocational aspirations of a legitimate nature.

Prisoners perceive other prisoners as having less commitment to staff-supported values than is, in fact, the case.

Inmate pressures on other inmates to avoid communication with officers varies directly with the extent to which there is an impersonal and authoritarian orientation of staff to inmates.

Staff influence on inmates varies directly with staff manifestation to inmates of the same types of personal behavior that cause a man to be liked in nonprison relationships.

   a. Inmates are most influenced by staff who act toward them in a friendly and considerate — rather than hostile — tone and manner.

   b. Inmates are most influenced by staff who treat them with fairness and predictability.

Promoting the isolation of inmates from each other fosters rehabilitation where the techniques for promoting isolation consist of:

   a. Providing physical arrangements of inmate housing which facilitate an inmates' achievement of privacy when he desires it;

   b. Separating inmates considered criminogenic influences on each other;

   c. Encouraging staff-desired patterns of inmate discrimination in choice of prisoner associates.

Custody grading systems foster rehabilitation by providing effective incentives to self-improvement activity, and to inmate discrimination in choice of associates, but they impede rehabilitation:

   a. if the rewards for conformity to prison regulations include such reduction of inmate-staff contacts in quarters as to facilitate domination by inmate elements there who seek hedonistic escape from the effort of rehabilitation;

   b. if they provide freedom without effectively imposing responsibility;

   c. if one of their consequences is such concentration of antirehabilitative inmates in certain units that they dominate other inmates there and seriously impede their reformation, particularly in a unit through which most inmates are expected to pass in their progression up a custody-graded hierarchy of units.

The administration of disciplinary penalties is most effective if it simultaneously:

   a. minimizes alienation of the rule-violating inmate from staff;

   b. maximizes his alienation from inmate supporters of his infraction;

   c. promotes in him a clear regret over having committed the infraction; but

   d. provides him with a perception of clearly available opportunities to pursue a course of behavior which will restore him to good standing in the prison and give him a more favorable self-conception than he had as a rule violator.

Prerelease arrangement of a parole job is not associated with markedly greater rates of success on parole than release on parole without a prearranged job.

Recidivism of adult male offenders varies inversely with their postrelease employment.

The ex-prisoner's primary barrier to employment is not so frequently his criminal record as it is his lack of extensive or skilled work experience.

As the date of their release approaches, the relationship between inmates and their parents or other blood relatives tends to improve ("absence makes the heart grow fonder"); therefore inmates increasingly expect postrelease assistance from some relatives.

Inmate hostility to persons in the free community diminishes as their release date approaches, at least as indicated by inmates less frequently expecting harm from specific persons, and more frequently expressing a willingness to accept help from anyone.

Over 90 percent of the men released from prison return to communities in which they previously resided.

Somewhat higher than average postrelease failure rates are associated with release to a community other than that of prior residence.

The most unfavorable postrelease residential arrangement, in terms of postrelease failure rates, is that in which the ex-prisoner lives alone.

Discord with relatives in the releasee's place of residence is highly associated with subsequent failure.

Prisoners generally encounter old friends soon after release, and their prison record is widely known in their postrelease social circles.

Most ex-prisoners re-encounter some prison acquaintances within a few months after their release.

Persistent renewal of prison contacts is highly associated with reimprisonment.

Most prisoners have real fears of suffering police harassment in their postrelease life.

Although such harassment does occur and is sometimes so unjust or corrupt as to be of legitimate public concern, both serious and undeserved police harassment probably is not suffered by more than a small per cent of ex-prisoners.

This half-century's most promising correctional development for alleviating postrelease problems of prisoners consists of the counseling centers in metropolitan areas to which prisoners scheduled for release are transferred some months before their release date, and from which they regularly go forth to enter the job market and to develop correctionally acceptable postprison social relationships, before they are released on a regular parole or on any other traditional types of release from prison.

The parole rules about which both prisoners expecting parole and men already on parole will be most apprehensive are rules against associating with other ex-criminals, drinking, travel, and being out of their homes late at night.

The performance of the parole supervision role can be scaled along two major dimensions, assistance and control, which differentiate four polar styles of role performance.

   a. paternal — high control, high assistance;
   b. punitive — high control, low assistance;
   c. welfare — low control, high assistance;
   d. passive — low control, low assistance.

When there is the possibility of performing either a criminal or a non-criminal act as alternative means for achieving certain ends, or where the only possibilities are to employ a criminal means or to forsake the ends that crime might serve, people take that course of action from which they anticipate the most favorable conception of themselves.

A person's self-conception in his pursuit of either criminal or noncriminal alternative actions is determined by both his prior experiences and his present circumstances.

After each release from prison, most prisoners are reformed, or recidivate, according to whether or not adequate change develops from their prior patterns of coping with dependence on relatives and with the need to achieve social and economic independence.

The correctional treatments of maximum reformative effect are those that enhance a prisoner's opportunities in legitimate economic pursuits and those that improve his conception of himself when he identifies with anticriminal persons.

Evaluation of correctional program effectiveness can be most conclusive and persuasive if the presentation of postrelease data is focused on the responsibilities which the correctional agency must meet.

Improvements in correctional operations suggested by research findings will be most readily supported if introduced as piecemeal innovations, and if an evaluation program is part of the innovation proposal.